Intelligent Renewable Energy Systems

Scrivener Publishing
100 Cummings Center, Suite 541J
Beverly, MA 01915-6106

Artificial Intelligence and Soft Computing for Industrial Transformation

Series Editor: Dr S. Balamurugan (sbnbala@gmail.com)

Scope: Artificial Intelligence and Soft Computing Techniques play an impeccable role in industrial transformation. The topics to be covered in this book series include Artificial Intelligence, Machine Learning, Deep Learning, Neural Networks, Fuzzy Logic, Genetic Algorithms, Particle Swarm Optimization, Evolutionary Algorithms, Nature Inspired Algorithms, Simulated Annealing, Metaheuristics, Cuckoo Search, Firefly Optimization, Bio-inspired Algorithms, Ant Colony Optimization, Heuristic Search Techniques, Reinforcement Learning, Inductive Learning, Statistical Learning, Supervised and Unsupervised Learning, Association Learning and Clustering, Reasoning, Support Vector Machine, Differential Evolution Algorithms, Expert Systems, Neuro Fuzzy Hybrid Systems, Genetic Neuro Hybrid Systems, Genetic Fuzzy Hybrid Systems and other Hybridized Soft Computing Techniques and their applications for Industrial Transformation. The book series is aimed to provide comprehensive handbooks and reference books for the benefit of scientists, research scholars, students and industry professional working towards next generation industrial transformation.

Publishers at Scrivener
Martin Scrivener (martin@scrivenerpublishing.com)
Phillip Carmical (pcarmical@scrivenerpublishing.com)

Intelligent Renewable Energy Systems

Edited by

Neeraj Priyadarshi
Akash Kumar Bhoi
Sanjeevikumar Padmanaban
S. Balamurugan
and
Jens Bo Holm-Nielsen

Scrivener
Publishing

WILEY

Wiley Global Headquarters
111 River Street, Hoboken, NJ 07030, USA

For details of our global editorial offices, customer services, and more information about Wiley products visit us at www.wiley.com.

Library of Congress Cataloging-in-Publication Data

ISBN 978-1-119-78627-6

Cover image: Pixabay.com
Cover design by Russell Richardson

Set in size of 11pt and Minion Pro by Manila Typesetting Company, Makati, Philippines

10 9 8 7 6 5 4 3 2 1

Contents

Preface

This book presents intelligent renewable energy systems integrating artificial intelligence techniques and optimization algorithms. The first chapter describes placement of distributed generation (DG) sources including renewable distributed generation (RDGs) such as biomass, solar PV, and shunt capacitor has been considered for the study purpose. The second chapter develops a new approach to chaotic particle swarm optimization (CPSO) technique. In the third chapter, comprehensive reviews of different artificial intelligence and machine learning techniques have been explicated. To bring out its advantages over other methods used in island detection, the traditional methods are first explained and then compared with artificial intelligence and machine learning island detection techniques. The performance of the intelligent controller is found to be good under steady conditions for grid connected photovoltaic systems and has been discussed in chapter four. Chapter five explains various uses of Genetic Algorithms (GA) and Solar PV forecasting are described; further, many stimulated algorithms which have been used in optimization, controlling, and methods of supervising of power for renewable energy analysis, which include hybrid power generation strategies are discussed. Chapter six presents the integration of 100 kW solar PV source to the 25 kV AC grid by using generalized r-s based SVPWM algorithm. Chapter seven aims to discuss the idea of hybrid system configuration, dynamic modeling, energy management, and control strategies. A multi-stage planning framework is proposed in chapter eight to divide the planning period into several stages so that investments can be made in each stage as per the requirements. A unique and a novel GUI is presented to design the entire solar PV systems has been discussed in Chapter nine. Chapter ten addresses micro-grid situational awareness using micro PMU. Role of AI & ML in smart grid entities such as Home Energy Management System (HEMS), Energy Trading, Adaptive Protection, Load Forecasting and Smart Energy Meter are presented in Chapter eleven. Chapter twelve presents a new method for energy loss allocation in radial distribution network

(RDN) with distributed generationin the context of deregulated power system. Chapter thirteen presents the optimization of controller parameters for FACTS and VSC based HVDC. Chapter fourteen describes Short Term load forecasting for a Captive Power Plant Using Artificial Neural Network. Chapter fifteen defines Real-time EV Charging Station Scheduling Scheme by using Global Aggregator.

Neeraj Priyadarshi
Akash Kumar Bhoi
Sanjeevikumar Padmanaban
S. Balamurugan
Jens Bo Holm-Nielsen
Editors

Optimization Algorithm for Renewable Energy Integration

Bikash Das[1], SoumyabrataBarik[2]*, Debapriya Das[3] and V. Mukherjee[4]

[1]*Department of Electrical Engineering, Govt. College of Engineering and Textile Technology, Berhampore, West Bengal, India*
[2]*Department of Electrical and Electronics Engineering, Birla Institute of Technology and Science Pilani, K. K. Birla Goa Campus, Goa, India*
[3]*Department of Electrical Engineering, Indian Institute of Technology, Kharagpur, West Bengal, India*
[4]*Department of Electrical Engineering, Indian Institute of Technology (Indian School of Mines), Dhanbad, Jharkhand, India*

Abstract

With the development of society, the electrical power demand is increasing day by day. To overcome the increasing load demand, renewable energy resources play an important role. The common examples of renewable energy resources are solar photovoltaic (PV), wind energy, biomass, fuel-cell, etc. Due to the various benefits of the renewable energy, the incorporation of renewable energy resources into the distribution network becomes an important topic in the field of the modern power system. The incorporation of renewable energy resources may reduce the network loss, improve voltage profile, and improve the reliability of the network. In this current research work, optimum placements of renewable distributed generations (RDGs) (viz. biomass and solar PV) and shunt capacitors have been highlighted. For the optimization of the locations and the sizes of the RDGs and the shunt capacitors, a multi-objective optimization problem is considered in this book chapter in presence of various equality and inequality constraints. The multi-objective optimization problem is solved using a novel mixed-discrete student psychology-based optimization algorithm, where the key inspiration comes from the behaviour of a student in a class to be the best one and the performance of the student is measured in terms of the grades/marks he/she scored in the examination

---

Corresponding author: soumyabratab@goa.bits-pilani.ac.in

Neeraj Priyadarshi, Akash Kumar Bhoi, Sanjeevikumar Padmanaban, S. Balamurugan and Jens Bo Holm-Nielsen (eds.) Intelligent Renewable Energy Systems, (1–40) © 2022 Scrivener Publishing LLC

and the efficacy of the proposed method is analyzed and compared with different other optimization methods available in the literature. The multi-objective DG and capacitor placement is formulated with reduction of active power loss, improvement of voltage profile, and reduction of annual effective installation cost. The placement of RDGs and shunt capacitors with the novel proposed method is implemented on two different distribution networks in this book chapter.

Keywords: Renewable energy integration, shunt capacitors, distributed generation, mixed discrete student psychology-based optimization algorithm, distribution networks

1.1 Introduction

In order to satisfy the increasing electricity load demand, electrical power generation needs to be scheduled properly [1–25]. Electrical power sources can be classified into two categories named as non-renewable and renewable sources. Non-renewable sources mainly include fossil fuels [26–45]. To generate electrical power from fossil-fuels, the fossil-fuels need to be burned. But the combustion of fossil-fuel causes pollution which affects the atmosphere. On the other hand, renewable energy resources cause zero or very little pollution. The main drawback of renewable energy resources is that the extraction of energy is dependent on nature [46–55]. In spite of having the disadvantages, the renewable energy resources are gaining more and more interest in the extraction of electrical power and to satisfy the increasing load demand.

To get better benefits, the placement of distributed generation (DG) to the distribution network needs proper strategy and planning [56–71]. Improper placement of DG may lead to increase in network loss, as well as may cause instability to the network. DG injects power into the distribution network. Based on the power injection, the DG sources can be classified into three categories *viz.*:

a) Unity power factor (UPF) DG,
b) Lagging power factor (LPF) DG and
c) Reactive power DG.

UPF DG injects active power only to the network whereas LPF DG injects both active and reactive power to the distribution network. On the other hand, reactive power DG generates only reactive power. An example of UPF DG is solar photovoltaic cells. Biomass and wind turbines can be considered as an example of LPF DG. The shunt capacitor injects reactive power to the network and it can be said as the reactive power DG.

Proper incorporation of renewable distributed generation (RDG) may reduce the network power loss, improve the voltage profile, improve the voltage stability index (VSI), improve reliability, etc. Due to the various benefits of the incorporation of distributed generation to the distribution network, various researchers have considered this topic as their research interest. The literature review reveals that for the placement of DG to the distribution network, various researchers have considered different approaches to optimize the location and the size of the DG sources. The approaches include analytical, classical optimization methods as well as the metaheuristic optimization algorithm. In order to reduce the active power loss of the distribution network, Acharya et al. [1] have proposed an analytical approach to optimize the size and location of the DG source. Gozel and Hocaoglu [2] have proposed another analytical expression to determine the optimum size and location of DG. This approach is based on the current injection method with an objective to reduce the network power loss. Wang and Nehair [3] have proposed an analytical approach to optimize the size of UPF DG [3]. Wang and Nehair have considered different types of load demands of the distribution network [3]. On the other hand, Hung et al. [4] have proposed an analytical expression to optimize the location and size of LPF DG which is capable of supplying both active and reactive power to the distribution network. It may be observed that most of the researchers have developed analytical expressions to determine the optimum size of the DG in order to reduce the network loss. Aman et al. [5] have proposed an analytical approach for optimum placement of DG considering active power loss reduction and improvement of voltage profile of the network. They have considered a voltage sensitivity analysis approach based on the power stability index to determine the size of DG using a stepwise iterative approach. Some researchers [6] have also considered classical optimization methods to optimize the size of DG. At that same time, an analytical approach to determine the optimum location of DG in the distribution network may also be seen in [7]. Analytical methods can be implemented easily and take less computation time. But the direct formulation of complex problems using the analytical method is quite difficult. The application of an analytical approach, to solve complex problems, may lead to inaccurate solutions due to the assumptions made during the problem formulation process.

To overcome the problem, some of the researchers have adopted the linear and nonlinear programming approach for optimizing the DG size [8]. A considerable number of researchers have applied the metaheuristic optimization algorithm for the DG placement problem. Different nature-inspired algorithms like genetic algorithm (GA) [9], tabu search [41], particle swarm optimization (PSO) [42, 43], combined GA-PSO [44], artificial bee colony (ABC) algorithm [45], harmony search algorithm [46, 47], differential evolution (DE) [48], teaching-learning based optimization (TLBO) [49] may be found in the literature. The application of different hybrid optimization algorithms to solve the DG placement problem may also be noticed in the literature [50–53]. In [54], the authors proposed a multi-objective GA-based approach for the optimal positioning of multiple types of DG to reduce investment costs, cost due to annual energy loss and increase the system reliability. Many of the researchers have taken into account the VSI as the primary objective function while optimizing the DG size [55, 56]. Various objective functions have been considered by different researchers to determine the size and the locations of the DG. In [57], considering the probabilistic behavior of renewable resources, the authors attempted to solve the DG optimization problem. Singh and Goswami [58] have considered nodal pricing methodology for optimizing the DG locations and capacity. They have also studied the economical aspect of DG incorporation into the distribution network. At that same time, in [59], the authors have studied the power penetration by the DG sources considering the average hourly load demand. Some other research works on the optimum DG placement problem may also be noticed in the literature [60–65].

In this current book chapter, placement of DG sources including RDGs (such as biomass, solar PV) and shunt capacitor has been considered for the study purpose. The study has been performed by considering a multi-objective function that includes reduction of active power loss, the betterment of voltage profile, and minimization of effective annual installation cost. To optimize the locations of considered DG sources, a novel optimizing technique named mixed-discrete student psychology-based optimization (SPBO) algorithm is used. The proposed algorithm is inspired by the natural behaviour of the students to be the best student in the class. The criteria to be the best student is to perform well in the examination and the student needs to give more effort to be the one. The study has been carried out considering the hourly average load demand of the distribution network for a day. In this book chapter, the proposed method is tested on two distribution networks namely 33-bus and 69-bus distribution networks.

The remaining book chapter is categorized as follows. In the next section, a new algorithm named mixed-discrete SPBO is presented. The problem formulation is discussed in Section 1.3. Section 1.4 presents the optimum DG placement in the distribution networks using the proposed mixed-discrete SPBO algorithm. Finally, the conclusions are drawn in Section 1.5.

1.2   Mixed Discrete SPBO

1.2.1   SPBO Algorithm

SPBO algorithm has been proposed by Das *et al.* [66]. Similar to other meta-heuristic methodology, SPBO also uses a set of populations. The population considered in SPBO is analogous to a group of students present in the class. In general, the performance of a student is analyzed based on the marks/grade obtained by the student in the examination. The student with the maximum marks/grade is considered as the best one in the class and the student is awarded accordingly. It is also very clear that in the test the students will aim to achieve the highest marks/grade for which they need to provide more effort in their study. The overall grade is the final score of the students in the examination. The overall grade of a student depends on the cumulative effort given by the student in each subject offered to them. The students enhance their performance in the examination by paying more attention and effort in their studies. SPBO is based on the psychology of the students who are trying to improve their performance in the examination as well as trying to get the highest marks/grade in the examination.

For the improvement of the overall performance, the students need to enhance their performance in each subject which are offered to them. However, the improvement of the students' performance is not the same for all the students. Improvement of the students' performance depends upon a few factors like the capability and efficiency of the student as well as how the student gets interested in the subject. If a student is interested in a subject, he/she will be more involved in that subject. As a result, the performance of the student will be improved in that subject. As the overall grades/marks depend on each subject, improvement in any subject will improve the student's overall performance. To improve performance, some students use to give similar or better kind of effort as given by the best student while some use to give more effort than that of the average student. If a student is less interested in a subject, then he/she will try to give the subject an average effort to improve his/her overall performance in the exam. The effort of a student can't be measured directly. Marks obtained by the student in a subject are the outcome of her/his effort given to that subject. So, it may be considered, in general, that the effort given by the student is equivalent to the marks/grade obtained. Considering all these facts and the psychology of the students, the students can be divided into four different categories (such as the best student, good student, average student, and the students trying to improve randomly) [66].

(a) Best student: The best student is to be considered as the student who scored the overall highest marks/grade in the examination. It is an obvious fact that the best student will always try to secure his/her position in the class. For securing his/her position, the best student should have to provide more effort towards each subject than the same given by the rest of the students in the class. Therefore, it can be concluded that the best student will always provide more effort than the same given by other students in the class. Mathematically, the student of this category can be visualized with the help of (Equation 1.1) [66]

$$X_{best\ new} = X_{best} + (-1)^D \times rand \times (X_{best} - X_j) \qquad (1.1)$$

where, X_{best} indicates the marks/grades obtained by the best student, X_j indicates the marks of the student, randomly selected, in the same subject, and *rand* generates a random number between 0 and 1. In (Equation 1.1), the D parameter randomly takes the value either 1 or 2. Marks obtained in the subjects by the best student may be increased or maybe decreased depending upon the student and the subjects. However, the primary objective of the best student in the class is to secure his/her position by continuously scoring the highest overall marks in the examination.

(b) Good student: If a student is interested in a subject, then he or she may strive to make more effort to enhance his or her performance in that subject. As a result, their overall performance in the examination will be improved. The students of this kind can be classified as subject wise good student. The effort given by all the students in this category may not be the same because the psychologies of the students are different. Some students try to give a similar or even better effort than the best student, where as; some students try to improve their performance by giving more effort after considering the effort given by the best student as well as the average effort given by the students of the class. This group of students may be further divided into two categories. The first category of this group of students is those who try to give similar or even better effort as given by the best student. This category of students gives effort to the subjects in which they are interested. So, their performance in that subject, as well as their overall performance, gets improved. Improvement of these kinds of students in a subject can be explained using (Equation 1. 2a) [66]. The other category of good students is those students who give effort considering the effort given by the best student as well as try to give more effort than the average effort of the class so that their performance in that subject, as well as overall performance, gets improved. Mathematically, the student of this category can be represented as (Equation 1. 2b) [66].

$$X_{newi} = X_{best} + [rand \times (X_{best} - X_i)]$$ (1.2a)

$$X_{newi} = X_i + [rand \times (X_{best} - X_i)] + [rand \times (X_i - mean)]$$ (1.2b)

Here, X_{newi} is the improved performance of the ith student in that subject; X_{best} and X_i are the marks/grade obtained in that subject by the best student and the ith student, respectively; *mean* represents the average marks obtained in the class in that particular subject and *rand* variable produces a random number between 0 and 1.

(c) **Average student:** In order to increase their overall success in the test, students with less interest in a subject aim to offer an average effort. The students of this category can be named as subject-wise average student. While giving average effort in a particular subject, students will try to improve their overall performance by paying more effort to the other subjects which are offered to them. The performance of this category of students may be explained with the help of (Equation 1. 3) [66]

$$X_{newi} = X_i + [rand \times (mean - X_i)]$$ (1.3)

where, X_i indicates the marks/grade of the ith student of the class in a subject, *mean* indicates the average marks obtained in that particular subject, and *rand* generates a random number between 0 and 1.

(d) **Students who try to improve randomly**: Except the three categories of students discussed above, there are certain students who strive to enhance their results without recognising the effort offered by rest of the students in the class. The students of these kinds always try to improve their performance randomly to some extent up to their limitations, depending upon their interest in the subject. Improvement of the students' performance based on this concept may be represented by (Equation 1. 4) [66]

$$X_{newi} = min + [rand \times (max - min)]$$ (1.4)

where *min* and *max* are the two variables that indicate the minimum and the maximum marks of the subject, respectively, and *rand* generates a random number between 0 and 1.

The process of getting interested in a subject for different students is not deterministic. It depends on the students' psychology. So, it may be said that the selection of different categories of students is a random process.

Incorporating the psychology of the aforementioned four categories of students, the SPBO algorithm can be visualized easily using the flowchart given in Figure 1.1. Each (student) population consists of various variables analogous to the subjects offered to the students. The students try to give the subjects effort so that their overall performance in the exam is improved. The fitness function is selected as the overall marks/grades obtained by the students. The effort given by the student is appreciated if her/his performance gets improved. Similarly, if the fitness function improves, a variable change is accepted. And, finally, the performance of the best student will be considered as the best solution or optimum solution. The performance of different optimization algorithms depends upon their own parameters. But SPBO has no such tuneable parameter.

1.2.2 Performance of SPBO for Solving Benchmark Functions

In order to evaluate the performance of SPBO for optimizing the benchmark functions, ten of the CEC-2005 benchmark functions are considered. The ten different CEC-2005 benchmark functions among twenty-five are presented in Table 1.1. To compare the performance of SPBO with other optimization methods, the results obtained by using SPBO are compared to those obtained by using the different optimization methods namely PSO, TLBO, CS, and SOS. Twenty-five individual runs are performed for each of the functions and for each of the algorithms.

The performance of the algorithms selected is evaluated on the basis of the optimal result obtained and on the basis of convergence mobility. For the purposes of analysis, the algorithms are found to converge when the gap between the optimal function result and the result obtained crosses below 1×10^{-5}. The results obtained below 1×10^{-5} are considered as equal to zero. The parameters of PSO, TLBO, CS and SOS are considered according to the dimension of the benchmark function. But SPBO does not have any parameter and the size of the population needs not vary according to the dimension of the benchmark functions. With the increase of dimension of the functions, the size of the population of the proposed SPBO needs not to be increased. That's why the population size of SPBO for all the considered benchmark functions is considered to be constant. It is considered as 20 for the proposed SPBO. In order to have a fair comparison of the performance of all the algorithms, the analysis is done based on the number of fitness function evaluations (NFFE) taken to converge.

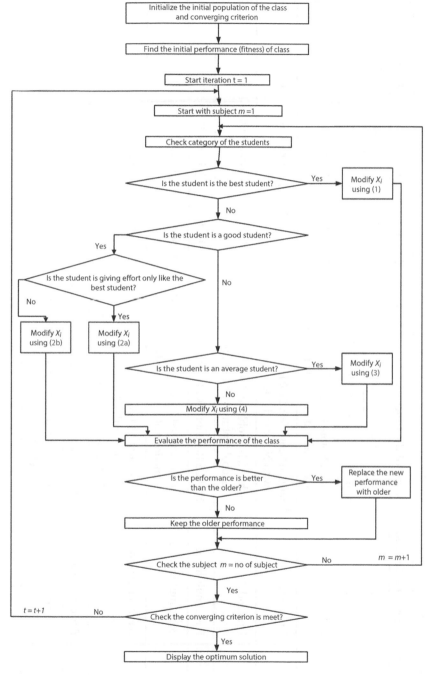

Figure 1.1 Flowchart of the SPBO algorithm.

Table 1.1 CEC 2005 benchmark function [67].

Problem	Type of the function	Name of the functions	$F(x^\star)$	Initial range	Bounds	Dimension (D)
F1	Unimodal	Shifted Sphere Function	-450	$[-100,100]^D$	$[-100,100]^D$	30
F2	Unimodal	Shifted Schwefel's Problem 1.2	-450	$[-100,100]^D$	$[-100,100]^D$	30
F3	Unimodal	Shifted Rotated High Conditioned Elliptic Function	-450	$[-100,100]^D$	$[-100,100]^D$	30
F4	Unimodal	Shifted Schwefel's Problem 1.2 with Noise in Fitness	-450	$[-100,100]^D$	$[-100,100]^D$	30
F5	Unimodal	Schwefel's Problems 2.6 with Global Optimum on Bounds	-310	$[-100,100]^D$	$[-100,100]^D$	30
F6	Basic multimodal	Shifted Rosenbrock's Function	390	$[-100,100]^D$	$[-100,100]^D$	30
F7	Basic multimodal	Shifted Rotated Griewank's Function without Bounds	-180	$[0,600]^D$	$[0,600]^D$	30
F8	Basic multimodal	Shifted Rotated Ackley's Function with Global Optimum on Bounds	-140	$[-32,32]^D$	$[-32,32]^D$	30
F9	Basic multimodal	Shifted Rastrigin's Function	-330	$[-5,5]^D$	$[-5,5]^D$	30
F10	Basic multimodal	Shifted Rotated Rastrigin's Function	-330	$[-5,5]^D$	$[-5,5]^D$	30

1.2.3   Mixed Discrete SPBO

In general, the optimization algorithm is used to optimize (minimize) the objective function by obtaining the optimum value of the variable vector $\mathbf{X}$. To optimize the variable vector $\mathbf{X}$, consist of some continuous and discrete variables, a mixed discrete version of SPBO may be used. For an n-dimensional problem that includes continuous and discrete variables, the variable vector may be represented as in (Equation 1.5).

$$[X] = [\ [X^{cont}],\ [X^{disc}]\ ] \tag{1.5}$$

where $[X^{cont}]$ and $[X^{disc}]$ are the continuous and discrete variable vectors, respectively. For the scenario of m continuous variables and remaining $(n\text{-}m)$ discrete variables, the $[X^{cont}]$ and $[X^{disc}]$ maybe expressed as in (Equation 1.6) and (Equation 1.7), respectively.

$$[X^{cont}] = [X_1, X_2, \ldots \ldots \ldots, X_m] \tag{1.6}$$

$$[X^{disc}] = [X_{m+1}, X_{m+2}, \ldots \ldots \ldots, X_n] \tag{1.7}$$

As mentioned earlier the mixed discrete SPBO is capable to handle both the continuous and discrete variables. In the mixed discrete SPBO, the continuous variables are updated as the conventional SPBO. The updating process of the continuous variables is the same as discussed in the previous section using four categories of students (namely best student, good student, average student, and students who want to improve randomly) with the help of (Equations 1.1–1.4). For the discrete variables, the discretization may be done with the help of the nearest vertex approach (NVA). The NVA method is normally based on finding out the Euclidean norm in the design space. The discrete variables may be expressed in terms of a hypercube, which are represented by the sets of ordered pair and can be represented as in (Equation 1.8)

$$H_{ij} = \left\{ \left(X_{ij}^L, X_{ij}^U\right) | X \in \mathbb{X}, j \in m+1, m+2, \ldots, n | m < n \right\} \tag{1.8}$$

where, X_{ij}^L and X_{ij}^I are the lower and upper limits of the discrete variables, in the hypercube. In the hypercube, the lower and upper limit can be defined by *floor* and *ceiling* functions as presented in (Equation 1.9) and (Equation 1.10), respectively.

$$X_{ij}^L = \lfloor X_{ij} \rfloor = max\{n_{ij} \in \mathbb{Z}^+ | n_{ij} \leq X_{ij}\} \tag{1.9}$$

$$X_{ij}^U = \lceil X_{ij} \rceil = min\{n_{ij} \in \mathbb{Z}^+ | n_{ij} \geq X_{ij}\} \tag{1.10}$$

where, $\mathbb{Z}^+$ is the set of integers. In the hypercube H, the closest vertex of the discrete variables can be determined using the NPV method as expressed in (Equation 1.11).

$$X_{ij}^{disc} = \begin{cases} X_{ij}^L, & if \; |X_{ij} - X_{ij}^L| \le |X_{ij} - X_{ij}^U| \\ X_{ij}^U, & if \; |X_{ij} - X_{ij}^L| > |X_{ij} - X_{ij}^U| \end{cases} \qquad (1.11)$$

where, X_{ij}^{disc} is the discrete version of the continuous variable X_{ij}. To restrict the variables within the boundary of minimum and maximum limit the same procedure may be used as used in the conventional SPBO algorithm.

1.3   Problem Formulation

1.3.1   Objective Functions

The selection of the locations and the proper sizes of the RDGs (biomass and solar PV) and shunt capacitors in the distribution networks depend on the selection of the proper objective functions. Improper placement of the RDGs and shunt capacitors leads to the maloperation of the distribution networks which includes the increment in active power loss, poor voltage profile, and huge installation cost. In this book chapter, the active power loss, voltage deviation, and the effective annual installation cost of RDGs and shunt capacitors are considered as the main objective functions. The multi-objective function is converted to the single objective function by using the weighted sum approach, where the weights for the objective functions are selected based on their preferences. The objective function with the weights is stated in (Equation 1.12).

$$(min) \; J(t) = w_1 PLI(t) + w_2 VDI(t) + w_3 ICI(t) \; \forall 1 \le t \le 24 \quad (1.12)$$

(a) Power Loss Index (PLI)
PLI is the ratio of the active power losses after and before the placement of RDGs and the shunt capacitors. PLI is defined as in (Equation 1.13).

$$PLI(t) = \frac{P_{loss}^{DG}(t)}{P_{loss}(t)} \qquad (1.13)$$

The $P_{loss}^{DG}(t)$ and $P_{loss}(t)$ are the active power loss after and before the placement of RDGs and shunt capacitors, respectively, at the time instant t.

The active power loss at any time instant t can be defined as in (Equation 1.14)

$$P_{loss}(t) = \frac{1}{2} \sum_{i,j=1}^{NBr} |I_{ij}(t)|^2 \Re (Z_{ij}) \tag{1.14}$$

where NBr is the total number of branches, Z_i is the branch impedance and $|I_{ij}|$ is the magnitude of the branch current, connected between bus-i and bus-j, defined as in (Equation 1.15).

$$|I_{ij}(t)| = \frac{1}{|Z_{ij}|} \sqrt{|V_i(t)|^2 + |V_j(t)|^2 - 2|V_i(t)||V_j(t)|cos\delta_{ij}} \tag{1.15}$$

After the RDGs and shunt capacitors connected to the distribution networks, the branch current magnitude $|I_{ij}|$ is modified by (Equation 1.16).

$$|I_{ij}^{DG}(t)| = \frac{1}{|Z_{ij}|} \sqrt{|V_i^{DG}(t)|^2 + |V_j^{DG}(t)|^2 - 2|V_i^{DG}(t)||V_j^{DG}(t)|cos\delta_{ij}^{DG}}$$

$$\tag{1.16}$$

Here, $|V_i^{DG}|$ and δ_{ij}^{DG} are the voltage magnitude and the load angle after inserting the DGs and shunt capacitors.

(b) Voltage Deviation Index (VDI)

Improvement in the voltage profile in the distribution network is measured by voltage deviation from the nominal voltage of 1.0 pu. The voltage deviation index is measured as the ratio of the voltage deviations (VDs) after and before the placement of the RDGs and shunt capacitors which are defined for the time instant t as

$$VDI(t) = \frac{VD^{DG}(t)}{VD(t)} \tag{1.17}$$

where VD^{DG} is defined as

$$VD^{DG}(t) = \sum_{i=1}^{NB} \left(|V_i^{DG}(t)| - 1.0 \right)^2 \tag{1.18}$$

$$VD(t) = \sum_{i=1}^{NB} (|V_i(t)| - 1.0)^2 \tag{1.19}$$

Here, $V_i^{DG}(t)$ and $V_i(t)$ are the voltage of ith bus after and before place-ment of DG to the distribution network. The value of voltage deviation near zero indicates an improved voltage profile.

(c) Installation Cost Index (ICI)
Total installation cost includes the cost of the RDGs and the shunt capaci-tors. Lifetime (LT) of the RDGs and the shunt capacitors are used to obtain the annual installation cost. The ICI is defined as

$$ICI(t) = \frac{Cost_{DG}(t)}{Cost_{peak}} \tag{1.20}$$

Here, $Cost_{DG}(t)$ is the effective annual installation cost of the DGs and shunt capacitors at time instant t, and can be defined as

$$Cost_{DG} = \frac{C_{bio} \times P_{bio}}{LT_{bio}} + \frac{C_{sol} \times P_{sol}}{LT_{sol}} + \frac{C_{cap} \times Q_{cap}}{LT_{cap}} \tag{1.21}$$

and the installation cost, considering the maximum sizes of DGs and shunt capacitors, is defined as

$$Cost_{peak} = \frac{C_{bio} \times P_{bio}^{max}}{LT_{bio}} + \frac{C_{sol} \times P_{sol}^{max}}{LT_{sol}} + \frac{C_{cap} \times Q_{cap}^{max}}{LT_{cap}} \tag{1.22}$$

In this book chapter, equal preference is given to each objective function in the weighted sum approach. Therefore, the weights for the three objec-tive functions are $w_1 = w_2 = w_3 = \frac{1}{3}$.

1.3.2 Technical Constraints Considered

The minimization of the weighted average of the three objective functions is subjected to the fulfilment of certain equality and inequality constraints as stated below [68],

(a) Equality Constraints
At any time instant t, the active and the reactive power balance for the dis-tribution network should be maintained by the equation as follows

$$P_{utility}(t) + P_{DG}(t) = \alpha_{pu}^{load}(t) \sum_{i=1}^{NB} PL_i^{peak} + P_{loss}(t)$$

$$Q_{utility}(t) + Q_{DG}(t) = \alpha_{pu}^{load}(t) \sum_{i=1}^{NB} QL_i^{peak} + Q_{loss}(t) \qquad (1.23)$$

This equality constraint is fulfilled by the load flow solution of the distribution networks. $P_{utility}$, $Q_{utility}$ are the active and reactive power taken from the utility, respectively, P_{DG}, Q_{DG} are the active and reactive power supplied by the RDGs, in order, and shunt capacitors, and α_{pu}^{load} is the percentage load level expressed in per unit.

(b) Inequality Constraints

(i)   The bus voltages of the distribution networks at any time instant must be within the minimum (V_{min}) and maximum (V_{max}) voltage level as in

$$V_{min} \leq V_i^{DG}(t) \leq V_{max} \qquad (1.24)$$

The placement of RDGs and the shunt capacitors may increase the bus voltage beyond the limit at low voltage level and decrease the bus voltage at high load level. Therefore, bus voltages are kept within the prescribed limit by introducing the penalty function defined as

$$f_V(t) = \tau_v \left[max\left\{0, \left(V_{min} - min\left(V_1^{DG}(t), V_2^{DG}(t), \cdots, V_{NB}^{DG}(t)\right)\right)\right\} + \right.$$

$$\left. max\left\{0, \left(max\left(V_1^{DG}(t), V_2^{DG}(t), \cdots, V_{NB}^{DG}(t)\right) - V_{max}\right)\right\}\right] \qquad (1.25)$$

(ii) The active and reactive power generation of the DGs should be within the specified limit given as

$$P_{DG}^{min} \leq P_{DG}(t) \leq P_{DG}^{max}$$

$$Q_{DG}^{min} \leq Q_{DG}(t) \leq Q_{DG}^{max} \qquad (1.26)$$

where $P_{DG}^{min}, P_{DG}^{max}$ are the minimum and the maximum limit of the active power injection of the DGs and $Q_{DG}^{min}, Q_{DG}^{max}$ are the minimum and the maximum limit of the reactive power injection of the DGs which are to be maintained at any time instant. These inequalities are maintained by introducing the penalty function as below

$$f_{PDG}(t) = \tau_{PDG}\left[max\left\{0,\left(P_{DG}^{min} - P_{DG}(t)\right)\right\} + max\left\{0,\left(P_{DG}(t) - P_{DG}^{max}\right)\right\}\right]$$

$$f_{QDG}(t) = \tau_{QDG}\left[max\left\{0,\left(Q_{DG}^{min} - Q_{DG}(t)\right)\right\} + max\left\{0,\left(Q_{DG}(t) - Q_{DG}^{max}\right)\right\}\right]$$

$$(1.27)$$

(iii) The total active and reactive power injections by the RDGs and shunt capacitors at any time instant should be less than the total active and reactive power load demand of the distribution network at the same instant. This inequality constraint is defined as

$$\sum_{i=1}^{N_{DG}} P_{DGi}(t) < \alpha_{pu}^{load} \sum_{i=1}^{NB} PL_i^{peak}$$

$$\sum_{i=1}^{N_{DG}} Q_{DGi}(t) < \alpha_{pu}^{load} \sum_{i=1}^{NB} QL_i^{peak} \qquad (1.28)$$

These inequality constraints are considered by introducing the two penalty functions as

$$f_{PDGtot}(t) = \tau_{PDGtot}\left[max\left\{0,\left(\sum_{i=1}^{N_{DG}} P_{DGi}(t) - \alpha_{pu}^{load}(t) \times \sum_{i=2}^{NB} PL_i^{peak}\right)\right\}\right]$$

$$f_{QDGtot}(t) = \tau_{QDGtot}\left[max\left\{0,\left(\sum_{i=1}^{N_{DG}} Q_{DGi}(t) - \alpha_{pu}^{load}(t) \times \sum_{i=2}^{NB} QL_i^{peak}\right)\right\}\right]$$

$$(1.29)$$

(iv) Branch currents, after the placement of DGs and shunt capacitors, should be within the maximum allowable level to maintain the feeder thermal limit. The branch current limit should be

$$|I_{ij}^{DG}(t)| \text{ or } |I_{ij}^{DG}(t)| \leq |I_{ij}^{max}| \qquad (1.30)$$

This limit is considered in the objective function with the help of a penalty function described as

$$f_{feed}(t) = \tau_{feed}[max\{0, max(I_{ij}^{feed} \text{ or } I_{ji}^{feed}) - I_{ij}^{feedmax}\}] \qquad (1.31)$$

After considering all the penalty functions, the objective function, to be minimized, is

$$(\min)J^{new}(t) = w_1 PLI(t) + w_2 VDI(t) + w_3 ICI(t) + f_V(t) + f_{PDG}(t) + f_{QDG}(t) +$$
$$f_{PDGtot}(t) + f_{QDGtot}(t) + f_{feed}(t) \qquad \forall 1 \leq t \leq 24$$

$$(1.32)$$

The values of the penalty factors τ_V, τ_{PDG}, τ_{QDG}, τ_{PDGtot}, τ_{QDGtot}, τ_{feed} are to be selected as very high value for a minimization problem. In this book chapter, the penalty values are selected as 10^{16} [68]. If any of the inequality constraints violates then the corresponding penalty function adds a very high value to the objective function.

1.4 Comparison of the SPBO Algorithm in Terms of CEC-2005 Benchmark Functions

For the comparison purpose, different algorithms (*viz.* PSO [69], TLBO [70], CS, and SOS) are considered in this book chapter and the parameters for the different algorithms considered are tabulated in Table 1.2 as below. The study has been carried out to analyze the performance of SPBO to solve CEC-2005 benchmark functions [67, 71]. The analysis has been done considering 30-dimensional problems. The comparison performance study of SPBO with PSO, TLBO, CS, SOS has been shown in Table 1.3. It may be noticed from Table 1.3, that the SPBO's performance is better compared to that given by the remaining optimization algorithms considered. SPBO stands 1st rank in nine of benchmark functions of CEC-2005 according to the optimum solution achieved as well as based on converging mobility. The mean of the result obtained in nine benchmark functions is better as compared to the mean achieved by PSO, TLBO, CS and SOS. In only one function (*i.e.* F8) SPBO stands 3rd. Compared to the other algorithms considered in this analysis, it can be found in the study that the performance of the proposed SPBO algorithm is better.

Table 1.2 Parameters of different algorithms for benchmark functions.

Algorithms	Parameters	Population size	Maximum NFFE
PSO	$C_1 = C_2 = 2$ $w_{max} = 0.9$, $w_{min} = 0.4$	If $D = 2$ Population =30	If $D = 2$ Max NFFE =12 × 10^4
TLBO	Teaching factor = either 1 or 2	If $D = 5$ Population =50	If $D = 5$ Max NFFE =2 × 10^5
CS	Levy co-efficient = 0.5 Discovery rate of alien eggs = 0.25	If $D = 10$ Population =50	If $D = 10$ Max NFFE =2 × 10^5
SOS	NA	If $D = 30$ Population = 100	If $D = 30$ Max NFFE =10 × 10^5
SPBO	NA	Population = 20	

An entry "NA" means not applicable.

So, it may be inferred that the proposed novel SPBO method works fine to solve ten CEC-2005 benchmark functions considered in this book chapter.

1.5 Optimum Placement of RDG and Shunt Capacitor to the Distribution Network

In this current book chapter, optimum placement of RDG (biomass and solar PV) and shunt capacitor has been considered for the study purpose. The DG optimization problem may be divided into two sections, such as optimization of the location of DG and optimization of the size of DG. To optimize both the location and size of the DGs simultaneously, mixed discrete SPBO has been used in this study. In the mixed discrete SPBO, the sizes of the DGs are considered as the continuous variables, and locations of the DGs are considered as the discrete variables. To optimize the sizes and locations of the biomass, solar PV, and shunt capacitor, a multi-objective

Table 1.3 Optimization result of CEC-2005 benchmark functions.

Functions	Attributes	PSO	TLBO	CS	SOS	SPBO
F1	Best *FF*	-450.0000	4.3423×10^3	285.0288	-450.0000	**-450.0000**
	Worst *FF*	-450.0000	1.2868×10^4	2.6304×10^4	-450.0000	**-450.0000**
	Mean	-450.0000	6.1561×10^3	9.2000×10^3	-450.0000	**-450.0000**
	Std. Dev	0	2.4294×10^3	8.1507×10^3	0	**0**
	Rank	3	5	4	2	**1**
F2	Best *FF*	-450.0000	-450.0000	-450.0000	-450.0000	**-450.0000**
	Worst *FF*	-450.0000	-450.0000	-449.9989	7.8615×10^8	**-450.0000**
	Mean	-450.0000	-450.0000	-449.9998	7.8615×10^7	**-450.0000**
	Std. Dev	0	0	3.3800×10^{-4}	2.3584×10^8	**0**
	Rank	2	3	4	5	**1**

(*Continued*)

Table 1.3 Optimization result of CEC-2005 benchmark functions. (*Continued*)

Functions	Attributes	PSO	TLBO	CS	SOS	SPBO
F3	Best FF	2.4082×10^6	1.2404×10^7	2.7113×10^6	1.4156×10^6	1.1252×10^6
	Worst FF	1.4310×10^7	9.0300×10^7	4.4354×10^6	6.8667×10^6	5.5039×10^6
	Mean	5.9320×10^6	7.4449×10^7	3.5213×10^6	3.0747×10^6	3.6913×10^6
	Std. Dev	3.6300×10^6	1.2404×10^7	7.8163×10^5	1.4156×10^6	1.2379×10^6
	Rank	3	5	4	2	1
F4	Best FF	-450.0000	-449.9981	-450.0000	-449.9957	-450.0000
	Worst FF	-450.0000	-449.7224	-450.0000	1.025×10^9	-450.0000
	Mean	-450.0000	-449.9655	-450.0000	1.0264×10^8	-450.0000
	Std. Dev	0	8.1216×10^{-2}	0	3.0745×10^8	0
	Rank	2	4	3	5	1
F5	Best FF	1.4051×10^4	1.0443×10^4	1.1914×10^4	7.9132×10^3	7.5236×10^3
	Worst FF	3.6183×10^4	1.7420×10^4	5.3257×10^4	1.8809×10^4	9.7728×10^3
	Mean	2.3954×10^4	1.3856×10^4	2.8358×10^4	1.1950×10^4	8.4225×10^3
	Std. Dev	7.0703×10^4	2.2846×10^3	1.0637×10^4	3.2094×10^3	3.1287×10^3
	Rank	5	3	4	2	1

(*Continued*)

Table 1.3 Optimization result of CEC-2005 benchmark functions. (*Continued*)

Functions	Attributes	PSO	TLBO	CS	SOS	SPBO
F6	Best *FF*	390.0070	405.8698	390.0033	390.0007	**390.0002**
	Worst *FF*	462.3391	407.8258	449.3571	457.6640	**390.0492**
	Mean	412.4370	406.5812	403.1944	401.5661	**390.0157**
	Std. Dev	25.1252	0.5722	16.8726	18.9630	**0.0176**
	Rank	4	5	3	2	**1**
F7	Best *FF*	-179.9926	4.2916×10^{3}	-179.9926	-179.9926	**-180.0000**
	Worst *FF*	-179.9803	8.2175×10^{3}	-179.9459	-179.8050	**-179.9901**
	Mean	-179.9764	5.8506×10^{3}	-179.9754	-179.9596	**-179.9943**
	Std. Dev	1.8121×10^{-2}	1.2183×10^{3}	1.7129×10^{-2}	5.3002×10^{-2}	**3.7955×10^{-3}**
	Rank	2	5	3	4	**1**
F8	Best *FF*	-119.5245	-119.3254	-119.9887	**-120.6199**	-119.5256
	Worst *FF*	-119.0590	-119.0550	-119.9010	**-120.2961**	-119.3143
	Mean	-119.2094	-119.1229	-119.9549	**-120.4613**	-119.3801
	Std. Dev	0.1392	7.3253×10^{-2}	2.3401×10^{-2}	**0.1028**	7.3663×10^{-2}
	Rank	4	5	2	**1**	3

(*Continued*)

Table 1.3 Optimization result of CEC-2005 benchmark functions. (*Continued*)

Functions	Attributes	PSO	TLBO	CS	SOS	SPBO
F9	Best *FF*	-321.0454	-164.8339	-172.7972	-293.1865	-330.0000
	Worst *FF*	-302.1412	-129.4599	-55.3934	-184.5407	-330.0000
	Mean	-313.3842	-147.5225	-123.7465	-241.1199	-330.0000
	Std. Dev	5.4141	11.0234	41.4742	42.6722	0
	Rank	2	4	5	3	1
F10	Best *FF*	-217.5703	-150.7517	-100.1658	-225.9089	-256.3699
	Worst *FF*	-92.2075	-104.3583	91.8576	-100.6526	-184.7313
	Mean	-153.3029	-125.7336	-9.2147	-151.2863	-213.3927
	Std. Dev	38.9758	14.0585	62.1465	38.1157	17.6163
	Rank	3	4	5	2	1

function is considered in this study. The objective function is described in (Equation 1. 12). The study has been carried out for a variable load demand for a day. Load demand of a network is not constant throughout the day. It varies with time, so as the power generation of the solar PV. Table 1.4 shows the load demand and electrical power generation from the solar PV for a day. The graphical representation of the variation of load demand (pu) and power generation from PV (pu) with respect to the different load hours of a day has been portrayed in Figure 1.2.

For the study purpose, two different distribution networks are considered. The first distribution network is a 33-bus distribution network having a total active power demand of 3715 kW with active power loss of 202.6771 kW [65] at the peak load level. The other one is 69-bus distribution network having active power demand as 3802.2 kW and, reactive power demand as 2694.6 kVAr [67]. The active power loss at the peak load level of the 69-bus distribution network is 224.96 kW.

The size of the solar PV can't be varied. The installed capacity of solar PV is constant. So, the size of the solar PV has been optimized for a particular hour. In this study, the size of the solar PV has been optimized for the 15th hour of the day correspond to which the load demand is 1.0 pu, and solar PV power generation is 0.7424 pu. The solar PV system generates and injects the active power to the distribution network. The active power injection from a solar PV plant for any particular hour can be expressed as in (Equation 1.33)

$$P_i^{solar} = PV \times solar_i \times GF \tag{1.33}$$

where PV and $solar_i$ are the solar PV installed capacity and solar power generation (in pu) for load hour of i. GF is the generation factor, having a value of (3.52/6.628) [68].

In this study, the biomass DG has been considered as the LPF DG having power factor being the same as the load demand. On the other hand, shunt capacitors available in the market are of standard size only. So, in this work, the sizes of shunt capacitors are considered to be as an integer multiple 25 kVAr. Table 1.5 presents the cost of different DGs and their lifetime. Using the mixed discrete SPBO, the location of the biomass DG, solar PV, and shunt capacitor has been optimized. As the location of the installed plants can't be moved from one bus to another bus, the locations of the considered DGs need to be kept constant.

Table 1.4 Variation of load demand (pu) and solar power generation (pu) with load hours.

Load hour	Load demand (pu) α_{pu}^{load}	Solar power generation (pu) [68]	Load hour	Load demand (pu) α_{pu}^{load}	Solar power generation (pu) [68]
1	0.64	0	13	0.99	1
2	0.6	0	14	1	0.9309
3	0.58	0	15	1	0.7424
4	0.56	0	16	0.97	0.5491
5	0.56	0	17	0.96	0.2827
6	0.58	0	18	0.96	0.0593
7	0.64	0.015	19	0.93	0
8	0.76	0.2143	20	0.92	0
9	0.87	0.5331	21	0.92	0
10	0.95	0.7653	22	0.93	0
11	0.99	0.894	23	0.87	0
12	1	0.9968	24	0.72	0

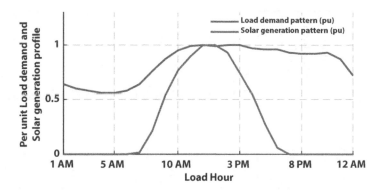

Figure 1.2 Variation of load demand (pu) and solar power generation (pu) with load hour.

Table 1.5 Cost and lifetime of different DGs.

	Biomass DG	Solar PV	Shunt capacitors
Cost ($)	3000/kW [60]	770/kW [60]	9/kVAr
Lifetime (years)	40	20	5

1.5.1 Optimum Placement of RDGs and Shunt Capacitors to 33-Bus Distribution Network

In this section, the optimum placement of biomass DG, solar PV, and shunt capacitors, to the 33-bus distribution network is discussed. Table 1.6 presents the optimum sizes and locations of biomass DG, solar PV, and shunt capacitors for different load hours of the 33-bus distribution networks. The reductions of active power loss and VDI for different load hours have been shown in Figures 1.3 and 1.4, respectively. From Table 1.6 and Figure 1.3, it may be noticed that the active power loss reduction after the placement of biomass DG, solar PV, and shunt capacitor is quite significant for all the load hours. After the placement of RDGs and shunt capacitors to bus numbers 14, 31, and 30, respectively, the active power loss of the 33-bus distribution network reduces from 202.6771 kW to 36.8247 kW for the 15th load hour. It may also be noticed that in presence of solar radiation, the active power loss reduction is higher compared to the same when the solar power generation is less or absent.

From Table 1.6 and Figure 1.4, it may be noticed that the improvement of the voltage profile of the 33-bus distribution network is very good for all the load hours of the day. Improvement of the voltage profile of the distribution network leads to the reduction of VDI. From Table 1.6 and

Table 1.6 Optimum placement of RDGs and shunt capacitors to the 33-bus distribution network.

Load hour	Optimum size of biomass DG (kW) Location – 14	Optimum size of solar PV (kW) Location – 31	Optimum size of shunt capacitor (kVAr) Location – 30	Active power loss before placement of DG (kW)	Active power loss after placement of DG (kW)	Base VDI (before placement of DG)	VDI after placement of DG
1	621.5083	1759.48	800	78.6548	29.4379	0.0453	0.0037
2	586.0025	1759.48	750	68.7376	25.8221	0.0396	0.0032
3	568.0646	1759.48	725	64.0501	24.1064	0.0369	0.003
4	550.005	1759.48	700	59.5413	22.4517	0.0343	0.0028
5	550.005	1759.48	700	59.5413	22.4517	0.0343	0.0028
6	568.0646	1759.48	725	64.0501	24.1064	0.0369	0.003
7	617.4665	1759.48	800	78.6548	28.7562	0.0453	0.0036
8	671.2714	1759.48	925	112.8660	31.2546	0.0651	0.0039
9	683.3	1759.48	1025	150.3564	30.2443	0.0868	0.0035
10	685.9	1759.48	1125	181.4934	31.9668	0.1048	0.0035
11	687.6	1759.48	1150	198.3321	33.0856	0.1146	0.0036
12	667.5	1759.48	1175	202.6771	32.981	0.1171	0.0033

(Continued)

Table 1.6 Optimum placement of RDGs and shunt capacitors to the 33-bus distribution network. (*Continued*)

Load hour	Optimum size of biomass DG (kW) Location – 14	Optimum size of solar PV (kW) Location - 31	Optimum size of shunt capacitor (kVAr) Location - 30	Active power loss before placement of DG (kW)	Active power loss after placement of DG (kW)	Base VDI (before placement of DG)	VDI after placement of DG
13	661.5	1759.48	1150	198.3321	32.0711	0.1146	0.0032
14	683.7	1759.48	1175	202.6771	33.5922	0.1171	0.0035
15	730.9	1759.48	1175	202.6771	36.8247	0.1171	0.0043
16	752.1	1759.48	1175	189.8051	39.7576	0.1096	0.0048
17	812.9	1759.48	1175	185.6225	50	0.1072	0.0066
18	866.0	1759.48	1225	185.6225	63.9226	0.1072	0.0086
19	861.3	1759.48	1175	173.3949	63.4637	0.1001	0.0087
20	851.4	1759.48	1175	169.4248	62.2863	0.0978	0.0083
21	851.4	1759.48	1175	169.4248	62.2863	0.0978	0.0083
22	861.3	1759.48	1175	173.3949	63.4637	0.1001	0.0087
23	813.6	1759.48	1100	150.3564	55.3269	0.0868	0.0074
24	691.0056	1759.48	900	100.7052	37.4156	0.0580	0.0048

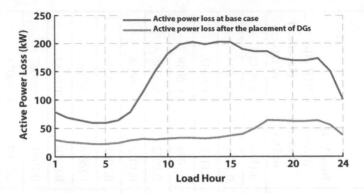

Figure 1.3 Variation of active power loss before and after placement of DGs to the 33-bus distribution network.

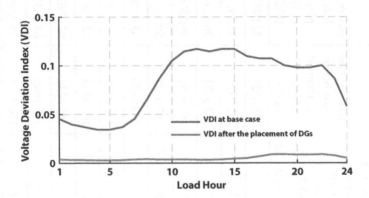

Figure 1.4 Variation of VDI before and after placement of DGs to the 33-bus distribution network.

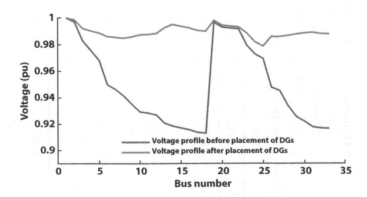

Figure 1.5 Voltage profile of the 33-bus distribution network before and after placement of DGs for 15th load hour.

Figure 1.4, the reduction of the VDI for all the load hours of the day may be noticed quite prominently. The voltage profile before and after the placement of DG to the 33-bus distribution network, for the 15th load hour, has been presented in Figure 1.5.

1.5.2   Optimum Placement of RDGs and Shunt Capacitors to 69-Bus Distribution Network

As mentioned earlier, using mixed discrete SPBO the sizes and locations of biomass DG, solar PV, and shunt capacitors have been optimized. The size of solar PV and the locations of the RDGs and shunt capacitors have been optimized considering 15th load hour of the day. The optimum locations of biomass DG, solar PV, and shunt capacitors are found to be bus numbers 61, 21, and 17, respectively. Table 1.7 presents the optimum sizes and locations of biomass DG, solar PV, and shunt capacitors obtained using the mixed discrete SPBO algorithm, with an objective to minimize the J for different load hours. Figure 1.6 presents the graphical representation of a comparative study of active power loss before and after placement of RDGs and shunt capacitors to 69-bus distribution networks. From Table 1.7 and Figure 1.6, it may be clearly noticed that, after the placement of RDGs and shunt capacitors to the distribution network, the active power loss reduces significantly for all the load hours of the day considered in this study. At the 15th load hour, the active power loss reduces from 224.96 kW to 11.2002 kW. Even in the absence of solar power injection, the active power loss reduction after the placement of RDGs and shunt capacitors is found to be quite significant for different load hours. Figure 1.7 shows the reduction VDI, after the placement of RDGs and shunt capacitors for all the load hours of the considered day. From Figure 1.7 and Table 1.7, it may be noticed that the reduction of VDI is quite significant for all the load hours, which implies a significant improvement of voltage profile after the placement of DGs to the distribution network corresponding to each load hours. Figure 1.8 shows the improvement of voltage profile after the placement of DGs to the distribution network for the 15th hour, using mixed discrete SPBO.

From the study, it is worth noting that after the placement of biomass DG, solar PV and shunt capacitors to the distribution networks, the active power loss, and VDI reduces quite significantly for both the considered distribution networks and for all the load hours of the considered day. The effective annual installation cost is also found to be less for both the considered distribution networks. It may also be said that the mixed discrete SPBO is quite capable to optimize the sizes and locations of the DGs, in order to achieve the desired objectives.

Table 1.7 Optimum placement of RDGs and shunt capacitors to the 69-bus distribution network.

Load hour	Optimum size of biomass DG (kW) Location – 61	Optimum size of solar PV (kW) Location - 21	Optimum size of shunt capacitor (kVAr) Location - 17	Active power loss before placement of DG (kW)	Active power loss after placement of DG (kW)	Base VDI (before placement of DG)	VDI after placement of DG
1	1098.3	963.8	375	86.4909	8.3858	0.0383	0.0027
2	1036.3	963.8	350	75.5157	7.3189	0.0334	0.0023
3	1003.4	963.8	350	70.3339	6.9606	0.0312	0.0021
4	973.4183	963.8	325	65.3533	6.3379	0.0290	0.002
5	973.4183	963.8	325	65.3533	6.3379	0.0290	0.002
6	1003.4	963.8	350	70.3339	6.9606	0.0312	0.0021
7	1096.2	963.8	375	86.4909	8.176	0.0383	0.0026
8	1251.2	963.8	425	124.4711	8.7507	0.0551	0.0024
9	1372.4	963.8	425	166.2875	8.4317	0.0735	0.0019
10	1456.4	963.8	425	201.1622	9.435	0.0888	0.0019
11	1495.3	963.8	425	220.0746	10.3757	0.0972	0.0019
12	1495.4	963.8	425	224.9605	10.8111	0.0993	0.0019

(Continued)

Table 1.7 Optimum placement of RDGs and shunt capacitors to the 69-bus distribution network. (*Continued*)

Load hour	Optimum size of biomass DG (kW) Location – 61	Optimum size of solar PV (kW) Location - 21	Optimum size of shunt capacitor (kVAr) Location - 17	Active power loss before placement of DG (kW)	Active power loss after placement of DG (kW)	Base VDI (before placement of DG)	VDI after placement of DG
13	1481.1	963.8	425	220.0746	10.5949	0.0972	0.0018
14	1504.2	963.8	425	224.9605	10.6459	0.0993	0.002
15	1523.5	963.8	475	224.9605	11.2002	0.0993	0.0024
16	1508.2	963.8	475	210.4930	11.3714	0.0929	0.0029
17	1525.2	963.8	525	205.7964	14.4862	0.0909	0.0044
18	1551.1	963.8	575	205.7964	19.078	0.0909	0.0063
19	1520.0	963.8	550	192.0793	18.7495	0.0848	0.0065
20	1505.6	963.8	550	187.6298	18.4184	0.0829	0.0063
21	1505.6	963.8	550	187.6298	18.4184	0.0829	0.0063
22	1520.0	963.8	550	192.0793	18.7495	0.0848	0.0065
23	1435.6	963.8	525	166.2875	16.3785	0.0735	0.0055
24	1219.6	963.8	425	110.9501	10.774	0.0491	0.0035

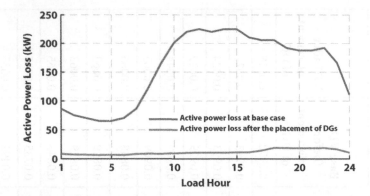

Figure 1.6 Variation of active power loss before and after placement of DGs to the 69-bus distribution network.

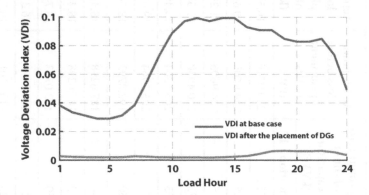

Figure 1.7 Variation of VDI before and after placement of DGs to the 69-bus distribution network.

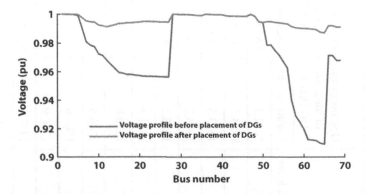

Figure 1.8 Voltage profile of 69-bus distribution network before and after placement of DGs for 15th load hour.

1.6 Conclusions

In this current book chapter, optimum placement of RDGs (such as bio-mass DG and solar PV) and shunt capacitors is studied with an objective to minimize a multi-objective function. The multi-objective function includes active power loss reduction, improvement of voltage profile, and reduction of effective annual installation cost. To optimize the size and the location of the DGs simultaneously, a new optimization algorithm named mixed discrete SPBO algorithm is used which is able to take care both the continuous and the discrete variables.

The proposed method has been coded in MATLAB software and compared with four different optimization methods, such as PSO, TLBO, CS and SOS, available in the literature. For the comparison purpose, the CEC-2005 benchmark functions have been considered, and the comparison has been made from the point of view of best FF, worst FF, mean, standard deviation and rank. For almost all benchmark functions, the proposed SPBO method has been provided the better results. Therefore, it can be concluded that the proposed method is superior than the other four methods considered in this book chapter.

The multi-objective RDGs and capacitors sizing and placement study has been carried out considering the variable load demand of a day. After the placement of biomass DG, solar PV, and shunt capacitors to the 33-bus and 69-bus distribution network using mixed discrete SPBO algorithm, it may be noticed that the active power loss reduction for all the load demands of the day and for both the considered distribution networks is quite significant. Significant reduction of VDI may also be noticed after the placement of DGs to both the distribution networks and for all the different load hours. The effective annual installation cost is also found to be less for both the distribution networks.

From the study, it may be concluded that the proper placement of biomass DG, solar PV, and shunt capacitors may lead to a significant reduction in active power loss, VDI, as well as effective annual installation cost, for both the considered 33-bus and 69-bus distribution networks. It is also worth mentioning that the mixed discrete version of SPBO is capable to optimize the sizes and locations of the DGs simultaneously in order to achieve the desired objective. It can also be concluded that the mixed discrete SPBO is very much capable to optimize both continuous and discrete variables simultaneously.

References

1. Acharya N., Mahat P., and Mithulananthan N. (2006) An analytical approach for DG allocation in primary distribution network. Int. J. Electr. Power Energy Syst. 28(10):669-678.
2. Gözel T., and Hocaoglu M.H. (2009) An analytical method for the sizing and sitting of distributed generators in radial systems. Electr. Power Syst. Res. 79(6):912-918.
3. Wang C., and Nehrir M.H. (2004) Analytical approaches for optimal placement of distributed generation sources in power system. IEEE Trans. Power Syst.19(4):2068-2076.
4. Hung D.Q., Mithulananthan N, and Bansal R. C. (2010) Analytical expressions for DG allocation in primary distribution networks. IEEE Trans. Energy Convers.25(3):814-820.
5. Aman M.M., Jasmon J., Mokhlis H., and Bakar A. (2012) Optimal placement and sizing of a DG based on new power stability index and line losses. Int. J. Electr. Power Energy Syst. 43(1):1296-1304.
6. Celli G.,Ghiani E., Mocci S., and Pilo F. (2005) A multi-objective evolutionary algorithm for the sizing and sitting of distributed generation. IEEE Trans. Power Syst. 20 (2): 750-757.
7. Falaghi H., and Haghifam M.R. (2007) ACO based algorithm for distributed generation sources allocation and sizing in distribution systems. In: Proc. IEEE Power Tech.: 555-560.
8. Al Abri R.S., El-Saadany E.F., and Atwa Y.M. (2013) Optimal placement and sizing method to improve the voltage stability margin in a distribution system using distributed generation. IEEE Trans. Power Syst. 28(1): 326–334.
9. Borges C.L.T., and Falcao D.M. (2006) Optimal distributed generation allocation for reliability, losses and voltage improvement. Int. J. Electr. Power Energy Syst. 28 (6):413-420.
10. Priyadarshi.; N;, Padmanaban, S.; Maroti, P.K.; Sharma. A.; An Extensive Practical Investigation of FPSO-Based MPPT for Grid Integrated PV System Under Variable Operating Conditions With Anti-Islanding Protection. IEEE System Journal, 2018, 13:1861 - 1871.
11. Priyadarshi, N.; Padmanaban, S.; Bhaskar, M.S.; Blaabjerg, F.; Sharma, A.; A Fuzzy SVPWM Based Inverter Control Realization of Grid Integrated PV-Wind System with FPSO MPPT Algorithm for a Grid-Connected PV/Wind Power Generation System: Hardware Implementation. IET Electric Power Appl., 2018, 12:962-971.
12. Priyadarshi, N.; Kumar, V.; Yadav, K.; Vardia, M.; An Experimental Study on Zeta buck-boost converter for Application in PV system. Handbook of distributed generation, Springer, DOI 10.1007/978-3-319-51343-0_13
13. Priyadarshi N.; Sharma A.K.; Priyam S.; An Experimental Realization of Grid-Connected PV System with MPPT Using dSPACE DS 1104 Control

Board. Advances in Smart Grid and Renewable Energy. Lecture Notes in Electrical Engineering, Springer, Singapore 2018, 435.

14. Priyadarshi N.; Sharma A.K.; Priyam S.; Practical Realization of an Improved Photovoltaic Grid Integration with MPPT. International Journal of Renewable Energy Research 2017, 7:1180-1891.

15. Priyadarshi N.; Sharma A.K.; Azam F.; A Hybrid Firefly-Asymmetrical Fuzzy Logic Controller based MPPT for PV-Wind-Fuel Grid Integration. International Journal of Renewable Energy Research 2017, 7: 1546-1560

16. Priyadarshi, N.; Anand, A.; Sharma, A.K.; Azam, F.; Singh, V.K.; Sinha, R. K.; An Experimental Implementation and Testing of GA based Maximum Power Point Tracking for PV System under Varying Ambient Conditions Using dSPACE DS 1104 Controller. International Journal of Renewable Energy Research, 2017, 7:255-265

17. Priyadarshi, N.; Padmanaban S.; Mihet-Popa L.; Blaabjerg, F.; Azam F.; Maximum Power Point Tracking for Brushless DC Motor-Driven Photovoltaic Pumping Systems Using a Hybrid ANFIS-FLOWER Pollination Optimization Algorithm. MDPI Energies 2018, 11:1-16

18. Priyadarshi, N.; Azam, F.; Bhoi, A.K.; Alam, S.; An Artificial Fuzzy Logic Intelligent Controller Based MPPT for PV Grid Utility. Lecture Notes in Networks and Systems 46, https://doi.org/10.1007/978-981-13-1217-5_88.

19. Padmanaban, S.; Priyadarshi, N.; Holm-Nielsen, J. B.; Bhaskar, M. S.; Azam, F.; Sharma, A.K.; A Novel Modified Sine-Cosine Optimized MPPT Algorithm for Grid Integrated PV System under Real Operating Conditions. IEEE Access, 2019, 7:10467-10477.

20. Padmanaban, S.; Priyadarshi, N.; Holm-Nielsen, J. B.; Bhaskar, M. S.; Hossain, E.; Azam, F.; A Hybrid Photovoltaic-Fuel Cell for Grid Integration With Jaya-Based Maximum Power Point Tracking: Experimental Performance Evaluation. IEEE Access, 2019, 7:82978-82990.

21. Priyadarshi, N.; Padmanaban, N.; Holm-Nielsen, J. B.; Blaabjerg, F.; Bhaskar, M.S.; An Experimental Estimation of Hybrid ANFIS–PSO-Based MPPT for PV Grid Integration Under Fluctuating Sun Irradiance. in IEEE Systems Journal. 2020, 14:1218-1229

22. Priyadarshi, N.; Padmanaban, N.; Bhaskar, M. S.; Blaabjerg, F.; Holm-Nielsen, J. B.; Azam, F.; Sharma, A.K.; A Hybrid Photovoltaic-Fuel Cell-Based Single-Stage Grid Integration With Lyapunov Control Scheme. IEEE Systems Journal, 2020, 14: 3334 - 3342

23. Priyadarshi, N.; Bhaskar, M. S.; Padmanaban, N.; Blaabjerg, F.; Azam, F.; New CUK–SEPIC converter based photovoltaic power system with hybrid GSA–PSO algorithm employing MPPT for water pumping applications. IET Power Electronics. 2020, 13:2824 – 2830

24. Priyadarshi, N.; Padmanaban, N.; Holm-Nielsen, J. B.; Bhaskar, M.S.; Azam, F.; Internet of things augmented a novel PSO-employed modified zeta converter-based photovoltaic maximum power tracking system: hardware realisation. IET Power Electronics. 2020, 13:2775 – 2781

25. Kamalapathi, K., Priyadarshi, N., Padmanaban, S., Holm-Nielsen, J.B., Azam, F., Umayal, C., Ramachandaramurthy, V.K. A Hybrid Moth-Flame Fuzzy Logic Controller Based Integrated Cuk Converter Fed Brushless DC Motor for Power Factor Correction. MDPI Electronics, 2018, 7: 288.

26. Priyadarshi, N., Padmanaban, S., Lonel, D., Mihet-Popa, L., Azam, F. Hybrid PV-Wind, Micro-Grid Development Using Quasi-Z-Source Inverter Modeling and Control—Experimental Investigation. MDPI Energies, 2018, 11:2277

27. Priyadarshi, N.; Ramachandaramurthy, V, K.; Padmanaban, S.; Azam, A.; An Ant Colony Optimized MPPT for Standalone Hybrid PV-Wind Power System with Single Cuk Converter. MDPI Energies, 2019, 12: 167

28. Azam, F.; Yadav, S.K.; Priyadarshi, N.; Padmanaban, S.; and Bansal, R.C.; A Comprehensive Review of Authentication Schemes in Vehicular Ad-Hoc Network, IEEE Access, 2021, 9:31309-31321, 2021, doi: 10.1109/ACCESS.2021.3060046.

29. Priyadarshi, N.; Sharma, A.K.; Bhoi, A. K.; Ahmad, S. N.; Azam, F.; Priyam, S.; A Practical performance verification of AFLC based MPPT for standalone PV power system under varying weather condition, International Journal of Engineering & Technology, 2018, 7:338-343

30. Azam F.; Priyadarshi N.; Nagar H.; Kumar S.; Bhoi A.K.; An Overview of Solar-Powered Electric Vehicle Charging in Vehicular Adhoc Network. in: Electric Vehicles. Green Energy and Technology. Springer, Singapore. https://doi.org/10.1007/978-981-15-9251-5_5

31. Azam, F.; Kumar, S.; Yadav, K.P.; Priyadarshi N.; Padmanaban, S.; An Outline of the Security Challenges in VANET, in Proc. of IEEE UPCON 2020, Nov, 2020.

32. Priyadarshi, N.; Azam, F.; Bhoi, A.K.; Sharma, A.K.; A Multilevel Inverter-Controlled Photovoltaic Generation. in Advances in Greener Energy Technologies. Springer, Singapore. 2020 https://doi.org/10.1007/978-981-15-4246-6_8

33. Priyadarshi, N.; Azam, F.; Bhoi, A.K.; Sharma, A.K.; Dynamic Operation of Grid-Connected Photovoltaic Power System. in Advances in Greener Energy Technologies. Springer, Singapore. 2020 https://doi.org/10.1007/978-981-15-4246-6_13

34. Priyadarshi, N.; Azam, F.; Bhoi, A.K.; Sharma, A.K.; A Proton Exchange Membrane-Based Fuel Cell Integrated Power System. in Advances in Greener Energy Technologies. Springer, Singapore. 2020 https://doi.org/10.1007/978-981-15-4246-6_18

35. Priyadarshi, N.; Azam, F.; Bhoi, A.K.; Sharma, A.K.; A Closed-Loop Control of Fixed Pattern Rectifier for Renewable Energy Applications. in Advances in Greener Energy Technologies. Springer, Singapore. 2020 https://doi.org/10.1007/978-981-15-4246-6_25

36. Priyadarshi, N.; Azam, F.; Bhoi, A.K.; Sharma, A.K.; A Four-Switch-Type Converter Fed Improved Photovoltaic Power System. in Advances

in Greener Energy Technologies. Springer, Singapore. 2020 https://doi.
org/10.1007/978-981-15-4246-6_29

37. Vardia, M.; Priyadarshi, N.; Ali, I.; Azam, F.; Bhoi, A.K.; Maximum Power
Point Tracking for Wind Energy Conversion System. in Advances in
Greener Energy Technologies. Springer, Singapore. 2020 https://doi.
org/10.1007/978-981-15-4246-6_36

38. Vardia, M.; Priyadarshi, N.; Ali, I.; Azam, F.; Bhoi, A.K.; Design of Wind
Energy Conversion System Under Different Fault Conditions. in Advances
in Greener Energy Technologies. Springer, Singapore. 2020 https://doi.
org/10.1007/978-981-15-4246-6_41

39 Choudhary, T.; Priyadarshi, N.; Kuma,r P.; Azam, F.; Bhoi A.K. (2020) A Fuzzy
Logic Control Based Vibration Control System for Renewable Application.
in Advances in Greener Energy Technologies. Springer, Singapore. 2020
https://doi.org/10.1007/978-981-15-4246-6_38

40. Priyadarshi, N.; Azam F.; Solanki, S. S.; Sharma, A.K.; Bhoi, A.K.; Almakhles,
D.; A Bio-Inspired Chicken Swarm Optimization-Based Fuel Cell System for
Electric Vehicle Applications. in Bio-inspired Neurocomputing. Studies in
Computational Intelligence, vol 903. Springer, Singapore. 2021 https://doi.
org/10.1007/978-981-15-5495-7_1

41. Gandomkar M.,Vikilian M., and Ehsan M.A. (2005) A genetic-based Tabu
search algorithm for optimal DG allocation in distribution systems. Electr.
Power Compon. Syst. 33:1351-1362.

42. Jamian J.J., Mustafa M.W., and Mokhlis H. (2015) Optimal multiple distributed generation output through rank evolutionary particle swarm optimization, Neurocomput. 152:190-198.

43. Gomez-Gonzalez M., Lopez A., and Jurado F. (2012) Optimization of distributed generation systems using a new discrete PSO and OPF. Electr. Power
Syst. Res. 84 (1): 174-180.

44. Moradi M.H., andAbedini M. (2012) A combination of genetic algorithm
and particle swarm optimization for optimal DG location and sizing in distribution systems.Int. J. Electr. Power Energy Syst. 34(1): 66-74.

45. Abu-Mouti F.S., and El-Hawary M.E. (2011) Optimal Distributed Generation
Allocation and Sizing in Distribution Systems via Artificial Bee Colony
Algorithm. IEEE Trans. Power Delivery. 26 (4): 2090-2101.

46. Rao R.S., Ravindra K., Satish K., and Narasimham S. (2012) Power loss minimization in distribution system using network reconfiguration in the presence of distributed generation. IEEE Trans Power Syst. 28: 317–325.

47. Kollu R.,Rayapudi S.R., and Sadhu V.L.N. (2014) A novel method for optimal
placement of distributed generation in distribution systems using HSDO.
Int.Trans. on Electr. Energy Syst. 24(4): 547-561.

48. Nayak M.R., Dash S.K., and Rout P. (2012) Optimal Placement and Sizing
of Distributed Generation in Radial Distribution System Using Different
Evolution Algorithm. In. Proc. third international conference on Swarm,
Evolutionary, and Memetic Computing.: 133-142.

49. Sultana S., and Roy P.K. (2014) Optimal capacitor placement in radial distribution systems using teaching learning based optimization. Int. J. Electr. Power Energy Syst. 54: 387-398.
50. Sadighizadeh M., Esmaili M., and Esmaili M. (2014) Application of the hybrid Big Bang-Big Crunch algorithm to optimal reconfiguration and distributed generation power allocation in distributed systems.Energy 76: 920-930.
51. Doagou-Mojarrad H., Gharehpetian G., Rastegar H., and Olamaei J. (2013) Optimal placement and sizing of DG (distributed generation) units in distribution networks by novel hybrid evolutionary algorithm. Energy 54: 129-138.
52. Aman M.M.,Jasmon G.B., Bakar A.H.A., and Mokhlis H. (2014) A new approach for optimum simultaneous multi-DG distributed generation units placement and sizing based on maximization of system loadability using HPSO (hybrid particle swarm optimization) algorithm. Energy 66: 202-215.
53. Singh A.K., and Parida S.K. (2015) Allocation of distributed generation using proposed DMSP approach based on utility and consumers aspects under deregulated environment. Int. J. Electr. Power Energy Syst. 68: 159-169.
54. Shaaban M.F., Atwa Y.M., and El-Saadany E.F. (2013) DG allocation for benefit maximization in distribution networks. IEEE Trans. Power Syst. 28(2): 639-649.
55. Ettchadi M.,Ghasemi H., and Vaez-Zedah S. (2013) Voltage stability-based DG placement in distribution network. IEEE Trans. Power Delivery 28(1):171-178.
56. Karatepe E.,Ugrandi F., and Hiyama T. (2015) Comparison of single and multiple-distributed generation concepts in terms of power loss, voltage profile and line flows under uncertainty scenarios. Renew. Sustain. Energy Rev. 48: 317-327.
57. Arefifar S.A., Mohamed Y.A.I., El-Fouly T.H.M. (2012) Supply-adequacy-based optimal construction of micro grids in smart distribution systems. IEEE Trans. Smart Grids 3(3):1491-1502.
58. Singh R.K., and Goswami S.K. (2010) Optimum allocation of distributed generations based on nodal pricing for profit, loss reduction and voltage improvement including voltage rise issue. Int. J. Electr. Power Energy Syst. 32(6): 637-644.
59. Prenc R., Skrlec D., and Komen V. (2013) Distributed generation allocation based on average daily load and power production curves. Int. J. Electr. Power Energy Syst. 53: 612-622.
60. Gampa S.R., and Das D. (2015) Optimum placement and sizing of DGs considering average hourly variation of loads. Int. J. Electr. Power Energy Syst. 66:25-40.
61. Jamil M., and Anees A.S. (2016) Optimal sizing and location of SPV (solar photovoltaic) based MLDG (multiple location distributed generator) in distribution system for loss reduction, voltage profile improvement with economical benefits. Energy 103:231-239.

62. Garcia J.A.M., and Mena A.J.G. (2013) Optimal distributed generation location and sizing using a modified teaching-learning based optimization algorithm. Int. J. Electr. Power Energy Syst. 50: 65-75.
63. Sultana U., Khairuddin A.B., Mokhtar A.S., Zareen N., and Sultana B. (2016) Grey wolf optimizer based placement and sizing of multiple distributed generation in the distribution system. Energy 111:525-536.
64. Devi S., and Geethanjali M. (2014) Application of modified bacterial foraging optimization algorithm for optimal placement and sizing of distributed generation. Expert Syst. Appl. 41(6):2772-2781.
65. Das B., Mukherjee V., and Das D. (2016) DG placement in radial distribution network by symbiotic organisms search algorithm for real power loss minimization. Appl. Soft Comput. 49:920-936.
66. Das B., Mukherjee V., and Das D. (2020) Student psychology based optimization algorithm: A new population based optimization algorithm for solving optimization problems. Adv. Engg. Soft. 146: 102804.
67. Sugantham P.N, Hansen N., Liang J.J., Deb K., Chen Y.P., Auger A., Tiwari S. (2005) Problem definitions and evaluation criteria for the CEC 2005 special session on real-parameter optimization. Nanyang Technol. Univ., Singapore, Tech. Rep. KanGAL #2005005, IIT Kanpur, India.
68. Barik S., Das D., and Bansal R. C. (2020) DG investment and allocation in active distribution networks, in Uncertainties in Modern Power Systems, Editor-Ahmed F. Zobaa, Shady H.E. Abdel Aleem, Academic Press, Elsevier, pp. 343-394.
69. Clerc, Maurice (2010) Particle swarm optimization. John Wiley & Sons 93.
70. Rao, R. Venkata (2016) Teaching-learning-based optimization algorithm. In Teaching learning based optimization algorithm, Springer, Cham, pp. 9-39.
71. Liao, Tianjun, Daniel Molina, Marco A. Montes de Oca, and Thomas Stützle (2014) A note on bound constraints handling for the IEEE CEC'05 benchmark function suite. Evolutionary computation 22(2): 351-359.

Chaotic PSO for PV System Modelling

Souvik Ganguli*, Jyoti Gupta and Parag Nijhawan

Department of Electrical and Instrumentation Engineering, Thapar Institute of Engineering and Technology, Patiala, Punjab, India

Abstract

This chapter develops a new approach to chaotic particle swarm optimization (CPSO) technique. Ten different chaotic maps are taken up for developing the chaotic PSO algorithms. The chaotic version produced is validated by two sets of test function namely the unimodal and multimodal benchmarks. The effectiveness of the proposed approach is justified by statistical tests. Even the majority of the test results are validated with the rank-sum test of Wilcoxon. Methods for estimating unknown parameters of the three-diode model are also checked further. The investigation uses two well-known commercial solar cell models. The techniques supersede the approaches that are currently commonly reported. The convergence curves genuinely explain better test results in speed and precision. The graphs I-V and P-V correspond closely with the ideal STC diagrams. Higher diode models can be used as a futuristic solution. Moreover, some additional could be applied to the test method to determine the effectiveness of the proposed strategy. Another development that can take place is the multi-objective optimization for the parameter estimation of different diode models.

Keywords: Particle swarm optimization (PSO), chaotic particle swarm optimization (CPSO), parameter identification, three diode model, Wilcoxon test

**Corresponding author*: souvik.ganguli@thapar.edu
Souvik Ganguli: ORCID: https://orcid.org/0000-0003-4192-398X

Neeraj Priyadarshi, Akash Kumar Bhoi, Sanjeevikumar Padmanaban, S. Balamurugan and Jens Bo Holm-Nielsen (eds.) Intelligent Renewable Energy Systems, (41–78) © 2022 Scrivener Publishing LLC

2.1   Introduction

Particle swarm optimization (PSO) is a metaheuristic approach linked to the population in which each solution, called a particle, flies around the multi-dimensional search space for problems [1–20]. Based on its own experience and the experience of neighbouring particles, each particle adapts its location during flight, with the best position experienced by itself and its neighbours. The path of the particle's swarm is determined by its past and its neighbour's experience [21–46]. Two factors decide the particle status in the search space: its location and its changed velocity [1].

PSO has gained a great deal of attention and widespread application in various fields [2–5]. However, the performance of a simple PSO depends very much on its parameters and often suffers from the problem of being trapped in local optima to converge prematurely [47–62]. There are several improvements of PSO suggested in the literature [6–10]. Chaotic PSO [11–14] is one such popular variant. In the world of engineering, it is a well-established fact that the theory of chaos can be used as a very useful technique for practical use [15, 16].

The acceleration coefficients, c_1 and c_2 as well as the inertia weight, w of the PSO algorithm can be varied chaotically to show the drastic improvements in the quality of solutions and convergence accuracy. Three instances have been considered in this chapter. In the first case, both c_1 and c_2 are varied chaotically while the inertia weight, w is kept fixed. On the second occasion, the inertia weight w is varied chaotically whereas the acceleration coefficients c_1 and c_2 are maintained constant. In the third instant, all the parameters are made to vary chaotically to expect a yet better outcome. However, the results of the first version of chaos enhanced PSO algorithms are showcased in the results section though. A set of ten chaotic maps [17, 18], widely popular in the literature are considered to assess the performance of the different chaotic versions of the PSO algorithms.

The newly developed chaotic particle swarm optimization (CPSO) techniques can be assessed to identify the parameters of mostly explored photovoltaic (PV) diode models viz. the three-diode model [19]. Unlike the experimental approach, the datasheet information of the different PV models is utilized to estimate the model parameters by setting up sum of square error (SSE) as the objective to minimize. The errors originate from the cumulative effects of the short circuit, open circuit and maximum power condition. Sufficient comparison is carried out with the existing techniques [20–27]. The performance of the new chaotic version of PSO turns out to be better than most of the methods with comparison is carried out.

The remaining chapter is constructed as enumerated. The proposed work is showcased in section-2.2. Section 2.3 narrates the simulation results with sufficient comparison and validity. In section-2.4, the salient conclusions are described giving a layout for the future work.

2.2   Proposed Method

Chaos is a random deterministic mechanism in a nonlinear system, which refers to the initial conditions. If there are minor variations in the initial values, the behaviour of the nonlinear system can change drastically. Moreover, a chaotic system has complex features, such as initial conditions of certainty, randomness, and sensitivity, and even a good internal structure. The diversity of the population should be maintained based on these characteristics, thereby preventing entry into an optimal local search and increasing the likelihood of achieving a global optimum. In the literature that is represented in Table 2.1, different types of such maps are used.

The acceleration coefficients, c1 and c2 as well as the inertia w of the PSO algorithm can vary chaotically to demonstrate drastic improvements in the quality and precision of the solutions. In this chapter, three cases were considered. In the first case, c1 and c2 differ chaotically as long as the weight of the inertia w is preserved. The inertia weight w is chaotically varied on the second occasion, while the acceleration coefficients c1 and c2 are constant. In the third moment, all parameters differ chaotically to anticipate a better result. However, in the results section, one can find results of the first case of the chaos motivated PSO algorithm. The chaotic particle swarm optimization (CPSO) developed in this chapter is thus used to test some benchmark mathematical functions and also to assess the parameters of the three-diode modelled industrial solar cells in the results section.

2.3   Results and Discussions

Five test functions are taken up for the study to justify the effectiveness of the proposed method. The fun-1 and fun-2 are unimodal while that of fun-3, fun-4 and fun-5 are multimodal. The characteristics of these test functions are provided in Table 2.2. Further details about the test functions can be found from [28]. The two varieties of the test problems are adopted to test the exploration and exploitation capabilities of the proposed methods.

The test problems considered are minimization problems. The search agents considered for the study is taken up as 30 while the maximum

Table 2.1 List of one-dimensional chaotic maps.

Map name	Definition
Chebyshev map	$x_{k+1} = \cos(k \cos^{-1}(x_k))$
Circle map	$x_{k+1} = x_k + b - (a - 2\pi) \sin(2\pi x_k) mod(1)$
Gauss map	$x_{k+1} = \begin{cases} 0 & x_k = 0 \\ 1/x_k mod(1) & otherwise \end{cases}$
Iterative map	$x_{k+1} = \sin(a\pi/x_k)$
Logistic map	$x_{k+1} = ax_k(1 - x_k)$
Piecewise map	$x_{k+1} = \begin{cases} \dfrac{x_k}{P} & 0 \leq x_k < P \\[2mm] \dfrac{x_k - P}{0.5 - P} & P \leq x_k < 0.5 \\[2mm] \dfrac{1 - P - x_k}{0.5 - P} & 0.5 \leq x_k < 1 - P \\[2mm] \dfrac{1 - x_k}{P} & 1 - P \leq x_k < 1 \end{cases}$
Sine map	$x_{k+1} = \dfrac{a}{4} \sin(\pi x_k)$
Singer map	$x_{k+1} = \mu(7.86x_k - 23.31x_k^2 + 28.75x_k^3 - 13.3028.75x_k^4)$
Sinusoidal map	$x_{k+1} = ax_k^2 \sin(\pi x_k)$
Tent map	$x_{k+1} = \begin{cases} \dfrac{x_k}{0.7} x_k & x_k < 0.7 \\[2mm] \dfrac{10}{3}(1 - x_k) & x_k \geq 0.7 \end{cases}$

number of iterations is considered to be 500 for the experiments conducted on the test functions. A host of latest techniques is taken up for comparison. Since the algorithms are stochastic, hence 30 independent test runs are taken up for the study. Somestatistical measures like the

Table 2.2 Unimodal and multimodal test problems and their details.

Test problems	Function name	Function type	Dim	Search limits	f_{min}
Fun-1	Sphere	Unimodal	100	[-100, 100]	0
Fun-2	Rosenbrock	Unimodal	100	[-30,30]	0
Fun-3	Rastrigin	Multimodal	100	[-5.12,5.12]	0
Fun-4	Ackley	Multimodal	100	[-32,32]	0
Fun-5	Griewank	Multimodal	100	[-600,600]	0

minimum, maximum, average and the standard deviation are reported in Table 2.3. The average gives an idea of the closeness of the value towards the ideal global minimum. The standard deviation, on the other hand, gives a measure of the stability of the algorithm. The best and worst values indicate the range in which the fitness function lies. Instead of the actual values of the fitness functions, the normalized values are presented in Table 2.3. The normalized values are obtained for all the statistical findings showcased in the table. Every column of this table thus lies between zero and unity. The zero value indicates the best value while unity represents the worst value of the test results considered. The best values are indicated with the aid of bold letters.

From the results of Table 2.3, it can be inferred, the chaotic versions of PSO technique proposed perform better than the algorithms used for comparison for the test function fun-1. It is worth mentioning here that the piecewise map generated PSO approach supersede all other maps for the test function fun-1. However, WOA outperforms all other methods for the test problems fun-2 to fun-5 wherein the chaotic PSO techniques comes out to be the second or the third-best methods. To be more specific, the Chebyshev map inspired PSO performs relatively better as compared to the other chaotic maps for the test functions fun-2 to fun-5. The results of the chaotic models are thus quite competitive with some of the widely cited methods used for comparison. The rank-sum test of Wilcoxon test [29] is also carried out to validate the test outcomes. In this non-parametric test, the p-values are calculated. The present investigation considers a confidence interval of 5%. This means that a p-value greater than 0.05 will be considered for the experiment. The p-values are reported in Tables 2.4 and 2.5 in two parts. The insignificant

Table 2.3 Results of the test problems with the proposed methods.

Test functions	Algorithms	Minimum	Maximum	Average	Std.
Fun-1	CPSO (Chebyshev)	4.9220E-12	5.5935E-11	4.9970E-11	8.6063E-11
	CPSO (Circle)	2.1817E-11	4.8535E-11	5.9996E-11	1.1474E-10
	CPSO (Gauss)	7.7247E-12	1.8470E-11	4.0600E-11	3.8188E-11
	CPSO (Iterative)	0	3.8849E-11	2.8304E-11	9.7277E-11
	CPSO (Logistic)	2.6950E-13	5.2877E-11	1.9058E-11	1.2452E-10
	CPSO (Piecewise)	1.0780E-12	0	0	0
	CPSO (Sine)	1.0055E-11	2.4357E-11	2.0024E-11	4.5864E-11
	CPSO (Singer)	3.8317E-12	8.0590E-12	1.3787E-11	1.9082E-12
	CPSO (Sinusoidal)	5.1180E-12	4.3423E-11	4.8850E-11	7.7760E-11
	CPSO (Tent)	4.1774E-11	2.2098E-11	3.9892E-11	6.0628E-12
	PSO [1]	7.1635E-04	5.1846E-03	2.4464E-03	6.8437E-03
	ALO [20]	5.4472E-02	1.1521E-01	7.4822E-02	1.6640E-01
	DA [21]	2.0181E-02	5.5916E-01	3.5921E-01	6.8213E-01

(Continued)

Table 2.3 Results of the test problems with the proposed methods. (*Continued*)

Test functions	Algorithms	Minimum	Maximum	Average	Std.
	MVO [22]	2.3212E-03	2.2265E-03	2.5443E-03	1.6348E-03
	MFO [23]	1	1	1	1
	WOA [24]	5.9304E-02	1.2056E-01	8.8498E-02	1.4998E-01
	GOA [25]	2.0800E-01	2.0578E-01	1.9983E-01	1.4254E-01
	SCA [26]	5.2598E-02	2.5807E-01	1.3142E-01	3.5890E-01
	SSA [27]	2.1591E-02	2.3428E-02	2.3370E-02	1.9675E-02
Fun-2	CPSO (Chebyshev)	7.6692E-05	1.6120E-04	1.4544E-04	2.1037E-04
	CPSO (Circle)	3.9302E-02	3.4300E-02	3.3354E-02	3.2940E-02
	CPSO (Gauss)	3.3695E-02	2.4020E-02	3.0213E-02	2.3231E-02
	CPSO (Iterative)	1.8405E-02	2.6856E-02	2.2825E-02	2.7802E-02
	CPSO (Logistic)	1.6327E-02	1.7577E-02	1.5302E-02	1.9719E-02
	CPSO (Piecewise)	4.5150E-02	2.9557E-02	3.2735E-02	3.0136E-02
	CPSO (Sine)	2.6562E-02	1.8098E-02	1.7060E-02	1.2328E-02
	CPSO (Singer)	1.7749E-02	1.5986E-02	1.4349E-02	1.3329E-02

(*Continued*)

Table 2.3 Results of the test problems with the proposed methods. (*Continued*)

Test functions	Algorithms	Minimum	Maximum	Average	Std.
	CPSO (Sinusoidal)	2.5474E-02	1.9563E-02	2.2749E-02	1.5910E-02
	CPSO (Tent)	3.7695E-02	3.0859E-02	3.1677E-02	3.0550E-02
	PSO [1]	4.5159E-05	3.8816E-04	1.0775E-04	3.9014E-04
	ALO [20]	3.6250E-03	6.8963E-03	5.0765E-03	8.4716E-03
	DA [21]	4.0692E-02	1.9347E-01	1.3613E-01	2.0455E-01
	MVO [22]	3.7133E-05	5.5901E-05	4.9340E-05	6.5166E-05
	MFO [23]	1	1	1	1
	WOA [24]	0	0	0	0
	GOA [25]	2.6077E-02	2.5408E-02	2.4200E-02	2.6956E-02
	SCA [26]	5.2918E-01	7.0354E-01	7.9452E-01	7.8355E-01
	SSA [27]	1.5344E-03	1.3896E-03	1.1790E-03	1.3538E-03
Fun-3	CPSO (Chebyshev)	2.9572E-01	4.9046E-01	4.2330E-01	7.2301E-01
	CPSO (Circle)	7.2774E-01	6.8376E-01	7.0073E-01	4.1280E-01
	CPSO (Gauss)	6.3685E-01	5.8543E-01	6.5030E-01	2.8178E-01

(*Continued*)

Table 2.3 Results of the test problems with the proposed methods. (Continued)

Test functions	Algorithms	Minimum	Maximum	Average	Std.
	CPSO (Iterative)	6.0026E-01	5.1314E-01	5.6839E-01	2.6769E-01
	CPSO (Logistic)	5.8189E-01	5.3960E-01	5.4761E-01	3.7178E-01
	CPSO (Piecewise)	7.2950E-01	6.1509E-01	6.8048E-01	2.5739E-01
	CPSO (Sine)	5.7241E-01	5.6224E-01	5.8562E-01	3.9456E-01
	CPSO (Singer)	6.1298E-01	6.1724E-01	5.8774E-01	4.5448E-01
	CPSO (Sinusoidal)	7.0735E-01	5.8097E-01	6.5679E-01	2.9932E-01
	CPSO (Tent)	7.4495E-01	5.8574E-01	6.6560E-01	2.7975E-01
	PSO [1]	2.1278E-01	2.9295E-01	2.4472E-01	2.6979E-01
	ALO [20]	3.9660E-01	4.8952E-01	4.6174E-01	4.8434E-01
	DA [21]	8.2912E-01	1	9.9359E-01	1
	MVO [22]	8.8720E-01	8.7238E-01	8.5841E-01	5.3449E-01
	MFO [23]	1	9.4651E-01	1	5.4178E-01
	WOA [24]	0	0	0	0
	GOA [25]	3.5350E-01	4.0924E-01	4.2082E-01	3.5393E-01

(Continued)

Table 2.3 Results of the test problems with the proposed methods. (*Continued*)

Test functions	Algorithms	Minimum	Maximum	Average	Std.
	SCA [26]	1.4517E-01	3.8151E-01	2.8491E-01	5.5689E-01
	SSA [27]	2.7921E-01	3.1297E-01	2.8972E-01	2.6631E-01
Fun-4	CPSO (Chebyshev)	1.5258E-01	3.0186E-01	2.3098E-01	1.7566E-01
	CPSO (Circle)	5.7716E-01	6.9651E-01	6.4360E-01	1.8667E-01
	CPSO (Gauss)	6.1134E-01	6.9608E-01	6.4669E-01	1.3762E-01
	CPSO (Iterative)	5.8210E-01	7.1850E-01	6.6167E-01	1.7600E-01
	CPSO (Logistic)	5.4829E-01	6.5485E-01	6.2283E-01	1.8248E-01
	CPSO (Piecewise)	5.9247E-01	6.5949E-01	6.4420E-01	1.2307E-01
	CPSO (Sine)	5.7769E-01	6.6972E-01	6.2669E-01	1.6068E-01
	CPSO (Singer)	5.6014E-01	6.9200E-01	6.2738E-01	1.7990E-01
	CPSO (Sinusoidal)	4.8896E-01	6.7856E-01	6.4091E-01	2.0839E-01
	CPSO (Tent)	6.1339E-01	6.8895E-01	6.6110E-01	1.4755E-01
	PSO [1]	1.8508E-01	3.5205E-01	2.6109E-01	2.0368E-01
	ALO [20]	5.9174E-01	7.7156E-01	6.9226E-01	2.5403E-01

(*Continued*)

Table 2.3 Results of the test problems with the proposed methods. (*Continued*)

Test functions	Algorithms	Minimum	Maximum	Average	Std.
	DA [21]	5.1110E-01	8.0184E-01	6.7902E-01	3.9172E-01
	MVO [22]	2.0952E-01	9.5757E-01	3.2183E-01	9.5990E-01
	MFO [23]	1	9.6616E-01	1	1.7834E-02
	WOA [24]	0	0	0	0
	GOA [25]	6.1482E-01	7.1762E-01	6.5695E-01	1.3104E-01
	SCA [26]	3.8439E-01	1	9.0752E-01	1
	SSA [27]	4.1455E-01	6.0874E-01	4.8643E-01	2.3589E-01
Fun-5	CPSO (Chebyshev)	6.5920E-03	1.6306E-02	1.1637E-02	2.2032E-02
	CPSO (Circle)	2.0194E-01	1.9814E-01	1.9630E-01	1.5929E-01
	CPSO (Gauss)	2.0341E-01	1.8098E-01	1.9873E-01	1.6283E-01
	CPSO (Iterative)	1.7303E-01	1.6612E-01	1.8876E-01	1.4806E-01
	CPSO (Logistic)	1.4868E-01	1.2814E-01	1.4176E-01	1.1474E-01
	CPSO (Piecewise)	1.9391E-01	1.9602E-01	2.0340E-01	1.8831E-01
	CPSO (Sine)	1.3257E-01	1.3970E-01	1.5750E-01	1.4841E-01

(*Continued*)

Table 2.3 Results of the test problems with the proposed methods. (*Continued*)

Test functions	Algorithms	Minimum	Maximum	Average	Std.
	CPSO (Singer)	1.7317E-01	1.9071E-01	1.4845E-01	1.7072E-01
	CPSO (Sinusoidal)	1.6774E-01	1.8986E-01	1.8278E-01	1.8159E-01
	CPSO (Tent)	2.0241E-01	1.9980E-01	2.0520E-01	1.8749E-01
	PSO [1]	3.5168E-03	7.8512E-03	5.1009E-03	9.3400E-03
	ALO [20]	5.0112E-02	1.0077E-01	7.7874E-02	1.4340E-01
	DA [21]	4.8176E-02	4.3043E-01	3.5241E-01	7.1776E-01
	MVO [22]	5.3734E-03	2.9032E-03	3.9989E-03	1.1421E-03
	MFO [23]	1	1	1	1
	WOA [24]	0	0	0	0
	GOA [25]	1.6539E-01	1.7016E-01	1.7250E-01	1.6360E-01
	SCA [26]	3.8594E-02	2.9077E-01	1.9576E-01	5.0507E-01
	SSA [27]	2.0035E-02	2.7542E-02	2.4920E-02	3.2029E-02

Table 2.4 Non-parametric test outcomes (part-1).

Test functions	Chaotic PSO methods	PSO	ALO	DA	MVO	MFO
Fun-1	CPSO (Chebyshev)	$\approx 10^{-5}$	$\approx 10^{-5}$	$\approx 10^{-5}$	$\approx 10^{-5}$	$\approx 10^{-5}$
	CPSO (Circle)	$\approx 10^{-4}$	$\approx 10^{-4}$	$\approx 10^{-4}$	$\approx 10^{-4}$	$\approx 10^{-4}$
	CPSO (Gauss)	$\approx 10^{-4}$	$\approx 10^{-4}$	$\approx 10^{-4}$	$\approx 10^{-4}$	$\approx 10^{-4}$
	CPSO (Iterative)	$\approx 10^{-4}$	$\approx 10^{-4}$	$\approx 10^{-4}$	$\approx 10^{-4}$	$\approx 10^{-4}$
	CPSO (Logistic)	$\approx 10^{-4}$	$\approx 10^{-4}$	$\approx 10^{-4}$	$\approx 10^{-4}$	$\approx 10^{-4}$
	CPSO (Piecewise)	$\approx 10^{-4}$	$\approx 10^{-4}$	$\approx 10^{-4}$	$\approx 10^{-4}$	$\approx 10^{-4}$
	CPSO (Sine)	$\approx 10^{-4}$	$\approx 10^{-4}$	$\approx 10^{-4}$	$\approx 10^{-4}$	$\approx 10^{-4}$
	CPSO (Singer)	$\approx 10^{-4}$	$\approx 10^{-4}$	$\approx 10^{-4}$	$\approx 10^{-4}$	$\approx 10^{-4}$
	CPSO (Sinusoidal)	$\approx 10^{-4}$	$\approx 10^{-4}$	$\approx 10^{-4}$	$\approx 10^{-4}$	$\approx 10^{-4}$
	CPSO (Tent)	$\approx 10^{-4}$	$\approx 10^{-4}$	$\approx 10^{-4}$	$\approx 10^{-4}$	$\approx 10^{-4}$
Fun-2	CPSO (Chebyshev)	0.0155	$\approx 10^{-8}$	$\approx 10^{-8}$	$\approx 10^{-5}$	$\approx 10^{-8}$
	CPSO (Circle)	$\approx 10^{-8}$	$\approx 10^{-8}$	$\approx 10^{-5}$	$\approx 10^{-8}$	$\approx 10^{-8}$
	CPSO (Gauss)	$\approx 10^{-8}$	$\approx 10^{-8}$	$\approx 10^{-5}$	$\approx 10^{-8}$	$\approx 10^{-8}$
	CPSO (Iterative)	$\approx 10^{-8}$	$\approx 10^{-7}$	$\approx 10^{-6}$	$\approx 10^{-8}$	$\approx 10^{-8}$

(Continued)

Table 2.4 Non-parametric test outcomes (part-1). (Continued)

Test functions	Chaotic PSO methods	PSO	ALO	DA	MVO	MFO
	CPSO (Logistic)	$\simeq 10^{-8}$	$\simeq 10^{-6}$	$\simeq 10^{-7}$	$\simeq 10^{-8}$	$\simeq 10^{-8}$
	CPSO (Piecewise)	$\simeq 10^{-8}$	$\simeq 10^{-8}$	$\simeq 10^{-5}$	$\simeq 10^{-8}$	$\simeq 10^{-8}$
	CPSO (Sine)	$\simeq 10^{-8}$	$\simeq 10^{-7}$	$\simeq 10^{-7}$	$\simeq 10^{-8}$	$\simeq 10^{-8}$
	CPSO (Singer)	$\simeq 10^{-8}$	$\simeq 10^{-6}$	$\simeq 10^{-7}$	$\simeq 10^{-8}$	$\simeq 10^{-8}$
	CPSO (Sinusoidal)	$\simeq 10^{-8}$	$\simeq 10^{-7}$	$\simeq 10^{-6}$	$\simeq 10^{-8}$	$\simeq 10^{-8}$
	CPSO (Tent)	$\simeq 10^{-8}$	$\simeq 10^{-8}$	$\simeq 10^{-6}$	$\simeq 10^{-8}$	$\simeq 10^{-8}$
Fun-3	CPSO (Chebyshev)	$\simeq 10^{-6}$	<u>0.2853</u>	$\simeq 10^{-8}$	$\simeq 10^{-8}$	$\simeq 10^{-8}$
	CPSO (Circle)	$\simeq 10^{-8}$	$\simeq 10^{-7}$	$\simeq 10^{-6}$	$\simeq 10^{-6}$	$\simeq 10^{-8}$
	CPSO (Gauss)	$\simeq 10^{-8}$	$\simeq 10^{-7}$	$\simeq 10^{-7}$	$\simeq 10^{-8}$	$\simeq 10^{-8}$
	CPSO (Iterative)	$\simeq 10^{-8}$	$\simeq 10^{-5}$	$\simeq 10^{-8}$	$\simeq 10^{-8}$	$\simeq 10^{-8}$
	CPSO (Logistic)	$\simeq 10^{-8}$	0.0021	$\simeq 10^{-8}$	$\simeq 10^{-8}$	$\simeq 10^{-8}$
	CPSO (Piecewise)	$\simeq 10^{-8}$	$\simeq 10^{-8}$	$\simeq 10^{-6}$	$\simeq 10^{-7}$	$\simeq 10^{-8}$
	CPSO (Sine)	$\simeq 10^{-8}$	$\simeq 10^{-8}$	$\simeq 10^{-7}$	$\simeq 10^{-8}$	$\simeq 10^{-8}$
	CPSO (Singer)	$\simeq 10^{-8}$	$\simeq 10^{-8}$	$\simeq 10^{-7}$	$\simeq 10^{-7}$	$\simeq 10^{-8}$

(Continued)

Table 2.4 Non-parametric test outcomes (part-1). (*Continued*)

Test functions	Chaotic PSO methods	PSO	ALO	DA	MVO	MFO
Fun-4	CPSO (Sinusoidal)	$\approx 10^{-8}$	$\approx 10^{-8}$	$\approx 10^{-6}$	$\approx 10^{-7}$	$\approx 10^{-8}$
	CPSO (Tent)	$\approx 10^{-8}$	$\approx 10^{-8}$	$\approx 10^{-6}$	$\approx 10^{-7}$	$\approx 10^{-8}$
	CPSO (Chebyshev)	0.0411	$\approx 10^{-8}$	$\approx 10^{-8}$	0.0239	$\approx 10^{-8}$
	CPSO (Circle)	$\approx 10^{-8}$	0.0123	0.1333	$\approx 10^{-5}$	$\approx 10^{-8}$
	CPSO (Gauss)	$\approx 10^{-8}$	0.0106	0.1478	$\approx 10^{-5}$	$\approx 10^{-8}$
	CPSO (Iterative)	$\approx 10^{-8}$	0.0962	0.5250	$\approx 10^{-5}$	$\approx 10^{-8}$
	CPSO (Logistic)	$\approx 10^{-8}$	$\approx 10^{-4}$	0.0256	$\approx 10^{-5}$	$\approx 10^{-8}$
	CPSO (Piecewise)	$\approx 10^{-8}$	0.0123	0.1333	$\approx 10^{-5}$	$\approx 10^{-8}$
	CPSO (Sine)	$\approx 10^{-8}$	$\approx 10^{-4}$	0.0294	$\approx 10^{-5}$	$\approx 10^{-8}$
	CPSO (Singer)	$\approx 10^{-8}$	0.0011	0.0315	$\approx 10^{-5}$	$\approx 10^{-8}$
	CPSO (Sinusoidal)	$\approx 10^{-8}$	0.0114	0.1806	$\approx 10^{-5}$	$\approx 10^{-8}$
	CPSO (Tent)	$\approx 10^{-8}$	0.1075	0.5075	$\approx 10^{-5}$	$\approx 10^{-8}$
Fun-5	CPSO (Chebyshev)	$\approx 10^{-8}$	$\approx 10^{-8}$	$\approx 10^{-7}$	$\approx 10^{-7}$	$\approx 10^{-8}$
	CPSO (Circle)	$\approx 10^{-8}$	$\approx 10^{-8}$	0.0013	$\approx 10^{-8}$	$\approx 10^{-8}$

(*Continued*)

Table 2.4 Non-parametric test outcomes (part-1). (*Continued*)

Test functions	Chaotic PSO methods	PSO	ALO	DA	MVO	MFO
	CPSO (Gauss)	$\approx 10^{-8}$	$\approx 10^{-7}$	0.0010	$\approx 10^{-8}$	$\approx 10^{-8}$
	CPSO (Iterative)	$\approx 10^{-8}$	$\approx 10^{-7}$	$\approx 10^{-4}$	$\approx 10^{-8}$	$\approx 10^{-8}$
	CPSO (Logistic)	$\approx 10^{-8}$	$\approx 10^{-6}$	$\approx 10^{-5}$	$\approx 10^{-8}$	$\approx 10^{-8}$
	CPSO (Piecewise)	$\approx 10^{-8}$	$\approx 10^{-8}$	0.0015	$\approx 10^{-8}$	$\approx 10^{-8}$
	CPSO (Sine)	$\approx 10^{-8}$	$\approx 10^{-6}$	$\approx 10^{-5}$	$\approx 10^{-8}$	$\approx 10^{-8}$
	CPSO (Singer)	$\approx 10^{-8}$	$\approx 10^{-6}$	$\approx 10^{-5}$	$\approx 10^{-8}$	$\approx 10^{-8}$
	CPSO (Sinusoidal)	$\approx 10^{-8}$	$\approx 10^{-7}$	$\approx 10^{-4}$	$\approx 10^{-8}$	$\approx 10^{-8}$
	CPSO (Tent)	$\approx 10^{-8}$	$\approx 10^{-8}$	0.0020	$\approx 10^{-8}$	$\approx 10^{-8}$

Table 2.5 Non-parametric test outcomes (part-2).

Test functions	Chaotic PSO methods	WOA	GOA	SCA	SSA
Fun-1	CPSO (Chebyshev)	$\approx 10^{-6}$	$\approx 10^{-5}$	$\approx 10^{-5}$	$\approx 10^{-5}$
	CPSO (Circle)	$\approx 10^{-5}$	$\approx 10^{-4}$	$\approx 10^{-4}$	$\approx 10^{-4}$
	CPSO (Gauss)	$\approx 10^{-5}$	$\approx 10^{-4}$	$\approx 10^{-4}$	$\approx 10^{-4}$
	CPSO (Iterative)	$\approx 10^{-5}$	$\approx 10^{-4}$	$\approx 10^{-4}$	$\approx 10^{-4}$
	CPSO (Logistic)	$\approx 10^{-5}$	$\approx 10^{-4}$	$\approx 10^{-4}$	$\approx 10^{-4}$
	CPSO (Piecewise)	$\approx 10^{-5}$	$\approx 10^{-4}$	$\approx 10^{-4}$	$\approx 10^{-4}$
	CPSO (Sine)	$\approx 10^{-5}$	$\approx 10^{-4}$	$\approx 10^{-4}$	$\approx 10^{-4}$
	CPSO (Singer)	$\approx 10^{-5}$	$\approx 10^{-4}$	$\approx 10^{-4}$	$\approx 10^{-4}$
	CPSO (Sinusoidal)	$\approx 10^{-5}$	$\approx 10^{-4}$	$\approx 10^{-4}$	$\approx 10^{-4}$
	CPSO (Tent)	$\approx 10^{-5}$	$\approx 10^{-4}$	$\approx 10^{-4}$	$\approx 10^{-4}$
Fun-2	CPSO (Chebyshev)	$\approx 10^{-8}$	$\approx 10^{-8}$	$\approx 10^{-8}$	$\approx 10^{-8}$
	CPSO (Circle)	$\approx 10^{-8}$	0.0275	$\approx 10^{-8}$	$\approx 10^{-8}$
	CPSO (Gauss)	$\approx 10^{-8}$	0.0531	$\approx 10^{-8}$	$\approx 10^{-8}$

(Continued)

Table 2.5 Non-parametric test outcomes (part-2). (*Continued*)

Test functions	Chaotic PSO methods	WOA	GOA	SCA	SSA
	CPSO (Iterative)	$\approx 10^{-8}$	<u>0.6359</u>	$\approx 10^{-8}$	$\approx 10^{-8}$
	CPSO (Logistic)	$\approx 10^{-8}$	0.0043	$\approx 10^{-8}$	$\approx 10^{-8}$
	CPSO (Piecewise)	$\approx 10^{-8}$	0.0499	$\approx 10^{-8}$	$\approx 10^{-8}$
	CPSO (Sine)	$\approx 10^{-8}$	0.0223	$\approx 10^{-8}$	$\approx 10^{-8}$
	CPSO (Singer)	$\approx 10^{-8}$	0.0012	$\approx 10^{-8}$	$\approx 10^{-8}$
	CPSO (Sinusoidal)	$\approx 10^{-8}$	<u>0.9031</u>	$\approx 10^{-8}$	$\approx 10^{-8}$
	CPSO (Tent)	$\approx 10^{-8}$	0.0385	$\approx 10^{-8}$	$\approx 10^{-8}$
Fun-3	CPSO (Chebyshev)	$\approx 10^{-9}$	<u>0.8392</u>	0.0020	$\approx 10^{-4}$
	CPSO (Circle)	$\approx 10^{-9}$	$\approx 10^{-8}$	$\approx 10^{-8}$	$\approx 10^{-8}$
	CPSO (Gauss)	$\approx 10^{-9}$	$\approx 10^{-8}$	$\approx 10^{-8}$	$\approx 10^{-8}$
	CPSO (Iterative)	$\approx 10^{-9}$	$\approx 10^{-7}$	$\approx 10^{-8}$	$\approx 10^{-8}$
	CPSO (Logistic)	$\approx 10^{-9}$	$\approx 10^{-7}$	$\approx 10^{-7}$	$\approx 10^{-8}$
	CPSO (Piecewise)	$\approx 10^{-9}$	$\approx 10^{-8}$	$\approx 10^{-8}$	$\approx 10^{-8}$
	CPSO (Sine)	$\approx 10^{-9}$	$\approx 10^{-7}$	$\approx 10^{-8}$	$\approx 10^{-8}$

(*Continued*)

Table 2.5 Non-parametric test outcomes (part-2). (*Continued*)

Test functions	Chaotic PSO methods	WOA	GOA	SCA	SSA
	CPSO (Singer)	≈ 10^{-9}	≈ 10^{-7}	≈ 10^{-8}	≈ 10^{-8}
	CPSO (Sinusoidal)	≈ 10^{-9}	≈ 10^{-8}	≈ 10^{-8}	≈ 10^{-8}
	CPSO (Tent)	≈ 10^{-9}	≈ 10^{-8}	≈ 10^{-8}	≈ 10^{-8}
Fun-4	CPSO (Chebyshev)	≈ 10^{-8}	≈ 10^{-8}	≈ 10^{-8}	≈ 10^{-8}
	CPSO (Circle)	≈ 10^{-8}	≈ 10^{-8}	≈ 10^{-4}	≈ 10^{-7}
	CPSO (Gauss)	≈ 10^{-8}	≈ 10^{-8}	≈ 10^{-4}	≈ 10^{-7}
	CPSO (Iterative)	≈ 10^{-8}	≈ 10^{-8}	≈ 10^{-4}	≈ 10^{-7}
	CPSO (Logistic)	≈ 10^{-8}	≈ 10^{-8}	≈ 10^{-4}	≈ 10^{-7}
	CPSO (Piecewise)	≈ 10^{-8}	≈ 10^{-8}	≈ 10^{-4}	≈ 10^{-7}
	CPSO (Sine)	≈ 10^{-8}	≈ 10^{-8}	≈ 10^{-4}	≈ 10^{-7}
	CPSO (Singer)	≈ 10^{-8}	≈ 10^{-8}	≈ 10^{-4}	≈ 10^{-7}
	CPSO (Sinusoidal)	≈ 10^{-8}	≈ 10^{-8}	≈ 10^{-4}	≈ 10^{-7}
	CPSO (Tent)	≈ 10^{-8}	≈ 10^{-8}	0.0011	≈ 10^{-7}
Fun-5	CPSO (Chebyshev)	≈ 10^{-8}	≈ 10^{-8}	≈ 10^{-8}	≈ 10^{-6}

(*Continued*)

Table 2.5 Non-parametric test outcomes (part-2). (*Continued*)

Test functions	Chaotic PSO methods	WOA	GOA	SCA	SSA
	CPSO (Circle)	$\approx 10^{-8}$	0.0810	0.4570	$\approx 10^{-8}$
	CPSO (Gauss)	$\approx 10^{-8}$	0.0439	0.5250	$\approx 10^{-8}$
	CPSO (Iterative)	$\approx 10^{-8}$	0.1636	0.7557	$\approx 10^{-8}$
	CPSO (Logistic)	$\approx 10^{-8}$	0.0084	0.2287	$\approx 10^{-8}$
	CPSO (Piecewise)	$\approx 10^{-8}$	0.0315	0.3942	$\approx 10^{-8}$
	CPSO (Sine)	$\approx 10^{-8}$	0.2287	0.5075	$\approx 10^{-8}$
	CPSO (Singer)	$\approx 10^{-8}$	0.0207	0.2616	$\approx 10^{-8}$
	CPSO (Sinusoidal)	$\approx 10^{-8}$	0.4094	0.8392	$\approx 10^{-8}$
	CPSO (Tent)	$\approx 10^{-8}$	0.0239	0.2853	$\approx 10^{-8}$

p-values are underlined for the readers. Some approximate orders are also mentioned in these table as well as few of these values were repetitive and quite significantly lower than 0.05. The similarity may either result due to the closeness of the data sets or else attributed to the fact that the lowest value is reached. Significantly lower values in comparison to 0.05 are represented in these tables by their orders only. Few significant values close to 0.05 are also presented. The direct insignificant values are also reported in these tables.

From the two Tables 2.4–2.5, it is found that about 94.22% of the results are significant. The invalid p-values are underlined. The parameters of a three-diode model are also obtained with the help of the proposed techniques. Two commercial solar cell models [30–31] are considered in the experiment. The datasheet of the models is provided in Tables 2.6. Standard search bounds available in the literature are taken up for the investigation.

The estimated parameters of the three-diode models are shown in Table 2.7 and 2.8 respectively. Apart from the parent PSO technique, metaheuristic approaches like SSA, MVO, DA and GOA are used for comparison.

The statistical measures of the fitness function, taken as the sum of square error (SSE), have been presented in Tables 2.9 and 2.10 respectively.

Table 2.6 Datasheet values of PV modules at STC conditions.

Manufacturer	Kyocera	Canadian solar
Model	KC200GT	CS6K-280M
Cell type	Multi-crystalline	Mono-crystalline
Pm [W]	200	280
Vm [V]	26.3	31.5
Im [A]	7.61	8.89
Vo [V]	32.9	38.5
Isc [A]	8.21	9.43
Ns[cells]	54	60
Ki	0.00318A/°C	0.053%/°C
Kv	−0.123V/°C	−0.31%/°C

Table 2.7 Estimated parameters of the three-diode model for Kyocera (KC200GT multi-crystal).

Methods	Ipv	Alpha1	Alpha2	Alpha3	Rs	Rsh	Io1	Io2	Io3
CPSO (Chebyshev)	8.2136	1.7464	1.5532	1.5683	0.1283	285.301	5.1E-07	4.8E-07	5.3E-07
CPSO (Circle)	8.2138	1.6907	1.5822	1.6302	0.1230	278.119	5.7E-07	4.5E-07	3.9E-07
CPSO (Gauss)	8.2133	1.4612	1.7156	1.7547	0.1256	309.348	5.3E-07	4.3E-07	5.7E-07
CPSO (Iterative)	8.2134	1.7232	1.6100	1.5658	0.1341	326.564	5.5E-07	5.1E-07	4.1E-07
CPSO (Logistic)	8.2129	1.6082	1.5063	1.6141	0.1295	367.112	5.9E-07	3.4E-07	3.3E-07
CPSO (Piecewise)	8.2137	1.5840	1.6980	1.4854	0.1268	284.687	3.4E-07	3.5E-07	3.9E-07
CPSO (Sine)	8.2141	1.7215	1.5140	1.6408	0.1209	255.447	5.2E-07	4.2E-07	5.5E-07
CPSO (Singer)	8.2133	1.6225	1.6279	1.5960	0.0994	268.863	4.9E-07	6.3E-07	5.1E-07
CPSO (Sinusoidal)	8.2139	1.6858	1.5840	1.6518	0.1147	243.558	4.3E-07	4.7E-07	7.1E-07
CPSO (Tent)	8.2133	1.7478	1.5258	1.5988	0.1200	304.642	6.7E-07	5.4E-07	4.7E-07
PSO [1]	6.4479	1.5459	1.6429	1.5911	0.1082	368.109	3.7E-07	5.1E-07	5.3E-07
SSA [27]	8.5018	1.7066	1.5223	1.5542	0.3153	322.346	7.6E-07	6.3E-07	7.3E-07
MVO [22]	8.1952	1.4770	1.3177	1.3435	0.0625	288.582	8E-07	4E-07	6E-07
DA [21]	9.5989	1.5756	1.2274	1.4454	0.0612	133.121	6.8E-07	3.6E-07	4.2E-07
GOA [25]	8.3456	1.4718	1.4873	1.6588	0.2662	438.823	4.1E-07	1.4E-07	6.6E-07

Table 2.8 Optimal parameter identification of the three-diode model for Canadian solar (CS6K 280M mono-crystalline).

Parameter/Algorithms	Ipv	Alpha1	Alpha2	Alpha3	Rs	Rsh	Io1	Io2	Io3
CPSO (Chebyshev)	9.4301	1.5479	1.5457	1.6803	0.0071	358.370	3.9E-07	2.3E-C7	2.8E-07
CPSO (Circle)	9.4301	1.6298	1.8864	1.6426	0.0051	407.717	4.6E-07	3.4E-07	4.4E-07
CPSO (Gauss)	9.4302	1.7427	1.8869	1.5916	0.0115	371.326	3.5E-07	3.6E-07	3.7E-07
CPSO (Iterative)	9.4301	1.5700	1.7139	1.7893	0.0038	349.276	3.6E-07	6.3E-07	3.5E-07
CPSO (Logistic)	9.4301	1.7652	1.7066	1.5909	0.0077	424.227	3.2E-07	3.1E-07	3.3E-07
CPSO (Piecewise)	9.4300	1.7513	1.4922	1.7977	0.0012	362.159	3.4E-07	4.2E-07	4.4E-07
CPSO (Sine)	9.4302	1.9159	1.4465	1.4272	0.0076	243.058	3.4E-07	9.5E-08	1.5E-07
CPSO (Singer)	9.4303	1.8398	1.6402	1.6807	0.0116	383.768	3.8E-07	3.8E-07	2.5E-07
CPSO (Sinusoidal)	9.4301	1.6340	1.5368	1.8102	0.0075	373.608	2.5E-07	3.6E-07	3.7E-07
CPSO (Tent)	9.4303	1.7207	1.7869	1.3637	0.0096	234.472	5.8E-07	3.3E-07	8.4E-08
PSO [1]	9.4300	1.7241	1.5977	1.7104	0.0016	348.100	2.7E-07	3.8E-07	5.1E-07
SSA [27]	9.5656	1.5878	1.7248	1.5705	0.1096	279.429	4.3E-07	5.9E-07	6.7E-07
MVO [22]	9.4711	1.3743	1.3580	1.4574	0.0027	341.157	0	6E-07	6E-07
DA [21]	8.6869	1.3408	1.7556	1.7724	0.4382	117.885	8.4E-07	8.4E-07	9.4E-09
GOA [25]	9.5874	1.4572	1.7606	1.6324	0.1462	499.944	3.8E-07	2.6E-07	4.5E-07

Table 2.9 Normalized statistical analysisof the error function for the three-diode model utilizing Kyocera (KC200GT multi-crystal).

Algorithms	Minimum	Average	Maximum	Standard deviation
CPSO (Chebyshev)	7.6078E-31	8.3950E-30	1.8192E-29	2.2203E-29
CPSO (Circle)	5.9329E-30	2.1604E-30	8.7418E-31	1.1655E-31
CPSO (Gauss)	2.3541E-30	8.0246E-31	9.5345E-31	8.7682E-31
CPSO (Iterative)	1.3695E-30	6.9444E-31	1.5503E-30	2.4235E-30
CPSO (Logistic)	2.1739E-30	1.3580E-30	2.4226E-31	1.0033E-31
CPSO (Piecewise)	1.0868E-30	1.6975E-31	3.5371E-31	1.1807E-30
CPSO (Sine)	**0**	1.2654E-30	1.5707E-30	4.0556E-30
CPSO (Singer)	5.622E-30	3.4413E-30	2.0995E-30	1.1708E-30
CPSO (Sinusoidal)	1.2061E-30	**0**	**0**	**0**
CPSO (Tent)	9.8554E-31	1.9444E-30	1.5817E-30	2.4612E-30
PSO [1]	4.0054E-28	4.4550E-28	5.7189E-28	5.3100E-28
SSA [27]	4.0909E-01	3.9351E-01	6.3056E-01	6.5562E-01
MVO [22]	5.0487E-02	6.4814E-02	9.9246E-02	1.0927E-01
DA [21]	1	1	1	1
GOA [25]	3.4634E-01	6.9598E-01	6.9498E-01	8.4437E-01

Once again, the normalized values of the error functions are reported. The best results of each column are highlighted with the help of bold letters.

The chaotic PSO algorithms outperform the basic PSO technique as well as some of the well-known methods widely reported in the literature. DA has the worst performance amongst the methods compared for both the models. The results of the CPSO are thus quite encouraging. The I-V and P-V graphs of the proposed techniques for the Kyocera (KC200GT multi-crystal) are drawn in Figures 2.1 and 2.2 respectively. The graphs resemble the original characteristics under ideal conditions.

The I-V and the P-V diagrams closely resemble the ideal characteristic curves at STC. The convergence characteristics of the proposed CPSO techniques for the Kyocera (KC200GT multi-crystal) are displayed in Figure 2.3. Several methods are also used for comparison.

Table 2.10 Normalized results of the sum of square error (SSE) for the three-diode model for Canadian solar (CS6K 280M mono-crystalline).

Algorithms	Minimum	Average	Maximum	S.D
CPSO (Chebyshev)	6.0743E-31	3.5963E-31	2.8884E-31	2.6239E-31
CPSO (Circle)	1.6015E-30	5.7088E-31	1.9872E-31	7.5971E-32
CPSO (Gauss)	2.2090E-31	4.0972E-32	0	0
CPSO (Iterative)	4.0234E-31	5.5176E-31	3.2288E-31	2.5086E-31
CPSO (Logistic)	2.2090E-31	4.6435E-32	2.4096E-31	4.0369E-31
CPSO (Piecewise)	4.9702E-31	3.3870E-31	3.2388E-31	4.4406E-31
CPSO (Sine)	4.9702E-31	2.4856E-31	3.2388E-31	3.9792E-31
CPSO (Singer)	4.9702E-31	5.1352E-31	3.2388E-31	4.0657E-31
CPSO (Sinusoidal)	5.5224E-32	0	1.9747E-31	2.6816E-31
CPSO (Tent)	0	1.0926E-32	3.2288E-31	4.0945E-31
PSO [1]	1.0016E-28	1.1566E-28	8.2734E-29	7.9016E-29
SSA [27]	1.5171E-01	1.0051E-01	5.4589E-02	3.8927E-02
MVO [22]	1.0424E-02	1.1745E-02	7.6492E-03	8.0738E-03
DA [21]	1	1	1	1
GOA [25]	9.2478E-02	1.1363E-01	8.4133E-02	8.9100E-02

The I-V and the P-V diagrams for the Canadian solar (CS6K 280M mono-crystalline) model are showcased in Figures 2.4 and 2.5 respectively.

The curves shown in Figures 2.4 and 2.5 closely match the actual characteristics at STC. The convergence curves of the suggested methods for the Canadian solar (CS6K 280M mono-crystalline) are drawn in Figure 2.6.

The convergence characteristics produce a good speed of convergence and better accuracy than the methods with which a comparison is carried out. Thus, our method gives satisfactory performance for the parameter estimation of the three-diode model as well. Higher diode models can be taken up as a futuristic approach. The constrained problem of optimization can also be considered to test the efficacy of the proposed approach. A multi-objective approach to the parameter estimation problem can also be thought of in times to come.

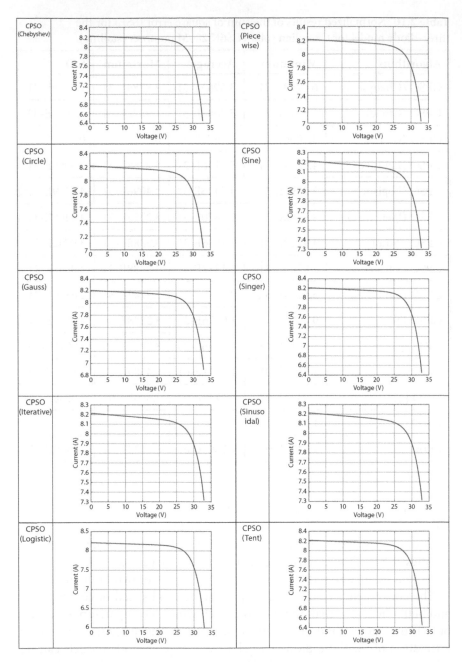

Figure 2.1 I-V curves for the proposed CPSO techniques Kyocera (KC200GT multi-crystal).

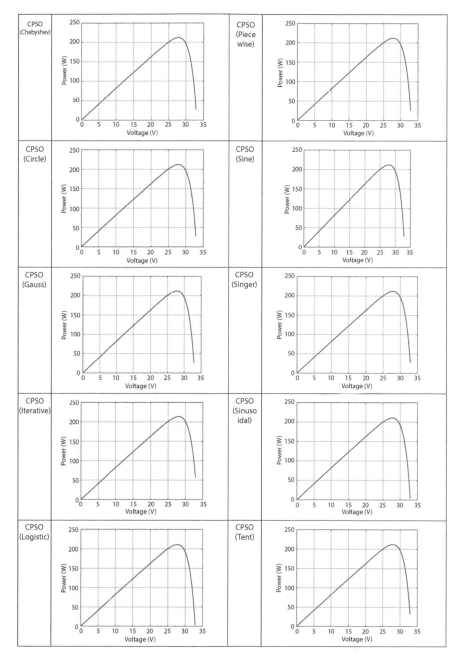

Figure 2.2 P-V curves of all the variants of CPSO Kyocera (KC200GT multi-crystal).

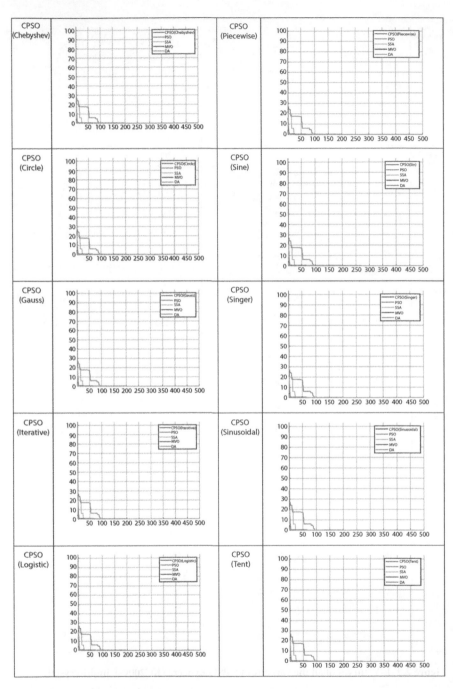

Figure 2.3 Convergence plots of each variant of CPSO with other compared algorithms Kyocera (KC200GT multi-crystal).

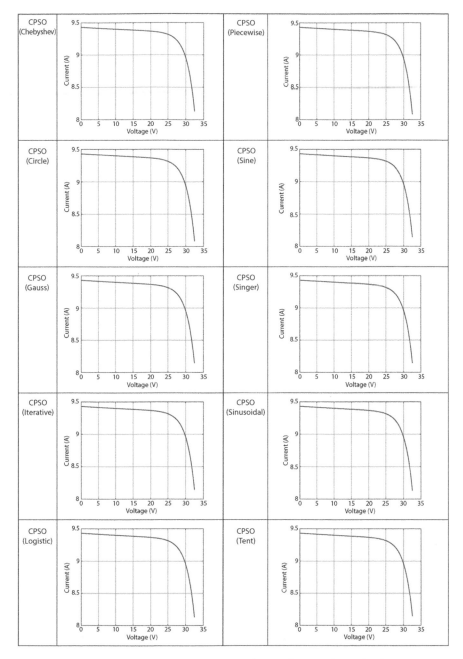

Figure 2.4 I-V curves of the proposed CPSO technique for Canadian solar (CS6K 280M mono-crystalline) model.

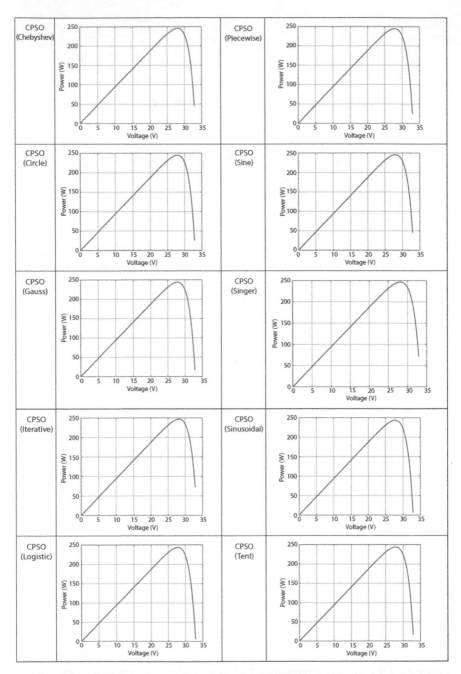

Figure 2.5 P-V curves of all variants of CPSO for Canadian solar (CS6K 280M mono-crystalline) model.

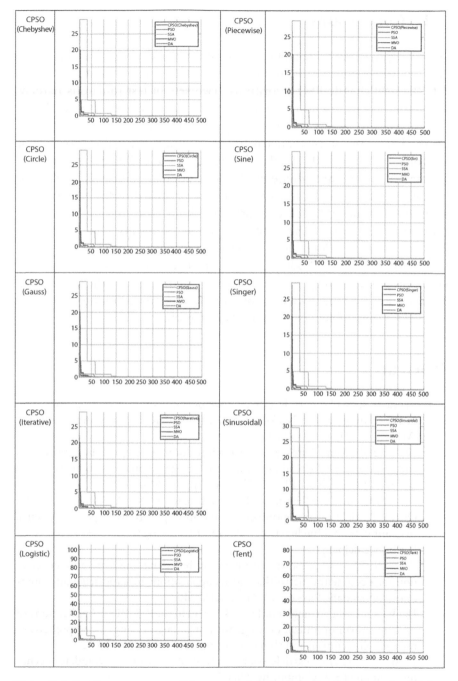

Figure 2.6 Convergences curves of the proposed methods for the Canadian solar (CS6K 280M mono-crystalline).

2.4   Conclusions

A new approach to the chaotic PSO technique is developed in this chapter. Ten widely popular one-dimensional chaotic maps are used to formulate the new chaotic PSO algorithms. Two sets of test functions namely, the unimodal and multimodal are considered to validate the developed chaotic version. Statistical measures justify the efficacy of the suggested method. Even the non-parametric test also signifies the majority of the test outcomes. The methods are also further tested to estimate the unknown parameters of the three-diode model. Two popular commercial solar cell models are used for the investigation. The proposed techniques outperform the existing and widely reported methods. The convergence curves truly justify better speed and accuracy of the test results. The I-V and the P-V graphs are in a close match with the ideal diagrams at STC. As a futuristic approach, higher diode models can be taken. To assess the feasibility of the proposed strategy, some constraints can be added to the test system. In near future, a multi-objective optimization approach may also be considered for the problem of parameter estimation.

References

1. Kennedy, J., & Eberhart, R. (1995, November). Particle swarm optimization. In Proceedings of ICNN'95-International Conference on Neural Networks (Vol. 4, pp. 1942-1948). IEEE.
2. Shi, Y. (2001, May). Particle swarm optimization: developments, applications and resources. In Proceedings of the 2001 congress on evolutionary computation (IEEE Cat. No. 01TH8546) (Vol. 1, pp. 81-86). IEEE.
3. AlRashidi, M. R., AlHajri, M. F., Al-Othman, A. K., & El-Naggar, K. M. (2010). Particle swarm optimization and its applications in power systems. In Computational Intelligence in Power Engineering (pp. 295-324). Springer, Berlin, Heidelberg.
4. Ye, F. (2017). Particle swarm optimization-based automatic parameter selection for deep neural networks and its applications in large-scale and high-dimensional data. PloS one, 12(12), e0188746.
5. Hajihassani, M., Armaghani, D. J., & Kalatehjari, R. (2018). Applications of particle swarm optimization in geotechnical engineering: a comprehensive review. Geotechnical and Geological Engineering, 36(2), 705-722.
6. Kiran, M. S. (2017). Particle swarm optimization with a new update mechanism. Applied Soft Computing, 60, 670-678.
7. Tian, D., & Shi, Z. (2018). MPSO: Modified particle swarm optimization and its applications. Swarm and evolutionary computation, 41, 49-68.

8. Wang, F., Zhang, H., Li, K., Lin, Z., Yang, J., & Shen, X. L. (2018). A hybrid particle swarm optimization algorithm using adaptive learning strategy. Information Sciences, 436, 162-177.

9. Xu, G., Cui, Q., Shi, X., Ge, H., Zhan, Z. H., Lee, H. P., ... & Wu, C. (2019). Particle swarm optimization based on dimensional learning strategy. Swarm and Evolutionary Computation, 45, 33-51.

10. Zhang, X., Liu, H., & Tu, L. (2020). A modified particle swarm optimization for multimodal multi-objective optimization. Engineering Applications of Artificial Intelligence, 95, 103905.

11. Xu, X., Rong, H., Trovati, M., Liptrott, M., & Bessis, N. (2018). CS-PSO: chaotic particle swarm optimization algorithm for solving combinatorial optimization problems. Soft Computing, 22(3), 783-795.

12. Tian, D., Zhao, X., & Shi, Z. (2019). Chaotic particle swarm optimization with sigmoid-based acceleration coefficients for numerical function optimization. Swarm and Evolutionary Computation, 51, 100573.

13. Tharwat, A., Elhoseny, M., Hassanien, A. E., Gabel, T., & Kumar, A. (2019). Intelligent Bézier curve-based path planning model using Chaotic Particle Swarm Optimization algorithm. Cluster Computing, 22(2), 4745-4766.

14. Wang, C., Yu, T., Shao, G., Nguyen, T. T., & Bui, T. Q. (2019). Shape optimization of structures with cutouts by an efficient approach based on XIGA and chaotic particle swarm optimization. European Journal of Mechanics-A/Solids, 74, 176-187.

15. Kaveh, A., & Javadi, S. M. (2019). Chaos-based firefly algorithms for optimization of cyclically large-size braced steel domes with multiple frequency constraints. Computers & Structures, 214, 28-39.

16. Yu, H., Zhao, N., Wang, P., Chen, H., & Li, C. (2020). Chaos-enhanced synchronized bat optimizer. Applied Mathematical Modelling, 77, 1201-1215.

17. Tharwat, A., & Hassanien, A. E. (2018). Chaotic antlion algorithm for parameter optimization of support vector machine. Applied Intelligence, 48(3), 670-686.

18. Sayed, G. I., Khoriba, G., & Haggag, M. H. (2018). A novel chaotic salp swarm algorithm for global optimization and feature selection. Applied Intelligence, 48(10), 3462-3481.

19. Abd Elaziz, M., & Oliva, D. (2018). Parameter estimation of solar cells diode models by an improved opposition-based whale optimization algorithm. Energy conversion and management, 171, 1843-1859.

20. Mirjalili, S. (2015). The ant lion optimizer. Advances in engineering software, 83, 80-98.

21. Mirjalili, S. (2016). Dragonfly algorithm: a new meta-heuristic optimization technique for solving single-objective, discrete, and multi-objective problems. Neural Computing and Applications, 27(4), 1053-1073.

22. Mirjalili, S., Mirjalili, S. M., & Hatamlou, A. (2016). Multi-verse optimizer: a nature-inspired algorithm for global optimization. Neural Computing and Applications, 27(2), 495-513.

23. Mirjalili, S. (2015). Moth-flame optimization algorithm: A novel nature-inspired heuristic paradigm. Knowledge-based systems, 89, 228-249.
24. Mirjalili, S., & Lewis, A. (2016). The whale optimization algorithm. Advances in engineering software, 95, 51-67.
25. Mirjalili, S. Z., Mirjalili, S., Saremi, S., Faris, H., & Aljarah, I. (2018). Grasshopper optimization algorithm for multi-objective optimization problems. Applied Intelligence, 48(4), 805-820.
26. Mirjalili, S. (2016). SCA: a sine cosine algorithm for solving optimization problems. Knowledge-based systems, 96, 120-133.
27. Mirjalili, S., Gandomi, A. H., Mirjalili, S. Z., Saremi, S., Faris, H., & Mirjalili, S. M. (2017). Salp Swarm Algorithm: A bio-inspired optimizer for engineering design problems. Advances in Engineering Software, 114, 163-191.
28. Jamil, M., & Yang, X. S. (2013). A literature survey of benchmark functions for global optimization problems. arXiv preprint arXiv:1308.4008.
29. de Barros, R. S. M., Hidalgo, J. I. G., & de Lima Cabral, D. R. (2018). Wilcoxon rank sum test drift detector. Neurocomputing, 275, 1954-1963.
30. Elazab, O. S., Hasanien, H. M., Alsaidan, I., Abdelaziz, A. Y., & Muyeen, S. M. (2020). Parameter estimation of three diode photovoltaic model using grasshopper optimization algorithm. Energies, 13(2), 497.
31. Qais, M. H., Hasanien, H. M., & Alghuwainem, S. (2020). Parameters extraction of three-diode photovoltaic model using computation and Harris Hawks optimization. Energy, 195, 117040.
32. Priyadarshi.; N; Padmanaban, S.; Maroti, P.K.; Sharma. A.; An Extensive Practical Investigation of FPSO-Based MPPT for Grid Integrated PV System Under Variable Operating Conditions With Anti-Islanding Protection. IEEE System Journal, 2018, 13:1861 - 1871.
33. Priyadarshi, N.; Padmanaban, S.; Bhaskar, M.S.; Blaabjerg, F.; Sharma, A.; A Fuzzy SVPWM Based Inverter Control Realization of Grid Integrated PV-Wind System with FPSO MPPT Algorithm for a Grid-Connected PV/Wind Power Generation System: Hardware Implementation. IET Electric Power Appl., 2018, 12:962-971.
34. Priyadarshi, N.; Kumar, V.; Yadav, K.; Vardia, M.; An Experimental Study on Zeta buck-boost converter for Application in PV system. Handbook of distributed generation, Springer, DOI 10.1007/978-3-319-51343-0_13
35. Priyadarshi N.; Sharma A.K.; Priyam S.; An Experimental Realization of Grid-Connected PV System with MPPT Using dSPACE DS 1104 Control Board. Advances in Smart Grid and Renewable Energy. Lecture Notes in Electrical Engineering, Springer, Singapore 2018, 435.
36. Priyadarshi N.; Sharma A.K.; Priyam S.; Practical Realization of an Improved Photovoltaic Grid Integration with MPPT. International Journal of Renewable Energy Research 2017, 7:1180-1891.
37. Priyadarshi N.; Sharma A.K.; Azam F.; A Hybrid Firefly-Asymmetrical Fuzzy Logic Controller based MPPT for PV-Wind-Fuel Grid Integration. International Journal of Renewable Energy Research 2017, 7: 1546-1560.

38. Priyadarshi, N.; Anand, A.; Sharma, A.K.; Azam, F.; Singh, V.K.; Sinha, R. K.; An Experimental Implementation and Testing of GA based Maximum Power Point Tracking for PV System under Varying Ambient Conditions Using dSPACE DS 1104 Controller. International Journal of Renewable Energy Research, **2017**, 7:255-265.

39. Priyadarshi, N.; Padmanaban S.; Mihet-Popa L.; Blaabjerg, F.; Azam F.; Maximum Power Point Tracking for Brushless DC Motor-Driven Photovoltaic Pumping Systems Using a Hybrid ANFIS-FLOWER Pollination Optimization Algorithm. MDPI Energies **2018**, 11:1-16.

40. Priyadarshi, N.; Azam, F.; Bhoi, A.K.; Alam, S.; An Artificial Fuzzy Logic Intelligent Controller Based MPPT for PV Grid Utility. Lecture Notes in Networks and Systems 46, https://doi.org/10.1007/978-981-13-1217-5_88.

41. Padmanaban, S.; Priyadarshi, N.; Holm-Nielsen, J. B.; Bhaskar, M. S.; Azam, F.; Sharma, A.K.; A Novel Modified Sine-Cosine Optimized MPPT Algorithm for Grid Integrated PV System under Real Operating Conditions. IEEE Access, **2019**, 7:10467-10477.

42. Padmanaban, S.; Priyadarshi, N.; Holm-Nielsen, J. B.; Bhaskar, M. S.; Hossain, E.; Azam, F.; A Hybrid Photovoltaic-Fuel Cell for Grid Integration With Jaya-Based Maximum Power Point Tracking: Experimental Performance Evaluation. IEEE Access, **2019**, 7:82978-82990.

43. Priyadarshi, N.; Padmanaban, N.; Holm-Nielsen, J. B.; Blaabjerg, F.; Bhaskar, M.S.; An Experimental Estimation of Hybrid ANFIS–PSO-Based MPPT for PV Grid Integration Under Fluctuating Sun Irradiance. in IEEE Systems Journal. **2020**, 14:1218-1229.

44. Priyadarshi, N.; Padmanaban, N.; Bhaskar, M. S.; Blaabjerg, F.; Holm-Nielsen, J. B.; Azam, F.; Sharma, A.K.; A Hybrid Photovoltaic-Fuel Cell-Based Single-Stage Grid Integration With Lyapunov Control Scheme. IEEE Systems Journal, **2020**, 14: 3334 - 3342.

45. Priyadarshi, N.; Bhaskar, M. S.; Padmanaban, N.; Blaabjerg, F.; Azam, F.; New CUK–SEPIC converter based photovoltaic power system with hybrid GSA–PSO algorithm employing MPPT for water pumping applications. IET Power Electronics. **2020**, 13:2824 – 2830.

46. Priyadarshi, N.; Padmanaban, N.; Holm-Nielsen, J. B.; Bhaskar, M.S.; Azam, F.; Internet of things augmented a novel PSO-employed modified zeta converter-based photovoltaic maximum power tracking system: hardware realisation. IET Power Electronics. **2020**, 13:2775 – 2781.

47. Kamalapathi, K., Priyadarshi, N., Padmanaban, S., Holm-Nielsen, J.B., Azam, F., Umayal, C., Ramachandaramurthy, V.K. A Hybrid Moth-Flame Fuzzy Logic Controller Based Integrated Cuk Converter Fed Brushless DC Motor for Power Factor Correction. MDPI Electronics, **2018**, 7: 288.

48. Priyadarshi, N., Padmanaban, S., Lonel, D., Mihet-Popa, L., Azam, F. Hybrid PV-Wind, Micro-Grid Development Using Quasi-Z-Source Inverter Modeling and Control—Experimental Investigation. MDPI Energies, **2018**, 11:2277.

49. Priyadarshi, N.; Ramachandaramurthy, V, K.; Padmanaban, S.; Azam, A.; An Ant Colony Optimized MPPT for Standalone Hybrid PV-Wind Power System with Single Cuk Converter. MDPI Energies, **2019**, 12: 167.

50. Azam, F.; Yadav, S.K.; Priyadarshi, N.; Padmanaban, S.; and Bansal, R.C.; A Comprehensive Review of Authentication Schemes in Vehicular Ad-Hoc Network, IEEE Access, **2021**, 9:31309-31321, 2021, doi: 10.1109/ACCESS.2021.3060046.

51. Priyadarshi, N.; Sharma, A.K.; Bhoi, A. K.; Ahmad, S. N.; Azam, F.; Priyam, S.; A Practical performance verification of AFLC based MPPT for standalone PV power system under varying weather condition, International Journal of Engineering & Technology, **2018**, 7:338-343.

52. Azam F.; Priyadarshi N.; Nagar H.; Kumar S.; Bhoi A.K.; An Overview of Solar-Powered Electric Vehicle Charging in Vehicular Adhoc Network. in: Electric Vehicles. Green Energy and Technology. Springer, Singapore. https://doi.org/10.1007/978-981-15-9251-5_5

53. Azam, F.; Kumar, S.; Yadav, K.P.; Priyadarshi N.; Padmanaban, S.; An Outline of the Security Challenges in VANET, in Proc. of IEEE UPCON 2020, Nov, 2020.

54. Priyadarshi, N.; Azam, F.; Bhoi, A.K.; Sharma, A.K.; A Multilevel Inverter-Controlled Photovoltaic Generation. in Advances in Greener Energy Technologies. Springer, Singapore. **2020** https://doi.org/10.1007/978-981-15-4246-6_8

55. Priyadarshi, N.; Azam, F.; Bhoi, A.K.; Sharma, A.K.; Dynamic Operation of Grid-Connected Photovoltaic Power System. in Advances in Greener Energy Technologies. Springer, Singapore. **2020** https://doi.org/10.1007/978-981-15-4246-6_13

56. Priyadarshi, N.; Azam, F.; Bhoi, A.K.; Sharma, A.K.; A Proton Exchange Membrane-Based Fuel Cell Integrated Power System. in Advances in Greener Energy Technologies. Springer, Singapore. **2020** https://doi.org/10.1007/978-981-15-4246-6_18

57. Priyadarshi, N.; Azam, F.; Bhoi, A.K.; Sharma, A.K.; A Closed-Loop Control of Fixed Pattern Rectifier for Renewable Energy Applications. in Advances in Greener Energy Technologies. Springer, Singapore. **2020** https://doi.org/10.1007/978-981-15-4246-6_25

58. Priyadarshi, N.; Azam, F.; Bhoi, A.K.; Sharma, A.K.; A Four-Switch-Type Converter Fed Improved Photovoltaic Power System. in Advances in Greener Energy Technologies. Springer, Singapore. **2020** https://doi.org/10.1007/978-981-15-4246-6_29

59. Vardia, M.; Priyadarshi, N.; Ali, I.; Azam, F.; Bhoi, A.K.; Maximum Power Point Tracking for Wind Energy Conversion System. in Advances in Greener Energy Technologies. Springer, Singapore. **2020** https://doi.org/10.1007/978-981-15-4246-6_36

60. Vardia, M.; Priyadarshi, N.; Ali, I.; Azam, F.; Bhoi, A.K.; Design of Wind Energy Conversion System Under Different Fault Conditions. in Advances

in Greener Energy Technologies. Springer, Singapore. **2020** https://doi.org/10.1007/978-981-15-4246-6_41

61. Choudhary, T.; Priyadarshi, N.; Kuma,r P.; Azam, F.; Bhoi A.K. (2020) A Fuzzy Logic Control Based Vibration Control System for Renewable Application. in Advances in Greener Energy Technologies. Springer, Singapore. **2020** https://doi.org/10.1007/978-981-15-4246-6_38

62. Priyadarshi, N.; Azam F.; Solanki, S. S.; Sharma, A.K.; Bhoi, A.K.; Almakhles, D.; A Bio-Inspired Chicken Swarm Optimization-Based Fuel Cell System for Electric Vehicle Applications. in Bio-inspired Neurocomputing. Studies in Computational Intelligence, vol 903. Springer, Singapore. **2021** https://doi.org/10.1007/978-981-15-5495-7_1

Application of Artificial Intelligence and Machine Learning Techniques in Island Detection in a Smart Grid

Soham Dutta[1], Pradip Kumar Sadhu[1], Murthy Cherikuri[2] and Dusmanta Kumar Mohanta[3]*

[1]Department of Electrical Engineering, IIT (ISM), Dhanbad, Jharkhand, India
[2]Department of Electrical and Electronics Engineering, NIST, Berhampur, Odisha, India
[3]Department of Electrical and Electronics Engineering, BIT, Mesra, Ranchi, Jharkhand, India

Abstract

Electricity grids are getting smarter day by day and simultaneously the importance of distributed generations (DGs) is increasing. The concept of DG has taken the power industry to a new height in terms of improved reliability and continuity. Integration of DGs has reduced dependency on main grid supply as they are sources of energy in a micro-grid and have the capacity to cater to the loads. However, as the penetration of these DGs has increased in energy system, various challenging uncertainties have evolved that are very different in nature from previously known traditional uncertainties. Among various types of modern uncertainties in smart grids, primary one is unintentional islanding of grids. It happens when the DGs continue to feed some portion of the load even after being disconnected from the main grid. Unintentional islanding comes with a large number of threats. Thus, it is very critical to detect the unintentional island incidents. The traditional methods used for island detections involves measurement of various parameters like voltage, frequency, etc. or the effect of injecting some intentional disturbances and analyzing the effects. The island cases are then identified by comparing the measured values with a threshold. However, the setting of the threshold

*Corresponding author: dkmohanta@bitmesra.ac.in

Neeraj Priyadarshi, Akash Kumar Bhoi, Sanjeevikumar Padmanaban, S. Balamurugan and Jens Bo Holm-Nielsen (eds.) Intelligent Renewable Energy Systems, (79–110) © 2022 Scrivener Publishing LLC

value is difficult because, if the value is less sensitive, the detection will not occur very accurately. However, if a highly sensitive value of threshold is set, it will cause false detection. So an appropriate tool is required to attain high sensitivity and also high accuracy. Thus, the island detection researchers incorporated artificial intelligence and machine learning techniques, which help in fulfilling this task effectively.

Keywords: Island detection, smart grid, microgrid, distributed generation, artificial intelligence, machine learning

3.1 Introduction

Electricity grids are getting smarter day by day and simultaneously the importance of distributed generations (DGs) is increasing [1–18]. The concept of DG has taken the power industry to a new height that has assured better reliability and continuity. The term DG means power generated from various decentralized sources for specific purposes. DG is mainly based upon renewable sources like wind turbines, fuel cells, solar panels etc [19–45]. DG has reduced our dependency on main grid supply as it itself behaves as a microgrid and has the capacity to supply small amount of loads like household loads. However, as the penetration of these DGs has increased in our supply system, various challenging uncertainties has evolved like islanding, faults and voltage dip that are very different in nature from previously known traditional faults [1, 2]. These need to be identifed and solved as it can be dangerous for the utility workers and for the whole supply system.

The concept of machine learning first emerged in the 1950s. Though it gained interest in the scientific community, it was limited to only equations and hypothesis. However, the progress in computers in the 1970s led to the rapid increase in the development of machine learning. Since then, it has been applied to a wide field [46–67]. Machine learning can be defined as a subdivision of artificial intelligence which uses different optimization, probabilistic and statistical tools to "learn" from previos examples [3]. After learning or training, it classifies new data. Thus, machine learning is successfully employed for analyzing and interpreting data [4]. It has also been extensively used in power systems for various applications. A major field of application is detection of islanding condition in a smart power system.

In the following sections, a comprehensive review of different artificial intelligence and machine learning techniques have been dealt. To bring out its advantages over other methods used in island detection, the traditional methods are first explained and then compared with artificial intelligence and machine learning island detection techniques.

3.1.1   Distributed Generation Technology in Smart Grid

Power generation and transmission is mainly administrated by the Government. The power industry has to maintain regulation and continuity of supply demand ratio [68–90]. However, there are always chances of power failure and irregularities of supply due to various reasons like faults, natural disaster etc. To deal with them, the system requires an alternate but reliable sources like DG. These are the best conclusive answers for modern day power requirements [5].

Modern development in the field of technology like rapid switching and capability to deal with the high voltage has pushed the power sector to a new height where DG can generate high amount of power in a much better and efficient way. DG is the answer to these rising power requirements as it helps to maintain continuity of supply [6].

3.1.2   Microgrids

Previously, the generation of power reliedonly on conventional energy sources like coal, diesel etc. However, these conventional sources cause high amount of pollution which leads to various issues like global warming and health hazards [91–106]. Thus, for providing better alternatives, the power engineers and scientists have focused on renewable and nonconventional energy sector. In search of better and quality sources of power generation, a smarter and faster approach must be adopted that would fulfill the current energy requirement in a environment friendly way as well as maintain the continuity of supply demands in an effective manner. As a result of these concerns, microgrid emerged [7–10]. Microgrids have the capability to operate as small power grids that can work in association with the various other small grid systems and also with the main-grid.

Microgrids have the following advantages:

- It can maintain the continuity of supply in the case of any localized fault that can disturb the main grid power.
- During intentional islanded mode it can supply the required active and reactive power demand.
- Microgrid in collaboration with main grid can serve the purpose of supplying the peak load demand.
- Surplus power generated by the microgrid can be sent back to the main grid.

3.1.2.1   Problems with Microgrids

Usually, the nature of power system networks is radial. The power flows from generation to distribution in one direction only. Based on this unidirectional power flow, monitoring, protection and control devices are designed. Hence, on integrating microgrids, the existing power system face technical issues like fuse-reclose coordination, increase fault level, voltage regulation, and unintentional islanding [11]. One of the most important concerns with microgrids is unintentional islanding.

3.2   Islanding in Power System

When a microgrid having one or more DGs and loads are electrically isolated from utility grid due to several reason like preplanned switching conditions for maintenance, equipment failure, switching incidents and electrical faults, the phenomenon is called as islanding condition [12, 13]. Figure 3.1 shows a typical microgrid system with a DG connection. Due to one of the following reasons stated above, if the circuit breaker "CB1" is tripped, then the DG and the load gets separated from the main grid. Thus, an islanded area is formed.

Islanding is categorized into two parts: unintentional island and intentional island. Intentional island operation does not pose any problem in the islanded system as they are preplanned. However, during unintended islanding, there can be a huge unbalance in generation and load which can lead to extensive damage to the islanded area [14]. In addition to it, unintentional islanding has the following concerns:

- In the islanding condition, the frequency and voltage in the islanded area significantly varies because the conventional grid is no further controlling frequency and voltage.
- Hazard can be created during islanding since the utility workers will misidentify an energized line as disconnected.
- During islanding, when the islanded part is reconnected to the utility grid, there can be a potential damage to the

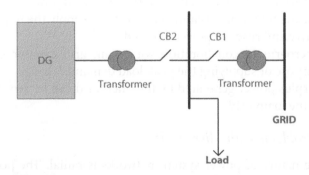

Figure 3.1 Typical microgrid system.

generators, due to the out-of-phase reclose which injects a high circulating current.

Thus, unintentional islanding must be properly detected for safe operation according to IEEE Standard 929-2000 and IEEE Standard 1547-2003.

3.3   Island Detection Methods

Islanding detection in a microgrid is essential for the protection of utility workers and to maintain supply in the islanded area. There are numerous methods developed by the researchers which are mainly classified into active, passive, hybrid, local, signal processing and classifier methods as shown in Figure 3.2. The principle of operation of all these methods are different [15]. A brief idea about these techniques is essential to understand the advantage of machine learning and artificial intelligence in island detection field.

3.3.1   Passive Methods

Passive methods deal with the comparison of parameter changes in a signal (like voltage, frequency, harmonic distortion etc.) with respect to a threshold value. Passive methods works best when the power difference between generation and load demand in the post islanded area is quite high. Passive methods are swift, reliable and do not introduces any system fluctuation, but they have

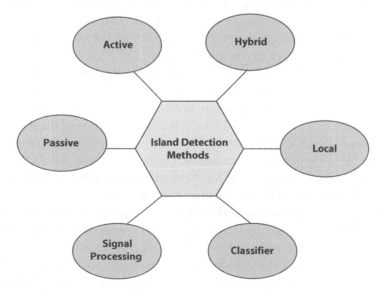

Figure 3.2 Island detection methods.

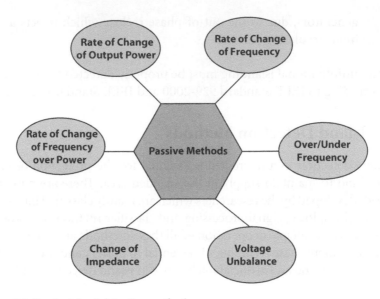

Figure 3.3 Passive island detection methods.

quite high non-detection zone (NDZ). Scientist has developedmany passive methods that can work effectively, some of which are given in Figure 3.3.

The easiest and the earliest passive island detection method is over/under frequency method. The frequency of the system does not vary much under normal condition but varies in a wide range under island condition [16]. When an islanding event occurs, the rate of change of output power (ROCOP) is larger than the ROCOP before the islanded condition [17]. This method is reliable when there is an unbalanced load present in the electrical distribution system.After islanding, the rate of change of the frequency (ROCOF) is considerably greater than the ROCOF when connected to the utility. This technique is effective when there is a large frequency mismatch present [18]. Usually, the rate of change of the frequency over power (ROCOFOP) in small DG system is significantly more than ROCOFOP of big generation structure. During islanding, this ROCOFOP differs [19]. Also, in research it has been discovered that for small power mismatch, this value is highly sensitive than the ROCOF over time.

The impedance of the main grid is lesser than the impedance of an island subsystem. However, during islanding event, the impedance present in the islanded grid portion will increase. This change of impedance is observed continuously to detect any islanding [20]. In voltage unbalance method, the percentage of the unbalance voltage in the system is checked for island detection [21]. This voltage unbalance becomes notable during island conditions.

3.3.2   Active Methods

Active method is based on introducing a small disruption or perturbation signal at point of common coupling (PCC) and measuring its counter effect. The perturbation signal will not give any significant variation in system parameters in grid connected mode but will give significant change when the system is islanded [22].

In case where the load and generation is matched, active method has advantage over the passive method. Active method by utilizing disruption signal can detect islanding with high efficiency and lower NDZ. However, on the other side, they degrade the power quality and increase the total harmonic distortion. Some common active island detection methods are depicted in Figure 3.4.

Active frequency drift chiefly work by slightly altering the current entering at PCC i.e. the inverter current in comparison with the main grid voltage [23]. This method is highly advantageous in case of photovoltaic plant in which microprocessor based controllers are being used. The main deciding parameter i.e. chopping frequency is quite small in normal loaded condition but increase to a large value in islanding case. To detect islanding, this chopping frequency is compared with a predefined value and whenever found higher, it indicates that islanding has happened.

Sandia frequency shiftworks on same principle as active frequency drift with additional addition of positive feedback to the frequency at phase locked

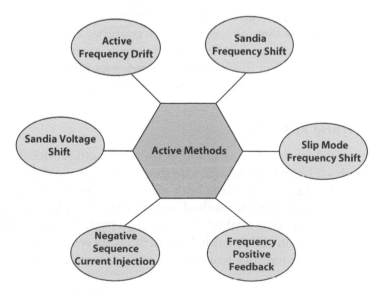

Figure 3.4 Active island detection methods.

loop [24]. When the system is operating in normal operating condition, a minute change in frequency has no noticeable effect but in islanded case the frequency error is increased due to PCC frequency which in turn increases the inverter frequency. This condition goes in loop until the frequency passes the predefined threshold and in this way islanding is detected. Non detection zone for Sandia frequency shift method is small but on the other side it degrades the power quality to a great extent and noise is introduced due to positive feedback. Sandia voltage shift has the same working principle as of sandia frequency shif but in this method, voltage amplitude requires positive feedback in PCC. Power and current output of inverter varies due to this positive feedback [25]. The amplitude of voltage is least affected during normal working condition but largely fluctuates in islanding mode. Under active techniques slip mode frequency shift is contemporary one and best one in terms of NDZ [26]. Slip mode frequency shift works on the positive feedback technique by applying this feedback to the inverter's current phase angle as per the fluctuation of frequency at PCC. For detecting islanding, slip mode frequency shift method uses a typical slip mode frequency shift curve. In islanded mode, the frequency and phase angle change as per the graph. For detecting islanding, the frequency has to cross a predefined threshold value. slip mode frequency shift method is highly efficient with no NDZ but slightly degrades the power quality.

In frequency positive feedback method, a phase shift, comparing the instantaneous frequency obtained from frequency locked loop unit with the nominal frequency, is generated to modify the reference phase angle [27]. Negative sequence current injection [28] works by inserting negative sequence current through voltage source converter and observing the negative sequence voltage at PCC. Under normal connection to the grid it has balance voltage but in islanded mode behavior of voltage is highly unbalance. This method is highly reliable with small NDZ.

3.3.3 Hybrid Methods

Hybrid method for detecting islanding is fusion of both previously mentioned methods i.e. passive and active methods of islanding detection. Due to this fusion, it has the benefits of both methods i.e. lower NDZ and less degradation of power. Hybrid method works by firstly applying the technique discussed in passive method and then applying the active technique for islanding detection [29]. Some hybrid methods are voltage and reactive power shift, positive feedback and voltage unbalance, voltage and reactive power shift, etc.

3.3.4 Local Methods

Local methods like transfer trip scheme and power line carrier communication (PLCC) utilizes a communication path between the DG and main utility section. As this method is mainly dependent upon communication signal, to avoid any interference of communication signal with the transmission power signal, the frequency of the signal is kept low. From expenditure point of view, local methods are very costly due to their communication channel requirement. This makes local methods unsuitable for single DG system [1]. Local methods have maximum advantage when use with multiple DG system as these methods have zero NDZ.

3.3.5 Signal Processing Methods

Signal processing island detection methods are advanced and modern methods. Owing to the huge penetration of signal processing tools in power system protection, these methods utilizes various signal processing tools for getting the characteristics or feautures of signals that are obtained from PCC for detecting islanding [30]. Some of the majortools are shown in Figure 3.5. The two main signal processing techniques extensively used for island detection are wavelet transform and Stockwell transform.

In literature, wavelet transform has been widely used as the signal processing tool in the past 20 years. The key benefit of wavelet transform is its capacity to develop a signal existing in frequency domain without

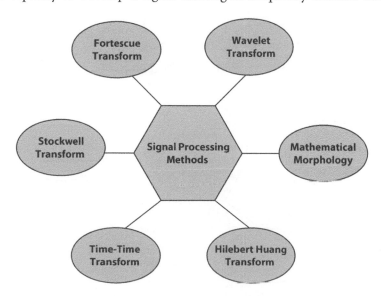

Figure 3.5 Signal processing island detection methods.

altering its time domain data. Thus, it finds its use in cases where both time & frequency is essential. Thus, it is extensively used in island detection [31–33]. Wavelet transform used for island detection has many variants, preferred depending on the kind of system used. There are chiefly three alternatives- discrete wavelet transform, continuous wavelet transform and wavelet packets transform. Stockwell transform is the extension of wavelet transform. It translates time domain into 2-D frequency domain. The main advantage of this tool is its uncomplex nature. The idea of multiresolution process of wavelet transform is simplified by Stockwell transform. Stockwell transform based islanding detection is presented in various literature [34–36], which clearly proves the edge Stockwell transform has over wavelet transform for island detection applications.

3.3.6 Classifer Methods

In all the previous mentioned island detection methods, it is very critical and difficult to set a suitable threshold. If the threshold value is insensitive, the detection won't occur very accurately, whereas if a highly sensitive value of threshold is set, it will cause false tripping of relays. So appropriate tool is required to attain high sensitivity and also high accuracy. Thus, came classifiers, which help in fulfilling this task effectively. Popular classifiers used for island detection are shown in Figure 3.6. As these methods employ machine learning and artificial intelligence algorithms, each algorirthm is detailed in the next sections.

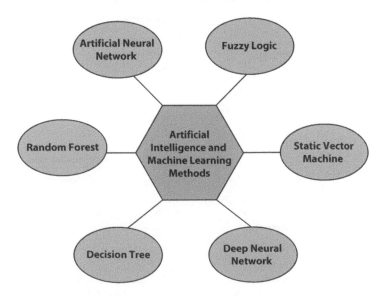

Figure 3.6 Classifier island detection methods.

3.4   Application of Machine Learning and Artificial Intelligence Algorithms in Island Detection Methods

Machine learning and artificial intelligence techniques are mainly used for the process of classification. Classification can be defined as a task of allocating objects to two or more numerous predefined classes. All the classifiers using machine learning and artificial intelligence has to be trained first. For training these classifiers, the input matrix/set and output matrix/set is developed. The input matrix or set is in the form as given by Equation (3.1), where xi represents the feature vectors. The corresponding output matrix or set (or classes) is in the form as given by Equation (3.2), where Cj represents the class labels.

$$MI = x1, x2, x3, x4, x5, \ldots \ldots, xi \qquad (3.1)$$

$$MO = Ca, Cb, Cc, Cd, Ce, \ldots \ldots, Cj \qquad (3.2)$$

The flowchart of the islanding classification techniques using machine learning and artificial intelligence is shown in Figure 3.7. The first step involves collection of the required signal from the grid that need to be accessed for island detection. In the next step, features or some values are obtained with active, passive or signal processing techniques. The extracted features are recorded and fed to the trained classifiers. These are trained using differentmachine learning and artificial intelligence techniques and from the input/output dataset provided by the developer of the algorithm. Island is detected when the classifiers identifies an instant that matches with those of island input matrix features. Thus, the training step is offline and the classification step is online [37]. The underlying principle of these machine learning and artificial intelligence techniques are explained in detail in the following subsections.

3.4.1   Decision Tree

Decision tree (DT) is similar to a flow chart i.e. it has a tree like structure with top down recursive approach [38]. Figure 3.8 represents a schematic diagram of a basic decision tree. The root nodes denotes the complete data set. In the first step, the root nodes are splitted into child nodes depending on a predictor variable. The node containing the purest data is designated as the child node which is further splitted. The child nodes are splitted

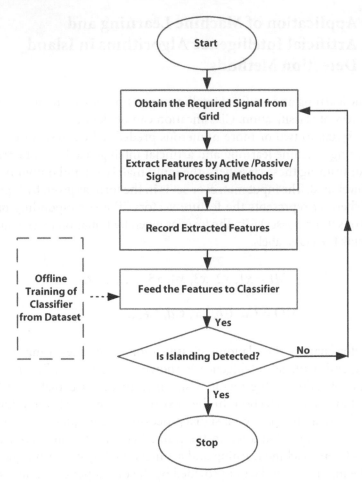

Figure 3.7 Flowchart of islanding classification techniques using machine learning and artificial intelligence.

continuously until a stage comes where it is not possible to split it into further nodes. The final nodes thus obtained after splitting are called leaf nodes. Thus, in case of islanding detection, the leaf nodes of the DT are the class labels i.e. islanding class and non islanding class.

There are various type of algorithms used for building a DT each having its own merits and demerits. Some of the widely used algorithms are CART, C 4.5 and ID3.11 parameters are used in [39] to train DT for island detection with 83% accuracy. To enhance the accuracy of island detection, adaptive boost algorithm is used in [40] to obtain high accuracy. The effect of noise is considered in [41] while detecting islanding instants. The accuracy

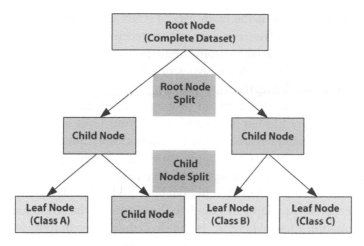

Figure 3.8 Schematic diagram of a decision tree.

obtained is 96%. Some more application of DT for island detection can be found in [42–45]. The advantages and disadvantges of DT are provided in the subsequent sections.

3.4.1.1 Advantages of Decision Tree

- Simple to understand
- Easy implementation
- Both numerical data as well as categorical data can be handled
- Needs mimimum data processing as it is outliers resistant.

3.4.1.2 Disadvantages of Decision Tree

- Overfitting problem
- Tuning of parameters is difficult
- Biasing problem if any class dominates

3.4.2 Artificial Neural Network

The principle of artificial neural network (ANN) is based on the biological neuron found in human brain. Since its inception, various types of neural networks have been formulated. In all the types, three characteristics are common - transfer functions of processing units, the connections formulas and the learning rules [46].

The processing unit is the main part of ANN and it corresponds to the cell body of a neuron. Numerous signals are received by the processing unit as weighted process variables from the response of other processing units [47, 48]. There are many ANN layout developed by researchers, forward propagating layout being the most common one. It is trained by error back propagation method. The forward propagation layout contains an input layer, one or more hidden layers and one output layer as represented in Figure 3.9. The data provided by the user acts as the input layer. The number of hidden layer varies with applications. It is generally ascertained by hit and trial method. With a sigmoidal function represented by Equation (3.3), the processing unit of each hidden layer and output layer adds up the input from preceding layer to calculate the output to the subsequent layer as per Equation (3.4), where, x_m is the preceding layer output, w_{mn} is the connection strength between m^{th} unit in the preceding layer and n^{th} unit

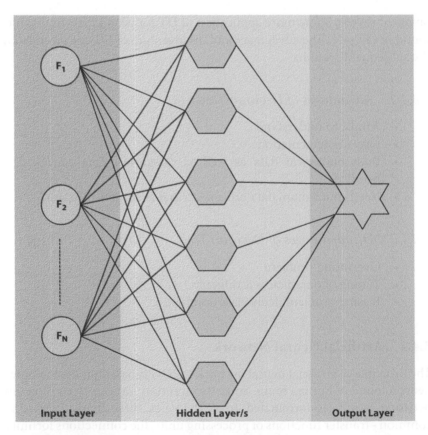

Figure 3.9 Schematic diagram of an artificial neural network.

in the present layer, δ is a value that influence the form of the sigmoidal function and $f(y_n)$ is output value to the subsequent layer.

$$f(y_n) = \frac{1}{1 + \exp(-\delta y_n)} \qquad (3.3)$$

$$y_n = \Sigma w_{mn} x_m \qquad (3.4)$$

ANN based hybrid island detection is proposed in [49]. 11% false rate detection is thus obtained. A low island conditon classification rate of nearly 0% is obtained in [50] where the three phase current signal is interpreted as a modal signal. Islanding detection in 2 normal power frequency cycles with high accuracy is achieved in [51]. Other modes of ANN such as self organising map, probabilistic neural network, back propagation method, etc. are also employed for island detection. Some other application of ANN for island detection can be found in [52, 53]. The advantges and disadvantages of ANN are provided in the subsequent sections.

3.4.2.1   Advantages of Artificial Neural Network

- Ability to do multiple jobs at the same time
- Fault tolerant nature i.e. it produces output even if some cell malfunctions
- Capability to perform under incomplete knowledge i.e after training it can produce result even if the input vector is incomplete

3.4.2.2   Disadvantages of Artificial Neural Network

- Difficult to explain the reason when it misbehaves
- Hardware constraint during parallel processing
- No logic for ascertaining number of hidden layers

3.4.3   Fuzzy Logic

Fuzzy logic (FL) can be defined as a superset of Boolean logic incorporating the notion of partial truth i.e. the values between totally false or totally true. In other words, FL replicates the human style of making a decision that includes all probable intermediary options between digital values NO and YES [54]. The schematic diagram of a FL is represented in Figure 3.10.

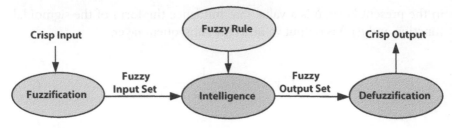

Figure 3.10 Schematic diagram of fuzzy logic.

FL has primarily has three main stages - fuzzification, assessment of rules (intelligence) and defuzzification.

In the fuzzification stage, the crisp system inputs are converted into fuzzy sets. Membership functions are used for fuzzification of numerical values. There are multiple membership functions available in literature. However, triangular membership function is the most used one. Generally, the input data is splitted into 5 steps. With the IF-THEN rules supplied by the user, human reasoning is done in the intelligence stage. After obtaining fuzzy inferences, the fuzzy set are converted into crisp value in the defuzzification stage.

A multi criteria based FL algorithm is proposed in [55]. The criterias include important parameters such as ROCOF, ROCOP, voltage, etc. Features extracted by Stockwell transform is fed in a fuzzy system in [56]. To tune the Sandia frequency shift parameters for island detection, FL is employed in [57]. Some other application of FL for island detection can be found in [58, 59]. The advantages and disadvantages of FL are provided in the subsequent sections.

3.4.3.1 Advantages of Fuzzy Logic

- Simple mathematics
- Easy to construct and understand
- Works well with noisy input data

3.4.3.2 Disadvantages of Fuzzy Logic

- No systematic design approach
- Accuracy is not always high
- Huge requirement of data

3.4.4   Artificial Neuro-Fuzzy Inference System

To combine the merits of FL and ANN, artificial neuro-fuzzy inference system (ANFIS) was developed. In ANFIS, the neural network handles the procedure of pattern recognition and adaptation to manage the fluctuating-situations and the fuzzy system handles the job of imprecision and uncertainty. It can also be interpreted as a technique in which the prior knowledge is splitted into subsets for reducing the search space and then using the back propagation method to regulate the fuzzy parameters [60, 61].

The schematic diagram of an ANFIS structure is shown in Figure 3.11. It mainly consists of five layers – fuzzification layer, product layer, normalisation layer, defuzzification layer and summation layer. Thus, ANFIS structure is similar to a first order Takagi-Sugeno system where the relationship between input and output follows linearity.

The strength of ANFIS in terms of reduced NDZ is highlighted in [62, 63]. An ANFIS based passive island detection method is mentioned in [64]. A hybrid island detection method used alongwith ANFIS can be found in [65]. The advantages and disadvantages of ANFIS are provided in the subsequent sections.

3.4.4.1   *Advantages of Artificial Neuro-Fuzzy Inference System*

- Mathematical models are not required
- Incorporates the merit of both ANN as well as FL
- High accuracy for complex problems

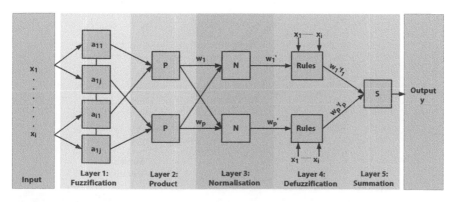

Figure 3.11 Schematic diagram of an artificial neuro-fuzzy inference system.

3.4.4.2 *Disadvantages of Artificial Neuro-Fuzzy Inference System*

- Familiarity with both ANN as well as FL is needed

3.4.5 Static Vector Machine

Static vector machine (SVM) is an adaptive statistical learning approach employed for regression and classification of problems efficiently and accurately [66]. The schematic diagram of SVM is shown in Figure 3.12. As shown in the figure, in a high dimensional space, to group the data space into different categories, an optimized hyperplane is built. The optimization of the hyperplane is done in the sense to separate the categories with a maximum margin. The nearest data points to the hyperplane of each of the classes is called the support vectors. Classification is achieved by SVM when the distance of the hyperplane from these support vectors become maximum. i.e. the margin value is maximum [67]. Thus, to select the optimal hyperplane, the constraint is as given in Equation (3.5), where y_i is the class variable and i varies from 1 to n.

$$\frac{2}{\|\rho\|} y_i (x\rho + \rho_0) \geq Margin \tag{3.5}$$

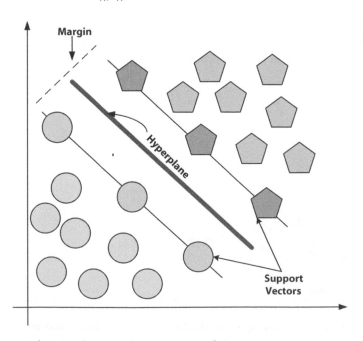

Figure 3.12 Schematic diagram of static vector machine.

The optimal hyperplane is easily achievable for linearly seperable data points with the help of Lagrangian functions. However, for non-linearly seperable data points, it becomes a difficult job. They are solved using some kernel functions e.g. liner kernel, Gaussian kernel and polynomial kernel.

SVM applied for island detection in CIGRE MV system can be found in [68]. Island detection for a hybrid DG based grid employing SVM is obtained in [69]. An accuracy of 98.7% is achieved for island detection using SVM in [70]. Some other application of SVM for island detection can be found in [1, 71]. The advantages and disadvanatges of SVM are provided in the subsequent sections.

3.4.5.1   Advantages of Support Vector Machine

- Easy classification of non-linear data
- Stability
- Reduced risk of overfitting

3.4.5.2   Disadvantages of Support Vector Machine

- Incorrect kernel can reduce accuracy
- Constaint of hardware requirement for quadratic programmimg
- Reduced performance with increase in number of samples

3.4.6   Random Forest

In simple language, random forest (RF) can be defined as a collection of untrimmed DT. By splitting the DT nodes in a randomised way, RF eliminates the demerits of DT i.e. it reduces the instability problems to small changes in the learning data and overfitting [72]. The schematic diagram of RF technique isdepicted in Figure 3.13. In the training process, a bootstrap sample is build from the input dataset. However, the constraint applied is that the number of training samples should be more than the bootstrap samples. For each bootstrap sample thus obtained, a tree is developed. The process of splitting of nodes is repeated until it reaches maximum depth. Thus, n number of trees are obtained [73].

In the classification process, for a data to be classified, all the n number of trees vote for its class. The data is assigned to the class for which the maximum number of trees votes. Thus, in this way the islanding instants are classified with RF technique.

A spectral kurtosis based island detection method employing RF to classify islanding events from other power system events is presented in [74].

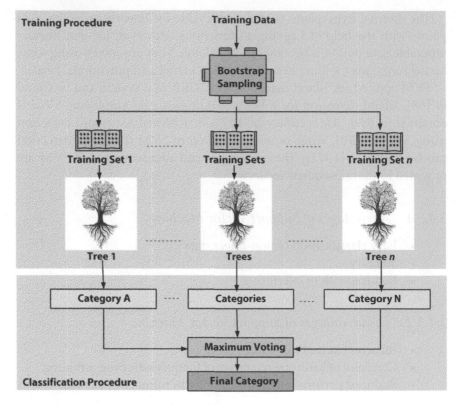

Figure 3.13 Schematic diagram of a random forest.

It has a high immunity to noise and possess an accuracy of 99.8% with a detection time of 20ms. A RF based universal island detection method capable of showing high accuracy and zero NDZ for both synchronous as well as inverter based DG is presented in [75]. The advantages and disadvantges of RF are provided in the subsequent sections.

3.4.6.1   Advantages of Random Forest

- Robustness to noise
- Ability to handle overfitting in case of large trees
- high accuracy

3.4.6.2   Disadvantages of Random Forest

- Less interpretability than DTs.
- Huge memory storage requirement
- Lengthier training period

3.4.7   Comparison of Machine Learning and Artificial Intelligence Based Island Detection Methods with Other Methods

The comparison of machine learning and artificial intelligence based island detection methods with other methods is given in Table 3.1. As seen from the table, each method of island detection has some advantages and disadvantages. However, classification technique with machine learning and artificial intelligence proves to be the most suitable method of island detection. These classifier methods does not affect the grid, can work in complex grids involving several DGs and unbalanced loads, the cost of implememting the algorithm is not high and has high accuracy. These characteristics have indeed motivated power system enginners and researchers to probe deeper into machine learning and artificial intelligence techniques.

3.5   Conclusion

Smart grids are the conclusive answer for grid management, providing the necessary dynamics to the system to increase its efficiency. Use of DGs has strengthened the utility's sustainability and thus constraints like islanding need to be dealt with coherently. Hence, scientist and researchers have always focused on islanding detection methods that are highly efficient and fast so that negative impacts of islanding can be avoided to a great extent. Coming on these track, the chapter stresses on various artificial intelligence and machine learning techniques that has opened several opportunities in a secured island detection method in smart grids. These artificial intelligence and machine learning techniques have many advantages over other island detection methods. Unlike, passive methods, these methods have zero NDZ and high accuracy. In comparison to active techniques, these techniques does not degrade the power quality of the grid as it does not introduce and disturbance signal to the grid. They are not costly unlike local methods. Moreover, they are more preferable over signal processing methods for complex grid structure. Thus, these methods proves to be beneficial in many aspects of island detection when compared with other methods. The above factors have contributed to its expanding application in island detection.

Further, with the increase in more complexity of the modern power system grid, the application of artificial intelligence and machine learning techniques in island detection will become more pronounced. For example, the grids are increasingly becoming more prone to cyber attacks with

Table 3.1 Comparison of machine learning and artificial intelligence based island detection methods with other methods.

Method	Consequence on grid	Suitability in complex grids	Cost of implementation	Accuracy
Passive	Nothing	High	Less	Low
Active	Exceedingly Worsens the Power Quality	Very low	Less	High
Hybrid	Worsens the Power Quality	Very low	Less	High
Local	Nothing	High	Very High	High
Signal Processing	Nothing	High	Less	High
Machine Learning and Artificial Intelligence	Nothing	Very High	Less	Very High

the shift in unidirectional traditional power system to bidirectional power flow information technology based power system. The grids are hugely exposed to false data injection, replay of data, blockage of data transfer, etc. The traditional island detection methods will fail under such conditions. However, if properly trained, the cyber attacks can be handled by the machine learning techniques. Thus, advanced methods such as reinforcement learning and extreme learning needs to be tested for island detection. Moreover, the increasing penetration of electric vehicles into the grid can make island detection a tedious job as the transients introduced due to these may be similar to island conditions. Thus, with the change in topology of the grid in future, artificial intelligence and machine learning will continue to play a significant role in detection island condition.

References

1. Dutta, S., Sadhu, P.K., Reddy, M.J.B. and Mohanta, D.K., 2018. Shifting of research trends in islanding detection method-a comprehensive survey. *Protection and Control of Modern Power Systems*, 3(1), p.1.
2. Anudeep, B. and Nayak, P.K., 2020. Transient energy-based combined fault detector and faulted phase selector for distribution networks with distributed generators. *International Transactions on Electrical Energy Systems*, 30(4), p.e12288.
3. Cheng, L. and Yu, T., 2019. A new generation of AI: A review and perspective on machine learning technologies applied to smart energy and electric power systems. *International Journal of Energy Research*, 43(6), pp.1928-1973.
4. Yannakakis, G.N. and Togelius, J., 2018. *Artificial intelligence and games* (Vol. 2). New York: Springer.
5. Chapman, B.R., 2017. Pricing Distributed Generation: Challenges and Alternatives. *Natural Gas & Electricity*, 33(8), pp.1-7.
6. Wu, Z., Yang, F. and Han, Q.L., 2014. A novel islanding fault detection for distributed generation systems. *International Journal of Robust and Nonlinear Control*, 24(8-9), pp.1431-1445.
7. Olivares, D.E., Mehrizi-Sani, A., Etemadi, A.H., Cañizares, C.A., Iravani, R., Kazerani, M., Hajimiragha, A.H., Gomis-Bellmunt, O., Saeedifard, M., Palma-Behnke, R. and Jiménez-Estévez, G.A., 2014. Trends in microgrid control. *IEEE Transactions on smart grid*, 5(4), pp.1905-1919.
8. Jimeno, J., Anduaga, J., Oyarzabal, J. and de Muro, A.G., 2011. Architecture of a microgrid energy management system. *European Transactions on Electrical Power*, 21(2), pp.1142-1158.
9. Rana, M.M., Bo, R. and Chen, H., 2019. Estimating and Controlling the Renewable Microgrid States Using IoT Infrastructure. *Asian Journal of Control*, 21(4), pp.2105-2113.

10. Arfeen, Z.A., Khairuddin, A.B., Larik, R.M. and Saeed, M.S., 2019. Control of distributed generation systems for microgrid applications: A technological review. *International Transactions on Electrical Energy Systems*, *29*(9), p.e12072.

11. Van Thong, V. and Belmans, R., 2010. Maximum penetration level of distributed generation with safety criteria. *European transactions on electrical power*, *20*(3), pp.367-381.

12. Dutta, S., Sadhu, P.K., Reddy, M.J.B. and Mohanta, D.K., 2018. Smart inadvertent islanding detection employing p-type μPMU for an active distribution network. *IET Generation, Transmission & Distribution*, *12*(20), pp.4615-4625.

13. Fernández-Porras, P., Panteli, M. and Quirós-Tortós, J., 2018. Intentional controlled islanding: when to island for power system blackout prevention. IET Generation, Transmission & Distribution, 12(14), pp.3542-3549.

14. Guler, T. and Gross, G., 2007. Detection of island formation and identification of causal factors under multiple line outages. *IEEE Transactions on Power Systems*, *22*(2), pp.505-513.

15. Shukla, A., Dutta, S. and Sadhu, P.K., An island detection approach by μ-PMU with reduced chances of cyber attack. *International Journal of Electrical Power & Energy Systems*, *126*, p.106599.

16. Yu, B., Matsui, M. and Yu, G., 2010. A review of current anti-islanding methods for photovoltaic power system. *Solar Energy*, *84*(5), pp.745-754.

17. Redfern, M.A., Usta, O. and Fielding, G., 1993. Protection against loss of utility grid supply for a dispersed storage and generation unit. *IEEE transactions on power delivery*, *8*(3), pp.948-954.

18. Freitas, W., Xu, W., Affonso, C.M. and Huang, Z., 2005. Comparative analysis between ROCOF and vector surge relays for distributed generation applications. *IEEE Transactions on power delivery*, *20*(2), pp.1315-1324.

19. Mahat, P., Chen, Z. and Bak-Jensen, B., 2008, April. Review of islanding detection methods for distributed generation. In 2008 third international conference on electric utility deregulation and restructuring and power technologies (pp. 2743-2748). IEEE.

20. Hamzeh, M., Farhangi, S. and Farhangi, B., 2008, August. A new control method in PV grid connected inverters for anti-islanding protection by impedance monitoring. In *2008 11th Workshop on Control and Modeling for Power Electronics* (pp. 1-5). IEEE.

21. Jang, S.I. and Kim, K.H., 2004. An islanding detection method for distributed generations using voltage unbalance and total harmonic distortion of current. *IEEE transactions on power delivery*, *19*(2), pp.745-752.

22. Zhang, R., Zhang, S., Wang, P. and Liu, X., 2014, June. A new active island detection method which is based on a novel disturbance way. In *2014 9th IEEE Conference on Industrial Electronics and Applications* (pp. 1214-1220). IEEE.

23. Xu, J., Zhou, H. and Fang, Y., 2019. An active frequency drift method for island problem of grid-connected photovoltaic power generation system. *IEEJ Transactions on Electrical and Electronic Engineering*, *14*(11), pp.1633-1638.

24. Azim, R., Li, F., Xue, Y., Starke, M. and Wang, H., 2017. An islanding detection methodology combining decision trees and Sandia frequency shift for inverter-based distributed generations. *IET Generation, Transmission & Distribution, 11*(16), pp.4104-4113.

25. Kim, M.S., Haider, R., Cho, G.J., Kim, C.H., Won, C.Y. and Chai, J.S., 2019. Comprehensive review of islanding detection methods for distributed generation systems. *Energies, 12*(5), p.837.

26. Gao, Y. and Ye, J., 2019, September. Improved Slip Mode Frequency-Shift Islanding Detection Method. In *2019 International Conference on Virtual Reality and Intelligent Systems (ICVRIS)* (pp. 152-155). IEEE.

27. Reddy, C.R., Goud, B.S., Reddy, B.N., Pratyusha, M., Kumar, C.V. and Rekha, R., 2020, June. Review of Islanding Detection Parameters in Smart Grids. In *2020 8th International Conference on Smart Grid (icSmartGrid)* (pp. 78-89). IEEE.

28. Karimi, H., Yazdani, A. and Iravani, R., 2008. Negative-sequence current injection for fast islanding detection of a distributed resource unit. *IEEE Transactions on power electronics, 23*(1), pp.298-307.

29. Seyedi, M., Taher, S.A., Ganji, B. and Guerrero, J.M., 2019. A hybrid islanding detection technique for inverter-based distributed generator units. *International Transactions on Electrical Energy Systems, 29*(11), p.e12113.

30. Raza, S., Mokhlis, H., Arof, H., Laghari, J.A. and Wang, L., 2015. Application of signal processing techniques for islanding detection of distributed generation in distribution network: A review. *Energy Conversion and Management, 96*, pp.613-624.

31. Buduma, P., Pinto, S.J. and Panda, G., 2018, December. Wavelet based islanding detection in a three-phase grid collaborative inverter system using FPGA platform. In *2018 8th IEEE India International Conference on Power Electronics (IICPE)* (pp. 1-6). IEEE.

32. Hashemi, F. and Mohammadi, M., 2016. Islanding detection approach with negligible non-detection zone based on feature extraction discrete wavelet transform and artificial neural network. *International Transactions on Electrical Energy Systems, 26*(10), pp.2172-2192.

33. Heidari, M., Seifossadat, G. and Razaz, M., 2013. Application of decision tree and discrete wavelet transform for an optimized intelligent-based islanding detection method in distributed systems with distributed generations. *Renewable and sustainable energy reviews, 27*, pp.525-532.

34. Mahela, O.P., Khan, B., Alhelou, H.H. and Siano, P., 2020. Power quality assessment and event detection in distribution network with wind energy penetration using stockwell transform and fuzzy clustering. *IEEE Transactions on Industrial Informatics, 16*(11), pp.6922-6932.

35. Kaushik, R., Mahela, O.P., Bhatt, P.K., Khan, B., Garg, A.R., Alhelou, H.H. and Siano, P., 2020. Recognition of Islanding and Operational Events in Power System With Renewable Energy Penetration Using a Stockwell Transform-Based Method. *IEEE Systems Journal.*

36. Mahela, O.P., Heydarian-Forushani, E., Alhelou, H.H., Khan, B., Garg, A.R. and Al-Sumaiti, A.S., 2020, October. Combined Stockwell and Hilbert Transforms Based Technique for the Detection of Islanding Events in Hybrid Power System. In *IECON 2020 The 46th Annual Conference of the IEEE Industrial Electronics Society* (pp. 2531-2536). IEEE.

37. Laghari, J.A., Mokhlis, H., Karimi, M., Bakar, A.H.A. and Mohamad, H., 2014. Computational Intelligence based techniques for islanding detection of distributed generation in distribution network: A review. *Energy conversion and Management, 88*, pp.139-152.

38. Myles, A.J., Feudale, R.N., Liu, Y., Woody, N.A. and Brown, S.D., 2004. An introduction to decision tree modeling. *Journal of Chemometrics: A Journal of the Chemometrics Society, 18*(6), pp.275-285.

39. El-Arroudi, K., Joos, G., Kamwa, I. and McGillis, D.T., 2007. Intelligent-based approach to islanding detection in distributed generation. *IEEE transactions on power delivery, 22*(2), pp.828-835.

40. Madani, S.S., Abbaspour, A., Beiraghi, M., Dehkordi, P.Z. and Ranjbar, A.M., 2012, October. Islanding detection for PV and DFIG using decision tree and AdaBoost algorithm. In *2012 3rd IEEE PES Innovative Smart Grid Technologies Europe (ISGT Europe)* (pp. 1-8). IEEE.

41. Lidula, N.W.A. and Rajapakse, A.D., 2012. A pattern-recognition approach for detecting power islands using transient signals—Part II: Performance evaluation. *IEEE Transactions on Power Delivery, 27*(3), pp.1071-1080.

42. Sun, R., Wu, Z. and Centeno, V.A., 2011, July. Power system islanding detection & identification using topology approach and decision tree. In *2011 IEEE power and energy society general meeting* (pp. 1-6). IEEE.

43. Senroy, N., Heydt, G.T. and Vittal, V., 2006. Decision tree assisted controlled islanding. *IEEE Transactions on Power Systems, 21*(4), pp.1790-1797.

44. Zhou, B., Cao, C., Li, C., Cao, Y., Chen, C., Li, Y. and Zeng, L., 2015. Hybrid islanding detection method based on decision tree and positive feedback for distributed generations. *IET Generation, Transmission & Distribution, 9*(14), pp.1819-1825.

45. Azim, R., Zhu, Y., Saleem, H.A., Sun, K., Li, F., Shi, D. and Sharma, R., 2015, February. A decision tree based approach for microgrid islanding detection. In *2015 IEEE Power & Energy Society Innovative Smart Grid Technologies Conference (ISGT)* (pp. 1-5). IEEE.

46. Merlin, V.L., Santos, R.C.D., Grilo, A.P., Vieira, J.C.M., Coury, D.V. and Oleskovicz, M., 2016. A new artificial neural network based method for islanding detection of distributed generators. *International Journal of Electrical Power & Energy Systems, 75*, pp.139-151.

47. Hopfield, J.J., 1988. Artificial neural networks. *IEEE Circuits and Devices Magazine, 4*(5), pp.3-10.

48. Fayyad, Y. and Osman, A., 2010, August. Neuro-wavelet based islanding detection technique. In *2010 IEEE Electrical Power & Energy Conference* (pp. 1-6). IEEE.

49. ElNozahy, M.S., El-Saadany, E.F. and Salama, M.M., 2011, July. A robust wavelet-ANN based technique for islanding detection. In *2011 IEEE Power and Energy Society General Meeting* (pp. 1-8). IEEE.

50. Abd-Elkader, A.G., Allam, D.F. and Tageldin, E., 2014. Islanding detection method for DFIG wind turbines using artificial neural networks. *International Journal of Electrical Power & Energy Systems, 62,* pp.335-343.

51. Kumar, D. and Bhowmik, P.S., 2018. Artificial neural network and phasor data-based islanding detection in smart grid. *IET Generation, Transmission & Distribution, 12*(21), pp.5843-5850.

52. Ahmadipour, M., Hizam, H., Othman, M.L. and Radzi, M.A., 2019. Islanding detection method using ridgelet probabilistic neural network in distributed generation. *Neurocomputing, 329,* pp.188-209.

53. Kumar, S.A., Subathra, M.S.P., Kumar, N.M., Malvoni, M., Sairamya, N.J., George, S.T., Suviseshamuthu, E.S. and Chopra, S.S., 2020. A novel islanding detection technique for a resilient photovoltaic-based distributed power generation system using a tunable-q wavelet transform and an artificial neural network. *Energies, 13*(16), p.4238.

54. Samantaray, S.R., Babu, B.C. and Dash, P.K., 2011. Probabilistic neural network based islanding detection in distributed generation. *Electric Power Components and Systems, 39*(3), pp.191-203.

55. Rosolowski, E., Burek, A. and Jedut, L., 2007. A new method for islanding detection in distributed generation. *Wroclaw University of Technology, Poljska.*

56. Samantaray, S.R., El-Arroudi, K., Joos, G. and Kamwa, I., 2010. A fuzzy rule-based approach for islanding detection in distributed generation. *IEEE transactions on power delivery, 25*(3), pp.1427-1433.

57. Vahedi, H. and Karrari, M., 2012. Adaptive fuzzy sandia frequency-shift method for islanding protection of inverter-based distributed generation. *IEEE Transactions on Power Delivery, 28*(1), pp.84-92.

58. Ghadimi, N., 2015. An adaptive neuro-fuzzy inference system for islanding detection in wind turbine as distributed generation. *Complexity, 21*(1), pp.10-20.

59. Dash, P.K., Barik, S.K. and Patnaik, R.K., 2014. Detection and classification of islanding and nonislanding events in distributed generation based on fuzzy decision tree. *Journal of Control, Automation and Electrical Systems, 25*(6), pp.699-719.

60. Hagh, M.T. and Ghadimi, N., 2015. Multisignal histogram-based islanding detection using neuro-fuzzy algorithm. *Complexity, 21*(1), pp.195-205.

61. Mlakić, D., Baghaee, H.R. and Nikolovski, S., 2018. A novel ANFIS-based islanding detection for inverter-interfaced microgrids. *IEEE Transactions on Smart Grid, 10*(4), pp.4411-4424.

62. Hashemi, F., Ghadimi, N. and Sobhani, B., 2013. Islanding detection for inverter-based DG coupled with using an adaptive neuro-fuzzy inference system. *International Journal of Electrical Power & Energy Systems, 45*(1), pp.443-455.

63. Shayeghi, H. and Sobhani, B., 2014. Zero NDZ assessment for anti-islanding protection using wavelet analysis and neuro-fuzzy system in inverter based distributed generation. *Energy conversion and management, 79*, pp.616-625.
64. Bitaraf, H., Sheikholeslamzadeh, M., Ranjbar, A.M. and Mozafari, B., 2012, May. Neuro-fuzzy islanding detection in distributed generation. In *IEEE PES Innovative Smart Grid Technologies* (pp. 1-5). IEEE.
65. Priyadarshi.; N;, Padmanaban, S.; Maroti, P.K.; Sharma. A.; An Extensive Practical Investigation of FPSO-Based MPPT for Grid Integrated PV System Under Variable Operating Conditions With Anti-Islanding Protection. IEEE System Journal, 2018, 13:1861 - 1871.
66. Priyadarshi, N.; Padmanaban, S.; Bhaskar, M.S.; Blaabjerg, F.; Sharma, A.; A Fuzzy SVPWM Based Inverter Control Realization of Grid Integrated PV-Wind System with FPSO MPPT Algorithm for a Grid-Connected PV/Wind Power Generation System: Hardware Implementation. IET Electric Power Appl., 2018, 12:962-971.
67. Priyadarshi, N.; Kumar, V.; Yadav, K.; Vardia, M.; An Experimental Study on Zeta buck-boost converter for Application in PV system. Handbook of distributed generation, Springer, DOI 10.1007/978-3-319-51343-0_13
68. Priyadarshi N.; Sharma A.K.; Priyam S.; An Experimental Realization of Grid-Connected PV System with MPPT Using dSPACE DS 1104 Control Board. Advances in Smart Grid and Renewable Energy. Lecture Notes in Electrical Engineering, Springer, Singapore 2018, 435.
69. Priyadarshi N.; Sharma A.K.; Priyam S.; Practical Realization of an Improved Photovoltaic Grid Integration with MPPT. International Journal of Renewable Energy Research 2017, 7:1180-1891.
70. Priyadarshi N.; Sharma A.K.; Azam F.; A Hybrid Firefly-Asymmetrical Fuzzy Logic Controller based MPPT for PV-Wind-Fuel Grid Integration. International Journal of Renewable Energy Research 2017, 7: 1546-1560
71. Priyadarshi, N.; Anand, A.; Sharma, A.K.; Azam, F.; Singh, V.K.; Sinha, R. K.; An Experimental Implementation and Testing of GA based Maximum Power Point Tracking for PV System under Varying Ambient Conditions Using dSPACE DS 1104 Controller. International Journal of Renewable Energy Research, 2017, 7:255-265
72. Priyadarshi, N.; Padmanaban S.; Mihet-Popa L.; Blaabjerg, F.; Azam F.; Maximum Power Point Tracking for Brushless DC Motor-Driven Photovoltaic Pumping Systems Using a Hybrid ANFIS-FLOWER Pollination Optimization Algorithm. MDPI Energies 2018, 11:1-16
73. Priyadarshi, N.; Azam, F.; Bhoi, A.K.; Alam, S.; An Artificial Fuzzy Logic Intelligent Controller Based MPPT for PV Grid Utility. Lecture Notes in Networks and Systems 46, https://doi.org/10.1007/978-981-13-1217-5_88.
74. Padmanaban, S.; Priyadarshi, N.; Holm-Nielsen, J. B.; Bhaskar, M. S.; Azam, F.; Sharma, A.K.; A Novel Modified Sine-Cosine Optimized MPPT Algorithm for Grid Integrated PV System under Real Operating Conditions. IEEE Access, 2019, 7:10467-10477.

75. Padmanaban, S.; Priyadarshi, N.; Holm-Nielsen, J. B.; Bhaskar, M. S.; Hossain, E.; Azam, F.; A Hybrid Photovoltaic-Fuel Cell for Grid Integration With Jaya-Based Maximum Power Point Tracking: Experimental Performance Evaluation. IEEE Access, 2019, 7:82978-82990.

76. Priyadarshi, N.; Padmanaban, N.; Holm-Nielsen, J. B.; Blaabjerg, F.; Bhaskar, M.S.; An Experimental Estimation of Hybrid ANFIS–PSO-Based MPPT for PV Grid Integration Under Fluctuating Sun Irradiance. in IEEE Systems Journal. 2020, 14:1218-1229

77. Priyadarshi, N.; Padmanaban, N.; Bhaskar, M. S.; Blaabjerg, F.; Holm-Nielsen, J. B.; Azam, F.; Sharma, A.K.; A Hybrid Photovoltaic-Fuel Cell-Based Single-Stage Grid Integration With Lyapunov Control Scheme. IEEE Systems Journal, 2020, 14: 3334 - 3342

78. Priyadarshi, N.; Bhaskar, M. S.; Padmanaban, N.; Blaabjerg, F.; Azam, F.; New CUK–SEPIC converter based photovoltaic power system with hybrid GSA–PSO algorithm employing MPPT for water pumping applications. IET Power Electronics. 2020, 13:2824 – 2830

79. Priyadarshi, N.; Padmanaban, N.; Holm-Nielsen, J. B.; Bhaskar, M.S.; Azam, F.; Internet of things augmented a novel PSO-employed modified zeta converter-based photovoltaic maximum power tracking system: hardware realisation. IET Power Electronics. 2020, 13:2775 – 2781

80. Kamalapathi, K., Priyadarshi, N., Padmanaban, S., Holm-Nielsen, J.B., Azam, F., Umayal, C., Ramachandaramurthy, V.K. A Hybrid Moth-Flame Fuzzy Logic Controller Based Integrated Cuk Converter Fed Brushless DC Motor for Power Factor Correction. MDPI Electronics, 2018, 7: 288.

81. Priyadarshi, N., Padmanaban, S., Lonel, D., Mihet-Popa, L., Azam, F. Hybrid PV-Wind, Micro-Grid Development Using Quasi-Z-Source Inverter Modeling and Control—Experimental Investigation. MDPI Energies, 2018, 11:2277

82. Priyadarshi, N.; Ramachandaramurthy, V, K.; Padmanaban, S.; Azam, A.; An Ant Colony Optimized MPPT for Standalone Hybrid PV-Wind Power System with Single Cuk Converter. MDPI Energies, 2019, 12: 167

83. Azam, F.; Yadav, S.K.; Priyadarshi, N.; Padmanaban, S.; and Bansal, R.C.; A Comprehensive Review of Authentication Schemes in Vehicular Ad-Hoc Network, IEEE Access, 2021, 9:31309-31321, 2021, doi: 10.1109/ACCESS.2021.3060046.

84. Priyadarshi, N.; Sharma, A.K.; Bhoi, A. K.; Ahmad, S. N.; Azam, F.; Priyam, S.; A Practical performance verification of AFLC based MPPT for standalone PV power system under varying weather condition, International Journal of Engineering & Technology, 2018, 7:338-343

85. Azam F.; Priyadarshi N.; Nagar H.; Kumar S.; Bhoi A.K.; An Overview of Solar-Powered Electric Vehicle Charging in Vehicular Adhoc Network. in: Electric Vehicles. Green Energy and Technology. Springer, Singapore. https://doi.org/10.1007/978-981-15-9251-5_5

86. Azam, F.; Kumar, S.; Yadav, K.P.; Priyadarshi N.; Padmanaban, S.; An Outline of the Security Challenges in VANET, in Proc. of IEEE UPCON 2020, Nov, 2020.

87. Priyadarshi, N.; Azam, F.; Bhoi, A.K.; Sharma, A.K.; A Multilevel Inverter-Controlled Photovoltaic Generation. in Advances in Greener Energy Technologies. Springer, Singapore. 2020 https://doi.org/10.1007/978-981-15-4246-6_8

88. Priyadarshi, N.; Azam, F.; Bhoi, A.K.; Sharma, A.K.; Dynamic Operation of Grid-Connected Photovoltaic Power System. in Advances in Greener Energy Technologies. Springer, Singapore. 2020 https://doi.org/10.1007/978-981-15-4246-6_13

89. Priyadarshi, N.; Azam, F.; Bhoi, A.K.; Sharma, A.K.; A Proton Exchange Membrane-Based Fuel Cell Integrated Power System. in Advances in Greener Energy Technologies. Springer, Singapore. 2020 https://doi.org/10.1007/978-981-15-4246-6_18

90. Priyadarshi, N.; Azam, F.; Bhoi, A.K.; Sharma, A.K.; A Closed-Loop Control of Fixed Pattern Rectifier for Renewable Energy Applications. in Advances in Greener Energy Technologies. Springer, Singapore. 2020 https://doi.org/10.1007/978-981-15-4246-6_25

91. Priyadarshi, N.; Azam, F.; Bhoi, A.K.; Sharma, A.K.; A Four-Switch-Type Converter Fed Improved Photovoltaic Power System. in Advances in Greener Energy Technologies. Springer, Singapore. 2020 https://doi.org/10.1007/978-981-15-4246-6_29

92. Vardia, M.; Priyadarshi, N.; Ali, I.; Azam, F.; Bhoi, A.K.; Maximum Power Point Tracking for Wind Energy Conversion System. in Advances in Greener Energy Technologies. Springer, Singapore. 2020 https://doi.org/10.1007/978-981-15-4246-6_36

93. Vardia, M.; Priyadarshi, N.; Ali, I.; Azam, F.; Bhoi, A.K.; Design of Wind Energy Conversion System Under Different Fault Conditions. in Advances in Greener Energy Technologies. Springer, Singapore. 2020 https://doi.org/10.1007/978-981-15-4246-6_41

94. Choudhary, T.; Priyadarshi, N.; Kuma,r P.; Azam, F.; Bhoi A.K. (2020) A Fuzzy Logic Control Based Vibration Control System for Renewable Application. in Advances in Greener Energy Technologies. Springer, Singapore. 2020 https://doi.org/10.1007/978-981-15-4246-6_38

95. Priyadarshi, N.; Azam F.; Solanki, S. S.; Sharma, A.K.; Bhoi, A.K.; Almakhles, D.; A Bio-Inspired Chicken Swarm Optimization-Based Fuel Cell System for Electric Vehicle Applications. in Bio-inspired Neurocomputing. Studies in Computational Intelligence, vol 903. Springer, Singapore. 2021 https://doi.org/10.1007/978-981-15-5495-7_1

96. Kermany, S.D., Joorabian, M., Deilami, S. and Masoum, M.A., 2016. Hybrid islanding detection in microgrid with multiple connection points to smart grids using fuzzy-neural network. *IEEE Transactions on Power Systems,* *32*(4), pp.2640-2651.

97. Matic-Cuka, B. and Kezunovic, M., 2014. Islanding detection for inverter-based distributed generation using support vector machine method. *IEEE Transactions on Smart Grid, 5*(6), pp.2676-2686.

98. Kim, H.C., Pang, S., Je, H.M., Kim, D. and Bang, S.Y., 2003. Constructing support vector machine ensemble. *Pattern recognition, 36*(12), pp.2757-2767.

99. Lidula, N.W.A. and Rajapakse, A.D., 2009, December. Fast and reliable detection of power islands using transient signals. In *2009 International Conference on Industrial and Information Systems (ICIIS)* (pp. 493-498). IEEE.

100. Mohanty, S.R., Ray, P.K., Kishor, N. and Panigrahi, B.K., 2013. Classification of disturbances in hybrid DG system using modular PNN and SVM. *International Journal of Electrical Power & Energy Systems, 44*(1), pp.764-777.

101. Mohanty, S.R., Kishor, N., Ray, P.K. and Catalo, J.P., 2014. Comparative study of advanced signal processing techniques for islanding detection in a hybrid distributed generation system. *IEEE Transactions on sustainable Energy, 6*(1), pp.122-131.

102. Baghaee, H.R., Mlakić, D., Nikolovski, S. and Dragičević, T., 2019. Support vector machine-based Islanding and grid fault detection in active distribution networks. *IEEE Journal of Emerging and Selected Topics in Power Electronics.*

103. Sylvester, E.V., Bentzen, P., Bradbury, I.R., Clément, M., Pearce, J., Horne, J. and Beiko, R.G., 2018. Applications of random forest feature selection for fine-scale genetic population assignment. *Evolutionary applications, 11*(2), pp.153-165.

104. Bradter, U., Kunin, W.E., Altringham, J.D., Thom, T.J. and Benton, T.G., 2013. Identifying appropriate spatial scales of predictors in species distribution models with the random forest algorithm. *Methods in Ecology and Evolution, 4*(2), pp.167-174.

105. Dutta, S., Reddy, M.J.B., Mohanta, D. and Sadhu, P., 2019. µPMU based Intelligent Island Detection–The first crucial step towards enhancing grid resilience with microgrid. *IET Smart Grid.* 3(2), pp.162 –173.

106. Faqhruldin, O.N., El-Saadany, E.F. and Zeineldin, H.H., 2014. A universal islanding detection technique for distributed generation using pattern recognition. *IEEE Transactions on Smart Grid, 5*(4), pp.1985-1992.

Intelligent Control Technique for Reduction of Converter Generated EMI in DG Environment

Ritesh Tirole[1]*, R R Joshi[2], Vinod Kumar Yadav[2], Jai Kumar Maherchandani[2] and Shripati Vyas[2]

[1]Dept. of Electrical Engineering, Sir Padampat Singhania University, Udaipur, India
[2]Dept. of Electrical Engineering, College of Technology and Engineering, Udaipur, India

Abstract

This chapter presents the intelligent control technique used for minimization of electromagnetic interference (EMI) generated in distributed generated (DG) environment. With the help of intelligent control technique, it is potentially found that EMI magnitude, generated in DG environment, can be reduce to permissible limits suggested by the CISPR standard for DG environment. The intelligent control technique reduces the EMI, improves the power quality, enhance the performance of system. The DG model of the system is developed in simulation environment to check the validity of the proposed intelligent control technique. The simulation result shows the efficacy of the proposed intelligent control technique in EMI reduction. From the results, it clearly indicates that, magnitude of the generated EMI, at various emission frequencies in DG environment, decreases considerably by using intelligent controller.

Keywords: Electromagnetic interference, distributed generation, linear impedance stabilization network (LISN), power quality, fuzzy logic controller

**Corresponding author*: ritesh.tirole@spsu.ac.in

Neeraj Priyadarshi, Akash Kumar Bhoi, Sanjeevikumar Padmanaban, S. Balamurugan and Jens Bo Holm-Nielsen (eds.) Intelligent Renewable Energy Systems, (111–130) © 2022 Scrivener Publishing LLC

4.1   Introduction

With the increase of economic development of any country, energy demand of it will increase multiple times [1–21]. To meet out this tremendous demand of energy, countries have been looking for different ways to harvest electricity from the natural resources [22–35]. Renewable energy is the promising solution to combat greenhouse emission, which is the greatest threat to the environment. Governmental agencies and the policy makers are also promoting renewable energy, because it could produce clean energy at minimum cost [36–47].

The distributed generation (DG), has all these capabilities like improved energy efficiency, low air emission to replace the conventional energy power plants. DG will be defined as low power capacity generators positioned at the client energy service provider or utility site and sometimes it may be stand-alone or connected to the medium electric distribution system. Various DG technologies are available like photovoltaic, wind, geothermal and ocean.

Regarding wind power, in *wind* power plant uses wind turbines are used to convert wind energy into electricity. The main components of wind power plants are wind generators (i.e. induction generators), power electronics converters like ac-dc converters or dc-ac converters.

A grid-connected solar photovoltaic (PV) system consists of PV modules that produce electricity from sunlight and power converters for energy extraction and grid interface control. The operation of a grid-connected solar PV system depends on the coordination of the electrical system and PV cells under variable weather and system conditions. Photovoltaic solar electricity can deliver and is delivering clean, reliable, on demand power in current markets worldwide. Although solar photovoltaic system provides electricity at zero emission, but at the same time major components of it, i.e. converters and inverters, creates electromagnetic interference, which causes lots of problem related to the functioning of these devise as well as power quality problems.

Any disturbance, which degrades, interrupts, limits the genuine performance, or obstructs any electrical or electronic system (i.e. equipment, transmission or distribution line etc.) can be termed as electromagnetic interference (EMI) [1, 2]. Electro-magnetic environment consist of emission control, electromagnetic vulnerability, electromagnetic pulse, precipitation static, electromagnetic compatibility (EMC) etc. are the integral part of EMI. EMI spread at any part of electromagnetic spectrum [2].

This chapter is organized in the following manner: 1) First it introduces the general configurations of a grid connected solar PV system in section 4.2; 2) Second, Section 4.3 presents the various control strategies used at grid connected solar PV system; 3) Third, Section 4.4 presents the electromagnetic interference and its causes in grid connected solar PV system. Section 4.5 presents the EMI simulation evaluation of various control strategies of the solar PV system. Finally, the paper concludes with the summary of major points.

4.2   Grid Connected Solar PV System

4.2.1   Grid Connected Solar PV System

Solar Photovoltaic system is classified into three types. A) Standalone type, B) Grid connected SPV system, and C) hybrid. The important components of a Grid Connected SPV system consist of PV array, controller circuit, Inverter, harmonic filter. Sometimes a low frequency transformer is also used in between inverter output and the grid. Schematic of Grid Connected PV system is shown in Figure 4.1.

PV cells are the core elements of any SPV system. By proper combination of PV cell either in series or in parallel or both, desired voltage or current can be produced by the PV module. Since the output magnitude of the PV module is not sufficient, strings of PV modules are used together to produce the required voltage and current. These strings of PV module are known as a PV array.

PV module converts the sunrays into DC power. A PV system is a combined assembly of one or more PV Arrays and have a balance of system components which are so, designed that they are used to convert solar energy into electrical form and can be used for a particular application alone or with some other sources of energy.

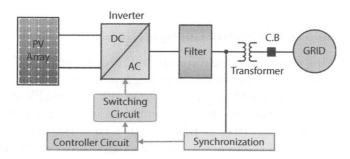

Figure 4.1 Grid connected solar PV system.

4.2.2   PhotoVoltaic Cell

It is a device, which generates electrical energy with the process of capturing the energy of photons by electrons known as Photovoltaic effect without using sun's heat energy. It produces electricity directly capturing (converting) falling sunlight into energy via the photovoltaic cells, which is a process in which the photons energetically break electrons free to cause/generate a flow of electricity, via the semiconducting material inside the PV cell. This effect is known as photoelectric effect. Semiconductor materials have a moderate gap between the conduction band and the valance band, so that electrons from valance band are able to jump into the conduction band by gaining adequate energy, which will be used for PV cells. Poly crystalline, single crystalline, thin film material are the popular name of PV cells.

4.2.3   PhotoVoltaic Array

PV cell is the basic unit of any PV module. The function of the PV cell is to generate electricity by solar energy. Commonly used material for PV cell is silicon. Series and parallel connection of multiple PV cells make a PV module. The power generated by a PV module is not sufficient to meet the demand of the grid. Therefore, numerous PV module are connected together to design a PV array. PV array is the combination of multiple PV modules, which generate the sufficient power to transfer it to grid. DC current is generated by the the PV array. To feed this generated electricity into the grid, conversion from DC to AC is essential. For that, the PV array uses inverters.

The structure of the PV array is simple. To obtain the required voltage, they are first linked in a series and then the strings of the array are linked in parallel to achieve the required current. The rating of PV array is in watt, kW or MW.

4.2.4   PhotoVoltaic System Configurations

For generating power from the PV array and feed, the process of generating power into the grid power conditioning system, using the dc-dc converter, inverter are required. In grid connected SPV systems, PV arrays and Power conditioning systems are each configured in different ways. These configuration is categorized as follows: A). Centralized configuration, B). Master slave configuration, C). String configuration, and D). Modular configuration.

4.2.4.1   Centralized Configurations

A centralized configuration is implemented for grid connected distribution systems. Here, the PV array is arranged in both parallel and series combinations for generating desired output current and voltage. Three-phase inverter in configuration with PV array is used to feed the generated power in to the grid. Centralized configuration of inverters is classified as per the kW capacity of the PV system.

4.2.4.2   Master Slave Configurations

In case of the master slave configuration, AC grid is fed through more than one (multiple) inverters, these inverters are connected in parallel to the grid. Through the parallel connection the reliability of the system increases, if one inverter stops functioning, due to any reason, another inverter will feed power to grid and continuity will be maintain. This configuration is suitable for large power SPV system. it has some limitations, like the mismatch of the PV modules characteristics, improper function in partial shading condition.

4.2.4.3   String Configurations

String configurations are grouped as single or multi string configurations. In the case of a single string configuration, the series of connected solar modules are used and the system is connected to AC grid. This type of configuration is popular in low power rooftop applications. For plant capacity up to 6 kW, multi string configuration is deployed.

4.2.4.4   Modular Configurations

The modular configuration is best suited for micro grid system. In this system, each PV array is connected to individual inverter, which is mounted on its panel. The advantage of modular configuration is reducing power loss in case of partial shading of PV array and design of the PV array will be flexible. It has some major limitation like high cost and increased thermal stress. This type of configuration applied for very low power rating, i.e. less than 1 kW.

4.2.5   Inverter Integration in Grid Solar PV System

The purpose of interface inverter implemented in grid-connected SPV system is to (1) ensure that SPV module must generate maximum power and

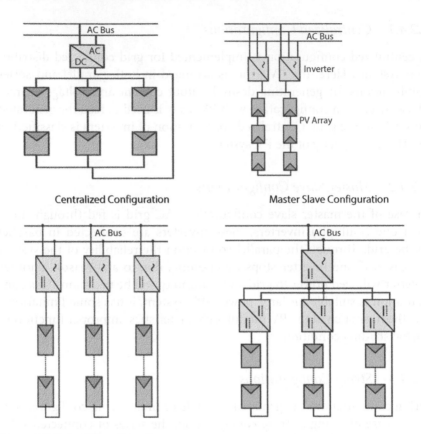

Figure 4.2 Solar PV configurations.

(2) the injected electric current to the grid should be sinusoidal in nature. Maximum power point tracking (MPPT) is used to ensure the maximum generation from SPV and to ensure sinusoidal current appropriate filters must be used. In a modern grid system, two-way communication, i.e. between the power grid and SPV array, will play a crucial role. To interface between SPV and grid, various inverters are available [6]. Various solar PV configurations are shown in Figure 4.2.

4.2.5.1   Voltage Source Inverter

Voltage source inverters (VSI) are the most popular type of Inverter configuration used to connect SPV to the grid system. In VSI, the output AC voltage is lower than the input DC voltage. Hence, to feed a 400-volt three-phase grid system at least 650-volt dc link voltage is required. In field conditions, at least 700 to 750 volt SPV module must be implemented to get the desired grid output, because of grid tolerance, i.e. 10% and the control reverse. Generally, neutral-point VSI is used for grid-connected SPV system. To minimize the Common mode voltage (CMV) neutral point is connected to the DC link at SPV module. In VSI, the additional DC-DC boost converter is essential if the SPV module of the grid is having the same or lower voltage rating as the AC grid system. To reduce the EMI interference, this topology is best suited for the SPV system.

4.2.5.2   Current Source Inverter

In this inverter integration configuration, the output current from the inverter is always constant irrespective of variation in the grid system and the input DC source act as a current source. The voltage of the grid will increase by use of this type of inverter. The CSI operates on maximum DC voltage and it may be an alternate solution to VSI integration configuration. This type of configuration requires fewer ancillaries to perform its operation systematically. The requirement of a DC-DC boost converter is eliminated when CSI is used in SPV grid interconnection.

4.3   Control Strategies for Grid Connected Solar PV System

The performance of grid connected SPV system governed by the accurate and peedy control of three phase inverters installed at grid side. The main cause of operational instability in this type of system arises because of deign issues present in switching controller. Linear controller, non-linear controller, robust controller, adaptive controller, predictive controller and intelligent controllers are the key switching controllers used in grid connected SPV system.

4.3.1   Grid Solar PV System Controller

4.3.1.1   Linear Controllers

In this type of switching controller, the control mechanism is based on principles of a linear control system. A *linear controller* generates a switching signal based on negative feedback. Integral members of this type of controllers are P, P-I, P-D and P-I-D.

4.3.1.2   Non-Linear Controllers

This type of switching controllers handle uncertainties of the SPV system to some extent because it has the nature of adaptableness. The output performance of the system is great when used as a nonlinear controller as compared to the linear controller.

4.3.1.3   Robust Controllers

Regarding *robust controllers*, the controllers are used to sustain the stability of SPV system by using closed loop technique. Here, the controller gets well-defined instructions from the system under specified criteria. In this type of controller, the output results produced by the system will be in stable condition even system exposed to abnormal conditions.

4.3.1.4   Adaptive Controllers

In adaptive control scheme, the output signals from the controller is being adjusted as per the requirement of SPV system operations. Here in this case, SPV system output will depends not only on the system parameters but also on other factors such as operating conditions etc.

4.3.1.5   Predictive Controllers

This controller capable of predicting the system behavior for future. It uses the well-defined optimization criteria of the system where it is used. In optimization criteria, predictive controller takes the complete system information to produce the optimal results.

4.3.1.6   Intelligent Controllers

In intelligent controller includes artificial intelligence (AI) techniques, i.e. genetic algorithm (GA), machine learning (ML), neural network (NN), and fuzzy logic (FL) for producing better results as they are capable of producing better results under dynamic conditions. Intelligent controllers are also implemented in systems where controlling is difficult by using earlier controller. The intelligent controller has the capability of learning, adaption and decision-making. The nature this type of controller is used in interdisciplinary applications.

4.4   Electromagnetic Interference

Electromagnetic interference (EMI) contains undesirable, spurious, conducted, and/or radiated signals of electrical nature that can cause intolerable degradation in the performance of any system or equipment. The EMI signals generate at very high frequencies and give rise to EMI magnitude. The gate control circuits of converters or inverters have a very low-level magnitude of voltage and current, and hence it can have an adverse effect of EMI generated by its own high power circuitry. EMI can also be taken as performance-degradation in equipment or devices. This EMI spread in the form of an undesirable signal/electromagnetic noise or even a modification of the medium of propagation itself.

Electromagnetic compatibility (EMC) is the capability of any power electronics system to (1) function appropriately in its intended electromagnetic environment, and (2) not become the source of EMI emission that pollutes the existing electromagnetic environment. Thus, the sensitive electrical or electronic equipment or control systems must co-exist in an electromagnetic environment without interrupting each other's operation. In addition, Electromagnetic Compatibility (EMC) can be perceived as the capability of any equipment functioning appropriately in its intended electromagnetic ambience.

4.4.1   Mechanisms of Electromagnetic Interference

The prime concerns of the Electromagnetic Compatibility are the generation, reception, and transmission of electromagnetic energy. When the source or an emitter generates emissions, a coupling or transfer path relays such emitted energy to a receiver. This receptor processes it, resulting in desirable or undesirable behaviour. Interference occurs when the resultant behaviour of the receptor is undesirable after receiving energy. Electromagnetic energy is transferred via unintended modes of coupling. However, this unintentional energy transfer creates interference.

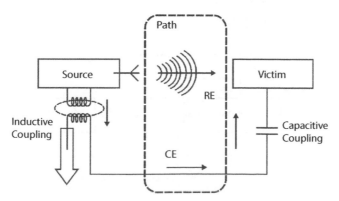

Figure 4.3 Source, victim and coupling path of EMI.

For understanding the phenomena of EMI, three components, as discussed earlier, must be understood clearly, the source of interference, coupling path and effect of disturbances on the victim circuit or receiver. These three components are obvious for EMI.

The source or culprit is the generator of electromagnetic energy; the coupling path is the transmitting medium of that energy between the apparatus, and the victim or receiver circuit is whose process is negatively impacted by the transmitted energy are shown in Figure 4.3. So, all three are necessary elements for EMI.

4.4.2 Effect of Electromagnetic Interference

EMI is considered to be a silent and an unknown threat. Electromagnetic interference affects several electronic and electrical devices and control systems. The equipment or the subsystems become susceptible to EMI when malfunctioning occurs due to this energy. The common effects of EMI are (i) Annoying Effects, (ii) Disturbing Effects, (iii) Catastrophic Situations, (iv) Thermal effect, and (v) Non-thermal effect.

4.5 Intelligent Controller for Grid Connected Solar PV System

4.5.1 Fuzzy Logic Controller

The main three blocks of the diagram are fuzzification, defuzzification, and inference engine are shown in Figure 4.4. The error E and change of error dE are the two inputs fed to the fuzzy logic controller.

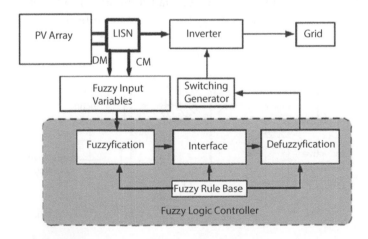

Figure 4.4 Block diagram of fuzzy logic controller.

Table 4.1 Rule base for fuzzy logic controller.

dE \ E	NB	NM	NS	ZE	P.S	P.M	P.B
NB	NB	NB	NB	NB	NB	NB	NB
NM	NM	NM	NM	NM	NM	NM	NM
NS	NS	NS	NS	NS	NS	NS	NS
ZE	ZE	ZE	ZE	ZE	ZE	ZE	ZE
PS	PS	PS	PS	PS	PS	PS	PS
PM	PM	PM	PM	PM	PM	PM	PM
PB	PB	PB	PB	PB	PB	PB	PB

According to the comprehensive behaviour of the SPV inverter system, the fuzzy rules are selected. Fuzzy decisions are made based on fuzzy rules to get minimum EMI generation due to the switching of inverter devices.

The fuzzy system rule base is created as shown in Table 4.1. It shows the set of rules of the fuzzy controller. All the fuzzy variables inputs are error variation E, change in error variation dE and output variation, i.e. duty cycle variation D. For expressing fuzzy rules, the syntax IF/THEN is always used. Here for EMI reduction, we use 49 rules like:

According to the comprehensive behaviour of the SPV inverter system, the fuzzy rules are selected. Fuzzy decisions are made based on fuzzy rules to get minimum EMI generation due to the switching of inverter devices.

The input is classified into seven membership functions or linguistic variables as Positive small (PS), Positive Medium (PM) and Positive big (PB), Negative Big (NB), Negative medium (NM), Negative small (NS), Zero error (ZE).

4.6   Results and Discussion

The proposed intelligent control technique for reduction of converter generated EMI in DG environment is investigated and validate through simulation under various conditions.

4.6.1   Generated EMI at the Input Side of Grid SPV System

Simulation results in Figure 4.5 shows the common mode (CM), Figure 4.6 shows differential mode (DM), and Figure 4.7 shows total EMI generated at the input side of the inverter circuit of a grid-connected SPV system.

Conventional switching scheme is used to deliver firing pulses to three-phase inverter switches. The magnitude of CM EMI measured is approximately in between 112 dBµV to 120 dBµV at 0.1 MHz frequency of emission. For frequency of emission ranges from 1 MHz to 5 MHz, 5 MHz to 15 MHz and 15 MHz to 30 MHz, the magnitude of generated CM EMI varies from 110 dBµV to 94 dBµV, 94 dBµV to 82 dBµV and 82 dBµV to 55 dBµV respectively. When compared, the generated CM EMI with the EMI standard CISPR 22 class A, it is found that the magnitude of generated CM EMI is higher than the prescribed limit of EMI magnitude in CISPR 22 Class A.

The generated magnitude of differential mode (DM) EMI, for the frequency of emission, ranges from 1 MHz to 5 MHz, 5 MHz to 15 MHz and 15 MHz to 30 MHz, varies from 109 dBµV to 84 dBµV, 84 dBµV to 80 dBµV and 80 dBµV to 52 dBµV respectively. When compare the generated DM EMI with the EMI standard CISPR 22, it is found that the magnitude of generated DM EMI is higher than the prescribed limit of EMI magnitude in CISPR 22.

The total EMI of inverter circuit at the input side of grid SPV system is higher than the recommended limit of EMI standards in CISPR 22 class A.

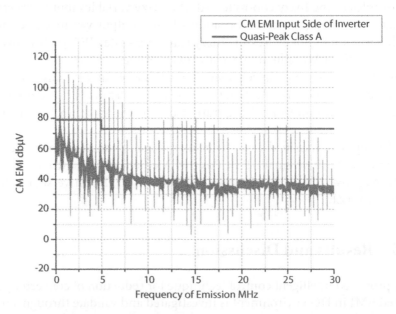

Figure 4.5 CM EMI at input side of inverter.

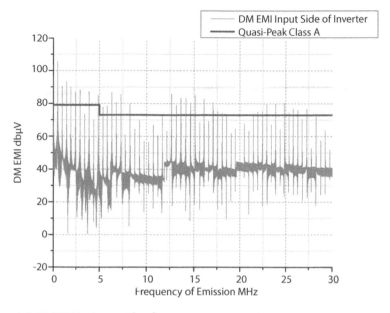

Figure 4.6 DM EMI at input side of inverter.

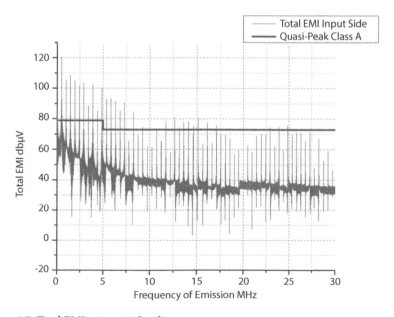

Figure 4.7 Total EMI at input side of inverter.

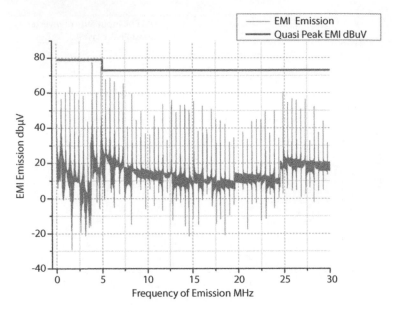

Figure 4.8 CM EMI at input side of inverter.

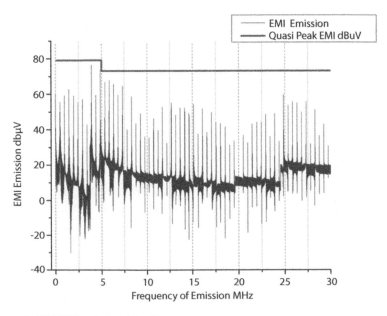

Figure 4.9 DM EMI at input side of inverter.

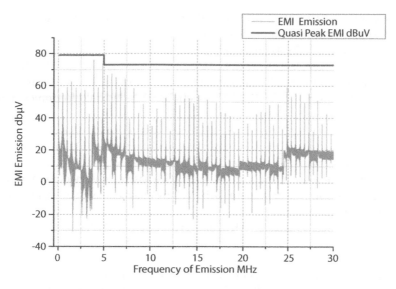

Figure 4.10 Total EMI at input side of inverter.

Figures 4.8, 4.9 and 4.10 shows, the reduction in the magnitude of EMI, when intelligent fuzzy logic controller is applied to the three-phase inverter of grid-connected Solar PV systems.

By implementing the intelligent fuzzy logic switching control technique will help in reducing the magnitude of generated EMI during the switching operation of the circuits. In case of intelligent control technique, the level of generated EMI magnitude is less than the CISPR 22 class A standards of EMC/EMI.

4.7 Conclusion

The performance of the intelligent controller is found to be good under steady conditions for grid connected photovoltaic systems. The generated EMI at various emission frequencies in DG environment, decreases considerably by using intelligent controller. It is seen that the EMI is significantly reduced to the permissible limit of CISPR and IEC standards.

References

1. Araneo, R., Lammens, S., Grossi, M., & Bertone, S. (2009). EMC issues in high-power grid-connected photovoltaic plants. IEEE Transactions on Electromagnetic Compatibility, 51(3 PART 2), 639–648.

2. Cecati, C., Ciancetta, F., & Siano, P. (2010). A multilevel inverter for photovoltaic systems with fuzzy logic control. IEEE Transactions on Industrial
   Electronics, 57(12), 4115–4125.
3. Kim, S. K., Jeon, J. H., Cho, C. H., Ahn, J. B., & Kwon, S. H. (2008). Dynamic
   modeling and control of a grid-connected hybrid generation system with
   versatile power transfer. IEEE Transactions on Industrial Electronics, 55(4),
   1677–1688.
4. Nguyen, X. H., & Nguyen, M. P. (2015). Mathematical modeling of photovoltaic cell/module/arrays with tags in Matlab/Simulink. Environmental
   Systems Research (Vol. 4). Springer Berlin Heidelberg.
5. Swami, R, Kumar V, and Joshi, R.R. "FPGA based Implementation of fuzzy
   logic DTC for induction motor drive fed by matrix converter," IETE Journal
   of research, August 2019.
6. N Priyadarshi, F Azam, AK Bhoi, AK Sharma: Dynamic Operation of
   Grid-Connected Photovoltaic Power System, Advances in Greener Energy
   Technologies, 2020.
7. Araneo, R., Lammens, S., Grossi, M., Bertone, S.: EMC issues in high-power
   grid-connected photovoltaic plants. IEEE Trans. Electromagn. Compat. 51,
   639–648 (2009).
8. Hedayati, M.H., John, V.: EMI and ground leakage current reduction in
   single-phase grid-connected power converter. IET Power Electron. 10,
   938–944 (2017).
9. Jiraprasertwong, J., Jettanasen, C.: Electromagnetic interference in photovoltaic system and mitigation of conducted noise at DC side. IEEE Reg. 10
   Annu. Int. Conf. Proceedings/TENCON. 915–920 (2017).
10. Xiao, W., El Moursi, M.S., Khan, O., Infield, D.: Review of grid-tied con-
    verter topologies used in photovoltaic systems. IET Renew. Power Gener. 10,
    1543–1551 (2016).
11. Román, E., Alonso, R., Ibañez, P., Elorduizapatarietxe, S., Goitia, D.:
    Intelligent PV module for grid-connected PV systems. IEEE Trans. Ind.
    Electron. 53, 1066–1073 (2006).
12. Roudet, J.: EMI Conducted Emission in the Differential Mode Emanating
    from an SCR: Phenomena and Noise Level Prediction. IEEE Trans. Power
    Electron. 10, 105–110 (1993).
13. Kouro, S., Leon, J.I., Vinnikov, D., Franquelo, L.G.: Grid-Connected
    Photovoltaic Systems: An Overview of Recent Research and Emerging PV
    Converter Technology. (2015).
14. Priyadarshi.; N;, Padmanaban, S.; Maroti, P.K.; Sharma. A.; An Extensive
    Practical Investigation of FPSO-Based MPPT for Grid Integrated PV System
    Under Variable Operating Conditions With Anti-Islanding Protection. IEEE
    System Journal, 2018, 13:1861–1871.
15. Priyadarshi, N.; Padmanaban, S.; Bhaskar, M.S.; Blaabjerg, F.; Sharma, A.;
    A Fuzzy SVPWM Based Inverter Control Realization of Grid Integrated
    PV-Wind System with FPSO MPPT Algorithm for a Grid-Connected PV/

Wind Power Generation System: Hardware Implementation. IET Electric Power Appl., 2018, 12:962–971.

16. Priyadarshi, N.; Kumar, V.; Yadav, K.; Vardia, M.; An Experimental Study on Zeta buck-boost converter for Application in PV system. Handbook of distributed generation, Springer, DOI 10.1007/978-3-319-51343-0_13

17. Priyadarshi N.; Sharma A.K.; Priyam S.; An Experimental Realization of Grid-Connected PV System with MPPT Using dSPACE DS 1104 Control Board. Advances in Smart Grid and Renewable Energy. Lecture Notes in Electrical Engineering, Springer, Singapore 2018, 435.

18. Priyadarshi N.; Sharma A.K.; Priyam S.; Practical Realization of an Improved Photovoltaic Grid Integration with MPPT. International Journal of Renewable Energy Research 2017, 7:1180–1891.

19. Priyadarshi N.; Sharma A.K.; Azam F.; A Hybrid Firefly-Asymmetrical Fuzzy Logic Controller based MPPT for PV-Wind-Fuel Grid Integration. International Journal of Renewable Energy Research 2017, 7: 1546–1560

20. Priyadarshi, N.; Anand, A.; Sharma, A.K.; Azam, F.; Singh, V.K.; Sinha, R. K.; An Experimental Implementation and Testing of GA based Maximum Power Point Tracking for PV System under Varying Ambient Conditions Using dSPACE DS 1104 Controller. International Journal of Renewable Energy Research, 2017, 7:255–265

21. Priyadarshi, N.; Padmanaban S.; Mihet-Popa L.; Blaabjerg, F.; Azam F.; Maximum Power Point Tracking for Brushless DC Motor-Driven Photovoltaic Pumping Systems Using a Hybrid ANFIS-FLOWER Pollination Optimization Algorithm. MDPI Energies 2018, 11:1–16

22. Priyadarshi, N.; Azam, F.; Bhoi, A.K.; Alam, S.; An Artificial Fuzzy Logic Intelligent Controller Based MPPT for PV Grid Utility. Lecture Notes in Networks and Systems 46, https://doi.org/10.1007/978-981-13-1217-5_88.

23. Padmanaban, S.; Priyadarshi, N.; Holm-Nielsen, J. B.; Bhaskar, M. S.; Azam, F.; Sharma, A.K.; A Novel Modified Sine-Cosine Optimized MPPT Algorithm for Grid Integrated PV System under Real Operating Conditions. IEEE Access, 2019, 7:10467–10477.

24. Padmanaban, S.; Priyadarshi, N.; Holm-Nielsen, J. B.; Bhaskar, M. S.; Hossain, E.; Azam, F.; A Hybrid Photovoltaic-Fuel Cell for Grid Integration With Jaya-Based Maximum Power Point Tracking: Experimental Performance Evaluation. IEEE Access, 2019, 7:82978–82990.

25. Priyadarshi, N.; Padmanaban, N.; Holm-Nielsen, J. B.; Blaabjerg, F.; Bhaskar, M.S.; An Experimental Estimation of Hybrid ANFIS–PSO-Based MPPT for PV Grid Integration Under Fluctuating Sun Irradiance. in IEEE Systems Journal. 2020, 14:1218–1229

26. Priyadarshi, N.; Padmanaban, N.; Bhaskar, M. S.; Blaabjerg, F.; Holm-Nielsen, J. B.; Azam, F.; Sharma, A.K.; A Hybrid Photovoltaic-Fuel Cell-Based Single-Stage Grid Integration With Lyapunov Control Scheme. IEEE Systems Journal, 2020, 14: 3334–3342

27. Priyadarshi, N.; Bhaskar, M. S.; Padmanaban, N.; Blaabjerg, F.; Azam, F.; New CUK–SEPIC converter based photovoltaic power system with hybrid GSA–PSO algorithm employing MPPT for water pumping applications. IET Power Electronics. 2020, 13:2824 – 2830

28. Priyadarshi, N.; Padmanaban, N.; Holm-Nielsen, J. B.; Bhaskar, M.S.; Azam, F.; Internet of things augmented a novel PSO-employed modified zeta converter-based photovoltaic maximum power tracking system: hardware realisation. IET Power Electronics. 2020, 13:2775 – 2781

29. Kamalapathi, K., Priyadarshi, N., Padmanaban, S., Holm-Nielsen, J.B., Azam, F., Umayal, C., Ramachandaramurthy, V.K. A Hybrid Moth-Flame Fuzzy Logic Controller Based Integrated Cuk Converter Fed Brushless DC Motor for Power Factor Correction. MDPI Electronics, 2018, 7: 288.

30. Priyadarshi, N., Padmanaban, S., Lonel, D., Mihet-Popa, L., Azam, F. Hybrid PV-Wind, Micro-Grid Development Using Quasi-Z-Source Inverter Modeling and Control—Experimental Investigation. MDPI Energies, 2018, 11:2277

31. Priyadarshi, N.; Ramachandaramurthy, V, K.; Padmanaban, S.; Azam, A.; An Ant Colony Optimized MPPT for Standalone Hybrid PV-Wind Power System with Single Cuk Converter. MDPI Energies, 2019, 12: 167

32. Azam, F.; Yadav, S.K.; Priyadarshi, N.; Padmanaban, S.; and Bansal, R.C.; A Comprehensive Review of Authentication Schemes in Vehicular Ad-Hoc Network, IEEE Access, 2021, 9:31309–31321, 2021, doi: 10.1109/ACCESS.2021.3060046.

33. Priyadarshi, N.; Sharma, A.K.; Bhoi, A. K.; Ahmad, S. N.; Azam, F.; Priyam, S.; A Practical performance verification of AFLC based MPPT for standalone PV power system under varying weather condition, International Journal of Engineering & Technology, 2018, 7:338–343

34. Azam F.; Priyadarshi N.; Nagar H.; Kumar S.; Bhoi A.K.; An Overview of Solar-Powered Electric Vehicle Charging in Vehicular Adhoc Network. in: Electric Vehicles. Green Energy and Technology. Springer, Singapore. https://doi.org/10.1007/978-981-15-9251-5_5

35. Azam, F.; Kumar, S.; Yadav, K.P.; Priyadarshi N.; Padmanaban, S.; An Outline of the Security Challenges in VANET, in Proc. of IEEE UPCON 2020, Nov, 2020.

36. Priyadarshi, N.; Azam, F.; Bhoi, A.K.; Sharma, A.K.; A Multilevel Inverter-Controlled Photovoltaic Generation. in Advances in Greener Energy Technologies. Springer, Singapore. 2020 https://doi.org/10.1007/978-981-15-4246-6_8

37. Priyadarshi, N.; Azam, F.; Bhoi, A.K.; Sharma, A.K.; Dynamic Operation of Grid-Connected Photovoltaic Power System. in Advances in Greener Energy Technologies. Springer, Singapore. 2020 https://doi.org/10.1007/978-981-15-4246-6_13

38. Priyadarshi, N.; Azam, F.; Bhoi, A.K.; Sharma, A.K.; A Proton Exchange Membrane-Based Fuel Cell Integrated Power System. in Advances in

Greener Energy Technologies. Springer, Singapore. 2020 https://doi.org/10.1007/978-981-15-4246-6_18

39. Priyadarshi, N.; Azam, F.; Bhoi, A.K.; Sharma, A.K.; A Closed-Loop Control of Fixed Pattern Rectifier for Renewable Energy Applications. in Advances in Greener Energy Technologies. Springer, Singapore. 2020 https://doi.org/10.1007/978-981-15-4246-6_25

40. Priyadarshi, N.; Azam, F.; Bhoi, A.K.; Sharma, A.K.; A Four-Switch-Type Converter Fed Improved Photovoltaic Power System. in Advances in Greener Energy Technologies. Springer, Singapore. 2020 https://doi.org/10.1007/978-981-15-4246-6_29

41. Vardia, M.; Priyadarshi, N.; Ali, I.; Azam, F.; Bhoi, A.K.; Maximum Power Point Tracking for Wind Energy Conversion System. in Advances in Greener Energy Technologies. Springer, Singapore. 2020 https://doi.org/10.1007/978-981-15-4246-6_36

42. Vardia, M.; Priyadarshi, N.; Ali, I.; Azam, F.; Bhoi, A.K.; Design of Wind Energy Conversion System Under Different Fault Conditions. in Advances in Greener Energy Technologies. Springer, Singapore. 2020 https://doi.org/10.1007/978-981-15-4246-6_41

43. Choudhary, T.; Priyadarshi, N.; Kuma,r P.; Azam, F.; Bhoi A.K. (2020) A Fuzzy Logic Control Based Vibration Control System for Renewable Application. in Advances in Greener Energy Technologies. Springer, Singapore. 2020 https://doi.org/10.1007/978-981-15-4246-6_38

44. Priyadarshi, N.; Azam F.; Solanki, S. S.; Sharma, A.K.; Bhoi, A.K.; Almakhles, D.; A Bio-Inspired Chicken Swarm Optimization-Based Fuel Cell System for Electric Vehicle Applications. in Bio-inspired Neurocomputing. Studies in Computational Intelligence, vol 903. Springer, Singapore. 2021 https://doi.org/10.1007/978-981-15-5495-7_1

45. Carrasco, J.M., Franquelo, L.G., Bialasiewicz, J.T., Member, S., Galván, E., Guisado, R.C.P., Member, S., Ángeles, M., Prats, M., León, J.I., Moreno-alfonso, N.: Power-Electronic Systems for the Grid Integration of Renewable Energy Sources : A Survey. Ieee Trans. Ind. Electron. 53, 1002–1016 (2006).

46. Kumary, S.V.S., Oo, V.A.A.M.T., Shafiullah, G.M., Stojcevski, A.: Modelling and power quality analysis of a grid-connected solar PV system. (2014).

47. N Priyadarshi, F Azam, A Sharma, AK Bhoi, M Kumar: A particle swarm optimization based fuzzy logic control for photovoltaic system, International Journal of Engineering & Technology, 2018.

5

A Review of Algorithms for Control and Optimization for Energy Management of Hybrid Renewable Energy Systems

Megha Vyas*, Vinod Kumar Yadav, Shripati Vyas†,
R.R. Joshi and Ritesh Tirole

Dept. of Electrical Engineering, CTAE, College, Udaipur, India

Abstract

Grid dependency for power supply in rural and far locations can be reduced by Hybrid renewable energy systems (HRES). These HRES systems can be achieved by combining various sources of energy such as solar, wind, diesel, and biomass energy; furthermore, it's imperative to implement an adept energy storage capacity system. An energy storage capacity system should facilitate controlling the energy systems intelligently and assure grid users that power is available to them. For a reliable supply of power to the last user or distribution end, the hybrid system's technical features can be examined by optimum sizing of source real design of control, which is an actual process of energy control, and also advocate sufficient reserves by large storage alternatives. In this chapter, various uses of Genetic Algorithms (GA) and solar PV forecasting are described, further many stimulated algorithms which have been used in optimization, controlling, and various methods of supervising power for renewable energy analysis (including hybrid power generation strategies), are discussed.

Keywords: Hybrid power sources, optimization algorithm, Genetic Algorithm, energy management system, solar PV

---

*Corresponding author: megha.vyas14@gmail.com
†Corresponding author: shripativyasjoni@gmail.com

Neeraj Priyadarshi, Akash Kumar Bhoi, Sanjeevikumar Padmanaban, S. Balamurugan and Jens Bo Holm-Nielsen (eds.) Intelligent Renewable Energy Systems, (131–156) © 2022 Scrivener Publishing LLC

5.1   Introduction

Generation of power from conventional energy sources or fossil fuels leads to emit the green-house gases that increases the global warming and due to these limitations, there is an urgent need of power generation sources which are non pollutable and viable in nature [1–20]. Solar and wind energy are the primary major energy sources used in terms of renewable energy, which are widely used, but issues of extreme weather and climate situations cannot be ignored and thus affect the subject of renewable energy in positive ways. It's important to emphasize using more renewable energy in the future [5, 6].

A combination of two or more energy sources with the add on storing capacity for a required load demand is called hybrid renewable energy systems. Hybrid renewable energy systmes are used and performed via pathways of alternative solutions for power production rather than conventional schemes [7, 8]. The schematic diagram of HRES as a combination of Solar and Wind is shown in Figure 5.1(a).

These systems can be employed as a connected grid or as isolated or can be used for backup purpose [21–40]. Such type of systems is beneficial in distant locations where conventional schemes (systems) are not possible or are not cost effective sources of energy [9, 10]. Moreover, these systems are less costly and more efficient; when utilizing HRES systems the result is not

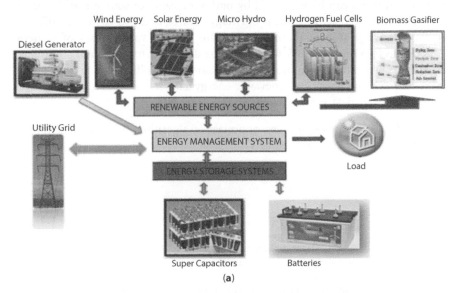

(a)

Figure 5.1 (a) HRES scheme with a combination of solar and wind energy [9]. (*Continued*)

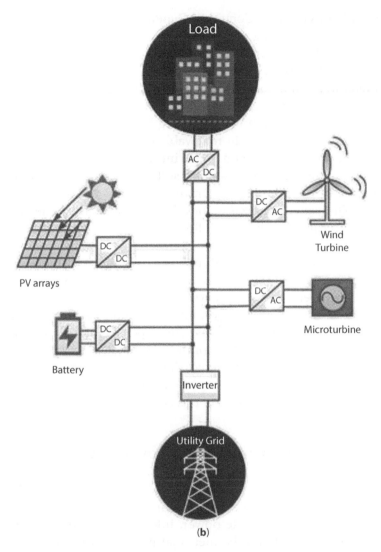

(b)

Figure 5.1 (Continued) (b) A schematic diagram for a hybrid grid connected system [12].

only a cost-effective benefit to consumers, the energy source is trustworthy, ecofriendly, and feasible [11] and also with a capacity of mitigating the whole development cost in a notable way [12]. Below is a schematic diagram of a simplified organization of a photo-voltaic, wind, and Micro-turbine [41–68] based HRES with battery as its storing device, is shown in Figure 5.1(b).

To further reliable power supplies and promote proper demand-side management, experts advocate the demand for research is in two areas:

1) Energy Management & Control, 2) Renewable Energy Sources [69–87]. Different soft computing and optimization techniques are becoming popular for solving optimization difficulties with a many purposes in past decades [88–101]. Further from data gathered through surveys and literature, it was found that a very little research has been conducted in energy management & control issues concerning renewable energy sources and how computing and optimization techniques as well as trouble shooting in renewable energy can be most efficient; whereas the attention is put on preparing a relative evolution of the utilizing and implementation of similar soft computing and optimization techniques. In the present chapter, the study gap between techniques for controlling and optimization of HRES is stated. The benefaction of this research can be outlined as follows:

1. Study of Genetic Algorithm, Solar PV forecasting based on techniques in the field of controller and improvement of hybrid renewable energy system.
2. A survey of Genetic algorithms evolved in last decade and their use in HRES analysis. The paper is classified as; the various issues related to controlling of HRES are presented in section 5.2, various forecasting techniques are analyzed in section 5.3 and the last section include statements of the discussions and analysis of present research.

5.2   Optimization and Control of HRES

The controlling of HRES has different conditions that involves The controlling of a HRES includes several features which have opportunity of elementary assets to generate power, information of the desired load requirement which should be met, real methods and the capacity of the HRES including or excluding storing choice of the hybrid system design, the option of actual power electronic converter [13–21]. The investigators researching in the area of HRES pivoted on the issue of magnitude optimization [22–29], optimum operating cost [30–35], controller design [36–38], controlling of actual and reactive power [39–42], and controlling of voltage and frequency [43]. In occurrence of grid connected HRES, reliability drew on execution estimation of the hybrid systems as perceived from the literature study. This paper mainly presents some well accepted techniques and mainly used algorithms for control of the HRES. Additionally, it also reveals some critical

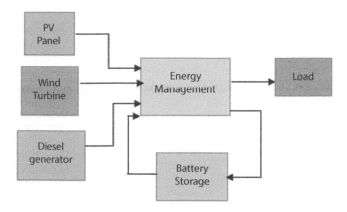

Figure 5.2 A hybrid renewable energy system energy management scheme [13].

issues. Also, there is an exhaustive discussion on latest and well-known algorithms as of the literature review, including Genetic Algorithms (GA), which arguing on the latest improvement methods that include implementation for the controlling purpose and for optimizing HRES depended systems in the given subsections. A hybrid renewable energy system energy management scheme shows in Figure 5.2.

5.3   Optimization Techniques/Algorithms

Various uses of optimizing methods for HRES are discussed by multitudes of researchers up to present day. Use of GA, methods for purpose of HRES controlling and optimizations are included and analyzed in further paragraphs. Every section begins with the breakdown of why and how the algorithm came to be and is followed by a short outline of the algorithm's foreground as well as the operating method. In final sections the Algorithm utilization for the purpose of HRES controlling and optimization, as stated within associated literature, is further talked about and summed up. A population and natural genetic algorithm, in which the entity's populace is altered, and derived from development and is further expressed as a progress of algorithm. A comprehensive method for the algorithm is presented in Figure 5.3. The algorithm gives rise to an arbitrary inceptive set of discrete facts and instructions, in short it's a series of instructions that tell the computer how to transform the set of facts about the data gathered from the world or from a certain selection of choices (data sets) gathered from a populace, that were chosen within certain parameters in which the computer follows a procedure or

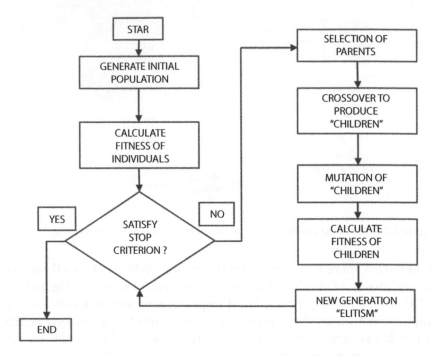

Figure 5.3 Flow chart of optimization employing Genetic Algorithm [45].

formula to solve the problem; these are utilized from sets of data gathered- or even at arbitrary in algorithm's every stage; also they work as the source for the upcoming repeated stages for the procedure. The three major stages of the algorithm that are generatated on a novel set of outcomes in successive repetitions are: assortment, intersect and alteration. The pretend code for GA is presented further:

5.3.1   Genetic Algorithms (GA)

John Holland evolved Genetic algorithms (GA) which further familiarized by Goldberg [44] were employed for reaching at results of composite optimization issues that can be either restrained or unrestrained in identity. The engineering and sciences are disciplines which use GA and are included as the desired technique for the normal cause. Select the beginning inhabitants of entities counts the fitness rates of every entity in the populace. Alter such invention up to execution of the criterion. Choose the healthy entities out of the populace for regeneration. Table 5.1 shows the uses of GA in the area of HRES and its optimization method. The hybrid system construction, terrestrial position of the use

Table 5.1 Application of Genetic Algorithms for Hybrid Renewable Energy system optimization [62].

Renewable energy system	Algorithm/application	Parameters considered/ optimization	Significant contribution/ remarks	Ref. no.
Hybrid Renewable Energy System	Controlling of apparatus structure and size, also simulates weather parameters for different climates	low cost, Battery SOC, LPSP	Better performance indexing, continuity of energy was a sign of efficiency of the system	13
Wind-Diesel-PV-battery scheme	Minimizing total operative cost using classical predictive controlling	Fuel cost, DG operation and preservation, and the life charges of battery and DG	Total 8% reduction in the whole cost is achieved yearly with cutback of 38.1% in functioning price by using scheme working as "load-following control strategy	34
Household PV linked to low voltage system including energy storing in scattered shape	GA and annealing simulation	Site, size of distributed storing methodologies	Satisfied end user, safety of personnel, less cost of billing, fiscal procedure of low voltage network, also includes a cutback in DG scheme along the grid	20

(Continued)

Table 5.1 Application of Genetic Algorithms for Hybrid Renewable Energy system optimization [62]. (*Continued*)

Renewable energy system	Algorithm/application	Parameters considered/ optimization	Significant contribution/ remarks	Ref. no.
MPPT based Grid connected PV	GA, CHC and DE type algorithm	Reduced sizing and sharing of PV modules in trackers, and inverter option	Comprehensive study of GA, CHC and DE algorithm, the DE along arbiter mutation is the major effective technique in PV based designed network	21
HRES along DG system	Genetic algorithm, PSO and BBO are characterized and optimum size of HRES	Sizing of separate components of HRES	Seven villages without electricity were selected for investigation, charging approach is best alternative while measured with load and crest saving scheme COE is Rupee's 5.65/kWh	14

of adopted work as well as the optimizing parameters is fore grounded as well as notable findings of the investigated work. Flow chart of optimization employing Genetic Algorithm show in Figure 5.3.

With the help of Table 5.1, we can sum up that GA exists its applications in the optimum planning and sizing [45–55], controlling of hybrid systems [56, 57], optimum economic functioning [58, 59], and optimization of parametric models of PV panels [60, 61]. Moreover, the issue of optimization of the scheme of controllers for energy management & reactive power management and in addition to optimizing transmission line tool positioning for reliability improvement has been finalized. Favorable realization of the impartial behavior utilizing GA for its performance to clarify high dimensional issues [62] has enlarged the curiosity of investigators to adopt of the algorithm for related difficulties.

With the help of facts given in Table 5.1, we can say that for HRES optimization the use of GA is very wide and other scholastic methods as iterative optimization techniques are in pain with the hereditary disadvantage of floundering at the local minima. The employment of GA prevents from situations because here is upgraded investigation in the investigated area for an optimum clarification. A genetic algorithm for optimization issue purpose show in Figure 5.4.

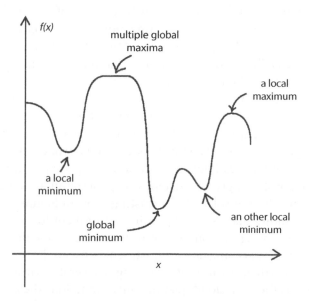

Figure 5.4 Genetic algorithms for optimization issue purpose.

GA executes crossover and transformation function which includes latest population launched in every iteration stage as a consequence the possibility of being surrounded in local minima is eliminated. The implementation of GA algorithms is self-reliant of the faulted external creation it worthy for multi-standard improvement paths. hence, we can say that the GA depended techniques are capable to efficiently give resolutions to single objective along with multi- objective optimization issues in the field of HRES [63].

5.4   Use of GA In Solar Power Forecasting

Renewable energy-based power plants are gaining more concentration of investigators because of its sprinkled verbalization during past ten years. Enlargement at a greater scale has made these sources to achieve the raised demand of electricity. This type of enlargement is for both the economic or political reason and also for constituting an acceptable atmosphere for our latest generation where power so that power can be generated from renewable sources like will solar and wind along no atmosphere contaminations. Higher authorities are also making huge efforts like carbon credit inducement, assistance for setting up of PV system, building up solar based government buildings etc. By surveying a lot of literature; we found that up to the year of 2035, among the whole electricity generation in the country the renewable energy depended generation will be a third of total [64]. When we discuss about greater range of interconnection of PV systems, it is needed to estimate everyday solar radiation time of the different climate field where PV system is usually to work from working and protection angle. There is also a need to think the researchers about power quality problems exists that is faced whole day due to irregular property of solar PV. One another parameter in a day type power production unit is Unit commitment. All day unit commitment of renewable power producing network builds it capable to operate the stored energy production network in a greater effective manner that reduces both the occasion and price and further, at the similar time boosts the grid consistency by penetrating power to the supplementary grid [65]. A solar PV forecasting show in Figure 5.5(a).

Figure 5.5 shows that Predicting unit commitment for all day systems assists the generating station operator to correctly handle the energy requirement and by keeping up an adjustment between the production and requirement. Further, because of involving a several environmental limitations such as thermal, cloud quantity, dirt limitations the accurate forecasting of PV power outcome becomes a more common place in regards to

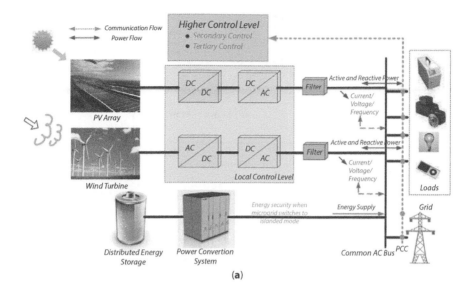

(a)

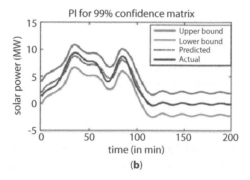

(b)

Figure 5.5 (a) Solar power forecasting [64]. (b) Forecasting of PI for 5 min ahead solar power prediction with 99% confidence [65].   (*Continued*)

work. Large counts/numbers of predicting method have been investigated by many investigators in past years. The whole methods were for long term forecasting of solar photo voltaic system. In this chapter, a comprehensive analysis of all predicting methods has been done that have been majorly employed in the past decades. Further, the research states regarding the artificial intelligence dependent extreme learning method for predicting the solar unseen system like considering a number of weights to the hidden layer and arbitrary choosing hidden bias is choose by using the GA to the controlling real time data that were composed from clear source data

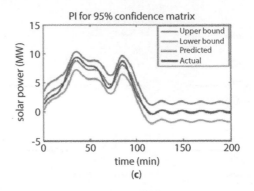

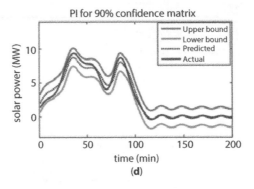

Figure 5.5 (Continued) (c) forecasting of PI for 5 min ahead solar power prediction with 95% confidence [66]. (d) forecasting of PI for 5 min ahead solar power prediction with 90% confidence [67].

depends on meteorological division [66]. Forecasting of PI for 5 min ahead solar power prediction with 99%, 95% and 90% confidence show in Figure 5.5(b)(c)(d).

Figure 5.4 GA in Solar power forecasting [65–67].

5.5   PV Power Forecasting

Selection of both the, input variable and consequence of eco-friendly feature disturb the exactness of established model [67]. Forecast of PV production functioning in an atmosphere be contingent in the succeeding referenced feature. PV forecasting of power generation of three types of forecasting show in Figure 5.6.

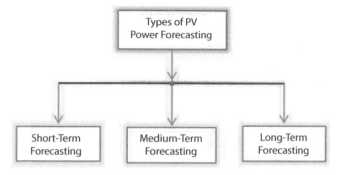

Figure 5.6 Forecasting of PV power generation [67].

5.5.1   Short-Term Forecasting

Economic load dispatch and informal delivery of power is a vital portion of intermittent power production and energy distribution systems, which include PV power production. Accurate solar power forecasting is paramount to enable accurate reading and data predictions for power management [68]. Short term predicting is really based on energy production for the short interim periods, but can advocate for integration of renewable energy sources into traditional power systems. It also facilitates efficient and responsible trade in efficient energy trading. Day ahead predicting allows the energy consumer and too distribution firm to assign the load

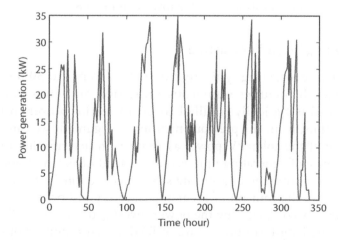

Figure 5.7 Short-term predicting [68].

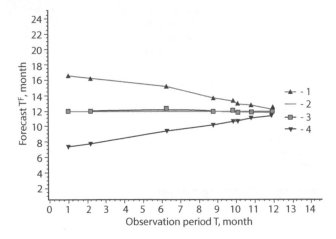

Figure 5.8 Medium term predicting [69].

rendering to accessibility of energy. The short-term predicting of power generation and time verses data show in Figure 5.7.

5.5.2   Medium Term Forecasting

Power systems continuously force some type of breakdown that needs intermittent preservation of the system. Medium term predicting typically differs from three to seven days. It allows the process and maintenance persons to assign the network and carry back them to the close for power transmission and distribution. The medium term predicting of forecast T_f month verses observation month show in Figure 5.8.

5.5.3   Long Term Forecasting

Long-term forecasting typically fluctuates from 7 to 30 days on to a year also. It includes numerous limitation and enormous diffi- cult control is typically fulfilled to estimate the power in respect of watt. Thus, from the previous mentioned argument we can say that predicting of the solar PV power assistances in determining the caus- ing assurance of generating unit, economic load dispatch of power, real time unit commitment, and storing scheme collection for the electricity market. From the four no of predicting technique short term forecast- ing is typically completed by the power investigator for solar PV system [69–70]. The long-term predicting of RMES verses number of neurons show in Figure 5.9.

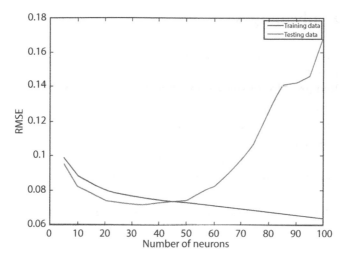

Figure 5.9 Long term forecasting [69].

5.6   Advantages

1. The availability of renewable power is whole day, a year, and even a cloudy climate.
2. Fossil fuels are needed much less.
3. The solar power has no pollution and produces no damaging gases after being setting up.
4. Maintenance of solar panel is significantly less, nearly zero.
5. Utility bills are very high as compared to the investment and production of solar energy in PV.
6. Surplus energy is a financial benefit that consumers and renewable energy companies can opt to sell back surplus (extra energy) to utilities for grid connected network.
7. There are endless opportunities for workers in the solar and PV production industries, as well as for the installers and their work can help create a strong economy.
8. The solar and PV systems are easy to install either ground or on structure.
9. There is a facility of grid free environment if enough energy is produced as requirement.
10. For use at night the batteries can be installed for storing power.

5.7 Disadvantages

1. Primary cost is high like material & installation and it takes a long time in return.
2. Require a lot of space and efficiency is not so more.
3. Require batteries as there is no solar power production in the middle of the night.
4. Based on geological position the structure of PV panels changes even for equal production of power.
5. There is much less energy production in cloudy/wintry seasons.
6. Speed of solar cars is not same as typical gas-powered cars.
7. Less solar generation in the winter season.

5.8 Conclusion

The power produced by solar PV system majorly rely on environment in which it is functioning and two more major factors such as the quantity of solar radiation and temperature. Purpose of GA to Forecasting of the Solar AC output system is analyzed in this research, after a huge investigation, it is concluded that the forecasting analysis by means of GA is greatly more suitable and exact in comparison of statistical technique. In the further paper of present series optimization of solar PV output with reference to two variables like temperature and solar radiation will be studied. Grid connected solar PV issues based on the forecasting result and their moderation techniques will be analyzed in forthcoming study.

Appendix A: List of Abbreviations

HRES	Hybrid Renewable Energy Systems
HGES	Hybrid Green Energy System
COE	Cost of Energy
SOC	State of Charge
DG	Distributed Generation
PV	Photovoltaic
WT	Wind Turbine
LV	Low Voltage
DE	Differential Evolution

GA	Genetic Algorithm
PI	Proportional Integral
FOR	Force Outage Rate
O&M	Operation and Maintenance
MPPT	Maximum Power Point Tracking
FESS	Fuel Energy Storage System
ELF	Equivalent Loss Factor
BESS	Battery Energy Storage System
UC	Ultra-Capacitor
FC	Fuel Cell
FESS	Flywheel Energy Storage Systems
WTG	Wind-Turbine Generator
DEG	Diesel Engine Generator
EMS	Energy Management System

References

1. Erdinc, O.; Uzunoglu, M.; Optimum design of hybrid renewable energy systems, Overview of different approaches, Renewable and Sustainable Energy Reviews. **2012**, 16,1412-1425.
2. Shaahidand, S. M.; Elhadidy, M. A.; Technical and economic assessment of grid-independent hybrid photovoltaic–diesel–battery power systems for commercial loads in desert environments, Renewable and Sustainable Energy Reviews. **2007**, 11, 1794-1810.
3. Zhou, Wei; Chengzhi, Zhou; Zhongshi, Lou; Lin Lu, Li; and Yang, Hongxing; Current status of research on optimum sizing of stand-alone hybrid solar–wind power generation systems Applied Energy, **2010**, 87, 380-389.
4. Elhadidyand, A. S; Shaahid, M; Parametric study of hybrid wind, solar, diesel power generating systems, Renewable Energy, **2000**, 21, 129-139.
5. Sharafi, Masoud; Elmekkawy, Tarek Y.; Multi-objective optimal design of hybrid renewable energy systems using PSO-simulation based approach, Renewable Energy, **2014**, 68, 67- 79.
6. Tezer, Tuba; Yaman, Ramazan; Yaman, Gülşen; Evaluation of approaches used for optimization of stand-alone hybrid renewable energy systems, Renewable and Sustainable Energy Reviews, **2017**, 73, 840-853.
7. Monaaf, D. A.; Al-falahi; Jayasinghe, S. D. G.; Enshaei, H; A review on recent size optimization methodologies for standalone solar and wind hybrid renewable energy system, Energy Conversion and Management, **2017**, 143, 252-274.
8. Nema, Pragya; Nema,R. K.; Rangnekar, Saroj; A current and future state of art development of hybrid energy system using wind and PV-solar, Renewable and Sustainable Energy Reviews, **2009**, 13,2096-2103.

9. Mahesh, Aeidapu; Sandhu, Kanwarjit Singh; Hybrid wind PV energy system development critical review and findings, Renewable and Sustainable energy review, **2015**, 52, 1135-1147.

10. Saharia, Barnam Jyoti; Munish Manas; Viability Analysis of PV, Wind Hybrid Distributed Generation in an Isolated Community of Northeastern India, *Distributed Generation & Alternative Energy Journal*, 32, 49-80.

11. Arif Hepbasli; A key review on energetic analysis and assessment of renewable energy resources for a sustainable future, Renewable and Sustainable Energy Reviews, **2008**, 12, 593-661.

12. R. Karki; R. Billinton; Reliability/cost implications of PV and wind energy utilization in small isolated power systems, IEEE Transactions on Energy Conversion, **2001**, 16, 368-373.

13. Michael S.; Okundamiya, Joy O.; Emagbetere; Emmanuel A.; Ogujor,; Design and control strategy for a hybrid green energy system for mobile telecommunication sites, Journal of Power Source, **2014**, 257, 335-343.

14. Subho Upadhyay; M.P. Sharma; Selection of a suitable energy management strategy for a hybrid energy system intramolecular area of India, Energy, **2016**, 94, 352-366.

15. Kalantar, M.; and Mousavi, S. M. G.; Dynamic behavior of a stand-alone hybrid power generation system of wind turbine, microturbine, solar array and battery storage, Applied Energy, **2010**, 87, 3051-3064.

16. SM Mousavi G; An autonomous hybrid energy system of wind, tidal, micro-turbine, battery storage, International Journal of Electrical Power and Energy Systems, **2012**, 43, 1144-1154.

17. Abd, El-Shafy; Nafeh, A.; Optimal economical sizing of a PV-wind hybrid energy system using genetic algorithm, *International Journal of Green Energy*, **2011**, 8, 25-43.

18. Khalil, Benmouiza; Mohammed, Tadj; Ali, Cheknane; Classification of hourly solar radiation using fuzzy c-means algorithm for optimal stand-alone PV system sizing, *International Journal of Electrical Power & Energy Systems*, **2016**, 82, 233-241.

19. Dirk, Magnor; Dirk, Uwe Sauer; Optimization of PV Battery Systems Using Genetic Algorithms, *Energy Procedia*, **2016**, 99, 332-340.

20. Crossland, A. F.; Jones, D.; Wade, N. S.; Planning the location and rating of distributed energy storage in LV networks using a genetic algorithm with simulated annealing, *International Journal of Electrical Power & Energy Systems*, **2014**, 59, 103-110.

21. Daniel, Gómez-Lorente; Isaac, Triguero; Consolación, Gil; EspínEstrella, A.; Evolutionary algorithms for the design of grid-connected PV-systems, Expert Systems with Applications, **2012**, 39, 8086-8094.

22. Seyed, Mahdi Moosavian; Mostafa, Modiri-Delshad; Nasrudin, Abd Rahim; Jeyraj, Selvaraj; Imperialistic competition algorithm, Novel advanced approach to optimal sizing of hybrid power system, *Journal of Renewable and Sustainable Energy*, **2013**, 5, 053141.

23. Martin, Paulitschke; Thilo, Bocklisch; Michael, Böttiger, Sizing Algorithm for a PV- battery-H2-hybrid System Employing Particle Swarm Optimization, *Energy Procedia*, **2015**, 73, 154-162.

24. Ahmed Fathy; A reliable methodology based on mine blast optimization algorithm for optimal sizing of hybrid PV-wind-FC system for remote area in Egypt, Renewable Energy, **2016**, 95, 367-380.

25. Hakimi, M. S.; Moghaddas-Tafreshi, M.; and zadehFard, H. Hassan; Optimal sizing of reliable hybrid renewable energy system considered various load types, Journal of Renewable and Sustainable Energy, **2011**, 3, 062701.

26. Yahiaoui, A. Benmansour, K.; and Tadjine, M.; Control, analysis and optimization of hybrid PV-Diesel-Battery systems for isolated aural city in Algeria, Solar Energy, **2016**, 137, 1-10.

27. Shang, Ce; Dipti, Srinivasan; and Reindl, Thomas; An improved particle swarm optimization algorithm applied to battery sizing for stand-alone hybrid power systems, *International Journal of Electrical Power & Energy Systems*, **2016**, 74, 104-117.

28. Priyanka, Paliwal; Patidar, N. P.; and Nema, R. K.; Determination of reliability constrained optimal resource mix for an autonomous hybrid power system using Particle Swarm Optimization, Renewable Energy, 2014, **63**, 194-204.

29. Amany, El-Zonkoly; Optimal placement and schedule of multiple grids connected hybrid energy systems, International Journal of Electrical Power & Energy Systems, **2014**, 61, 239-247.

30. Hongbin, Wu; Xingyue, Liu; and Ming, Ding; Dynamic economic dispatch of a microgrid: Mathematical models and solution algorithm, *International Journal of Electrical Power & Energy Systems*, **2014**, 63, 336-346.

31. Mohammad, Sarvi; and Isa, Nasiri Avanaki; An optimized Fuzzy Logic Controller by Water Cycle Algorithm for power management of Stand-alone Hybrid Green Power generation, Energy Conversion and Management, **2015**, 106, 118-126.

32. Cheng, Yu-Shan; Man-Tsai, Chuang; Yi-Hua, Liu; Shun-Chung, Wang; and Zong-Zhen, Yang; A particle swarm optimization-based power dispatch algorithm with roulette wheel re-distribution mechanism for quality constraint, Renewable Energy, **2016**, 88, 58-72.

33. Hakimi, M.; and Moghaddas-Tafreshi, S. M.; Optimization of smart microgrid considering domestic flexible loads, *Journal of Renewable and Sustainable Energy*, **2012**, 4, 042702.

34. Rodolf, Dufo-López; Alfredo, L.; Fernández-Jiménez, Ignacio J.; Ramírez-Rosado, J.; Sergio Artal-Sevil, José A.; Domínguez-Navarro; and Jose, L. Bernal-Agustín; Daily operation optimization of hybrid stand-alone system by model predictive control considering ageing model, Energy Conversion and Management, **2017**, 134, 167-177.

35. Ismail, M. S.; Moghavvemi, M.; and Mahlia, T. M. I.; Genetic algorithm-based optimization on modeling and design of hybrid renewable energy systems, Energy Conversion and Management, **2014**, 85, 120-130.

36. Rajvir, Kaur; Vijayakumar, Krishnasamy; Kaleeswari, Muthusamy; and Periasamy, Chinnamuthan; A novel proton exchange membrane fuel cell-based power conversion system for telecom supply with genetic algorithm assisted intelligent interfacing converter, Energy Conversion and Management, **2017**, 136, 173-183.

37. Rochdi, Bouchebbat; and Sofiane, Gherbi; A Novel Optimal Control and Management Strategy of Stand-Alone Hybrid PV/Wind/Diesel Power System, *Journal of Control, Automation and Electrical Systems*, 2017, **28**, 284-296.

38. Dulal, Ch Das; AK, Roy; and Sinha, N.; GA based frequency controller for solar thermal– diesel–wind hybrid energy generation energy storage system, *International Journal of Electrical Power & Energy System*, 2012, **43**, 262-279.

39. Vijayakumar, D.; and Malathi, V.; A real-time management and evolutionary optimization scheme for a secure and flexible smart grid towards sustainable energy, *International Journal of Electrical Power & Energy Systems*, **2014**, 62, 540-548.

40. Lei, Yu; Minyou, Chen; David, C. Yu; Liang, Zhang; Fan, Yang; and Jinqian, Zhai; A novel information exchange particle swarm optimization for microgrid multi-objective dynamic optimization control, *Journal of Renewable and Sustainable Energy*, **2014**, 6, 023114.

41. Borni,A.; Abdelkrim, T.; Zaghba,L.; Bouchakour, A.; Lakhdari, A.; and Zarour,L.; Fuzzy logic, PSO based fuzzy logic algorithm and current controls comparative for grid-connected hybrid system, *AIP Conference Proceedings*, **2017**, 1814, 020006.

42. Pablo, García-Triviño; Antonio, José Gil-Mena; Francisco, Llorens-Iborra; Carlos, Andrés García-Vázquez; Luis, M.; Fernández, Ramírez; and Francisco, Jurado; Power control based on particle swarm optimization of grid-connected inverter for hybrid renewable energy system, Energy Conversion and Management, **2015**, 91, 83-92.

43. Soumya, R. Mohanty; Nand, Kishor; and Prakash, K. Ray; Robust H-infinite loop shaping controller based on hybrid PSO and harmonic search for frequency regulation in hybrid distributed generation system, *International Journal of Electrical Power & Energy System*, **2014**, 60, 302-316.

44. Goldberg,DE; Genetic Algorithms in Search, Optimization, and Machine Learning, Addison Wesley, Reading, Massachusetts, **1989**.

45. Gupta, R. A.; Kumar,R., and Bansal, A. K.; Economic analysis and design of stand-alone wind/photovoltaic hybrid energy system using Genetic algorithm, International Conference on Computing, Communication and Applications, **2012**, 1-6.

46. Jemaa, A. B.; Hamzaoui, A.; Essounbouli,N.; Hnaien, F.; and Yalawi, F.; Optimum sizing of hybrid PV/wind/battery system using Fuzzy-Adaptive Genetic Algorithm,in 3rd International Conference on Systems and Control, **2013**, 810-814.

47. Ould Bilal, V. Sambou; Kébé, C. M. F.; Ndiaye, P. A., and Ndongo, M.; Methodology to Size an Optimal Stand-Alone PV, wind, diesel, battery System Minimizing the Levelized cost of Energy and the CO2 Emissions, *Energy Procedia*, **2012**, 14,1636-1647.

48. Ould Bilal, B.; Sambou,V.; Ndiaye, P. A.; Kébé, C. M. F., and Ndongo, M.; Study of the Influence of Load Profile Variation on the Optimal Sizing of a Standalone Hybrid PV, Wind, Battery, Diesel System, *Energy Procedia*, **2013**, 36, 1265-1275.

49. Phrakonkham, S.; Remy, G.; Diallo, D.; and Marchand, C.; Pico vs Micro Hydro based Optimized Sizing of a Centralized AC Coupled Hybrid Source for Villages in Laos, *Energy Procedia*, **2012**, 14, 1087-1092.

50. Eftichios, Koutroulis; Dionissia, Kolokotsa; Antonis, Potirakis; and Kostas, Kalaitzakis; Methodology for optimal sizing of stand-alone photovoltaic, wind-generator systems using genetic algorithms, Solar Energy, **2006**, 80,1072-1088.

51. Hongxing, Yang; Wei, Zhou; Lin, Lu; and Zhaohong, Fang; Optimal sizing method for stand- alone hybrid solar–wind system with LPSP technology by using genetic algorithm,Solar Energy, 2008, **82**, 354-367.

52. Tomonobu, Senjyu; Daisuke, Hayashi; Atsushi, Yona; Naomitsu, Urasaki; and Toshihisa, Funabashi; Optimal configuration of power generating systems in isolated island with renewable energy, Renewable Energy, **2007**, 32, 1917-1933.

53. Jeremy, Lagorse; Abdellatif, Miraoui; Sizingoptimizationofastand-alone street lighting system powered by a hybrid system using fuel cell, PV and battery, Renewable Energy, **2009**, 34,683-691.

54. Priyadarshi.; N;, Padmanaban, S.; Maroti, P.K.; Sharma. A.; An Extensive Practical Investigation of FPSO-Based MPPT for Grid Integrated PV System Under Variable Operating Conditions With Anti-Islanding Protection. IEEE System Journal, 2018, 13:1861–1871.

55. Priyadarshi, N.; Padmanaban, S.; Bhaskar, M.S.; Blaabjerg, F.; Sharma, A.; A Fuzzy SVPWM Based Inverter Control Realization of Grid Integrated PV-Wind System with FPSO MPPT Algorithm for a Grid-Connected PV/ Wind Power Generation System: Hardware Implementation. IET Electric Power Appl., 2018, 12:962-971.

56. Priyadarshi, N.; Kumar, V.; Yadav, K.; Vardia, M.; An Experimental Study on Zeta buck-boost converter for Application in PV system. Handbook of distributed generation, Springer, DOI 10.1007/978-3-319-51343-0_13

57. Priyadarshi N.; Sharma A.K.; Priyam S.; An Experimental Realization of Grid-Connected PV System with MPPT Using dSPACE DS 1104 Control Board. Advances in Smart Grid and Renewable Energy. Lecture Notes in Electrical Engineering, Springer, Singapore 2018, 435.

58. Priyadarshi N.; Sharma A.K.; Priyam S.; Practical Realization of an Improved Photovoltaic Grid Integration with MPPT. International Journal of Renewable Energy Research 2017, 7:1180-1891.

59. Priyadarshi N.; Sharma A.K.; Azam F.; A Hybrid Firefly-Asymmetrical Fuzzy Logic Controller based MPPT for PV-Wind-Fuel Grid Integration. International Journal of Renewable Energy Research 2017, 7: 1546-1560.

60. Priyadarshi, N.; Anand, A.; Sharma, A.K.; Azam, F.; Singh, V.K.; Sinha, R. K.; An Experimental Implementation and Testing of GA based Maximum Power Point Tracking for PV System under Varying Ambient Conditions Using dSPACE DS 1104 Controller. International Journal of Renewable Energy Research, 2017, 7:255-265.

61. Priyadarshi, N.; Padmanaban S.; Mihet-Popa L.; Blaabjerg, F.; Azam F.; Maximum Power Point Tracking for Brushless DC Motor-Driven Photovoltaic Pumping Systems Using a Hybrid ANFIS-FLOWER Pollination Optimization Algorithm. MDPI Energies 2018, 11:1-16.

62. Priyadarshi, N.; Azam, F.; Bhoi, A.K.; Alam, S.; An Artificial Fuzzy Logic Intelligent Controller Based MPPT for PV Grid Utility. Lecture Notes in Networks and Systems 46, https://doi.org/10.1007/978-981-13-1217-5_88.

63. Padmanaban, S.; Priyadarshi, N.; Holm-Nielsen, J. B.; Bhaskar, M. S.; Azam, F.; Sharma, A.K.; A Novel Modified Sine-Cosine Optimized MPPT Algorithm for Grid Integrated PV System under Real Operating Conditions. IEEE Access, 2019, 7:10467-10477.

64. Padmanaban, S.; Priyadarshi, N.; Holm-Nielsen, J. B.; Bhaskar, M. S.; Hossain, E.; Azam, F.; A Hybrid Photovoltaic-Fuel Cell for Grid Integration With Jaya-Based Maximum Power Point Tracking: Experimental Performance Evaluation. IEEE Access, 2019, 7:82978-82990.

65. Priyadarshi, N.; Padmanaban, N.; Holm-Nielsen, J. B.; Blaabjerg, F.; Bhaskar, M.S.; An Experimental Estimation of Hybrid ANFIS–PSO-Based MPPT for PV Grid Integration Under Fluctuating Sun Irradiance. in IEEE Systems Journal. 2020, 14:1218-1229.

66. Priyadarshi, N.; Padmanaban, N.; Bhaskar, M. S.; Blaabjerg, F.; Holm-Nielsen, J. B.; Azam, F.; Sharma, A.K.; A Hybrid Photovoltaic-Fuel Cell-Based Single-Stage Grid Integration With Lyapunov Control Scheme. IEEE Systems Journal, 2020, 14: 3334–3342.

67. Priyadarshi, N.; Bhaskar, M. S.; Padmanaban, N.; Blaabjerg, F.; Azam, F.; New CUK–SEPIC converter based photovoltaic power system with hybrid GSA–PSO algorithm employing MPPT for water pumping applications. IET Power Electronics. 2020, 13:2824–2830.

68. Priyadarshi, N.; Padmanaban, N.; Holm-Nielsen, J. B.; Bhaskar, M.S.; Azam, F.; Internet of things augmented a novel PSO-employed modified zeta converter-based photovoltaic maximum power tracking system: hardware realisation. IET Power Electronics. 2020, 13:2775–2781.

69. Kamalapathi, K., Priyadarshi, N., Padmanaban, S., Holm-Nielsen, J.B., Azam, F., Umayal, C., Ramachandaramurthy, V.K. A Hybrid Moth-Flame Fuzzy Logic Controller Based Integrated Cuk Converter Fed Brushless DC Motor for Power Factor Correction. MDPI Electronics, 2018, 7: 288.

70. Priyadarshi, N., Padmanaban, S., Lonel, D., Mihet-Popa, L., Azam, F. Hybrid PV-Wind, Micro-Grid Development Using Quasi-Z-Source Inverter Modeling and Control—Experimental Investigation. MDPI Energies, 2018, 11:2277.

71. Priyadarshi, N.; Ramachandaramurthy, V, K.; Padmanaban, S.; Azam, A.; An Ant Colony Optimized MPPT for Standalone Hybrid PV-Wind Power System with Single Cuk Converter. MDPI Energies, 2019, 12: 167.

72. Azam, F.; Yadav, S.K.; Priyadarshi, N.; Padmanaban, S.; and Bansal, R.C.; A Comprehensive Review of Authentication Schemes in Vehicular Ad-Hoc Network, IEEE Access, 2021, 9:31309-31321, 2021, doi: 10.1109/ACCESS.2021.3060046.

73. Priyadarshi, N.; Sharma, A.K.; Bhoi, A. K.; Ahmad, S. N.; Azam, F.; Priyam, S.; A Practical performance verification of AFLC based MPPT for standalone PV power system under varying weather condition, International Journal of Engineering & Technology, 2018, 7:338-343.

74. Azam F.; Priyadarshi N.; Nagar H.; Kumar S.; Bhoi A.K.; An Overview of Solar-Powered Electric Vehicle Charging in Vehicular Adhoc Network. in: Electric Vehicles. Green Energy and Technology. Springer, Singapore. https://doi.org/10.1007/978-981-15-9251-5_5

75. Azam, F.; Kumar, S.; Yadav, K.P.; Priyadarshi N.; Padmanaban, S.; An Outline of the Security Challenges in VANET, in Proc. of IEEE UPCON 2020, Nov, 2020.

76. Priyadarshi, N.; Azam, F.; Bhoi, A.K.; Sharma, A.K.; A Multilevel Inverter-Controlled Photovoltaic Generation. in Advances in Greener Energy Technologies. Springer, Singapore. 2020 https://doi.org/10.1007/978-981-15-4246-6_8

77. Priyadarshi, N.; Azam, F.; Bhoi, A.K.; Sharma, A.K.; Dynamic Operation of Grid-Connected Photovoltaic Power System. in Advances in Greener Energy Technologies. Springer, Singapore. 2020 https://doi.org/10.1007/978-981-15-4246-6_13

78. Priyadarshi, N.; Azam, F.; Bhoi, A.K.; Sharma, A.K.; A Proton Exchange Membrane-Based Fuel Cell Integrated Power System. in Advances in Greener Energy Technologies. Springer, Singapore. 2020 https://doi.org/10.1007/978-981-15-4246-6_18

79. Priyadarshi, N.; Azam, F.; Bhoi, A.K.; Sharma, A.K.; A Closed-Loop Control of Fixed Pattern Rectifier for Renewable Energy Applications. in Advances in Greener Energy Technologies. Springer, Singapore. 2020 https://doi.org/10.1007/978-981-15-4246-6_25

80. Priyadarshi, N.; Azam, F.; Bhoi, A.K.; Sharma, A.K.; A Four-Switch-Type Converter Fed Improved Photovoltaic Power System. in Advances in Greener Energy Technologies. Springer, Singapore. 2020 https://doi.org/10.1007/978-981-15-4246-6_29

81. Vardia, M.; Priyadarshi, N.; Ali, I.; Azam, F.; Bhoi, A.K.; Maximum Power Point Tracking for Wind Energy Conversion System. in Advances in

Greener Energy Technologies. Springer, Singapore. 2020 https://doi.org/10.1007/978-981-15-4246-6_36

82. Vardia, M.; Priyadarshi, N.; Ali, I.; Azam, F.; Bhoi, A.K.; Design of Wind Energy Conversion System Under Different Fault Conditions. in Advances in Greener Energy Technologies. Springer, Singapore. 2020 https://doi.org/10.1007/978-981-15-4246-6_41

83. Choudhary, T.; Priyadarshi, N.; Kuma,r P.; Azam, F.; Bhoi A.K. (2020) A Fuzzy Logic Control Based Vibration Control System for Renewable Application. in Advances in Greener Energy Technologies. Springer, Singapore. 2020 https://doi.org/10.1007/978-981-15-4246-6_38

84. Priyadarshi, N.; Azam F.; Solanki, S. S.; Sharma, A.K.; Bhoi, A.K.; Almakhles, D.; A Bio-Inspired Chicken Swarm Optimization-Based Fuel Cell System for Electric Vehicle Applications. in Bio-inspired Neurocomputing. Studies in Computational Intelligence, vol 903. Springer, Singapore. 2021 https://doi.org/10.1007/978-981-15-5495-7_1

85. Ould Bilal, B.; Sambou, V.; Ndiaye,P. A.; Kébé,C. M. F.; and Ndongo, M.; Optimal design of ahybridsolar–wind-battery system using them minimization of the annualized cost system and the minimization of the loss of power supply probability, LPSP, Renewable Energy, **2010**, 35, 2388-2390.

86. Alireza, Maheri,Multi-objective design optimization of standalone hybrid wind-PV-diesel systems under uncertainties, Renewable Energy, **2014**, 66,650-661.

87. Rodolfo, Dufo-Lópezand; José, L., Bernal-Agustín; Design and control strategies of PV-Diesel systems using genetic algorithms, Solar Energy, **2005**,79,33-46.

88. Rodolfo, Dufo-López; José, L., Bernal-Agustín; and Javier, Contreras; Optimization ofcontrol strategies for stand-alone renewable energy systems with hydrogen storage,Renewable Energy, 2007, **32**,1102-1126.

89. Zhao, Y.S.;Zhan,J.; Zhang, Y.; Wang,D.P.; andZou,B.G.; The optimal capacity configuration of an independent Wind, PV, hybrid power supply system based on improved PSO algorithm, in *IET Conference Proceedings*, Institution of Engineering and Technology, **2009**, 159-159.

90. Hong, Y. Y.; Lian, R. C.; Optimal Sizing of Hybrid Wind, PV, Diesel Generation in a Stand-Alone Power System Using Markov-Based Genetic Algorithm, IEEE Transactionson Power Delivery, **2012**, 27,640-647.

91. Junfeng, Rong; Bing, Wang; Bo, Liu; and Xiaorui, Zha; Parameter Optimization of PV based on Hybrid Genetic Algorithm, IFAC-PapersOnLine, **2015**, 48,568-572.

92. Daming, X.; Longyun, K.Liuchen, C.; Binggang,C.; Optimalsizing of stand-alone hybrid wind, PV power systems using genetic algorithms, in Canadian Conference on Electrical and Computer Engineering, **2005**, 1722-1725.

93. Zahraee, S. M.; KhalajiAssadi, M.; Saidur, R.; Application of Artificial Intelligence Methods for Hybrid Energy System Optimization, Renewable and Sustainable Energy Reviews, **2016**, 66,617-630.

94. Bala, B. K.; Saiful Azam, Siddique; Optimal design of a PV-diesel hybrid system forelectrification of an isolated island, Sandwip in Bangladesh using genetic algorithm, Energy for Sustainable Developmen, 2009, **13**, 137-142.

95. Kaur, A.; Nonnenmacher, L.; Pedro, HTC.; Coimbra, CFM.; Benefitsof solar forecasting for energy imbalance markets. RenewEnergy, **2016**, 86:819–30. http://dx.doi.org/10.1016/j.

96. Tao, Y.; and Chen,Y.; Distributed PV power forecasting using geneticalgorithm based neural network approach,*Proceedings of the International Conference on Advanced Mechatronic Systems, Kumamoto,* **2014**, 557-560.

97. Harendra, Kumar Yadav; Yash, Pal; Madan, Mohan Tripathi; A novelGA-ANFIS hybrid model for short-term solar PV power forecasting inIndian electricity market, *Journal of Information and Optimization Sciences,*2019, 40, 377-395.

98. Chow, SKH; Lee, EWM; Li, DHW; Short-term prediction of photovoltaic energy generation by intelligent approach, Energy Build, **2012**, 55, 660–667.

99. Fernandez, Jimenez LA; Muñoz, Jimenez A; Falces, A.; Mendoza, Villena M.; Garcia, Garrido E.; Lara, Santillan PM.; Zorzano, AlbaE.; Zorzano, Santamaria PJ.; Shortterm power forecasting system for photovoltaic plants, Renewable Energy, **2012**, 44, 311–317.

100. Bacher, P.; Madsen, H.; Nielsen, HA; Online short-term solar powerforecasting, Solar Energy, **2009**, 83, 1772–1783.

101. Yona, A.; Senjyu, T.; Saber, AY.; Funabashi, T.; Sekine, H.; Kim, CH.; Application of neural network to one-dayahead 24 hours generatingpower forecasting of photovoltaic system, in Intelligent Systems Applications to Power Systems, International Conference, **2008**, 1–6.

6

Integration of RES with MPPT by SVPWM Scheme

Busireddy Hemanth Kumar[1] and Vivekanandan Subburaj[2*]

[1]Department of EEE, Sree Vidyanikethan Engineering College, Tirupathi, India
[2]School of Electrical and Electronics Engineering, REVA University, Bengaluru, India

Abstract

This chapter presents the integration of 100 kW solar PV source to the 25 kV AC grid by using generalized r-s based SVPWM algorithm. A generalized SVPWM algorithm is used to control the twenty seven-level diode clamped multilevel inverter (DCMLI). This higher level MLI produces the AC voltage harmonic content less than 5% for higher modulation indices, which is required at the point of common connection (PCC). Hence filter requirement is not necessary at the inverter output in order to reduce the harmonics. And the incremental conductance MPPT algorithm is used to obtain the maximum output from the PV source. In order to phase and frequency lock between the voltage at the PCC and the grid system voltage, a Phase Lock Loop (PLL) is used collectively with the controller. Simulation results for the variation of solar PV inputs like temperature and irradiance on the PV array voltage, PV array power, DC bus voltage, inverter output voltages and active power injected into the AC grid is discussed.

Keywords: Pulse width modulation, renewable energy sources, MPPT algorithm, multilevel inverter, THD and AC grid

Corresponding author: vivekeee810@gmail.com

Neeraj Priyadarshi, Akash Kumar Bhoi, Sanjeevikumar Padmanaban, S. Balamurugan and Jens Bo Holm-Nielsen (eds.) Intelligent Renewable Energy Systems, (157–178) © 2022 Scrivener Publishing LLC

6.1 Introduction

Multilevel inverters (MLI) [1] were introduced in 1981, and have developed rapidly over the last two decades. MLI provides [2] lower harmonic distortion, lower frequency for turning on and off the switches and provides lower switch level stresses [2] compared to conventional two-level VSI. In addition, to withstand the high voltage and/or high current requirement, by adding several switches in series or parallel for high power applications. Owing to the intrinsic variations in system characteristics [2], this contributes to current/voltage sharing problems. For high-power applications, MLIs have a suitable alternative, and are thus usually used.

Number of voltage levels of a sinusoidal voltage denotes the generalized structure of MLIs, normally derived from the voltage sources of a capacitor. In general, the phase output voltage levels > 3, so the inverters are termed as MLIs [2].

The neutral point (NP) MLI are discussed in [1], in which the starting 3 levels output voltage in the inverter load side are known as neutral point clamped inverter; which is done by adding two capacitors in a series and its midpoint [1]. The NP is clamped to the center of each unit pair with the aid of clamping diodes. The quasi-square waveform is extracted from the three-level inverter output [3].

The diode-clamp approach is introduced for higher inverter levels. As the level of the inverter increases, additional voltage steps are applied to the produced output waveform, creating a staircase wave much like the lower harmonic content sinusoidal wave. Eventually, an infinite number of voltage levels can be reached by the output voltage waveform with zero harmonic distortion. Regrettably, not just because of unbalanced voltage issues, but even because of circuit structure, voltage clamping conditions, and packaging restrictions, the number of voltage levels achievable is very limited [3].

6.2 Multilevel Inverter Topologies

Several independent multilevel inverter topologies have been presenetd in scientific research literature over the past few decades/years. MLI is divided into two categories based on quantity of independent DC voltage sources, which are included in their structure [4]. Some of the known topolgoies of the inverter are developed using the the diode clamped (DC) or neutral point clamped (NPC), cascaded H-bridge (CHB), the flying capacitor

(FC), and/or the capacitor clamped inverter [4–7]. The choice of the necessary topology of the MLI is based on the particular application.

6.2.1   Cascaded H-Bridge (CHB) Topology

In 1975, Baker constructed the MLI topology for semiconductors [8]. The connection of MLI is with a serial connection with one phase which is known as CHB [1].

The H bridge inverter is mainly used to produce three voltage levels separately. Each of the leg has simply two potential switching instants and to prevent the DC-link capacitor short circuits. Therefore, four separate switching states for single phase H-bridge are available. The basic configuration of single phase H-bridge is shown in Figure 6.1. The various variations of output voltage produced with this bridge, are shown in Table 6.1.

A single H bridge inverter generates $\pm V_{DC}$ voltage levels and 0 [1]. For more inverter performance stages, it offers the versatility of expansion. One independent cell is assumed to be the configuration of each H-bridge cell. The individual phases neutral points is joined together for n-level three phase inverter. The number of voltage ranges that can be reached at the line voltage is 2^{n-1}.

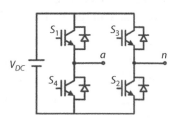

Figure 6.1 Single phase H-bridge inverter.

Table 6.1 Pulse pattern of H-bridge.

Switching combination		Output voltage V_{an}
Switches ON	**Switches OFF**	
S_1, S_2	S_3, S_4	$+V_{DC}$
S_1, S_3	S_2, S_4	0
S_2, S_4	S_1, S_3	0
S_3, S_4	S_1, S_2	$-V_{DC}$

6.2.1.1   Neutral Point Clamped (NPC) Topology

Following the description and completion of the first CHB MLI, Baker proposed diode clamped (DC) or neutral-point-clamped (NPC) MLI in 1980 [9]. The topology for the three-level single phase and a five-level structure are shown in Figures 6.2 (a) and (b) respectively.

In the output voltage waveform, the inclusion of the zero voltage stage decreases the harmonic distortion. The NPC topology of three levels causes the supply voltage to be twice the voltage rating of the unit. For a given system rating, this causes output power to double.

The NPC topology can be realized at higher inverter levels by increasing the diode and capacitor count. On the other hand, due to capacitor voltage balance concerns, the NPC implementation was largely limited to a three-level inverters. As a consequence, for large range of switching frequency applications, the three-level NPC VSI is the best topology.

Moreover, among the open solutions for the industry, this topology has the best converter performance. Diode clamped multilevel inverters are considered in this work.

6.2.1.2   Flying Capacitor (FC) Topology

In 1992, Foch and Meynard released the FC converter as an MLI and multilevel chopper. The output voltage in the DCMLIs is connected by

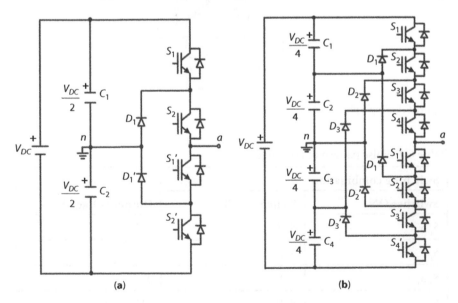

(a)   (b)

Figure 6.2 Basic topology of NPC: (a) three-level and (b) five-level.

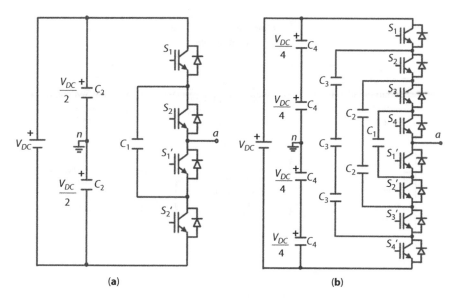

Figure 6.3 Generalised circuit of inverter: (a) three-level and (b) five-level.

diodes. In this topology the capacitors clips the required voltage from the source then it is flying capacitor (FC). Due to the high cost of capacitors the FCMLI topologies, which are shown in Figures 6.3 (a) and (b) are not efficient for low to medium power level application.

6.3   Multilevel Inverter Modulation Techniques

The simplest control techniques 3ϕ two-level voltage source inverter (VSI) by turning on and off the switches in 120° and 180° respectively. Such methods are easy to monitor the inverter's output frequency, but the output voltage magnitude can not be controlled; and thus they are rarely used.

The pulse width modulation (PWM) techniques are used for basic switching sequence for turning ON and OFF the inverter topology switches. Different classification of switching techniques [10–12] are used such as sinusoidal PWM (SPWM), space vector PWM (SVPWM), and selective harmonic elimination (SHE) etc., must be used if the output voltage magnitude is required appropriately.

For the two-level VSI, these are well developed and widely documented approaches, and have therefore been generalized to effectively modulate multilevel inverters as well. Owing to the large number of power electronic switches, difficulty increases when expanding these techniques for multilevel inverter modulations.

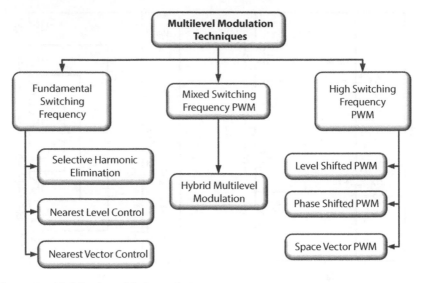

Figure 6.4 Multilevel modulation techniques.

In the other hand, with the rise in inverter levels, redundancy switching states are rising, providing more choices for choosing switching states depending on the application. As a result, more multilevel modulation approaches have been built based on the application and the MLI structure.

Each and every form of modulation has its own benefits and drawbacks. Multilevel modulation techniques are explained and it shown in Figure 6.4 and the detail explanation are follows in the upcoming topics.

6.3.1   Fundamental Switching Frequency (FSF)

The FSF provides low level switching losses. Space Vector Control (SVC), Selective Harmonic Exclusion (SHE), and Nearest Level Control are three distinct techniques under this group (NLC). The theoretical history of modulation methods for the multilevel converter is given in this section.

6.3.1.1   Selective Harmonic Elimination Technique for MLIs

Generally, for high power application, lower switching frequency control methods are used. If traditional SPWM or SVPWM techniques work at lower switching frequencies, the inverter output voltage results in low-order harmonics.

The predefined switching angles per quarter cycle of the fundamental frequency was determined on the basis of the SHE method, based on a fourier analysis, in order to remove the unnecessary lower order harmonics [13]. The undesired harmonic components are reduced to zero in this process, while the amplitude of the fundamental variable is reached according to the desired value. In order to achieve switching angles, this approach requires the comprehension of computational approaches to solve offline non-linear equations. Initially proposed for a two-level inverter, the SHE approach has been applied to MLIs.

All of these methods require computational methods [1]. By using the look-up tables switching sequences, the solutions can be obtained which are saved for unresolved indices of modulation [1]. Due to that, SHE based algorithms are not appropriate for applications with high dynamic efficiency.

6.3.1.2   Nearest Level Control Technique

The NLC technique's operating theory of first quarter waveform is shown in Figure 6.5(a) [1], where, $V_{dc}/2$ is the maximum approximation error that this method introduces. The implementation of the closest level for the degree of voltage is shown in Figure 6.5(b).

In the NLC system, the time-average synthesis does not track the reference signal between two stages. So, it is not a scheme of modulation.

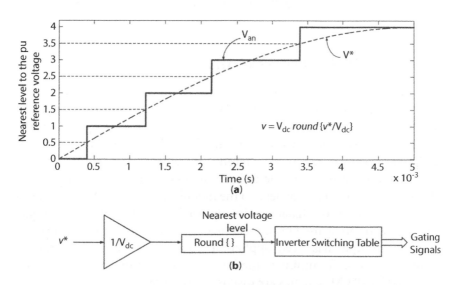

Figure 6.5 Nearest level selection: (a) waveform synthesis and (b) control diagram.

6.3.1.3 Nearest Vector Control Technique

NVC, which is a MLIs lower switching frequency techniques scheme, is also known as the nearest vector control (NVC) technique. To address the drawbacks of the SHE technique, such as slow dynamic response and the need for offline calculations, NVC was implemented in [14] as an alternative to the SHE technique. NVC provides less reference vector error and does not need any complicated calculations needed for the space vector PWM.

The nearest stationary voltage vector to the V_{ref} is discovered at each moment in time and then enabled for each sampling time, so it is called as nearest to vector control. This approach has a basic operating principle; however, it is not as straightforward to realize this technique since it is capable of finding the closest voltage vector must be required.

6.3.2 Mixed Switching Frequency PWM

A mixture of low frequency switching approaches and high frequency PWM techniques is mixed frequency switching. This method of modulation is often applied for asymmetrical MLIs where the various levels process unlike amount of power. The low-power cell usually operates with PWM, while the higher-power cells operate with lower frequencies [11].

6.3.3 High Level Frequency PWM

The CBPWM and the SVPWM are two separate approaches in this category.

6.3.3.1 CBPWM Techniques for MLI

The carrier-dependent PWM is defined by a contrast with a carrier high-frequency waveform of a modulating (reference) signal (triangular). The carrier waveforms are classed as triangular, sawtooth, trapezoidal. The most common triangular waveform is used for PWM. A periodic unipolar or bipolar waveform can be the reference waveform.

The conversion pulses to the inverter are determined depending on the intersections between the carrier and the modulating signals. Due to its versatility and low distortion characteristics, sinusoidal PWM (SPWM) techniques have been commonly used in classical two-level six switch inverters [15].

This technique has been applied to multilevel inverter control for related purposes. To minimize the harmonic distortion in MLIs, various multi-carrier PWM schemes are discussed as follows:

6.3.3.1.1   Level Shifted PWM

The carrier-dependent PWM for M-level MLI uses the same frequency and the same peak-to-peak amplitude set of neighboring (M-1) level carrier (triangular) waves. The waveforms of the carrier occupy the entire amplitude of the spectrum that the converter will produce.

Three SPWM techniques for carrier provisions are generally referred to be in phase disposition (PD) which is shown in Figure 6.6(a), the phase opposition disposition (POD) is shown in Figure 6.6(b) and the alternative phase opposition disposition (APOD) is shown in Figure 6.6(c).

The reference waveform, carrier waveforms, and the five level inverter output voltage are shown in Figure 6.7. The carriers (V_{cr1}, V_{cr2}, V_{cr3}, V_{cr4}) voltages are given in (6.1).

$$v_{out} = \begin{cases} \dfrac{V_{DC}}{2} & : & v_{ref} > v_{cr1} \\[2mm] \dfrac{V_{DC}}{4} & : & v_{cr1} > v_{ref} > v_{cr2} \\[2mm] 0 & : & v_{cr2} > v_{ref} > v_{cr3} \\[2mm] -\dfrac{V_{DC}}{4} & : & v_{cr3} > v_{ref} > v_{cr4} \\[2mm] -\dfrac{V_{DC}}{2} & : & v_{cr4} > v_{ref} \end{cases} \qquad (6.1)$$

The switching instants of the inverter are given by comparing the V_{ref} with triangular waveforms to obtain the appropriate output voltage as given in the (6.1).

6.3.3.1.2   Phase Shifted PWM (PSPWM)

The PSPWM approaches an evolution to standard PWM structures, especially developed for CHB and FC MLIs. In general, all topologies are

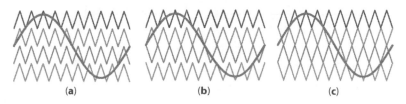

(a)   (b)   (c)

Figure 6.6 (a) PD, (b) POD and (c) APOD.

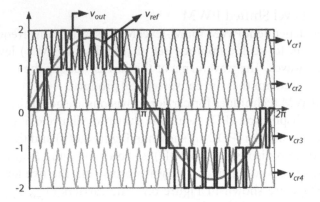

Figure 6.7 Five-level converter output voltage with PD-LSPWM.

modular. So, modulating each cell individually may be used by using the same reference signal. (M-1) adjacent level carrier (triangular) waves of the similar frequency and the equal peak to peak amplitude set are used by the PS-PWM system. A phase shift is implemented among the carrier signals of neighboring cells in such a way that the switching instants are obtained accordingly.

As coupled together, this generates a stepped multilevel waveform. When the phase change between carriers is $360°/(M-1)$ for the FCMI and $360°(or)180°/k$ for the CHB Inverter (k is H-bridge cells count) for the multilevel PWM waveform at the inverter output, the lowest harmonic distortion is obtained. This dissimilarity is due to the information that the CHB and FC inverters respectively emit two levels and three levels.

An example in [1] the operating theory is explained in Figure 6.8, for the five-level CHB inverter. Both H-bridge cells are operated by the same

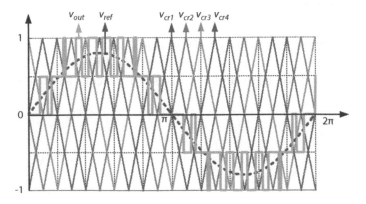

Figure 6.8 Five level converter of phase shifted waveform, nature of the output voltage.

carrier frequency and single modulating signal, equally transmitted by the use of switches and also by the average power controlled by each cell. Another fascinating property is the output voltage of 5 level inverter has switches that are k times the switching frequency of each cell. Due to phase changes among the airlines, this occurs. An inverter then creates an output voltage with a lower harmonic distortion.

6.3.3.2 Pulse Width Modulation Algorithms Using Space Vector Techniques for Multilevel Inverters

The space vector algorithm is also a PWM technique, but the distinction is that, based on the reference, the switching times, commonly known as dwell times, are discovered [1]. Consequently, it is important to first grasp the fundamentals of SVPWM as applied to two-level inverters [5].

The conventional SVPWM strategies, however, suffer from the disadvantage of requiring pre-stored look-up tables involved. Because of this, for higher inverter levels, computing burden and device memory requirements are high, i.e. the complexity increases as the inverter level also increases. These methods are, however, not the generalized SVPWM for MLIs.

For higher power applications, the number of levels requires to be high but in SVMMI are less by added with the SVPWM techniques [16–19], which do not need any look-up tables, are needed.

6.4 Grid Integration of Renewable Energy Sources (RES)

Solar photovoltaic array (100 kW) is considered as RES, which is integrated to the AC grid (25 kV) through DC-DC, DC-AC converters and a transformer [20, 21]. As the PV source is usable to produce output voltage to the desired value. Hence, it is recommended to use boost converter to meet the load constraints. In this application, to extract maximum power point tracking (MPPT) from the PV source, incremental and conductance algorithm [22, 23] is used. The proposed SVPWM algorithm is used to generate pulses to the twenty seven- level DC MLI as per the application.

6.4.1 Solar PV Array

PV cell produces DC power, which directly converts the solar energy in to electricity. Its output depends on the solar irradiation and environmental conditions. Figure 6.9, shows the solar cell equivalent circuit, which has

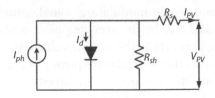

Figure 6.9 Single diode model of PV cell.

a current source (I_{ph}), diode, a series and parallel resistors. The two characteristics of solar cell such as P-V and I-V are non-linear nature. For the single diode model I-V characteristic equation is given by

$$I_{PV} = I_{ph} - \underbrace{I_o \left[\exp\left(\frac{V_{PV} + I_{PV} R_s}{V_t a} - 1 \right) \right]}_{I_d} - \frac{V_{PV} + I_{PV} R_s}{R_{sh}} \quad (6.2)$$

where

I_o is the diode saturation current,
I_d is diode current,
V_t is junction thermal voltage which is given by

$$V_t = \frac{kATn_s}{q} \quad (6.3)$$

where q is an electron charge (1.6×10^{-19} C),

T is the working temperature,
A is the ideal factor of diode,
k is Boltzmann's constant (1.38×10^{-23} J/K) and
n_s is number of series connected cells.

If such solar PV cells are in series connection then it is known as solar PV panel/module. Similarly, multiple solar panels are connected in series as well as in parallel, it is said to be solar PV array. In practice, more the surface area of array, will produce more the electricity. In this work, the SunPower SPR-305E-WHT-D solar PV module is taken and it's specifications as shown in Table 6.2 at STC conditions i.e., Irradiation: 1000 w/m² and temperature: 25°C.

Table 6.2 Specifications of SunPower SPR-305E-WHT-D module at STC.

Parameter	Values
Maximum Power (P_{max})	305.226W
Voltage at P_{max} (V_{mp})	54.7V
Current at P_{max} (I_{mp})	5.58A
Short circuit current (I_{sc})	5.96A
Open circuit voltage (V_{oc})	64.2V
Temperature co-efficient of open circuit voltage	-0.273 %/°C
Temperature co-efficient of short circuit current	0.062%/°C
Temperature co-efficient of power	-0.386%/°C
No. of series cells	96
No. of Parallel cells	1

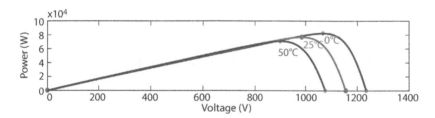

Figure 6.10 P-V Array characteristics at different temperature and constant irradiance.

To obtain 100kW solar PV, 14 parallel strings are considered. Each string has 24 solar modules. i.e., N_s= 24 & N_p=14. The PV characteristics for PV array is shown in Figure 6.10 at three different temperatures and constant irradiance of 1000 W/m².

6.4.2   Maximum Power Point Tracking (MPPT)

To pull out the maximum power from PV array, two established MPPT tracking algorithms are normally used, such as perturbation and observation (P&O) and incremental conductance (IC) techniques. In INC method, it is not required to calculated PV array power where as P&O method requires PV array power for every iteration. So, the dynamic response for

IC method is high compared to P&O method [23]. In this work, IC MPPT algorithm is used and it is explained as follows. The IC method is depends on PV curve slope i.e., $\dfrac{dP}{dV}$. This value depends on the location of the operating point in PV curve, which means

- If operating point lies exactly at the MPP then $\dfrac{dP}{dV} = 0$.
- If operating point lies left side of MPP then $\dfrac{dP}{dV} > 0$.
- If operating point lies right side of MPP then $\dfrac{dP}{dV} < 0$.

Based on the above conditions, the MPP is easily found in terms of the increment in an array conductance. The IC conditions is obtained as follows

We know $\dfrac{dP}{dV} = \dfrac{d(VI)}{dV} = I + V\dfrac{dI}{dV}$ then

If $\dfrac{\Delta I}{\Delta V} = -\dfrac{I}{V}$;operating point is lies at MPP

If $\dfrac{\Delta I}{\Delta V} > \dfrac{I}{V}$;operating point is lies at left side of MPP

If $\dfrac{\Delta I}{\Delta V} < \dfrac{I}{V}$;operating point is lies at right side of MPP $\qquad$ (6.4)

6.4.3 Power Control Scheme

The grid-linked solar photovoltaic (PV) twenty seven level DC MLI control system as shown in Figure 6.11. In the control system, there are two control loops: an external control loop which controls the DC link voltage. And, the internal loop, the regulation of the active and reactive current components (I_{dref} and I_{qref}). The Reference I_d current is the output of a DC voltage external controller.

The current reference of I_q is set to zero to maintain the operation of the unity power factor. V_d and V_q are the current controller outputs and, using reverse park transformation, are converted to three modulating signals. Then the modulating signals are given to the improved generalized SVPWM technique [19] to produce the switching pulses to the CHB MLI. The inverter output voltage is passed through the filter to eliminate

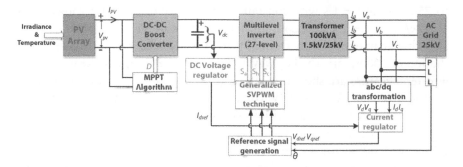

Figure 6.11 Control scheme of grid-tied solar photovoltaic (PV) twenty seven-level DCMLI.

harmonics and given to a step-up transformer, in order to enhance the voltage level up to grid voltage (25kV) for the synchronization.

6.5   Simulation Results

The twenty seven grid tied PV system has been simulated using MATLAB/ SIMULINK platform. The parameters of the PV module modelled were set to emulate the SunPower SPR-305E-WHT-D module rated at 100kw, with approximately 78.12 A and 1.312kV V output current and voltage respectively at MPP conditions. The specifications of the PV modules is shown in Table 6.3. The various system parameters are considered are listed in Table 6.3. For the PV inputs, a step change in irradiation from 1000w/m²

Table 6.3 Simulation parameters.

Parameter	Value
DC Voltage	2600 V
Output Power	100 kW
Sampling Frequency	5kHz
Grid voltage	25 kV
Transformer rating	100 kVA, 1.5kV/25kV
Grid frequency	50 Hz
DC link capacitor	100 mf
Line inductance	5 mH

to 750w/m² at t = 1 s with constant temperature of 25°c and 750w/m² to 1000w/m² at t = 2 s with constant temperature of 50°c is applied. Also, a step change in temperature from 25°c to 50°c at t = 1.5 s with constant irradiation of 1000w/m². The key waveforms for the PV inputs like irradiance and temperature are shown in Figure 6.12. Figure 6.13 shows the output response of the PV array (PV voltage and PV power) with incremental and conductance MPPT algorithm with respect to the PV inputs, shown in Figure 6.12. The DC output voltage of the DC-DC boost converter is maintained at 2600V with the help of MPPT controller that uses the Integral Regulator plus Incremental Conductance technique, which is shown in Figure 6.14. The inverter output line voltage is shown in Figure 6.15, which is operating at an average value of 0.85 modulation index.

Hence the output voltage harmonic distortion is lies in the specified limit (<5%). The twenty seven level inverter line voltage THD with respect to M, is shown in Table 6.4. With the help of step-up transformer, the inverter output voltage is stepped to 25kV which is the grid voltage. The individual waveforms for the grid voltage and injected current in to the grid, whose THD value is less than 5% are shown in Figure 6.15. Figure 6.16 shows the

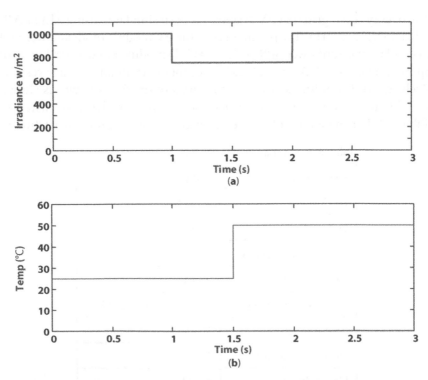

Figure 6.12 PV inputs (a) change in irradiance and (b) change in temperature.

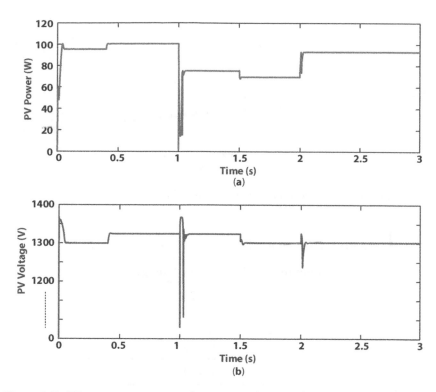

Figure 6.13 PV output response w.r.t change in irradiance and temperature (a) power and (b) voltage.

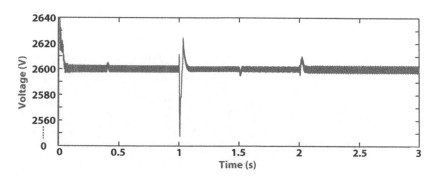

Figure 6.14 Boost converter output voltage.

grid side output voltage of the step-up transformer and injected grid current at the AC grid. Figure 6.17, shows the injected grid current is inphase with voltage. Hence, the power injected into the grid is at unity power

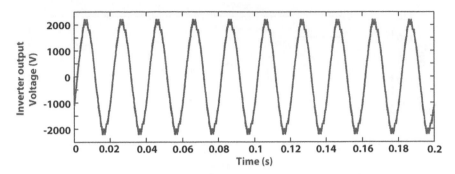

Figure 6.15 Twenty seven level inverter output line voltage.

Table 6.4 Harmonic distortion of line voltage w.r.t M.

Modulation Index (M)	Line Voltage THD %
1.0	2.24
0.9	2.55
0.8	2.75
0.7	3.09
0.6	3.76

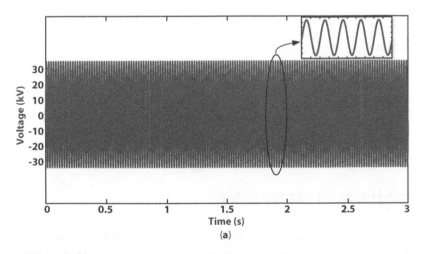

Figure 6.16 Voltage and injected current at the grid (a) output voltage of the step-up transformer and (b) injected grid current.   (*Continued*)

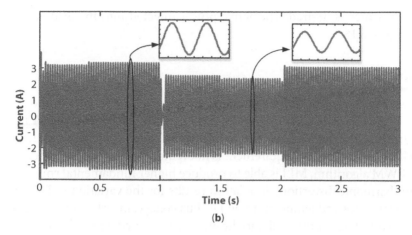

Figure 6.16 (Continued) Voltage and injected current at the grid (a) output voltage of the step-up transformer and (b) injected grid current.

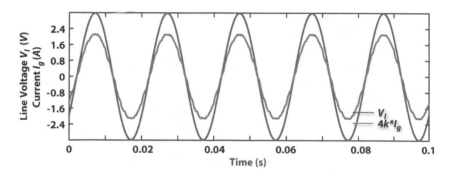

Figure 6.17 Line current and voltage injected in to the grid.

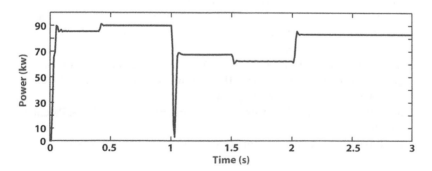

Figure 6.18 Power injected in to the grid w.r.t, PV array inputs.

factor, which is desired. The active power injected into the grid is shown in Figure 6.18.

6.6   Conclusion

This chapter presents the integration of 100kw solar PV array to the 25KV AC grid with twenty seven-level DCMLI by using an generalized SVPWM algorithm. The higher level inverter provides the AC voltage in less than 5% THD. Hence, the filter requirement is not required. By using the generalized SVPWM algorithm, MLI is able to produce higher fundamental rms voltage with harmonic distortion. Simulation results for the variation of PV inputs like irradiance and temperature on DC bus voltage, inverter voltage, current injected and power injected into the grid are presented. From the results, it is shown that power injected into the grid is at unity power factor.

References

1. A. Nabae, I. Takahashi, and H. Akagi, "A new neutral-point-clamped PWM inverter", IEEE Transaction of Industrial Applications, vol. 17, no. 5, pp. 518–523, Sept. 1981.
2. G. Walker, and G. Ledwich, "Bandwidth considerations for multilevel converters", IEEE Transaction on Power Electronics, vol. 14. no. 1, pp. 74–81, Jan. 1999.
3. J. S. Lai and F. Z. Peng, "Multilevel converters – A new breed of power converters", IEEE Transaction of Industrial Applications, vol. 32, no. 3, pp. 509–517, May/June 1996.
4. J. Rodriguez, L. G. Franquelo, S. Kouro, J. I. Leon, R. C. Portillo, M. A. M. Prats, and M. A. Perez, "Multilevel converters: An enabling technology for high-power applications", Proceedings of IEEE, vol. 97, no. 11, pp. 1786–1817, Nov. 2009.
5. Bin Wu, High-power converters and ac drives, IEEE Press, 2006.
6. L. Tolbert, F. Z. Peng, and T. Habetler, "Multilevel converters for large electric drives", IEEE Transaction of Industrial Applications, vol. 35, no. 1, pp. 36–44, Jan./Feb. 1999.
7. J. Rodriguez, J. S Lai, and F. Z. Peng, "Multilevel inverters: a survey of topologies, controls, and applications", IEEE Transaction on Industrial Electronics, vol. 49, no. 4, pp. 724–738, Aug. 2002.
8. R. H. Baker and L.H. Bannister, "Electric power converter", U.S. Patent 3 867 643, Feb. 1975.
9. R. H. Baker, "Switching circuit", U.S. Patent 4 210 826, Jul. 1980.

10. J. Holtz, "Pulsewidth modulation for electronic power conversion," Proceedings of the IEEE Conference, vol. 82, no. 8, pp. 1194–1214, Aug. 1994.

11. D. G. Holmes and T. A. Lipo, "Pulse Width Modulation for Power Converters", New York: Wiley, 2003

12. Prabaharan, Natarajan, and Kaliannan Palanisamy. "A comprehensive review on reduced switch multilevel inverter topologies, modulation techniques and applications." Renewable and Sustainable Energy Reviews, vol. 7, pp. 1248–1282, Sep 2017.

13. L. G. Franquelo, J. Napoles, R. C. P. Guisado, J. I. Leon, and M. A. Aguirre, "A flexible selective harmonic mitigation technique to meet grid codes in three-level PWM converters", IEEE Transaction on Industrial Electronics, vol. 54, no. 6, pp. 3022–3029, Dec. 2007.

14. J. Rodriguez, L. Moran, P. Correa, and C. Silva, "A vector control technique for medium-voltage multilevel inverters", IEEE Transaction on Industrial Electronics, vol. 49, no. 4, pp. 882–888, Aug. 2002.

15. B. P. McGrath and D. G. Holmes, "Multicarrier PWM strategies for multilevel inverters," IEEE Transactions on Industrial Electronics, vol. 49, no. 4, pp. 858–867, Aug 2002.

16. Ahmed, I, Borghate, V. B, Matsa, A, Meshram, P. M, Suryawanshi, H.M, Chaudhari, M. A, "Simplified space vector modulation techniques for multilevel inverters", IEEE Transaction on Power Electronics, vol. 31, no. 12, pp. 8483–8499, 2016.

17. B. Hemanth Kumar, Makarand M. Lokhande, Raghavendra Reddy Karasani and Vijay B. Borghate, "A Modified Space Vector PWM Approach for Nine-Level Cascaded H-Bridge Inverter," Arabian Journal for Science and Engineering, vol. 4, no. 3, pp. 2131–2149, Mar. 2019.

18. I. Ahmed and M. A. Chaudhari, Optimized space vector pulse-width modulation technique for a five-level cascaded H-bridge inverter, Journal of Power Electronics, vol. 14, pp. 937–945, 2014.

19. B. Hemanth Kumar, Makarand M. Lokhande, Raghavendra Reddy Karasani and Vijay B. Borghate, "An Improved Space Vector Pulse Width Modulation for Nine-Level Asymmetric Cascaded H-Bridge Three-Phase Inverter," Arabian Journal for Science and Engineering, vol. 44, no. 3, pp. 2453–2465, Mar. 2019.

20. E. Villanueva, P. Correa, J. Rodriguez, and M. Pacas, "Control of a single-phase cascaded H-bridge multilevel inverter for grid-connected photovoltaic systems," IEEE Trans. Ind. Electron., vol. 56, no. 11, pp. 4399–4406, Nov. 2009.

21. S. Alepuz, S. Busquets-Monge, J. Bordonau, J. Gago, D. Gonzalez, and J. Balcells, "Interfacing renewable energy sources to the utility grid using a three-level inverter," IEEE Trans. Ind. Electron., vol. 53, no. 5, pp. 1504–1511, Oct. 2006.

22. T. Esram and P. L. Chapman, "Comparison of photovoltaic array maximum power point tracking techniques," IEEE Trans. Energy Convers., vol. 22, no. 2, pp. 439–449, Jun. 2007.
23. M. A. Elgendy, B. Zahawi, and D. J. Atkinson, "Assessment of the incremental conductance maximum power point tracking algorithm," IEEE Trans. Sustain. Energy, vol. 4, no. 1, pp. 108–117, Jan. 2013.

7

Energy Management of Standalone Hybrid Wind-PV System

Raunak Jangid[1]*, Jai Kumar Maherchandani[1], Vinod Kumar[1] and Raju Kumar Swami[2]

[1]Department of Electrical Engineering, College of Technology and Engineering, Udaipur, India
[2]Department of Electrical Engineering, Pacific University, Udaipur, India

Abstract

The given piece of work shows control scheme along with energy management for hybrid system comprising wind turbine & solar photovoltaic (SPV) generation systems with a battery bank, and an AC domestic load. It is accompanied by DC bus and has MPPT controllers based on optimal torque (OT). Further for storing energy battery is used through DC-DC converter (bidirectional) with DC bus. Interface of AC with DC bus is provided with the help of fuzzy-based controlled inverter. Hybrid generation systems that can maintain continuous load power demand and provide satisfied operation on the main constraints. The developed control strategy can control various devices and different power interface circuitry. The continuous power is ensured by coordinating an efficient control strategy with all sources. Simulation studies have been performed to determine the performance of the system with various input parameters such as specific solar radiation, temperature, wind speed, and battery charge or discharge conditions. Simulation test results reflect variable power output and verify performance of integrated system with a control strategy for real-time installation.

Keywords: SPV array, wind turbine, battery, optimal torque, energy management unit, standalone hybrid system

*Corresponding author: raunakee.85@gmail.com

Neeraj Priyadarshi, Akash Kumar Bhoi, Sanjeevikumar Padmanaban, S. Balamurugan and Jens Bo Holm-Nielsen (eds.) Intelligent Renewable Energy Systems, (179–198) © 2022 Scrivener Publishing LLC

7.1   Introduction

The Renewable energy sources (RES) have been relied upon more regularly now a days [1–17]. It has provided us the other option for clean energy generation compared to conventional sources. PV systems and wind systems can easily be taken as the alternate source of generation for the area located remotely [18–32]. With combination of both is system i.e. to have hybrid system further decreases standalone power supply growth cost. Nonetheless, it's a reliable option for power supply [1, 2]. A power system is said to be hybrid when it comprises of fossil powered generator along with RES [3]. But the RES like wind and solar PV array has some disadvantages too. These are dependent on the surrounding environment as in the case of wind systems its output changes as the speed of wind changes. Same is true for PV array as it varies with the solar radiation [33–47]. Hence, the output of these RES is different for different day and month of the year. In order to develop the infrastructure of grid in remote area the transportation cost of fuel and infrastructure is extensively increases in such case the standalone RES hybrid system is suitable for the remote location installation as those type of location doesn't have access of the grid. To make it a more reliable system these are associated with battery for all the working conditions [4]. Using a RES hybrid system that has the facility of storage of energy can easily keep out diesel powered generator. The hybrid system discussed here there are several topologies [5]. This includes the conditioning of power and energy storage systems (ESS) also it emphasizes on optimal control for maximum transfer of energy [6–9]. Presented work aims to the idea of hybrid system configuration, dynamic modeling, energy management, and control strategies. The author proposes and investigates an efficient control strategy for standalone hybrid solar-wind system energy management for different operating conditions. Due to the uninterrupted demand for energy, batteries backups are used in the hybrid system. Therefore, the suggested system is efficient for working under variable load conditions.

7.2   Hybrid Renewable Energy System Configuration & Modeling

Figure 7.1 shows the developed control strategy for energy management is implemented on stand-alone hybrid wind-solar PV systems. For efficient energy management between WES, solar PV and battery storage system (BSS), an fuzzy logic controller (FLC) based energy management unit (EMU) is proposed. This unit control the power flow amid dc bus and different sources.

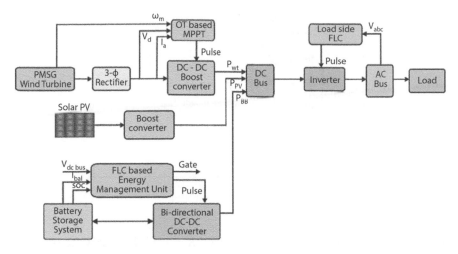

Figure 7.1 Block diagram of FLC based energy management unit (EMU) for stand-alone hybrid PV-WECS.

7.3   PV System Modeling

PV cell's equivalent circuit [10] is given in Figure 7.2. I_{ph} = Cell/Module photocurrent (A). R_{sh} = Intrinsic shunt resistance of cell & R_s = cell series resistances. R_{sh} has a large value whereas R_s is very small, therefore, for the purpose of analysis both can be neglected [11]. The generation of electrical power takes place in PV system by PV arrays. These PV arrays are arrangement of single unit modules in either series or parallel. One module unit of PV is created by grouping several PV cells. In Figure 7.3 PV array's equivalent circuit is outlined.

The expression for solar cell characteristics for voltage-current relations is as [12, 13]. Table 7.1 shows the electrical characteristics data of sun power SPR-305E-WHT-U module.

$$I_{ph} = [I_{SC} + K_i (T - 298)] * I_r / 1000$$

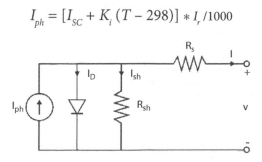

Figure 7.2 Equivalent circuit for PV.

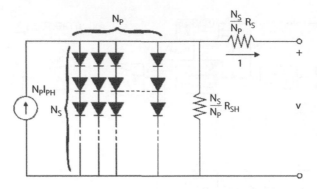

Figure 7.3 Solar arrays.

I_{sc} = current in short circuit condition (A), K_i = cell's I_{sc} at 25°C & 1000W/m², T = operating temperature (K), I_r = solar irradiation (W/m²).

Expression for reverse saturation current (I_{rs}) of PV module [12].

$$I_{rs} = I_{sc} / [\exp(qV_{oc} / N_S \, knT) - 1]$$

q = electron charge = $1.6 \times 10{-19}$C, V_{oc} = voltage in open circuit condition (V), Ns = cells connected no. in series, n = diode ideality factor, k = Boltzmann's constan t = $1.3805 \times 10{-23}$J/K.

Table 7.1 Electrical characteristics data of sun power SPR-305E-WHT-U module.

Parameter	Value
Rated value of power (W_{mp})	305.226 W
Voltage value when power has maximum value (V_{mp})	54.7 V
Current value when power has maximum value (I_{mp})	5.58 A
Voltage when Open circuit (V_{OC})	64.2 V
Current in Short circuit condition (I_{SC})	5.96 A
Total Series-connected modules per string	11
Total Parallel strings	3
System's Maximum value of voltage	700 V
Operating temperature range	−40°C to 80°C

Expression for module saturation current (I_0) is given below and it changes with cell temperature,

$$I_0 = I_{rs}\left[\frac{T}{T_r}\right]^3 \exp\left[\frac{q\times E_{g0}}{nk}\left(\frac{1}{T}-\frac{1}{T_r}\right)\right] \tag{7.1}$$

T_r = nominal temperature = 298.15K, E_{g0} = semiconductor's band gap energy = 1.1eV.PV module output current,

$$I = N_P \times I_{ph} - N_P \times I_0 \times \left[\exp\left(\frac{V/N_S + I\times R_s/N_P}{n\times V_t}\right)-1\right] - I_{sh} \tag{7.2}$$

With $V_t = \dfrac{k\times T}{q}$ and $I_{sh} = \dfrac{V\times N_P/N_S + I\times R_S}{R_{sh}}$

Np = PV modules connected no. in parallel, V_t = diode thermal voltage (V).

7.4 Wind System Modeling

It can be seen from the block diagram optimal torque with MPPT method shown in Figure 7.4. MPPT tool execute a torque reference accomplished of extracting maximum power at any wind speed. The curve T_{opt} is expressed by [14]. Table 7.2 shows the parameters of wind turbine model.

$$T_{opt} = K_{opt} * \omega_{opt}^2 \tag{7.3}$$

$$K_{opt} = 0.5 * \rho\, A * \left(\frac{r_m}{\lambda_{opt}}\right)^3 * C_{P\text{-}max} \tag{7.4}$$

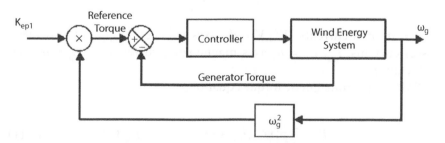

Figure 7.4 Optimal torque control with MPPT method.

Table 7.2 Parameter of wind turbine model.

Parameter	Value
Mechanical power output at nominal rating (W)	8.5e3
Electrical generator's value of Base power (VA)	8.5e3/0.9
Wind speed's base value (m/s)	12
Maximum power when wind's speed is at base value (nominal rated mechanical power's p.u.)	0.8
Rotational speed's base value (base generator speed's p.u.)	1
Pitch angle beta to display (beta >=0)(deg)	0

PMSG currents are:

$$\frac{di_{md}}{dt} = \frac{1}{L_d}(v_d - R_{st}i_d + \omega L_q i_{mq}), \tag{7.5}$$

$$\frac{di_{mq}}{dt} = \frac{1}{L_d}(v_q - R_{st}i_q + \omega L_q i_{md} - \omega \psi_{PM}), \tag{7.6}$$

$$i_d = \frac{1}{R_c}\left(L_d \frac{di_{md}}{dt} - \omega L_q i_{mq} + R_c i_{md}\right), \tag{7.7}$$

$$i_q = \frac{1}{R_c}\left(L_q \frac{di_{mq}}{dt} - \omega L_d i_{md} + \omega \psi_{PM} + R_c i_{mq}\right), \tag{7.8}$$

$$i_{cd} = i_d - i_{md}, \tag{7.9}$$

$$i_{cq} = i_q - i_{mq}, \tag{7.10}$$

$i_d, i_q = d_q$ axes currents, $V'_d, V_q = d_q$ axes voltages, $i'_{cd}, i_{cq} = d_q$ axes iron losses currents, $i_{md}, i_{mq} = d_q$ axes magnetizing currents, $L_d, L_q = d_q$ axes inductances.

PMSG Electromagnetic torque equation,

$$T_e = \frac{2}{3}p\left[\psi_{PM}i_{mq} + (L_d - L_q)i_{md}\,i_{mq}\right] \tag{7.11}$$

7.5   Modeling of Batteries

Figure 7.5 displays the blocks that are used to build the battery equivalent circuit. Its parameters have been set so as to get best rechargeable battery.

Mathematical modeling of battery is based on the equation written below for different types i.e. nickel-cadmium (Ni-Cd) & Ni-metal-hydride based [15].

Discharge Model

$$(i^*>0)\, f_1(it,i*,i,Exp) = E_0 - K.\frac{Q}{Q-it}.i^* - K.\frac{Q}{Q-it}.it + \text{Laplace}^{-1}\left(\frac{Exp(s)}{Sel(s)}.0\right)$$

Charge Model

$$(i^*<0)\, f_2(it,i*,i,Exp) = E_0 - K.\frac{Q}{|it|+0.1.Q}.i^* - K.\frac{Q}{Q-it}.it + \text{Laplace}^{-1}\left(\frac{Exp(s)}{Sel(s)}.\frac{1}{s}\right).$$

E_{Batt} = nonlinear voltage (Volt), E_0 = constant voltage (Volt), Exp(s) = exponential zone dynamics (Volt), Sel(s) = battery mode, when battery discharge s = 0 & when it is charging s = 1. K = polarization constant (Ah^{-1}),

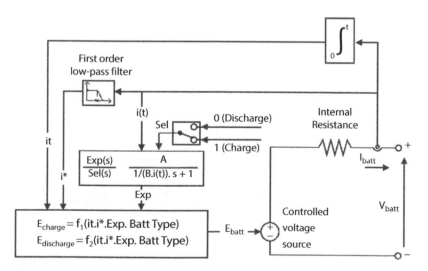

Figure 7.5 Battery equivalent circuit.

i* = current dynamics at low frequency (A), I = battery current (A), extracted capacity (Ah), Q = maximum battery capacity (Ah).

7.6   Energy Management Controller

FLC is an inference enabling apposite human reasoning abilities. It has faster, smoother response, better control performance, robustness and overall system stability than conventional controllers and less control complexity [16]. The two fuzzy logic controller designed and implemented for efficient energy management of the developed system. One for the generation of battery reference current (CFLC) and another one for the SOC control (SOCFLC). If the system is highly nonlinear in nature it will suits that system. Both of above mentioned methods were implemented so as to achieve controlling of output power along with the charging-discharging process in battery. Since these are very efficient, can provide the proposed hybrid system management of energy as shown in Figure 7.6.

7.7   Simulation Results and Discussion

This system presents, following different Simulink studies designed to investigate applications of proposed control strategy with energy management model for hybrid generation system in stand-alone power generation mode.

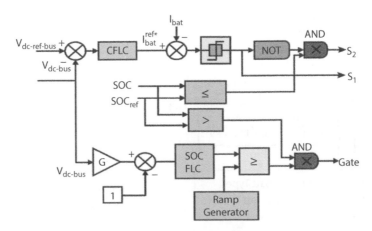

Figure 7.6 Developed FLC based energy management unit.

7.7.1 Simulation Response at Impulse Change in Wind Speed, Successive Increase in Irradiance Level and Impulse Change in Load

This case present the scenario of impulse change in wind speed in stepped manner amid (12-8) m/s & further to 10 m/s and successive increase in irradiance level in stepped manner from 600W/m² to 800W/m² and further to 1000W/m² at varying load from 6.6 kW to 16 kW and further to 7.1 kW. The simulation results are shown below. Figure 7.7 (a) shows simulation results of PV system with the effect of successive increase in irradiance level. Figure 7.7 shows the Irradiance (W/m²), PV Temperature (⁰C), PV voltage (volt) and PV output power (kW). Figure 7.7 (a) and (d)

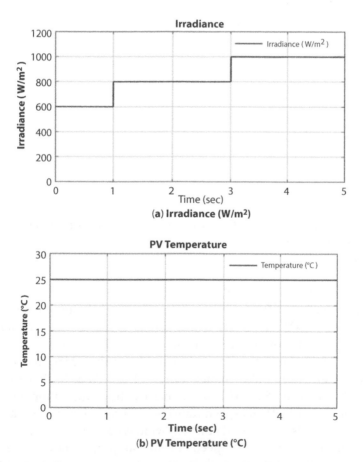

(a) Irradiance (W/m²)

(b) PV Temperature (°C)

Figure 7.7 Graph, PV system with irradiance change from 600W/m² to 800W/m², 800W/m² to 1000W/m² waveforms.   (*Continued*)

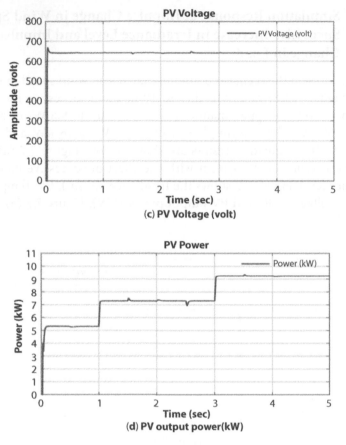

Figure 7.7 (Continued) Graph, PV system with irradiance change from 600W/m² to 800W/m², 800W/m² to 1000W/m² waveforms.

clearly shows that at 600W/m² the power output is 5.4 kW. At t=1 sec when irradiance increased from 600W/m² to 800W/m² the power output also increased to 7.4 kW. At t=3 sec when irradiance increased from 800W/m² to 1000W/m², the power output further increased to 9.5 kW.

Figure 7.8(a) shows the simulation results of the PMSG based WECS with wind speed's impulse change amid (12-8) m/s & further to 10 m/s (ω_s, ω_m, P_{ac}). Figure 7.8 (a), (b) and (c) clearly shows that at input of 12m/s (wind speed, ωs) & PMSG speed (ωm) is 1410 rpm. Power output is 6430 Watt. When t is 2sec the speed at which wind is i.e. the input is falls to 8m/s from 12m/s while the PMSG speed falls to 940 rpm, the power output also decreased to 1925 Watt. On reaching 4 sec input rises to 10m/s then PMSG speed rises to 1175 rpm, the power output also increased to 3770 Watt.

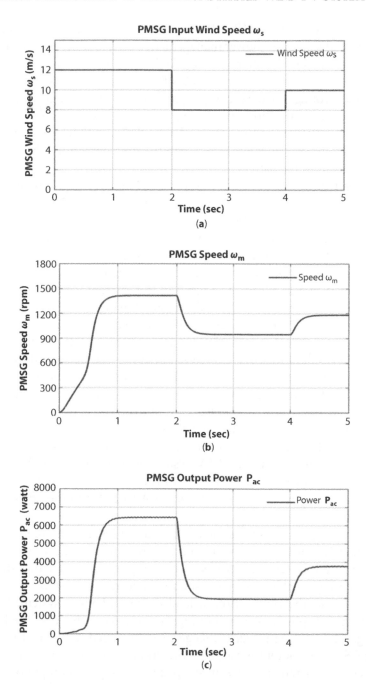

Figure 7.8 Graph of Input wind speed change from 12m/s to 8m/s, 8m/s to 10m/s waveform of (a) input wind speed ωs, (b) PMSG Speed ω_m and (c) PMSG output power *Pac*.

DC link receives hybrid (PV+WECS) system's output, which is regulated by developed scheme of power management based on FLC algorithm. This link is associated with battery through DC-DC Buck-Boost converter.

Figure 7.9 shows simulation results of battery storage system. It shows the battery voltage, battery current and battery SOC (State of change). Figure 7.9 (a) clearly shows result that the voltage of the battery remains constant at 330V. At the time of simulation Battery's SOC is 60% initially. Because the power generated is less than the load demanded the power in excess is given to the battery.

As seen from battery current waveform in Figure 7.9 (b) initially at time t = 0.5 sec PV system working at 600W/m² and WECS at 12m/s the current fed to the battery is about 18A.

As the battery is getting current from the hybrid system so it started charging and SOC is started increasing. At time t = 1 sec power output from the PV system increase as irradiance level changed from 600W/m² to 800 W/m² and WECS at 12m/s. As a result of this current fed to the battery is also increased from 18A to 22A and the rate of rising of SOC also increased shown in Figure 7.9 (c). Further, at time t = 2 sec power output of PV system irradiance 800 W/m² and WECS decrease as ωs falls from 12m/s to 8m/s. As a result of this, current fed to battery is also decreased from 20A to 10A and the rate of rising of SOC also increased. Further, at time t = 3 sec power output from the PV system increase as irradiance changed from 800W/m² to 1000 W/m² and power output from the WECS as input wind speed 8 m/s. As a result of this, current fed to the battery is also increased from 10A to 16A and the rate of rising of SOC also increased. Further, at time t = 4 sec power output of PV system as irradiance 1000 W/m² and WECS increase as ωs raises from 8m/s to 10m/s. As a result of this, current fed to the battery is also increased from 16A to 21A and the rate of rising of SOC further increase.

Figure 7.10 (a) shows the simulation result of DC bus reference voltage and actual DC bus voltage, switching pulses switch S_1 and S_2 of DC-DC buck-boost converter & controller output. Figure 7.10 (a) shows that the control strategy is able to keep constant voltage across DC bus.

In this case, the comparison of load demand, battery system, WECS, and PV system power is shown in Figure 7.11. As in this case the load is varying. Also, during impulse change in wind speed in stepped manner, so WECS power output is varying correspondingly. Also, during successive increase in irradiance level in stepped manner, power output of the PV system is varying correspondingly. As seen from the result that during the time interval, 0 to 1-sec load remain unchanged PV system output is also constant. The load demanded can be fulfill by PV only. As WECS is not in

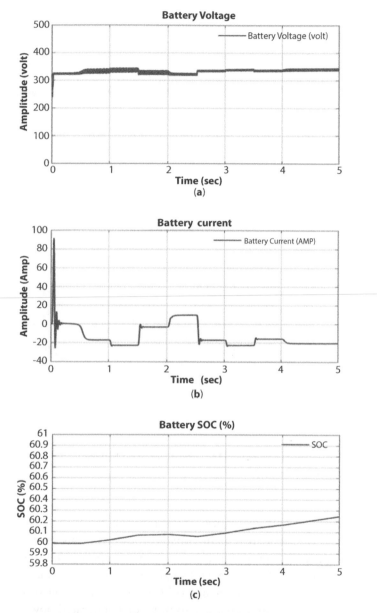

Figure 7.9 Graphed results for battery system, waveforms.

steady-state operation so power generation initially is very low, after a time delay of about 0.5-sec WECS power output increases. Hence, the hybrid system output power is more than load demand such that after 0.5sec excess

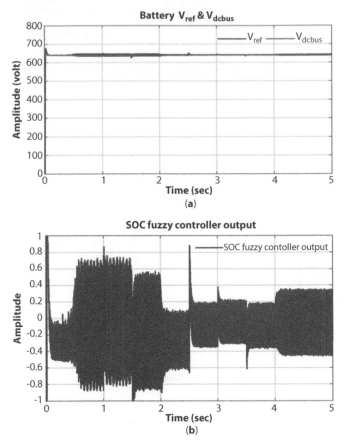

Figure 7.10 Simulation results for EMU, waveform of (a) battery V_{ref} & V_{dcbus} (volt), (b) SOC fuzzy controller output.

power is flows to battery. Figure 7.11 shows the result that when at time interval 1 to 1.5-sec load remain constant power output of PV system is increased and WECS output is also constant than power fed to the battery is also increased. Further, at time interval 1.5 to 2-sec load suddenly change the power output of PV system and WECS remain unchanged than power fed to the battery is also decreased. So now total generated power from the PV system and WECS is less than the demanded load situation so as from time interval 1.5-sec extra power consumption through battery system.

Firstly, at time interval 2 to 2.5-sec load remain constant power output of the PV system remains unchanged and WECS suddenly changed than power fed to the battery is also decreased. So now total power generated from the PV and WECS is less than the demanded load situation so as from

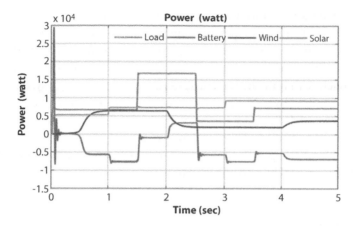

Figure 7.11 Power levels of load, battery, wind and solar system.

time interval 2 to 2.5-sec extra power consumption through the battery system. Second, at time interval 2.5 to 3-sec load suddenly changed the power output of the PV system & WECS remain unchanged than power given to battery also raises. Hence, the hybrid system output power is more than load demand such that amid (2.5-3) sec excess power is flows to battery. Further, at time interval 3 to 3.5-sec load remain constant power output of the PV system suddenly increase and WECS remain unchanged than power given to battery also raises. So now total generated power of proposed system is more than the demanded load situation so as from time interval 3 to 3.5 sec the excess generated power stored in battery system. Next, at time interval 3.5 to 4-sec load suddenly change, power output of PV system and WECS remain unchanged than power fed to the battery is also decreased. So now total generated power from the PV system & WECS is less than the demanded load situation so as from time interval 3.5 to 4-sec extra power consumption through the battery system. Then, at time interval 4 to 5-sec load remain constant power output of the PV system remains unchanged and WECS suddenly changed than power, which is fed to the battery is also increased. So now the total generated power from the PV system and WECS is more than the demanded load situation therefore between time interval 4 to 5 sec excess generated power stored in the battery system.

7.8 Conclusion

The work presented here displays hybrid system i.e. PV-WCES with EMU and the control schemes for it. Through the analysis under various scenario of power generation as well as the power fed to load the controller implemented is tested and found performing well. At this very point the SOC for the battery is maintained with respect to the limits of either maximum or minimum. To be specific, it tends to be above 80% which is taken care of by the approach with how the hybrid system works. The whole system is realized and simulated via MATLAB/Simulink. The results of the simulation of this very model shows that it is able to maintain a balance amid supply-demand in an effective manner irrespective of the fact of the sudden changes in load along with the change in generated power. Hence the OT and FLC based EMU performs well to serve the purpose.

References

1. Nema, P.; Nema, R.K.; Rangnekar, S.; "A Current and Future state of art development of Hybrid Energy system using Wind and PV Solar". *Elsevier Renewable and Sustainable Reviews.* **2009**, 13, 2096-2103.
2. Sassi, A.; Zaidi, N.; Nasri, O.; Slama, J.B.H.; "Energy management of PV/wind/battery hybrid energy system based on batteries utilization optimization". *IEEE International Conference on Green Energy Conversion Systems.* **2017**, 1-7.
3. Rehman, S.; Alam, M.M.; Meyer, J.P.; Al-Hadhrami, L.M.; "Feasibility study of a wind-PV-diesel hybrid power system for a village". *Elsevier Renewable Energy.* **2012**, 38, 258–268.
4. Khan, B.H.; Non-Conventional Energy Resources. Tata McGraw-Hill Pub. Co. **2009**.
5. Dali, M.; Belhadj, J.; Roboam, X.; "Hybrid solar-wind system with battery storage operating in grid–connected and standalone mode: Control and energy management-experimental investigation". *Energy.* **2010**, 35, 2587–2595.
6. Kamal, T.; Karabacak, M.; Hassan, S. Z.; Li, H.; Arsalan, A.; Rajkumar, R. K.; "Integration and control of an off-grid hybrid wind/PV generation system for rural applications". *International Conference on Innovations in Electrical Engineering and Computational Technologies.* **2017**, 1-6.
7. Akram, U.; Khalid, M.; Shafiq, S.; "Optimal sizing of a wind/solar/battery hybrid grid-connected microgrid system". *IET Renewable Power Generation.* **2018**, 12, 72–80.
8. Basaran, K.; Cetin, N.S.; Borekci, S.; "Energy management for on-grid and off-grid PV/wind and battery hybrid systems". *IET Renewable Power Generation.* **2017**, 11, 642-649.
9. Hosseinzadeh, M.; Salmasi, F.R.; "Power management of an isolated hybrid AC/DC micro-grid with fuzzy control of battery banks". IET Renewable Power Generation. **2015**, 9, 484–493.

10. Nguyen, X. H.; Nguyen, M. P.; "Mathematical modeling of photovoltaic cell/ module/arrays with tags in Matlab/Simulink". *Environmental Systems*. **2015**, 4, 1-13.
11. Pandiarajan, N.; Muthu, R.; "Mathematical modeling of photovoltaic module with Simulink". *IEEE International Conference on Electrical Energy Systems* **2011**, 258-263.
12. Salmi, T.; Bouzguenda, M.; Gastli, A.; Masmoudi, A.; "Matlab/simulink based modelling of solar photovoltaic cell". *International Journal of Renewable Energy Research*, **2015**, 2, 1-6.
13. Deshmukh, S.; Thorat, A. R.; Korachagaon, I.; Modelling and Analysis of PV Standalone System with Energy Management Scheme. *IEEE International Conference on Electronics, Computing and Communication Technologies*. **2020**.
14. M.; A.; I.; A.; H.; "Maximum Power Extraction from Utility-Interfaced Wind Turbines. *New Developments in Renewable Energy*", **2013**,1-34.
15. Priyadarshi.; N;, Padmanaban, S.; Maroti, P.K.; Sharma. A.; "An Extensive Practical Investigation of FPSO-Based MPPT for Grid Integrated PV System Under Variable Operating Conditions With Anti-Islanding Protection". IEEE System Journal, 2018, 13:1861–1871.
16. Priyadarshi, N.; Padmanaban, S.; Bhaskar, M.S.; Blaabjerg, F.; Sharma, A.; "A Fuzzy SVPWM Based Inverter Control Realization of Grid Integrated PV-Wind System with FPSO MPPT Algorithm for a Grid-Connected PV/ Wind Power Generation System: Hardware Implementation". IET Electric Power Appl., 2018, 12:962-971.
17. Priyadarshi, N.; Kumar, V.; Yadav, K.; Vardia, M.; "An Experimental Study on Zeta buck-boost converter for Application in PV system". Handbook of distributed generation, Springer, DOI 10.1007/978-3-319-51343-0_13
18. Priyadarshi N.; Sharma A.K.; Priyam S.; An Experimental Realization of Grid-Connected PV System with MPPT Using dSPACE DS 1104 Control Board. Advances in Smart Grid and Renewable Energy. Lecture Notes in Electrical Engineering, Springer, Singapore 2018, 435.
19. Priyadarshi N.; Sharma A.K.; Priyam S.; Practical Realization of an Improved Photovoltaic Grid Integration with MPPT. International Journal of Renewable Energy Research 2017, 7:1180-1891.
20. Priyadarshi N.; Sharma A.K.; Azam F.; A Hybrid Firefly-Asymmetrical Fuzzy Logic Controller based MPPT for PV-Wind-Fuel Grid Integration. International Journal of Renewable Energy Research 2017, 7: 1546-1560
21. Priyadarshi, N.; Anand, A.; Sharma, A.K.; Azam, F.; Singh, V.K.; Sinha, R. K.; An Experimental Implementation and Testing of GA based Maximum Power Point Tracking for PV System under Varying Ambient Conditions Using dSPACE DS 1104 Controller. International Journal of Renewable Energy Research, 2017, 7:255-265
22. Priyadarshi, N.; Padmanaban S.; Mihet-Popa L.; Blaabjerg, F.; Azam F.; Maximum Power Point Tracking for Brushless DC Motor-Driven

Photovoltaic Pumping Systems Using a Hybrid ANFIS-FLOWER Pollination Optimization Algorithm. MDPI Energies 2018, 11:1-16

23. Priyadarshi, N.; Azam, F.; Bhoi, A.K.; Alam, S.; An Artificial Fuzzy Logic Intelligent Controller Based MPPT for PV Grid Utility. Lecture Notes in Networks and Systems 46, https://doi.org/10.1007/978-981-13-1217-5_88.

24. Padmanaban, S.; Priyadarshi, N.; Holm-Nielsen, J. B.; Bhaskar, M. S.; Azam, F.; Sharma, A.K.; A Novel Modified Sine-Cosine Optimized MPPT Algorithm for Grid Integrated PV System under Real Operating Conditions. IEEE Access, 2019, 7:10467-10477.

25. Padmanaban, S.; Priyadarshi, N.; Holm-Nielsen, J. B.; Bhaskar, M. S.; Hossain, E.; Azam, F.; A Hybrid Photovoltaic-Fuel Cell for Grid Integration With Jaya-Based Maximum Power Point Tracking: Experimental Performance Evaluation. IEEE Access, 2019, 7:82978-82990.

26. Priyadarshi, N.; Padmanaban, N.; Holm-Nielsen, J. B.; Blaabjerg, F.; Bhaskar, M.S.; An Experimental Estimation of Hybrid ANFIS–PSO-Based MPPT for PV Grid Integration Under Fluctuating Sun Irradiance. in IEEE Systems Journal. 2020, 14:1218-1229

27. Priyadarshi, N.; Padmanaban, N.; Bhaskar, M. S.; Blaabjerg, F.; Holm-Nielsen, J. B.; Azam, F.; Sharma, A.K.; A Hybrid Photovoltaic-Fuel Cell-Based Single-Stage Grid Integration With Lyapunov Control Scheme. IEEE Systems Journal, 2020, 14: 3334–3342

28. Priyadarshi, N.; Bhaskar, M. S.; Padmanaban, N.; Blaabjerg, F.; Azam, F.; New CUK–SEPIC converter based photovoltaic power system with hybrid GSA–PSO algorithm employing MPPT for water pumping applications. IET Power Electronics. 2020, 13:2824–2830

29. Priyadarshi, N.; Padmanaban, N.; Holm-Nielsen, J. B.; Bhaskar, M.S.; Azam, F.; Internet of things augmented a novel PSO-employed modified zeta converter-based photovoltaic maximum power tracking system: hardware realisation. IET Power Electronics. 2020, 13:2775–2781

30. Kamalapathi, K., Priyadarshi, N., Padmanaban, S., Holm-Nielsen, J.B., Azam, F., Umayal, C., Ramachandaramurthy, V.K. A Hybrid Moth-Flame Fuzzy Logic Controller Based Integrated Cuk Converter Fed Brushless DC Motor for Power Factor Correction. MDPI Electronics, 2018, 7: 288.

31. Priyadarshi, N., Padmanaban, S., Lonel, D., Mihet-Popa, L., Azam, F. Hybrid PV-Wind, Micro-Grid Development Using Quasi-Z-Source Inverter Modeling and Control—Experimental Investigation. MDPI Energies, 2018, 11:2277

32. Priyadarshi, N.; Ramachandaramurthy, V, K.; Padmanaban, S.; Azam, A.; An Ant Colony Optimized MPPT for Standalone Hybrid PV-Wind Power System with Single Cuk Converter. MDPI Energies, 2019, 12: 167

33. Azam, F.; Yadav, S.K.; Priyadarshi, N.; Padmanaban, S.; and Bansal, R.C.; A Comprehensive Review of Authentication Schemes in Vehicular Ad-Hoc Network, IEEE Access, 2021, 9:31309-31321, 2021, doi: 10.1109/ACCESS.2021.3060046.

34. Priyadarshi, N.; Sharma, A.K.; Bhoi, A. K.; Ahmad, S. N.; Azam, F.; Priyam, S.; A Practical performance verification of AFLC based MPPT for standalone PV power system under varying weather condition, International Journal of Engineering & Technology, 2018, 7:338-343

35. Azam, F.; Priyadarshi N.; Nagar H.; Kumar S.; Bhoi A.K.; An Overview of Solar-Powered Electric Vehicle Charging in Vehicular Adhoc Network. in: Electric Vehicles. Green Energy and Technology. Springer, Singapore. https://doi.org/10.1007/978-981-15-9251-5_5

36. Azam, F.; Kumar, S.; Yadav, K.P.; Priyadarshi N.; Padmanaban, S.; An Outline of the Security Challenges in VANET, in Proc. of IEEE UPCON 2020, Nov, 2020.

37. Priyadarshi, N.; Azam, F.; Bhoi, A.K.; Sharma, A.K.; A Multilevel Inverter-Controlled Photovoltaic Generation. in Advances in Greener Energy Technologies. Springer, Singapore. 2020 https://doi.org/10.1007/978-981-15-4246-6_8

38. Priyadarshi, N.; Azam, F.; Bhoi, A.K.; Sharma, A.K.; Dynamic Operation of Grid-Connected Photovoltaic Power System. in Advances in Greener Energy Technologies. Springer, Singapore. 2020 https://doi.org/10.1007/978-981-15-4246-6_13

39. Priyadarshi, N.; Azam, F.; Bhoi, A.K.; Sharma, A.K.; A Proton Exchange Membrane-Based Fuel Cell Integrated Power System. in Advances in Greener Energy Technologies. Springer, Singapore. 2020 https://doi.org/10.1007/978-981-15-4246-6_18

40. Priyadarshi, N.; Azam, F.; Bhoi, A.K.; Sharma, A.K.; A Closed-Loop Control of Fixed Pattern Rectifier for Renewable Energy Applications. in Advances in Greener Energy Technologies. Springer, Singapore. 2020 https://doi.org/10.1007/978-981-15-4246-6_25

41. Priyadarshi, N.; Azam, F.; Bhoi, A.K.; Sharma, A.K.; A Four-Switch-Type Converter Fed Improved Photovoltaic Power System. in Advances in Greener Energy Technologies. Springer, Singapore. 2020 https://doi.org/10.1007/978-981-15-4246-6_29

42. Vardia, M.; Priyadarshi, N.; Ali, I.; Azam, F.; Bhoi, A.K.; Maximum Power Point Tracking for Wind Energy Conversion System. in Advances in Greener Energy Technologies. Springer, Singapore. 2020 https://doi.org/10.1007/978-981-15-4246-6_36

43. Vardia, M.; Priyadarshi, N.; Ali, I.; Azam, F.; Bhoi, A.K.; Design of Wind Energy Conversion System Under Different Fault Conditions. in Advances in Greener Energy Technologies. Springer, Singapore. 2020 https://doi.org/10.1007/978-981-15-4246-6_41

44. Choudhary, T.; Priyadarshi, N.; Kuma,r P.; Azam, F.; Bhoi A.K. (2020) A Fuzzy Logic Control Based Vibration Control System for Renewable Application. in Advances in Greener Energy Technologies. Springer, Singapore. 2020 https://doi.org/10.1007/978-981-15-4246-6_38

45. Priyadarshi, N.; Azam F.; Solanki, S. S.; Sharma, A.K.; Bhoi, A.K.; Almakhles, D.; A Bio-Inspired Chicken Swarm Optimization-Based Fuel Cell System for Electric Vehicle Applications. in Bio-inspired Neurocomputing. Studies in Computational Intelligence, vol 903. Springer, Singapore. 2021 https://doi.org/10.1007/978-981-15-5495-7_1

46. Omar, N.; Monem, M. A.; Firouz, Y.; Salminen, J.; Smekens, J.; Hegazy, O.; Gaulous, H.; Mulder, G.; Bossche, P. V.; Coosemans, T.; Mierlo, J. V.; Lithium iron phosphate based battery — Assessment of the aging parameters and development of cycle life model. *Applied Energy*. **2014**, 113, 1575–1585.

47. Saidi. A; Harrouz, A.; Colak, I.; Kayisli, K.; Bayindir, R.; Performance Enhancement of Hybrid Solar PV Wind System Based on Fuzzy Power Management Strategy: A Case Study. *IEEE International Conference on Smart Grid*. **2019**, 126-131.

8

Optimization Technique Based Distribution Network Planning Incorporating Intermittent Renewable Energy Sources

Surajit Sannigrahi* and Parimal Acharjee

Department of Electrical Engineering, NIT Durgapur, West Bengal, India

Abstract

In the circumstances of rapid load growth, the Distribution Company must undertake an appropriate strategy for distribution network planning so that customers can be supplied with an uninterrupted and superior power. Accordingly, a planning strategy is adopted in this chapter for distribution network considering the integration of renewable sources. As renewable sources cause bi-directional power flows and voltage limits violation, network reconfiguration technology is also utilized in this study to solve the afore-mentioned issues of the network. The key aim of the network planning is maximizing the potential benefits of Distribution Company by enhancing bus voltage, maximizing economic benefit and reducing emission. To address these technical, economic and environmental issues, different logical indexes such as system voltage enhancement index (SVEI), economic feasibility index (EFI) and emission cost reduction index (ECRI) are formulated. Since the values of these objectives are in different ranges, it will be difficult to choose appropriate values of weighting factor to formulate single–objective problem from multi-objective problem. To solve the issue, fuzzy logic is utilized in this chapter, which can bring the objective functions between 0 and 1 using the membership functions. In this chapter, instead of the traditional single-level planning model where all the planning investment are made at the beginning of the planning period, a multi-stage planning model is developed to divide the planning horizon into several stages so that the planning investments can be made in each planning stage according to the need. Therefore, cost-effective planning solutions

*Corresponding author: surajit710@yahoo.in

Neeraj Priyadarshi, Akash Kumar Bhoi, Sanjeevikumar Padmanaban, S. Balamurugan and Jens Bo Holm-Nielsen (eds.) Intelligent Renewable Energy Systems, (199–242) © 2022 Scrivener Publishing LLC

can be obtained. Moreover, the uncertainty of wind turbine system is taken into account and it is modeled using Weibull probability distribution function. In addition, the time-varying characteristics of different types of loads are also taken to account and unlike the traditional load flow method, a voltage-dependent load flow technique is applied for a realistic system planning. Furthermore, the discrete version of rooted tree optimization technique (DRTO) is utilized here to solve the planning problem and its effectiveness is proved by comparing with other standard techniques based on convergence characteristic, solution quality, simulation time, failure rate and Wilcoxon signed rank test. Moreover, regarding the distribution network planning, various planning cases are taken into account to find out the most suitable one for practical implementation.

Keywords: Distribution network planning, renewable energy sources, wind turbine DG, multi stage planning, uncertainty, discrete rooted tree optimization technique

8.1   Introduction

Nowadays, under the circumstance of power system restructuring, distribution companies all over the world are experiencing the rapid growth of load demand of different consumers such as commercial, residential and industrial [1–4]. To meet the constant load growth of distribution network, the substation capacity needs to be upgraded [5]. On the other hand, with the growth of load, the power flow through the feeder increases and in the near future, the power flow may reach the maximum power flow capability of the feeder. In such a situation, to maintain stability, the feeders' capacity enhancement decisions need to be undertaken by the planning engineers [6]. The process of upgrading substation and feeders' capacity is very costly investments; however, the distribution company has to undertake these decisions to continue the reliable power supply to the consumers during the planning period [5–8]. In such context, distribution companies are looking for any planning alternative for maximizing the network assets utilization so that the requirement of upgradation can be delayed. On the contrary, during electricity production from conventional power plants, fossil fuels are burnt that produces a huge amount of greenhouse gases, causing several atmospheric pollutions [9]. To reduce greenhouse gases emission, the government of many progressive countries has imposed emission costs on distribution company [9]. Therefore, any device that can generate clean and green energy has become a preferable choice for distribution companies so that the power taken from the grid can be reduced. These issues drive the attention of planning engineers to implement renewable energy-based and environmentally friendly distributed generation (DG) technology, especially in distribution networks [11–14].

DG technology can provide a wide range of benefits by reducing loss and improving bus voltage [11–14]. Apart from this, due to the active power generation from DG units, a significant portion of the consumers' load demand can be met [15, 16]. Therefore, the overall load of the network is reduced. Accordingly, the grid supplied power and the imposed cost due to pollutant emission are also reduced [11]. Moreover, the requirement of undertaking substation upgradation decision is also eliminated or further delayed to the later stage [15]. However, the incorporation of DG leads to a bi-directional line flow in the network. Furthermore, there may be an addition of new load points that can make the situation worse [17], which seeks further attention from the planning engineers.

Network reconfiguration, a process of changing the network configuration, can reduce the bi-directional power flow in the network [16, 18, 19]. Accordingly, the power flow can be evenly distributed among the feeders by changing the status of installed tie switches, which improves the network stability and eliminate the need for the feeder upgradation process. Moreover, the alteration of tie switches during the reconfiguration process helps to isolate the faulty systems during a fault, which improves overall system reliability [16].

In most literature, a single-stage or static model was designed regarding network planning. This model made the planning investment at the beginning considering the projected demand at the end of the planning period [1, 2, 6, 12]. Suppose, to carry out a planning study, the planning horizon is taken as 15 years. In this model, researchers projected the load demand at the end of the planning horizon and using these values, they determined the suitable planning investments which are to be implemented at the beginning. The static model is easy to execute from optimization viewpoint, but the obtained solutions will not be cost-effective [15, 17]. This is due to the fact that it may not be possible for distribution companies to implement such huge investments at a single time. This motivates the authors to develop a multi-stage or dynamic planning model for dividing the planning period into several stages so that the planning of the distribution network can be implemented at each stage. In this case, firstly, the planning horizon is divided into various planning stages namely, planning stage 1 (0–5 years), planning stage 2 (6–10 years) and planning stage 3 (11–15 years) and the loads and renewable power generations are projected for these planning stages and accordingly, planning is carried out gradually. As a result, the proposed model can handle the continuous growth of the load demand optimally and generate a more cost-effective planning solution as compared to the static model [15, 17].

Literature review indicates that the researchers mostly took technical and economic factors as the primary objectives to conduct the network planning process [17–21]. In [17], authors considered economic aspects to carry out the planning of active distribution system. The economic factors consist of the investment, operation and maintenance cost. DG Integration in distribution network was carried out with reconfiguration in [18] with an aim to minimize energy loss. Minimization of loss and operational cost was taken as the objectives in [19]. Authors in [20] conducted the DG integration process accounting technical and economic factors such as voltage deviation, yearly DG investment cost, and purchasing grid electricity. Simultaneous reconfiguration and placement of solar PV array and DSTATCOM is executed in [21] to maximize the technical aspects of the distribution network. Loss, voltage magnitude and feeder load balancing were considered as technical aspects. Considering a global concern about the environment in recent time, the environmental factors must be addressed regarding network planning [10, 11]. In such context, this chapter designs the planning framework considering the technical, environmental, and economic aspects for efficient planning investments, which was missing in existing articles.

As different objective functions are simultaneously accounted for network planning, the obtained values of objectives will not be in the same range. Thus, the multi-objectives problem cannot be converted to a single objective problem due to the difficulty in choosing the desired value of weighting factors as per the objectives [21, 22]. Hence, the values of objectives need to be logically brought in the same range and to do so, Fuzzy logic can be used. Utilizing Fuzzy logic, the membership values can be determined for all the objective functions according to the specified maximum and minimum value of the objective [23].

In the distribution network, there are different types of consumers and the load of these consumers is not constant; rather it alters from hour to hour, season to season. As presented in [18, 19], time-varying characteristics of system load were considered for the planning purpose. Therefore, the network must be analyzed utilizing a multi-level load model in order to properly design the planning framework. However, there are articles where only the peak load level was taken to carry out distribution network planning [24, 25]. Moreover, the multi-load level based voltage-dependent power flow method should be conducted instead of the standard load flow method [19, 26]. Furthermore, researchers usually considered DG as a constant power source, which is impractical as the power output of renewable energy-based DG is highly intermittent in nature [1, 11, 16]. Therefore, the high-level uncertainty associated with the renewable-based DG must be taken into account to make the study practical.

As the proposed planning framework considers multiple planning alternatives, the problem becomes complex in nature and due to the complexity, the general optimization techniques may not perform satisfactorily regarding solution quality, convergence time, convergence characteristics, and robustness. This motivates the authors to apply a computationally efficient and nature-inspired rooted tree optimization (RTO) technique for carrying out the planning process [27]. As the problem formulated in this chapter is discrete, the standard RTO technique is converted to discrete RTO (DRTO) to adapt with the problem [28]. Furthermore, to convert the proposed problem with multiple objective functions to a single objective problem, this chapter utilizes Fuzzy logic that brings all the objectives in the same range by developing membership functions. The main focuses of this chapter are stated below:

- A multi-stage planning framework is proposed to divide the planning period into several stages so that investments can be made in each stage as per the requirements.
- Regarding the network planning, new load points addition, yearly load growth, feeder reconfiguration, and the network reinforcement options such as feeder and substation capacity up-gradation are taken as planning alternatives that are utilized in coordination with DG integration.
- The high-level uncertainty of the power output of wind turbine DG (WTDG) and the time-varying characteristics of different consumers' demands are taken to design the planning model.
- Considering a global concern about the environment in recent time, the environmental aspect is considered along with the technical and economic aspects. Moreover, logical formulas are proposed to address these aspects.
- The problem regarding the conversion of single-objective problem from a multi-objectives problem is overcome by utilizing fuzzy logic that can bring the objectives between 0 and 1 (in the same range) by developing membership function.
- To solve the planning problem that is discrete in nature, a more efficient discrete RTO (DRTO) technique is proposed.

8.2 Load and WTDG Modeling

This section describes the modeling of different consumers' load demand and the uncertainty in WTDG's output.

8.2.1 Modeling of Load Demand

The power demand of different types of consumers in a distribution network alters from time to time [19, 26]. Therefore, before carrying out the planning study, planning engineers must consider the daily load profile of these consumers and accordingly, in this chapter, the time-varying characteristics of loads are taken into account and Figure 8.1 graphically represents different load characteristics. Moreover, the voltage dependencies of residential,

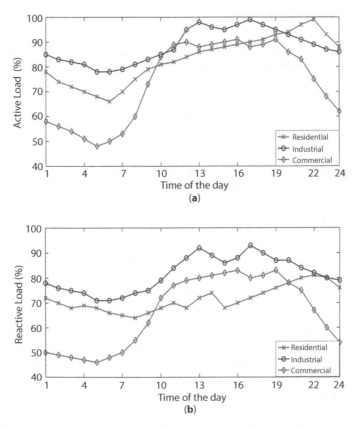

Figure 8.1 Time-varying characteristics of (a) Active and (b) Reactive power demand for different customers.

Table 8.1 Values of exponential parameters for commercial, industrial and residential loads.

	Commercial (C)	Industrial (I)	Residential (R)
P	0.6	0.1	1.7
Q	2.5	0.6	2.6

industrial, and commercial loads are designed in equations (8.1)–(8.2). Table 8.1 presents the components of active and reactive power [26].

$$P = P_n \left\{ X_{com} \left(\frac{V}{V_n} \right)^{C_P} + Y_{ind} \left(\frac{V}{V_0} \right)^{I_P} + Z_{res} \left(\frac{V}{V_0} \right)^{R_P} \right\} \tag{8.1}$$

$$Q = Q_n \left\{ X_{com} \left(\frac{V}{V_n} \right)^{C_Q} + Y_{ind} \left(\frac{V}{V_n} \right)^{I_Q} + Z_{res} \left(\frac{V}{V_n} \right)^{R_Q} \right\} \tag{8.2}$$

where P_n and Q_n are the active and reactive power load at nominal voltage (V_n), whereas X, Y, and Z are load percentage in different buses.

8.2.2   Modeling of WTDG

The power output of WTDG depends upon the wind speed of the location where the device is installed [11]. The geographical location and weather conditions have a significant influence on the wind speed, which makes the WTDG power output intermittence in nature [20, 24]. Therefore, for a practical analysis of network planning, the stochastic nature of the wind speed should be properly studied. Accordingly, in this chapter, Weibull probability distribution function ($f_{wt}(w)$) is utilized to present the randomness in wind speed as given below [8]:

$$f_{wt}(w) = \frac{M}{C} \left(\frac{w}{C} \right)^{M-1} exp \left(-\left(\frac{w}{C} \right)^M \right) \tag{8.3}$$

$$M = \left(\frac{\sigma_w}{\mu_w} \right)^{-1.086} ; C = \frac{\mu_w}{\Gamma \left(1 + \frac{1}{M} \right)} \tag{8.4}$$

where C and M denote the scale and shape parameters, respectively. Wind speed is denoted as w. The mean and standard deviation of wind speed is presented as σ_w and μ_w, respectively.

The average value of WTDG output $\left(P_{wt}^t \right)$ can be calculated as:

$$P_{wt}^t = \sum_{j=1}^{N_j} P_{wt}^j \times p_w(j) \tag{8.5}$$

$$p_w(j) = \int_{wl}^{wu} f_{wt}(w)\,dw \tag{8.6}$$

$$P_{wt}^j = \begin{cases} 0 & 0 \leq w^j \leq w_{in}, w^j \geq w_{out} \\ P_{rated}\left(\dfrac{w^j - w_{in}}{w_{rated} - w_{in}} \right) & w_{in} \leq w^j \leq w_{rated} \\ P_{rated} & w_{rated} \leq w^j \leq w_{out} \end{cases} \tag{8.7}$$

where N_j is the number of states. P_{wt}^j and $p_w(j)$ are WTDG power output and wind speed probability, respectively in state j. The wind speed limits are represented as w_u and w_l. P_{rated} is the rated power output of WTDG. w_{out}, w_{in}, and w_{rated} are the cut out, cut in, and rated speed of wind turbine. Equation 8.7 indicates that if the wind speed is less than the cut in value or more than the cut out value, the power output of the wind DG is zero. On the other hand, a wind speed in the range of rated value and cut out value will give a rated power output. Beside, a variable value of wind power output is obtained if the wind speed lies between cut in and rated value.

In this chapter, historical wind speed data is collected for the town Kanyakumari, India. From the data, the standard deviation and mean of wind speed is calculated for 24 hours as graphically represented in Figure 8.2. Then, each time segment is divided into 20 wind speed states between 1 and 20 at a step of 1 and the Weibull probability distribution function is generated for all the states of each time segment. The power generation of WTDG for t^{th} time segment is calculated by multiplying the probability distribution and maximum power generation at each state. Figure 8.3 represents the variation of WTDG power output for 24 hours time period. Here, the technical parameters of WTDG are taken as P_{rated}: 250 kW; w_{out}: 25 m/s; w_{in}: 3 m/s; and w_{rated}: 12 m/s.

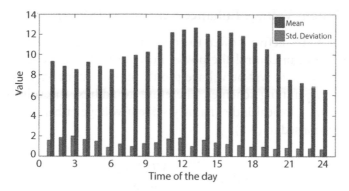

Figure 8.2 Standard deviation and Mean of the wind speed.

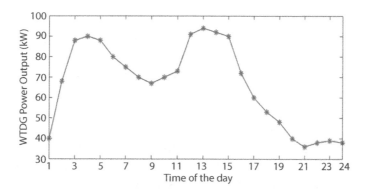

Figure 8.3 Power output of WTDG for different times of the day.

8.3 Objective Functions

In the existing articles, the technical and economic factors were mostly considered to conduct the distribution network planning [17–21]. However, considering the increasing environmental concern in recent days, environmental aspects have become an important factor that must be considered regarding the planning process [10, 11]. In such context, this chapter designs a planning study considering all the aspects and to address these aspects, authors have formulated logical indexes such as system voltage enhancement index (SVEI), economic feasibility index (EFI) and emission cost reduction index (ECRI) which are explained below.

8.3.1   System Voltage Enhancement Index (SVEI)

WTDG provides active power to the network, whereas the reconfiguration process can control the power flow through the feeders [18, 19]. Consequently, there will be voltage profile improvement with the utilization of these planning schemes. Therefore, to address the voltage profile enhancement, a logical index namely system voltage enhancement index (SVEI) is proposed in (8.8):

$$SVEI = \frac{\sum_{t \in S_t} VP_t^{wp} \times \Delta t}{\sum_{t \in S_t} VP_t^{wop} \times \Delta t} \tag{8.8}$$

$$VP_t^{wp} = \sum_{b \in S_b} \left\{ \left(V_t^{b,wp} - V^{min} \right) \times \left(V^{max} - V_t^{b,wp} \right) \right\} \tag{8.9}$$

$$VP_t^{wop} = \sum_{b \in S_b} \left\{ \left(V_t^{b,wop} - V^{min} \right) \times \left(V^{max} - V_t^{b,wop} \right) \right\} \tag{8.10}$$

$$S_t = \{1, 2, \ldots \ldots, N_t\}; \quad S_b = \{1, 2, \ldots \ldots, N_b\}$$

where VP_t^{wp} and VP_t^{wop} are the overall voltage profile at t^{th} time segment with and without planning, respectively. N_t and N_b are the numbers of time segments and buses. The maximum and minimum voltage limits is indicate as V^{max} and V^{min}. $V_t^{b,wp}$ and $V_t^{b,wop}$ are the voltage of bth bus at t^{th} time segment with and without planning, respectively.

8.3.2   Economic Feasibility Index (EFI)

Before the commencement of any planning project, it is important to check the economic feasibility of the planning project. Based on this viewpoint, a formula namely Economic Feasibility Index (EFI) is developed considering the ratio of total economic benefit and total investment cost of the distribution company.

To meet the consumers' demand, the distribution company buys power from the electrical grid [16, 24]. However, with active power generation, WTDG can meet a significant amount of consumers' load demand [16, 24]. Thus, there is a reduction of grid-supplied power, which provides substantial economic benefits to the distribution company. On the other hand, the expenses for the system planning comprise the investment and maintenance cost of WTDG, upgradation cost of substation and feeders, and the line building cost for new load point addition.

$$EFI = \frac{TEB}{TIC} \tag{8.11}$$

The total investment cost (TIC) of the distribution company can be calculated as shown below:

$$TIC = \sum_{st \in S_{st}} (1+\gamma)^{(1-st) \times K} \times \left\{ IN_{st}^{sub} + IN_{st}^{fed} + IN_{st}^{line} + IN_{st}^{WTDG} + MC_{st}^{WTDG} \right\} \tag{8.12}$$

$$S_{st} = \{1, 2, \ldots \ldots, N_{st}\}$$

$$IN_{st}^{sub} = \sum_{ss \in S_{ss}} \sum_{sa \in S_{sa}} Cost_{ss}^{sub,sa} \tag{8.13}$$

$$S_{ss} = \{1, 2, \ldots \ldots, N_{ss}\}; \quad S_{sa} = \{1, 2, \ldots \ldots, N_{sa}\}$$

$$IN_{st}^{fed} = \sum_{f \in S_f} \sum_{fa \in S_{fa}} Cost_f^{fed,fa} \times l_f \tag{8.14}$$

$$S_f = \{1, 2, \ldots \ldots, N_f\}; \quad S_{fa} = \{1, 2, \ldots \ldots, N_{fa}\}$$

$$IN_{st}^{line} = \sum_{nf \in S_{nf}} Cost_{nf}^{fed} \times l_{nf} \tag{8.15}$$

$$S_{nf} = \{1, 2, \ldots \ldots, N_{nf}\}$$

where N_{st} is the number of planning stages and the duration of each stage is presented as K. γ is the bank interest. The investment cost regarding substation upgrade, feeders upgrade, and new line construction for planning stage st are presented as IN_{st}^{sub}, IN_{st}^{fed}, and IN_{st}^{line}, respectively. N_{ss} and N_f are the number of substations and feeders to be upgraded, whereas N_{sa} and N_{fa} are the alternatives for substation and feeder upgrade, respectively. $Cost_{ss}^{sub,sa}$ and $Cost_f^{fed,fa}$ indicate the cost of upgrading ss[th] substation and f[th] feeders using sa[th] and fa[th] alternative. $Cost_{nf}^{fed}$ is the cost of nf[th] feeder construction. l_{nf} is the length of nf[th] feeder.

The installation (IN_{st}^{WTDG}) and maintenance cost (MC_{st}^{WTDG}) of WTDG units is formulated in equation (8.16) and (8.18), respectively. As a huge amount of land is required to install the device, the cost of land ($Cost_{land}$) is taken into account to calculate IN_{st}^{WTDG} as shown in equation (8.16).

$$IN_{st}^{WTDG} = Cost_{land} + Cost_{ins}^{WTDG} \times \sum_{b \in S_b} Cap_b^{WTDG} \times U_b \times L_b \tag{8.16}$$

$$L_b = \begin{cases} 1 & \textit{if } \text{WTDG unit installed at bus b} \\ 0 & \textit{if } \text{WTDG unit not installed at bus b} \end{cases} \quad (8.17)$$

$$MC_{st}^{WTDG} = \Sigma_{t \in S_t} OP_{st,t}^{WTDG} \times Cost_{main}^{WTDG} \times N_{st}^{days} \times \Delta t \times f(\gamma, K) \quad (8.18)$$

$$f(\gamma, K) = \left(\frac{1 - (1 + \gamma)}{\gamma} \right)^{-K} \quad (8.19)$$

where $Cost_{ins}^{WTDG}$ is the installation cost of WTDG per MW, whereas the maintenance cost of WTDG per MWh of energy generation is indicated as $Cost_{main}^{WTDG}$. Cap_b^{WTDG} is the capacity of WTDG installed at bth bus. U_b is the number of units installed at bus b. The output power of WTDG at tth time segment of stth planning stage is shown as $OP_{st,t}^{WTDG}$. N_{st}^{days} presents the number of days in each planning stage. Δt is the duration of each time segment. The present value of the annuity function is calculated using $f(\gamma, K)$.

The total economic benefit (TEB) of the distribution company can be calculated using equation (8.20).

$$TEB = \Sigma_{st \in S_{st}} (1 + \gamma)^{(1-st) \times K} \times \{ Sav_{st}^{\Delta ap} + Sav_{st}^{\Delta rp} \} \quad (8.20)$$

The economic benefit obtained due to the reduction of grid-supplied active power ($Sav_{st}^{\Delta ap}$) can be calculated as

$$Sav_{st}^{\Delta ap} = \Sigma_{t \in S_t} \Sigma_{b \in S_b} \left[\left(AP_{st,t,b}^{load} + AP_{st,t}^{loss,wop} \right) - \left(AP_{st,t,b}^{load} + AP_{st,t}^{loss,wp} - OP_{st,t}^{WTDG} \right) \right] \times$$
$$Cost_{st,t}^{grid,ap} \times N_{st}^{days} \times \Delta t \times f(\gamma, K)$$

$$(8.21)$$

After simplifying the above equation, we get

$$Sav_{st}^{\Delta ap} = \Sigma_{t \in S_t} \Sigma_{b \in S_b} \left[\left(AP_{st,t}^{loss,wop} - AP_{st,t}^{loss,wp} + OP_{st,t}^{WTDG} \right) \right] \times Cost_{st,t}^{grid,ap} \times N_{st}^{days} \times \Delta t \times f(\gamma, K)$$

$$(8.22)$$

Similarly, the economic benefit obtained due to the reduction of grid-supplied reactive power (Sav_{st}^{ap}) can be calculated as

$$Sav_{st}^{\Delta rp} = \sum_{t \in S_t} \sum_{b \in S_b} \left[\left(RP_{st,t}^{loss,wop} - RP_{st,t}^{loss,wp} \right) \right] \times Cost_{st,t}^{grid,rp} \times N_{st}^{days} \times \Delta t \times f(\gamma, K)$$

(8.23)

where $AP_{st,t,b}^{load}$ is the load of bth bus at tth time segment of stth planning stage. $AP_{st,t}^{loss,wop}$ and $AP_{st,t}^{loss,wp}$ are the active loss without and with planning at tth time segment of stth planning stage, whereas the reactive loss without and with planning at tth time segment of stth planning stage are indicated as $RP_{st,t}^{loss,wop}$ and $RP_{st,t}^{loss,wp}$, respectively. $Cost_{st,t}^{grid,ap}$ and $Cost_{st,t}^{grid,rp}$ is the price of grid supplied active and reactive power.

8.3.3 Emission Cost Reduction Index (ECRI)

Conventional power plants significantly contribute to greenhouse gases emission into the atmosphere during power generation, which leads to various ecological and health-related issues [6]. To counter these problems, the producers and consumers of electricity are being imposed emission costs to reduce environmental pollution [10]. The negative environmental impact created by conventional power plants can be reduced with the addition of renewable energy sources [6, 16]. This is because renewable energy sources can generate clean and green electricity without any emission of pollutants. Thus, in the current situation, environmental aspects must be considered along with the economic and technical aspects and accordingly, a formula namely emission cost reduction index (ECRI) is formulated as shown in (8.24) to address the environmental impacts.

$$ECRI = \frac{TEC_{wp}}{TEC_{wop}}$$

(8.24)

$$TEC_{wp} = \sum_{g \in S_g} C_g \times \sum_{st \in S_{st}} (1+\gamma)^{(1-st) \times K} \times \sum_{t \in S_t} \sum_{b \in S_b} \left(AP_{st,t,b}^{load} + AP_{st,t}^{loss} - OP_{st,t}^{WTDG} \right) \times$$
$$N_{st}^{days} \times \Delta t \times f(\gamma, K)$$

(8.25)

$$TEC_{wop} = \sum_{g \in S_g} C_g \times \sum_{st \in S_{st}} (1+\gamma)^{(1-st) \times K} \times \sum_{t \in S_t} \sum_{b \in S_b} \left(AP_{st,t,b}^{load} + AP_{st,t}^{loss} \right) \times N_{st}^{days} \times \Delta t$$
$$\times f(\gamma, K)$$

(8.26)

$$S_g = \{CO_2, NO_x, SO_x, CO\}$$

where TEC_{wp} and TEC_{wop} are the total emission cost with and without system planning, respectively. The emission cost for g^{th} pollutant is indicated as C_g.

8.4   Mathematical Formulation Based on Fuzzy Logic

In this chapter, the system planning framework is designed considering technical, economic, and environmental objectives namely SVEI, EFI, and ECRI. As the considered objectives are in different ranges, the multi-objective problem cannot be easily converted into a single objective problem using the weighted sum approach [22]. In this context, Fuzzy logic is used to bring them in the same range by determining membership function. To maximize the overall system benefits, SVEI and EFI need to be maximized, whereas ECRI requires to be minimized. Based on this factor, the fuzzy membership functions (MF) are developed for all the objective functions as presented below.

8.4.1   Fuzzy MF for SVEI

The fuzzy MF for $SVEI$ (M_{SVEI}) can be shown in Figure 8.4(a).
According to the figure, the following equation can be derived.

$$M_{SVEI} = \begin{cases} 0 & \text{if } SVEI \leq SVEI_{min} \\ \dfrac{SVEI - SVEI_{min}}{SVEI_{max} - SVEI_{min}} & \text{if } SVEI_{min} < SVEI < SVEI_{max} \\ 1 & \text{if } SVEI \geq SVEI_{max} \end{cases} \quad (8.27)$$

where the fuzzy membership value (MV) for objective function $SVEI$ is represented as M_{SVEI}. The upper and lower limits of $SVEI$ are denoted as $SVEI_{max}$ and $SVEI_{min}$, respectively.

According to equation (8.27), if the value of $SVEI$ is less or equal to $SVEI_{min}$, then the fuzzy MV is assigned as 0, and if $SVEI$ exceeds or is equal to $SVEI_{max}$, then unity value of fuzzy MV is considered. When $SVEI$ is greater than $SVEI_{min}$ and less than $SVEI_{max}$, a fuzzy MV in between 0 and 1 is assigned as per equation (8.27).

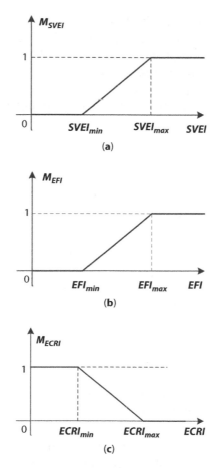

Figure 8.4 Membership functions for (a) *SVEI*, (b) *EFI* and (c) *ECRI*.

8.4.2   Fuzzy MF for EFI

The fuzzy MF for *EFI* (M_{EFI}) is presented in Figure 8.4(b).
According to the figure, the following equation can be derived.

$$M_{EFI} = \begin{cases} 0 & \text{if } EFI \leq EFI_{min} \\ \dfrac{EFI \text{ - } EFI_{min}}{EFI_{max} - EFI_{min}} & \text{if } EFI_{min} < EFI < EFI_{max} \\ 1 & \text{if } EFI \geq EFI_{max} \end{cases} \quad (8.28)$$

where the fuzzy MV for objective function *EFI* is represented as M_{EFI}. The upper and lower limits of *EFI* are denoted as EFI_{max} and EFI_{min}, respectively.

According to equation (8.28), if the value of *EFI* is less or equal to EI_{min}, then the fuzzy MV is assigned as 0, and if *EFI* exceeds or is equal to EFI_{max}, then a fuzzy MV of 1 is considered. On the other hand, when *EFI* lies within EFI_{min} and EFI_{max}, a fuzzy MV between 0 and 1 is assigned as per equation (8.28).

8.4.3   Fuzzy MF for ECRI

Figure 8.4(c) presents the fuzzy MF for *ECRI*.

According to the figure, the following equation can be derived.

$$M_{ECRI} = \begin{cases} 1 & \text{if } ECRI \leq ECRI_{min} \\ \dfrac{ECRI_{max} - ECRI}{ECRI_{max} - ECRI_{min}} & \text{if } ECRI_{min} < ECRI < ECRI_{max} \\ 0 & \text{if } ECRI \geq ECRI_{max} \end{cases} \quad (8.29)$$

where the fuzzy MV for objective function *ECRI* is represented as M_{ECRI}. The upper and lower limits of *ECRI* are denoted as $ECRI_{max}$ and $ECRI_{min}$, respectively.

M_{ECRI} is formulated in such a way that if the *ECRI* is less or equal to $ECRI_{min}$, then a fuzzy MV of 1 is considered, whereas a fuzzy MV of 0 is assigned if *ECRI* exceeds $ECRI_{max}$. On the other hand, when *ECRI* lies between $ECRI_{min}$ and $ECRI_{max}$, a fuzzy MV between 0 and 1 is assigned as per equation (8.29).

Based on the fuzzy MV computed for *SVEI*, *EFI* and *ECRI*, a single objective function 'F' is calculated in (8.30) using proper weighting factors:

$$\text{Maximize } F = \mu_1 \times M_{SVEI} + \mu_2 \times M_{EFI} + \mu_3 \times M_{ECRI} \quad (8.30)$$

Here, equal importance is given to each objective and accordingly, the value of μ_1, μ_2, and μ_3 is taken as 0.333 subjected to equation (8.31).

$$\sum_{k=1}^{3} \mu_k = 1 \wedge \mu_k \in [0,1] \quad (8.31)$$

The security constraints considered for the planning process are presented below:

Active and reactive line flow constraints:

$$AP_{st,t}^{grid} + OP_{st,t}^{WTDG} - \sum_{b \in S_b} AP_{st,t,b}^{load} - AP_{st,t}^{loss} = 0 \quad \forall st \in S_{st}, \forall t \in S_t \quad (8.32)$$

$$RP_{st,t}^{grid} - \sum_{b \in S_b} RP_{st,t,b}^{load} - RP_{st,t}^{loss} = 0 \quad \forall st \in S_{st}, \forall t \in S_t \quad (8.33)$$

Voltage constraint:

$$|V^{min}| \leq |V_b| \leq |V^{max}| \quad \forall b \in S_b \quad (8.34)$$

Power flow constraint:

$$S_f \leq S_f^{max} \quad \forall f \in S_f \quad (8.35)$$

WTDG size constraint:

$$\sum_{b \in S_b} Cap_b^{WTDG} \times U_b \times L_b \leq \sum_{b \in S_b} AP_{st,t,b}^{load} \quad (8.36)$$

System Radiality:

For maintaining the radial structure of the distribution network during the reconfiguration process, the topology of the distribution network must satisfy equation (8.37).

$$N_b = N_f - 1 \quad (8.37)$$

8.5   Solution Algorithm

8.5.1   Standard RTO Technique

RTO technique is designed based on the tree roots' behavior when they are searching for the water source [27]. The orientation or location of these tree roots is changed based on the wetness degree (WND) of the root head. In search of water, the roots move randomly and whenever any root finds any source of water, they call others to change their orientations or locations so that they can come near to the water source. In this technique, the tree roots with less value of *WND* upgrade their locations according to the best root that has the highest value of *WND*. Further, the orientation of the tree roots with a considerably superior *WND* is updated by preserving their previous orientations. Besides, the roots that have the worst values of *WND* are replaced by randomly generated new roots.

Initially, the population matrix (PM) consisting of n number of roots is generated randomly. Then, as per equation (8.38), *WND* is evaluated for each of the roots and thereafter, they are sorted in a descending manner according to *WND*.

$$WND_i = 1 - \frac{F_i}{\max(F)}, \quad i = 1, 2, \dots n \tag{8.38}$$

where the *WND* and fitness value of ith root is denoted as F_i and WND_i, respectively.

After completing the sorting of tree roots, the orientations/locations of the roots are updated in the following process.

1. The rate of the random root (R_R)

R_R represents a percentage of roots that will orient themselves randomly so that the diversity of the optimization technique is increased. The roots will update their orientation according to equation (8.39) and will replace the previous generation roots having less *WND*.

$$R_{i,d}^{it+1} = R_{r,d}^{it} + C_1 \times WND_i \times randn \times \frac{\left| R_d^{max} + R_d^{min} \right|}{it} \tag{8.39}$$

where *it* and d denote iteration number and dimension. The newly oriented root for the $(it+1)^{th}$ iteration is shown as $R_{i,d}^{it+1}$, whereas $R_{r,d}^{it}$ is the randomly selected root. R_d^{max} and R_d^{min} are the maximum and minimum limit of the dth dimension.

2. The rate of the nearest root to water (R_N)

R_N represents a percentage of roots that will orient themselves to come closer the wetter place according to the best root ($R_{best,d}^{it}$) that have the highest value of *WND*. The updated roots will act as a successor of the roots having weak wetness in the previous generation. The orientation occurs according to the following equation.

$$R_{i,d}^{it+1} = R_{best,d}^{it} + C_2 \times WND_i \times randn \times \frac{\left| R_d^{max} + R_d^{min} \right|}{it \times n} \qquad (8.40)$$

3. The rate of the continuous root in its orientation (R_c)

R_c indicates a specific number of roots that have a considerably better value of *WND* as compared to other roots. As the present location of these roots is very near to the source of water, they will be continuing their orientations as per the previous generation as presented in equation (8.41).

$$R_{i,d}^{it+1} = R_{i,d}^{it} + C_3 \times WND_i \times rand \times \left(R_{best,d}^{it} - R_{i,d}^{it} \right) \qquad (8.41)$$

where $R_{i,d}^{it}$ represents the ith root in itth iteration.

Considering appropriates values for R_R, R_N, and R_C, the current generation of roots update their orientations/locations using equation (8.42). Then it is checked that whether the new positions of the tree roots lie within the prescribed limits or not.

$$R_{i,d}^{it+1} = \begin{cases} R_{r,d}^{it} + C_1 \times WND_i \times randn \times \dfrac{\left| R_d^{max} + R_d^{min} \right|}{it} & for\ i = 1\ to\ (R_R \times n) \\[4mm] R_{best,d}^{it} + C_2 \times WND_i \times randn \times \dfrac{\left| R_d^{max} + R_d^{min} \right|}{it \times n} & for\ i = (R_R \times n) + 1\ to\ (R_R + R_N) \times n \\[4mm] R_{r,d}^{it} + C_3 \times WND_i \times rand \times \left(R_{best,d}^{it} - R_{i,d}^{it} \right) & for\ i = \left((1 - R_C) \times n \right) + 1\ to\ n \end{cases}$$

$$(8.42)$$

Once the locations are updated, the roots are arranged in descending order based on the updated *WND*. When the convergence criterion is met, this process stops.

8.5.2   Discrete RTO (DRTO) Algorithm

The original RTO technique, as presented in the previous section, is appropriate to sole the continuous optimization problems [27]. However, here, the planning problem is formulated considering new load point addition, WTDG placement, and tie switch allocation for reconfiguration, which makes the problem discrete in nature. Therefore, to solve the formulated problem, the standard RTO technique is modified to discrete RTO (DRTO) as discussed in the following section [28].

Suppose, the discrete search space for three decision variables D_1, D_2 and D_3 in case of any optimization problem are shown in equations (8.43), (8.44), and (8.45), respectively.

$$D_1 = [4 \ 11 \ 13 \ 10 \ 25 \ 44] \Rightarrow E_1 = 6 \tag{8.43}$$

$$D_2 = [7 \ 10 \ 2 \ 13 \ 9] \Rightarrow E_2 = 5 \tag{8.44}$$

$$D_3 = [25 \ 1 \ 21 \ 9 \ 17 \ 1 \ 4] \Rightarrow E_3 = 7 \tag{8.45}$$

The population matrix (M) is initialized between 0 and 1 (in continuous space) for D_1, D_2, and D_3 at the beginning of DRTO as shown below:

$$M = \begin{bmatrix} 0.34 & 0.22 & 0.77 \\ 0.25 & 0.15 & 0.52 \\ \vdots & \vdots & \vdots \\ 0.21 & 0.54 & 0.40 \end{bmatrix} \tag{8.46}$$

Therefore, equation (8.46) indicates that corresponding to the 1st population, the value of K_1, K_2, and K_3 is 0.34, 0.22, and 0.77, respectively. Before fitness calculation of the 1st population, the values of D_1, D_2, and D_3 corresponding to K_1, K_2, and K_3 need to find out.

$$\mu_1 = 1 + (E_1 \times K_1) \Rightarrow 1 + (6 \times 0.34) = 2.04 \tag{8.47}$$

$$\mu_2 = 1 + (E_2 \times K_2) \Rightarrow 1 + (5 \times 0.22) = 1.10 \tag{8.48}$$

$$\mu_3 = 1 + (E_3 \times K_3) \Rightarrow 1 + (7 \times 0.77) = 5.39 \tag{8.49}$$

$$\beta_1 = \min(\lfloor \mu_1 \rfloor, E_1) \Rightarrow \min(\lfloor 2.04 \rfloor, 6) = 2 \tag{8.50}$$

$$\beta_2 = \min(\lfloor \mu_2 \rfloor, E_2) \Rightarrow \min(\lfloor 1.10 \rfloor, 5) = 1 \tag{8.51}$$

$$\beta_3 = \min(\lfloor \mu_3 \rfloor, E_3) \Rightarrow \min(\lfloor 5.39 \rfloor, 7) = 5 \tag{8.52}$$

$$D_1|_{K_1} = D_1(\beta_1) = D_1(2) = 11 \tag{8.53}$$

$$D_2|_{K_2} = D_2(\beta_2) = D_2(1) = 7 \tag{8.54}$$

$$D_3|_{K_3} = D_3(\beta_3) = D_3(5) = 17 \tag{8.55}$$

8.5.3   Computational Flow

This chapter proposes DRTO technique to conduct the distribution network planning problem considering WTDG and reconfiguration to maximize technical, economic, and environmental benefits. The stepwise process of applying DRTO technique to solve the planning process is given below:

Step 1: Define load data, line data, variation of different consumers' loads, and mean and standard deviation of wind speed.
Step 2: Determine the power output of WTDG for a 24 hours time period using equations (8.3)–(8.7).
Step 3: Initialize parameters of DRTO algorithm such as number of Roots, the values of $\{R_R, R_N, R_C\}$ and $\{C_1, C_2, C_3\}$, number of planning stages (PS_{max}) and maximum number of iteration (T_{max}).
Step 4: Set the planning stage (PS) =1.
Step 5: Randomly initialize the population matrix (PM) that consist of n number of roots as given below:

$$PM = [R_1, R_2, R_3, \ldots \ldots, R_n]^T \tag{8.56}$$

where R_1, R_2, R_3, and R_n represent 1st, 2nd, 3rd and n^{th} root of the population, respectively.

In this chapter, the planning study is conducted considering reconfiguration, WTDG and new load point addition. Hence, the location of tie switches, newly built feeders for the addition of new load and size and site of WTDG are chosen to be the decision variable. The population structure of nth root is shown in equation (8.57).

$$R_n = \{\overbrace{TS_1^n, TS_2^n, \ldots, TS_x^n}^{\substack{\text{Location of} \\ \text{Tie Switches}}}, \overbrace{NF_1^n, NF_2^n, \ldots, NF_y^n}^{\substack{\text{Newly built} \\ \text{feeders}}}, \overbrace{S_1^{DG,n}, S_2^{DG,n}, \ldots, S_z^{DG,n}}^{\substack{\text{Size of} \\ \text{WTDG}}}, \overbrace{L_1^{DG,n}, L_2^{DG,n}, \ldots, L_z^{DG,n}}^{\substack{\text{Location of} \\ \text{WTDG}}}\}$$
$$\tag{8.57}$$

Step 6: Set the iteration number (T) = 1.
Step 7: Carry out the voltage-dependent load flow analysis using the backward-forward method for all the time segments.
Step 8: If obtained solutions satisfy the security, calculate *SVEI*, *EFI* and *ECRI* using equations (8.8), (8.11), and (8.24), respectively. Thereafter, calculate the fuzzy membership value using equations (8.27), (8.28), and

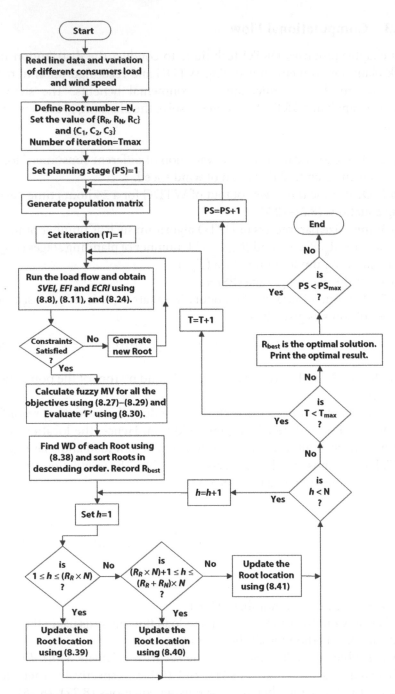

Figure 8.5 Flow chart of the proposed approach.

(8.29), respectively; and then evaluate the fuzzy objective function using equation (8.30).

Step 9: After calculating 'F' for all the roots in Step 8, evaluate *WND* as per equation (8.38) and sort the roots in descending order. Store the best root (R_{best}).

Step 10: Update the roots position using (8.42) and check the limit of the updated roots. If the root is not in the limit, rearrange the root within the search space.

Step 11: Increase the iteration (T) by 1 i.e. T=T+1.

Step 12: Check if the maximum iteration number is reached, print the optimal results, otherwise repeat Steps 7–11.

Step 13: Find the best solution for the planning stage PS.

Step 14: Increase the planning stage (PS) by 1 i.e. PS=PS+1.

Step 15: Check if the maximum planning stage (PS_{max}) is reached, print the optimal results, otherwise repeat Steps 5–14.

The flow chart of the proposed methodology is represented in Figure 8.5.

8.6   Simulation Results and Analysis

The performance of the proposed planning strategy is tested considering the modified 33-bus network as the test system. The standard 33-bus network consists of 33 buses and 32 feeders as shown in Figure 8.6 and the detailed parameters of the test network can be found in [29]. After modifications, four new load points namely 34, 35, 36, and 37 are added with the existing network and candidate buses to access, demand, and year of connection of the new load points are presented in Table 8.2. The planning strategy is conducted for a 15 year time period and the time period is divided into three planning stages. The load growth of the consumers is considered to be 5% yearly.

In this chapter, all the loaded buses are taken as the candidate location for incorporating WTDG units. Moreover, the rated capacity of each WTDG unit is chosen as 250 KW i.e. this device is providing only active power. The technical parameter related to WTDG can be referred to [11, 30] and the values of the environmental and economic parameters are presented in Table 8.3 [16–17, 20]. Initially, the substation capacity is 5 MVA and A1 conductor type is used for all the feeders. Details data regarding the alternatives for substation and feeder upgradation are displayed in Tables 8.4–8.5 [5, 6].

As displayed in Table 8.6, this chapter considers different planning cases to facilitate network engineers to choose the best planning option. In case 1, as indicated in Table 8.6, the base case planning is conducted where new load point addition and substation and feeders upgradation are taken as planning alternatives. On the other hand, network planning is conducted utilizing WTDG incorporation in case 2. Moreover, in case 3,

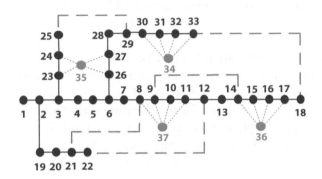

Figure 8.6 Schematic representation of the modified 33-bus system.

Table 8.2 Load demand, candidate buses to access, and year of connection of the new load points for 33-bus system.

New loads	Load value (KVA)	Candidate buses	Year of connection
Bus 34	60 + j35	30, 31, 32, 33	6
Bus 35	28 + j19	23, 24, 25, 26	9
Bus 36	115 + j80	14, 15, 16, 17	11
Bus 37	58 + j35	8, 9, 10, 11	12

Table 8.3 Economic and environmental data.

Parameters	Values	Parameters	Values
$Cost_{ins}^{WTDG}$	750000 $/MW	l_{nf}	1 km
$Cost_{main}^{WTDG}$	10 $/MWh	C_{CO2}	0.00288 $/Kg
γ	10 %/year	C_{Sox}	0.75 $/Kg
K	5 year	C_{NOx}	1.00 $/Kg
l_f	1 km	C_{CO}	0.125 $/Kg

both reconfiguration and WTDG incorporation are utilized for planning purposes.

Regarding the network planning, MATLAB version 2017a is chosen as the coding platform and the optimization is carried out in a computer with Intel(R) Core(TM) i5-6600 CPU. Both the maximum iteration and population size are set to 200. The values of R_R, R_N, and R_C are chosen as 0.3, 0.4, and 0.3, respectively.

8.6.1   Obtained Results for Different Planning Cases

The investment plans regarding upgradation of substation and feeders, newly build lines, location and size of WTDG, and tie switch allocation for stages 1–3 are presented in Table 8.7 for all the planning cases. Table 8.7 indicates that the total number of WTDG units incorporated during the planning period is 16 and 18, respectively for planning cases 2 and 3. Therefore, it can be concluded that the utilization of reconfiguration scheme can help

Table 8.4 Alternatives for substation and feeder upgradation.

Substation			Feeders			
Type	S_{max} (MVA)	Cost (USD)	Type	R (Ω/km)	X (Ω/km)	I_{max} (A)
S1	7	0.336	A1	0.5240	0.0900	219
S2	10	0.672	A2	0.3780	0.0860	304
S3	20	1.344	A3	0.2990	0.0830	384
S4	30	2.016	A4	0.1950	0.0800	590
S5	40	2.688	A5	0.1740	0.0780	661

Table 8.5 Cost of upgrading feeders ($\times 10^3$USD).

	A1	A2	A3	A4	A5
A1	-	7.5	13.5	21.5	29.5
A2	-	-	11	18.5	25.5
A3	-	-	-	14	22
A4	-	-	-	-	17.5

Table 8.6 Different planning cases.

Planning alternatives	Case 1	Case 2	Case 3
Network Reinforcements	√	√	√
New load points addition	√	√	√
DG incorporation	√	√	√
Reconfiguration	×	×	√

the distribution company to incorporate more WTDG units in the network. On the contrary, it is also observed that the capacity of substation 1 needs to be upgraded to 10 MVA (Type S2), 7 MVA (Type S1) and 7 MVA (Type S1), respectively for planning case 1, 2 and 3, which indicates that the presence of WTDG eliminates the need for upgrading substation to a higher capacity by meeting a significant portion of the consumers' load growth. Moreover, comparing the substation upgradation decision as undertaken in planning cases 2 and 3, it is revealed that the incorporation of WTDG in combination with reconfiguration can further delay the substation upgradation process to later stage. On the other hand, Table 8.7 also reveals that the number of feeder capacity enhancement decisions during the planning period as undertaken by the distribution company is the lowest in planning case 3. This is because WTDG units can act as a local active power source and the reconfiguration process can monitor the overall power flow; thus, the need for enhancing feeder capacity can be eliminated or delayed further.

The values of the objective functions, as obtained in different planning stages, are tabulated in Table 8.8 for all the planning cases. Based on the optimization results, it can be confirmed that compared to the base case (planning case 1), there is a notable improvement in techno-economic and environmental benefits for planning cases 2 and 3. Table 8.8 indicates that the obtained values of SVEI, EFI, and ECRI for planning case 3 are better than that of planning case 2. Therefore, this analysis concludes that with regard to the improvement of system voltage, reduction of pollutants emission and maximization of financial benefit, simultaneous reconfiguration with WTDG incorporation is more superior as compared to only WTDG allocation.

The stage-wise analysis of economic performances for planning cases 1–3 is summarized in Table 8.9. As shown in the table, although there is no installation and maintenance cost of WTDG units in planning case 1, the distribution company has to invest 165000.4 $, 436020.1 $, 438080.3 $, respectively in stage 1, 2, and 3; this is due to undertaking the upgradation

Table 8.7 Stage-wise investment plans for different planning cases.

Planning stage	Substation upgrade	Feeder upgrade	New lines	WTDG locations (units)	Reconfiguration
Planning case 1					
1	-	A3(1-2, 2-3), A2(3-4, 4-5)	-	-	-
2	S1 (Bus 1)	A4(1-2, 2-3), A3(3-4), A2(5-6)	34-30, 35-23	-	-
3	S2 (Bus 1)	A5(1-2), A4(3-4), A3 (4-5, 5-6), A2(6-26)	36-14, 37-9	-	-
Planning case 2					
1	-	A2(1-2, 2-3)	-	6(2), 14(2), 25(2), 33(1)	-
2	S1 (Bus 1)	A3(1-2), A2(2-3, 3-4)	34-30, 35-23	11(1), 24(2), 30(1)	-
3	-	A4(1-2), A3(2-3), A2(4-5, 5-6)	36-14, 37-9	3(1), 7(3), 16(1)	-
Planning case 3					
1	-	A2(1-2)	-	6(3), 21(2), 29(2), 33(1)	7-9-28-32-34
2	-	A3(1-2), A2(2-3)	34-30, 35-23	14(2), 24(2), 31(1)	7-10-28-32-34
3	S1 (Bus 1)	A4(1-2), A2(3-23)	36-14, 37-9	5(1), 13(2), 25(2)	7-10-28-32-36

Table 8.8 Obtained values of objectives for different planning cases.

Case	Stages	SVEI	EFI	ECRI
Planning Case 1	1	1.000	0	1.0000
	2	1.000	0	1.0000
	3	1.000	0	1.0000
Planning Case 2	1	1.277	0.916	0.7396
	2	1.298	1.403	0.6781
	3	1.321	2.078	0.6088
Planning Case 3	1	1.294	0.976	0.7076
	2	1.324	1.929	0.6251
	3	1.349	2.112	0.5631

decision of substation and feeders to meet the yearly load growth of the consumers. Moreover, the value of the obtained benefit is 0 in planning case 1 as there is no reduction of the grid-energy purchasing cost. On the other hand, due to the presence of WTDG units in planning cases 2 and 3, the grid-energy purchasing cost is reduced that results in significant economic benefits for the distribution company as displayed in Table 8.9. It is interesting to note that during stage 1 of both the planning cases 2 and 3, the total economic benefit (TEB) is less as compared to total investment cost (TIC). As a result, the values of EFI for planning cases 2–3 are obtained less than 1 during stage 1 as presented in Table 8.8. Moreover, Table 8.9 reveals that considering the entire planning period, the total benefits acquired by the distribution company is 849196.1$ and 1389629.6$, respectively for planning cases 2 and 3, which concludes that reconfiguration plays an important role to maximize the economic benefits.

The stage-wise analysis of environmental performances for planning cases 1–3 are summarized in Table 8.10. The table indicates that for planning case 1, the energy taken from the grid during stage 1, 2 and 3 is 119837, 144584, and 167929 MWh, respectively, which is reduced to {88629, 98046, 102229}, and {84797, 90381, 94564}, respectively in planning case 2 and 3. As there is a reduction in the grid supplied power, the emission of hazardous pollutants such as CO_2, NO_x, SO_x, and CO is also reduced. Therefore, distribution companies will get benefitted due to the imposed penalty cost of pollutant emission. The emission cost of different pollutants for planning cases 1–3 are given in

Table 8.9 Detail analysis of economic performances of planning cases 1–3.

Case	Stages	TIC ($)	TEB ($)	Net benefit ($)	Total benefit ($)
Planning Case 1	1	165000.4	0	-165000.4	0
	2	436020.1	0	-436020.1	
	3	438080.3	0	-438080.3	
Planning Case 2	1	1504976.9	1378830.0	-126146.9	849196.1
	2	922404.6	1294386.4	371981.8	
	3	559490.1	1162851.3	603361.2	
Planning Case 3	1	1623545.0	1585208.0	-38337.0	1389629.6
	2	791359.1	1526193.2	734834.2	
	3	623113.2	1316245.7	693132.5	

Table 8.10 Detail analysis of Economic performances of planning cases 1–3.

Case	Stages	Grid-supplied energy (MWh)	CO_2 emission cost ($)	NO_x emission cost ($)	SO_x Emission Cost ($)	CO Emission Cost ($)	Emission cost	Total emission cost
Planning Case 1	1	119837	214508	582407	345130	1618	4345918	9971911
	2	144584	258805	702677	416401	1952	3250892	
	3	167929	300593	816136	483636	2267	2375101	
Planning Case 2	1	88629	158646	430738	255252	1196	3214168	6864564
	2	98046	175503	476505	282373	1324	2204521	
	3	102229	182990	496834	294420	1380	1445875	
Planning Case 3	1	84797	151786	412112	244215	1145	3075181	6444824
	2	90381	161783	439253	260298	1220	2032177	
	3	94564	169270	459582	272345	1277	1337466	

Table 8.10. The emission cost of these pollutants is taken from [20]. The table indicates that compared to case 1, emission costs for all the planning stages are reduced for cases 2–3. Moreover, the total emission cost indicates that in case 2 and 3, emission cost is reduced by 31.16% and 35.37%, respectively, which establishes the environmental feasibility of planning case 3.

In this study, the distribution network planning is executed considering the maximization of techno-economic-environmental aspects. System voltage enhancement index is taken an objective function to address the technical aspects. However, active and reactive power losses are also vital parameters that need to be analyzed for effective network planning. In this regard, the average values of active and reactive power losses are determined for different cases and a planning stage-wise graphical representation is shown

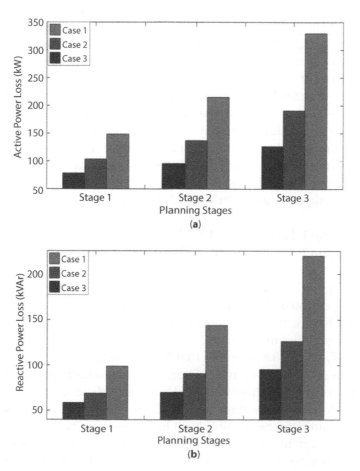

Figure 8.7 (a) Active and (b) Reactive power loss for different planning stages.

in Figures 8.7(a) and 8.7(b), respectively for active and reactive power loss. These figures clearly indicate that for all the planning stages, power losses are reduced in cases 2–3 in comparison with the base case i.e. case 1. Moreover, by comparing cases 2 and 3, it is concluded that the highest reduction of line losses occurs in case 3. Therefore, from the viewpoint of power losses, the implementation of case 3 will be most suitable for planning engineers.

8.6.2   Analysis of Voltage Profile and Power Flow Under the Worst Case Scenarios:

The simulation results indicate that the integration of WTDG units provides a wide range of benefits to the distribution network. However, there are various technical and regulatory issues such as voltage level violation, and power flow violation that may arise in the presence of WTDG. For example, if the power output of WTDG is very high at the time of low load, voltage magnitude of some buses and power flow through some feeders may violate the maximum permissible limit. On the other hand, if the power output of WTDG is very low at the time of high load, then voltage magnitude of many buses may fall below the minimum permissible limit. During the execution of the system planning, the main concern of the planning engineers is that the voltage magnitude and power flow must satisfy the permissible limit even in the most extreme situations. Therefore, to check the impact of proposed planning investment plans on the bus voltage and power flow of the test network, two severe load/generation scenarios are considered as shown below and thereafter, the impact is analyzed.

Scenario 1: Maximum load and Minimum WTDG power output.
Scenario 2: Minimum load and Maximum WTDG power output.

The graphical representation of system voltage for different planning cases is represented in Figures 8.8(a) and 8.8(b), respectively for scenarios 1 and 2 whereas, the power flow in the test network for planning cases 1–3 corresponding to scenario 1 and 2 is shown in Figures 8.9 and 8.10, respectively. Figure 8.8(a) reveals that in the case of scenario 1, the voltage magnitude of 24 and 17 number of buses falls below the minimum permissible limit of system voltage (0.95 P.U.), respectively in the planning cases 1 and 2. However, the voltage magnitude of only three buses is obtained below the minimum permissible limit in the planning case 3. Moreover, in the case of scenario 2, the bus voltage of all the buses reaches closer to the desired system voltage (1.0 P.U.) for planning case 3 as depicted in Figure 8.8(b). On the other hand, regarding the power flow, it is evident from

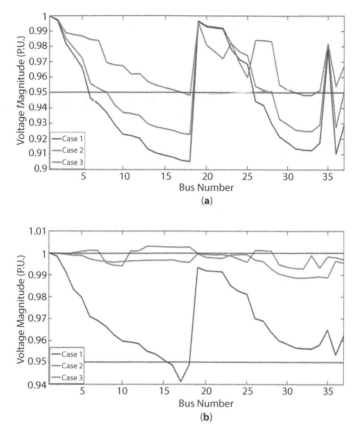

Figure 8.8 Bus voltages of the test network in (a) Scenario 1 and (b) Scenario 2.

Figures 8.9 and 8.10 that for both the scenarios, the feeders' power flow can be monitored to the permissible limit in planning case 3 due to the utilization of reconfiguration that can evenly distribute the power flow among the feeders. As a result, the requirement to undertake the feeder capacity enhancement decision can be further delayed or eliminated. Therefore, this analysis establishes the superiority of integrating WTDG in combination with the reconfiguration for distribution network planning.

8.6.3   Comparison Between Different Algorithms

The performance of the proposed DRTO algorithm is checked by comparing with optimization techniques; namely discrete particle swarm optimization (DPSO) technique [26] and discrete teaching learning-based optimization (TLBO) technique [28] based on solutions quality, simulation

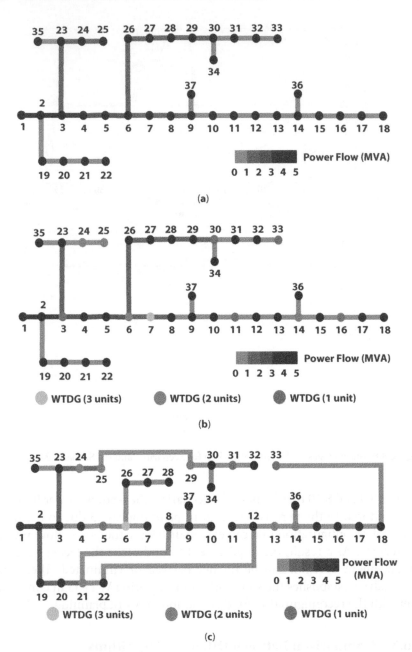

Figure 8.9 Power flow in the test network for planning (a) case 1, (b) case 2 and (c) case 3 corresponding to scenario 1.

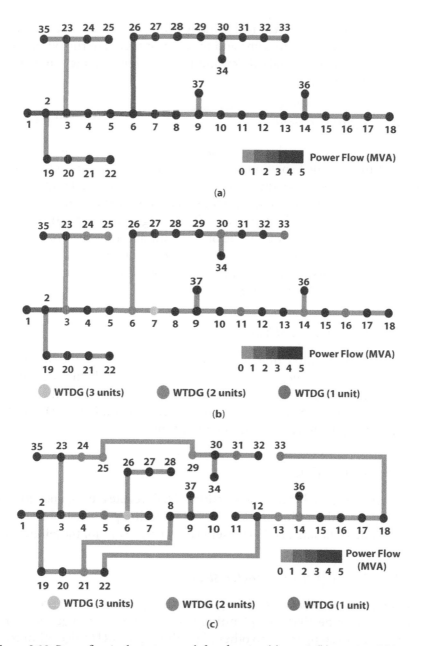

Figure 8.10 Power flow in the test network for planning (a) case 1, (b) case 2 and (c) case 3 corresponding to scenario 2.

time, and failure rate as presented in Table 8.11. The number of population and iteration are taken the same and these techniques are run 30 times to obtain the mean and standard deviation of solutions, average simulation time and failure rate.

8.6.3.1   Solution Quality

In this study, a lower value of standard deviation and a higher value of mean of the obtained solution are desirable from an optimization viewpoint. Therefore, to check the solution quality of different techniques, each technique is trial 30 times and the obtained results are shown in Table 8.10. The table shows that for both the case of planning cases 2 and 3, the highest value of mean and the lowest value of standard deviation are obtained for the proposed DRTO algorithm, establishing its superior solution quality compared to others. On the contrary, DPSO presents the worst quality of solutions for both planning cases.

8.6.3.2   Computational Time

The average simulation time, as shown in Table 8.11, is the lowest for the proposed technique, establishing the computational efficiency of the DRTO technique. On the other hand, DTLBO technique takes the highest simulation time. Therefore, as compared to DRTO and DPSO, DTLBO is the most computationally inefficient algorithm.

8.6.3.3   Failure Rate

Table 8.10 indicates that the lowest values of failure rate are obtained for the proposed algorithm, which makes the DRTO technique more robust compared to others. Besides, DPSO presents the worst results for the failure rate.

8.6.3.4   Convergence Characteristics

The computational characteristic is graphically represented in Figure 8.11(a) and 8.11(b), respectively for planning case 2 and 3. These figures clearly indicate that in comparison to other algorithms, the DRTO algorithm converges to the highest value of 'F' and DRTO also take the minimum of iteration to converge to the final 'F' value. Therefore, from the viewpoint of convergence characteristics, the proposed algorithm is the most superior technique as compared to others.

Table 8.11 Comparison of different optimization techniques.

Cases	Algorithms	Objective function		Simulation time (sec)	Failure rate
		Mean	Standard deviation		
Planning Case 2	DPSO	0.41533	0.000612	102.3	11
	DTLBO	0.41765	0.000524	112.5	9
	DRTO	0.41932	0.000388	98.4	7
Planning Case 3	DPSO	0.43976	0.000893	115.3	13
	DTLBO	0.44315	0.000741	123.1	10
	DRTO	0.44614	0.000577	108.5	8

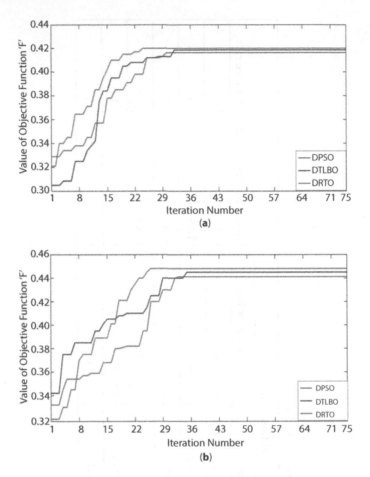

Figure 8.11 Convergence characteristic for all techniques for (a) Planning case 2 and (b) Planning case 3 in 33-bus test network.

8.6.3.5   *Wilcoxon Signed Rank Test (WSRT)*

This statistical tool is applied in this study to analyze and compare the performances of different optimization techniques [31]. Here, the superiority of the proposed DRTO technique as compared to other techniques is established utilizing WSRT. The null hypothesis (H_0) and alternative hypothesis (H_1) is described below:

H_0: MD = 0 i.e. the median difference between the two samples are equal.

Table 8.12 WSRT based comparison between different algorithms.

Comparison	Rank +	Rank -	p values
Planning Case 2			
DRTO vs DPSO	389	76	0.0013
DRTO vs DTLBO	378	87	0.0028
Planning Case 3			
DRTO vs DPSO	385	80	0.0017
DRTO vs DTLBO	380	85	0.0024

H_1: MD ≠ 0 i.e. the median difference between the two samples are not equal.

The significance level is considered to be 0.05. Hence, the value of probability (p) greater than 0.05 represents a failure to reject the H_0, while the value of p less than 0.05 denotes rejection of H_0. To compare these algorithms on the basis of p-value, each algorithm is trial run 30 times to obtain 30 sets of 'F' values that are taken into account for data analysis. The proposed DRTO technique is chosen to be the control algorithm and Table 8.12 shows the obtained p-values for different cases of comparison. The table indicates that for planning case 2, the p-values are calculated as 0.0013 and 0.0028, respectively when the proposed algorithm is compared with DPSO and DTLBO. On the other hand, for planning case 3, the p-values are calculated as 0.0017 and 0.0024, respectively when the proposed DRTO algorithm is compared with DPSO and DTLBO. The obtained results clearly demonstrate that in every case, the obtained value of p is below the 0.05, which indicates null hypothesis rejection. Therefore, a significant difference is there in the performance of different algorithms and the proposed algorithm predominantly outperforms others.

8.7   Conclusion

In the viewpoint of recent energy market deregulation, this chapter proposed DRTO algorithm to carry out the distribution network planning with the objective of maximizing technical, economic and environmental benefits. A multi-stage model is formulated to divide the planning period into three equal stages to carry put the planning investments. The upgradation of substation and feeders' capacity, new point addition, reconfiguration and WTDG incorporation are taken as the planning alternatives. The time-wise variation of different consumers' load and the uncertainty in the WTDG power output are also taken into account. Moreover, logical indexes are developed to compute the techno-economic and environmental impacts.

The planning model formulated in this chapter was tested on 33-bus distribution network considering different planning cases to assist the distribution network engineers. Simulation results reveal that in comparison to planning case 1 (i.e. base case), the values of SVEI and EFI are improved and there is a reduction in the value of ECR in all the stages for planning case 2 and 3, which indicates that incorporation of these devices can improve system voltage, maximize economic benefit and reduce emission cost. However, the improvement of system voltage, maximization of economic benefits, and the reduction of emission are the highest in planning case 3, which establishes the superiority of utilizing reconfiguration in the presence of WTDG to increase the potential benefits of the network. A detailed environmental analysis demonstrates that compared to planning case 1, there is a 31.16% and 35.37% reduction of pollutant emission cost, respective in planning case 2 and 3, which demonstrates the environmental feasibility of planning case 3. Moreover, planning case 3 also results in the lowest values of both the power losses for all the stages. On the other hand, the results also reveal that the incorporation of these planning alternatives can delay or eliminate the need for upgrading substation and feeders' capacity. Further, in comparison with planning case 2, planning case 3 i.e. the implementation of WTDG in combination with reconfiguration can further delay the substation upgrading decisions. Moreover, in planning case 3, the number of feeders upgrading decisions that the distribution utilities need to undertake is the lowest. Furthermore, it is possible to incorporate more number of WTDG units with the utilization of reconfiguration scheme, which eventually decreases the grid dependency. In addition, two worst case scenarios are taken into account for voltage and power flow analysis and the results conclude that in planning case 3, the highest number of buses attains the permissible voltage limit and the power flow through most feeders kept in control. Hence, the analysis concludes that integrating WTDG in combination with reconfiguration is essential for effective distribution network planning. Furthermore, the proposed DRTO algorithm presents superior results regarding convergence characteristics, convergence time, solution quality and failure rate in comparison to other techniques. Moreover, Wilcoxon signed rank test (WSRT) is also conducted that establish the proposed algorithm as the most superior one.

In the situation of constantly increasing load, the multi-stage planning framework, as presented in this chapter, could serve as reliable references to the planning engineers for practical implementation.

References

1. Hemmati, R., Hooshmand, R.A., Taheri, N., 2015. "Distribution network expansion planning and DG placement in the presence of uncertainties". International Journal of Electrical Power and Energy Systems, 73:665–673.
2. Junior, B.R.P., Cossi, A.M., Mantovani, J.R.S., 2013. "Multiobjective Short-Term Planning of Electric Power Distribution Systems Using NSGA-II". Journal of Control, Automation and Electrical System. 24:286-299.
3. Zhang, X., Karady, G.G., Ariaratnam, S.T., 2014. "Optimal allocation of CHP based distributed generation on urban energy distribution networks". IEEE Transactions on Sustainable Energy. 5(1):246–251.
4. Hien, N.C., Mithulananthan, N., Bansal, R.C., 2013. "Location and sizing of distributed generation units for loadabilty enhancement in primary feeder". IEEE Systems Journal. 7(4):797–806.
5. Hincapie, I.R.A., Gallego, R.A., Mantovani, R.J.R.S., 2019. "A decomposition approach for integrated planning of primary and secondary distribution networks considering distributed generation". International Journal of Electrical Power and Energy Systems. 106:146-157.
6. Home-Ortiza, J. M., Melgar-Domingueza, O.D., Pourakbari-Kasmaei, M., Mantovani, J.R.S., 2019. "A stochastic mixed-integer convex programming model for long-term distribution system expansion planning considering greenhouse gas emission mitigation". International Journal of Electrical Power and Energy Systems. 108:86-95.
7. Gao, Y., Hu, X., Yang, W., Liang, H., Li, P., 2017. "Multi-Objective Bilevel Coordinated Planning of Distributed Generation and Distribution Network Frame Based on Multiscenario Technique Considering Timing Characteristics". IEEE Transactions on Sustainable Energy. 8(4):1415-1429.
8. Capitanescu, F., Ochoa, L.F., Margossian, H., Hatziargyriou, N. D., 2015. "Assessing the Potential of Network Reconfiguration to Improve Distributed Generation Hosting Capacity in Active Distribution Systems". IEEE Transactions on Power Systems. 30(1):346-356.
9. Zidan, A., Shaaban, M.F., El-Saadany, E.F., 2013. "Long-term multi-objective distribution network planning by DG allocation and feeders' reconfiguration". International Journal of Electrical Power System Research. 105:95–104.
10. Zangeneh, A., Jadida, S., Rahimi-Kian, A., 2009. Promotion strategy of clean technologies in distributed generation expansion planning. Renewable Energy. 34(12):2765-2773.
11. García, J.A.M., Mena, A.J.G., 2013. "Optimal distributed generation location and size using a modified teaching–learning based optimization

algorithm". International Journal of Electrical Power & Energy Systems. 50:65-75.

12. Barati, F., Jadid, S., Zanganeh, A., 2017. A new approach for DG planning at the viewpoint of the independent DG investor, a case study of Iran. International Transaction on Electrical Energy System. 27(6):e2319.

13. Ali, E.S., Abd-Elazim, S.M., Abdelaziz, A.Y., 2018. Optimal allocation and sizing of renewable distributed generation using ant lion optimization algorithm. Electrical Engineering. 100:99–109.

14. Kayalvizhi, S., Vinod Kumar, D.M., 2018. Optimal planning of active distribution networks with hybrid distributed energy resources using grid-based multi-objective harmony search algorithm. Applied Soft Computing. 67:387–398.

15. Shen, X., Shahidehpour, M., Zhu, S., Han, Y., Zheng, J., 2018. Multi-Stage Planning of Active Distribution Networks Considering the Co-Optimization of Operation Strategies. IEEE Transactions on Smart Grid. 9(2):1425-1433.

16. Koutsoukis, N.C., Siagkas, D.O., Georgilakis, P.S., Hatziargyriou, N.D., 2017. Online Reconfiguration of Active Distribution Networks for Maximum Integration of Distributed Generation. IEEE Transactions on Automation Science and Engineering. 14(2):437-448.

17. Li, R., Wang, W., Wu, X., Tang, F., Chen, Z., 2019. Cooperative planning model of renewable energy sources and energy storage units in active distribution systems: A bi-level model and Pareto analysis. Energy. 168:30–42.

18. Esmaeilian, H.R., Fadaeinedjad, R., 2015. Energy loss minimization in distribution systems utilizing an enhanced reconfiguration method integrating distributed generation. IEEE Systems Journal. 9(4):1430–1439.

19. Hamida, I.B., Salah, S.B., Msahli, F., Mimouni, M.F., 2018. Optimal network reconfiguration and renewable DG integration considering time sequence variation in load and DGs. Renewable Energy. 121:66–80.

20. Liu, K., Sheng, W., Liu, Y., Meng, X., Liu, Y., 2015. Optimal sitting and sizing of DGs in distribution system considering time sequence characteristics of loads and DGs. International Journal of Electrical Power and Energy Systems. 69:430–440.

21. Tolabi, H.B., Ali, M.H., Rizwan, M., 2015. Simultaneous reconfiguration, optimal placement of DSTATCOM, and photovoltaic array in a distribution system based on fuzzy-ACO approach. IEEE Transactions on Sustainable Energy. 6(1):210-218.

22. Gampa, S.R., Das, D., 2016. Optimum placement of shunt capacitors in a radial distribution system for substation power factor improvement using fuzzy GA method. International Journal of Electrical Power and Energy Systems. 77:314-326.

23. Gampa, S.R., Das, D., 2015. Optimum placement and sizing of DGs considering average hourly variations of load. International Journal of Electrical Power & Energy Systems. 66:25-40.

24. Tabares, A., Franco, J.F., Lavorato, M., Rider, M.J., 2016. Multistage Long-Term Expansion Planning of Electrical Distribution Systems Considering Multiple Alternatives. IEEE Transactions on Power Systems. 31(3):1900-1914.
25. Das, B., Mukherjee, V., Das, D., 2016. DG placement in radial distribution network by symbiotic organisms search algorithm for real power loss minimization. Applied Soft Computing. 49:920-936.
26. Rahmani-andebili, M., 2016. Distributed generation placement planning modeling feeder's failure rate and customer's load type. IEEE Transactions on Industrial Electronics. 63(3):1598–1606.
27. Labbi, Y., Attous, D.B., Gabbar, H.A., Mahdad, B., Zidan, A., 2016. A new rooted tree optimization algorithm for economic dispatch with valve-point effect. International Journal of Electrical Power and Energy Systems. 79:298–311.
28. Lotfipour, A., Afrakhte, H., 2016. A discrete Teaching–Learning-Based optimization algorithm to solve distribution system reconfiguration in presence of distributed generation. International Journal of Electrical Power and Energy Systems. 82:264–273.
29. Taher, S.A., Afsari, S.A., 2014. Optimal location and sizing of DSTATCOM in distribution systems by immune algorithm. International Journal of Electrical Power and Energy Systems. 60:34-44.
30. Kayal, P., Chanda, C.K., 2015. Optimal mix of solar and wind distributed generations considering performance improvement of electrical distribution network. Renewable Energy. 75:173-186.
31. Derrac, J., Garcia., S., Molina, D., Herrera, F., 2011. A practical tutorial on the use of nonparametric statistical tests as a methodology for comparing evolutionary and swarm intelligence algorithms. Swarm and Evolutionary Computation. 1:3-18.

9

User Interactive GUI for Integrated Design of PV Systems

SushmitaSarkar[1]*, K. UmaRao[1], Prema V[2], Anirudh Sharma C A[1], Jayanth Bhargav[1] and ShrikeshSheshaprasad[1]

*[1]Dept. of Electrical & Electronics Engineering, RV College of Engineering®,
Bengaluru, India*
*[2]Dept. of Electrical & Electronics Engineering, B.M.S. College of Engineering,
Bengaluru, India*

Abstract

All over the world, penetration of solar PV in electrical grids has seen a steep increase in the last decade. This includes both low power solar roof top installations and large-scale solar farms. Consciousness about climate change and encouraging government policies especially in developing countries have made investment in solar PV farms an attractive option for private investors. Further large amount of infertile land in tropical countries has also boosted installation of PV farms in such spaces. Two important decisions for any PV system are the space required for panel installation and the cost incurred. The cost depends on the type of installation. Popular models are standalone PV micro grid, large farms and that are grid-tied and those that are not tied to the grid. Based on the model, the required power electronics has to be designed. Currently, there are no open-source design tool to help the consumer/investor to design the specifications and ratings of different components. In this paper, a unique and a novel GUI is presented to design the entire solar PV systems. Further break-up of cost components, standards and configuration for inverters are also presented in the GUI.

Keywords: Economic gross evaluation, grid-tied PV system, PV power plants, PV system design, stand-alone PV system

*Corresponding author: sushmitasarkar@rvce.edu.in

Neeraj Priyadarshi, Akash Kumar Bhoi, Sanjeevikumar Padmanaban, S. Balamurugan and Jens Bo Holm-Nielsen (eds.) Intelligent Renewable Energy Systems, (243–266) © 2022 Scrivener Publishing LLC

9.1   Introduction

India's power generation sector is dominated by fossil fuels, especially coal, accounting for about three-fourths of the total electricity generated in 2017-18 [1–15]. With the fossil fuels depleting at a startling rate, renewable power resources prove to be a dependable option. Solar Power industry in India is rapidly developing with the country's installed capacity reaching 25.21GW as of December 31st, 2018 [1]. In 2015, the Government of India raised it's target of 20GW to 100GW of solar capacity by 2022 including 40 GW from rooftop solar [16–30]. Depleting fossil fuels has paved way for utilization of renewable forms of energy like solar, although solar is economically not very feasible, with government tax rebates and incentives it makes it more sustainable [3]. However, the technology to tap this solar energy on a large scale is yet to take off. The widely used solar modules have an efficiency of around 10-20% with the maximum efficiency achieved till now being around 22-24%. Advancements in solar panel technology, government policies and enhanced infrastructure has led to increased use of solar PVs in industries and in the domestic sector. A decision on the use of solar PV for power generation depends largely on the available irradiance in a location [31–45]. The irradiance data is available in the Meteonorm data base which is an open-source software that provides irradiance data for various locations for every month. This data can be used to depict the available generation for a given type of panel at the location of installation.

Extensive design tools for PV system design are available, which provide the user with design parameters for all kinds of solar installations. Engineers, architects and researchers use the existing PV system design tools in a myriad of applications. These system design tools provide a detailed description of the procedures and various models that are used for the purpose of PV installation. Most of these software systems import data from meteonorm database and from various other reliable sources. The design tools are also used for educational purposes since they contain a detailed contextual explanation of the technical aspects involved in designing of PV systems. These software systems (programs) and tools are either licensed and costly or do not have a detailed user-friendly interface (UI), giving the consumer or investor an idea of economic aspects along with the technical design specifications.

Various GUI models have been designed. Reference [4] gives an overview of the design of a GUI for a PV array monitoring system involving the monitoring of irradiance, short-circuit current, open circuit voltage, maximum power, fill factor, and also efficiency of PV array. Reference [5] discusses design of GUI for an optimal hybrid energy system and displays the optimal number of wind generators and number of panels with optimal cost installation and savings based on the customer input.

In this paper, the detailed design procedure for the design of different solar PV systems such as stand-alone micro grid, grid tied PV farm etc. are presented. Further, a novel GUI has been developed that provides the user an open source, user-friendly design tool to give an overview of both the technical and economic aspects for PV installation. With the in-house design, the specific lacuna in the existing PV system design tools has been addressed.

The organization of the paper is as follows: Section 9.2 discusses the various types of PV systems and the complete design equations that are developed for optimal sizing of the systems. In Section 9.3, economic aspects and evaluations related to the various components of PV systems, installation, operation, and maintenance are discussed. Section 9.4 of the paper provides the commercial standards in India that have to be followed for installation and testing of PV systems. In Section 9.5, the complete development of a User-Interactive Integrated Design Tool Front End is discussed. Section 9.6 presents the results for design of PV systems using the developed GUI.

9.2   PV System Design

A photovoltaic (PV) system mainly caters to three important applications: Stand-alone system, Grid-tied system and Large power plants. The design and calculations for these systems are discussed in the sections below.

9.2.1   Design of a Stand-Alone PV System

A standalone system is an off-grid system usually used in locations that have limited access to public utilities and public electricity. Environmentally conscious consumers and those interested in renewable energy or green power are also opting for standalone PV systems. During daylight hours, the PV (photo voltaic/renewable energy) system is fed to the load directly and the excess of energy is stored in the batteries and during cloudy days and during night, energy is supplied to the load from the battery [6]. Depending upon the solar array configuration, battery banks are installed with particular specifications [7, 8]. In a standalone system, a charge controller plays a vital role to prevent over-charging or over-discharging of the batteries. Although optional, it is widely used in most of the roof-top standalone systems. The total investment for a stand-alone system consists

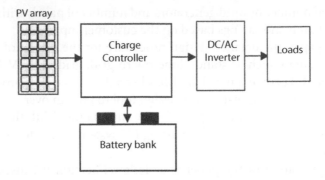

Figure 9.1 Block diagram of a stand-alone PV system.

of the Module Cost, Maintenance Cost, Battery and Inverter costs. Stand-alone systems have low maintenance but high initial and low upkeep cost with comfortable expansion of panels and batteries. Figure 9.1 depicts a block diagram of a typical stand-alone system.

In a stand-alone system, the user has to input the lumped load data, location, type of PV module and the consumption pattern. The design of a stand-alone system consists of the following calculations.

9.2.1.1   Panel Size Calculations

The panel sizing is expressed in terms of kW_{peak}. kW_{peak} represents the maximum power generated by the panel for 100% irradiance. kW_{peak} is calculated using (i) daily energy required (ii) energy required to provide storage for required number (No.) of days of autonomy.

kW_{peak1}, to meet daily demand is given in Equation (9.1a):

$$kW_{peak1} = \frac{\text{Total Demand in kWh}}{\text{Hours of sunlight in a day}} \qquad (9.1a)$$

kW_{peak2}, to meet energy demand for autonomy is:

$$kW_{peak2} = \frac{\text{Avg. daily demand in kWh} * \text{Days of autonomy}}{\text{No. of days of uninterrupted generation} * \text{Hours of sunlight in a day}}$$

$$(9.1b)$$

In equation 9.1(b), the numerator indicates the energy requirement for the required days of autonomy and the denominator accounts the no.

of sunshine hours available for the probabilistic availability of PV power. The total peak power kW_{peak}, is calculated by summing equation (9.1a) and (9.1b).

$$kW_{peak} = kW_{peak1} + kW_{peak2}$$

A safe average of 28 days in a month, which is true for most places in India, is considered for uninterrupted generation from the panel. During the uninterrupted generation period the panel produces enough power to charge the battery to be able to meet the average daily demand for the user defined days of autonomy.

9.2.1.2 Battery Sizing

In order to reduce the overall cost of the PV system it is important to reduce the investment on the battery. Therefore, appropriate battery sizing is important. A general thumb rule to size the battery as per the load demand. However, this is not necessary as the battery sizing can be reduced considering that the battery does not supply the load during hours of sunlight. Also, days of autonomy are met taking into consideration the probabilistic loss of generation in a given month. The battery sizing is thus dictated by the kW_{peak} rating of the panel, number of hours of sunlight available, days of autonomy specified by the consumer and the consumer load usage pattern. This usage pattern majorly affects the storage. For instance, if most of the load is used during non-sunlight hours the storage required is very high compared to a scenario in which most of the load is used during peak sun hours.

Depth of discharge (DoD): The depth of discharge indicates the percentage of the battery that has been discharged relative to the overall capacity of the battery [9]. It is not advisable to discharge the battery completely to ensure longevity of the battery. A standard DoD is around 90% of the battery capacity. In equation (9.2), the sizing of battery is done based on average hours of sunlight.

$$kWh \text{ Battery} = kW_{peak} \times \text{Hours of Sunlight - Load Units during}$$
$$\text{Hours of Sunlight} \qquad (9.2)$$

$$\text{Battery Ah} = (kWh \text{ Battery} \times 1000) / (\text{Battery Voltage} \times \text{Percentage}$$
$$\text{Depth of Discharge}) \qquad (9.3)$$

The sizing can be increased by 20% to account for days of lesser sunlight.

9.2.1.3   Inverter Design

Design of inverter plays a key role in the solar PV system in terms of performance and cost. The rating of the inverter must be carefully chosen such that the input rating is 25–30% more than kW_{peak}. For a stand-alone system the operating voltage of the inverter need to be more than the nominal voltage of the battery. For grid-tied systems the input rating needs to be equal to the rating of the PV array. The inverter cost is included in the Electrical Power Conditioning System Cost (EPC) as mentioned in Table 9.1. A detailed market survey is conducted to study different types of inverters and is classified as Level-0 to Level-3 as mentioned in Table 9.2.

Table 9.1 Cost estimate of PV system.

Estimate breakdown	Components	Percentage of total cost
Electrical Power Conditioning System Cost (EPC)	Grid Tie Inverter, Array Junctionboxes, Main Junction box, Array/subJunction box, PVC insulated copper cables.	23%
Testing, Erection and Commissioning cost (TEC)	Solar PV module roof topmounting structure.	10%
Annual Maintenance Charges (AMC)	Panel cleaning, Retro Commissioning, Upkeep of monitoring systems, Site maintenance, Critical and non-critical reactive repair, Warranty enforcement	10%
Other Infrastructure cost	AC Distribution unit and DC Distribution unit with switch gears, Earthing kit, Bidirectional meter, Lightning Arrestor, Installation Accessories for power plants, Processing and Application fee.	17%
Module Cost	Cost of the Solar PV module(Mono crystalline/poly crystalline/thin film panel)	40%

Table 9.2 Market survey data for PV system design.

Design component	Description/value	
Area of Panel	8m² per kW for Large Power plants	
	6m² per kW for Stand-alone and Grid-tied systems	
Battery Cost	INR 6.7 per Watt Hour	
Maximum power per string	100kW for large power plants	
Maximum operating current for battery charging	40A for stand-alone systems	
Inverter Configurations for Large Power Plants	Level	No. of Inverters
	Level 0 - Centralized Inverter	1
	Level 1 - String Inverter	2
	Level 2 - String Inverter	5
	Level 3 - String Inverter	10

9.2.1.4   Loss of Load

PV generation varies throughout the year owing to the intermittent nature of solar radiation. Therefore, there is a possibility that the stand-alone system may not be capable of delivering the complete load in all the seasons of the year. If this has to be achieved, it will increase the energy storage cost. Hence, the loss of energy in meeting the load demand is quantified as, the excess of load over generation as a percentage of the load demand, all expressed in electrical units (kWh) defined as the loss of load.

$$\text{Loss of Load} = (\text{Load Demand in Units - Generation in Units}) / (\text{Load Demand in Units}) \times 100 \tag{9.4}$$

9.2.1.5   Average Daily Units Generated

Based on the available solar energy and irradiance, power generated is calculated accounting for the type of solar cells and hours of sunlight. A plot of average units generated is displayed for different months in a year. Equation (9.5) gives the power generated by the PV panel.

$$\text{Power Generated} = \text{Panel Efficiency} \times \text{Irradiance}$$
$$\times \text{Hours of Sunlight} \times \text{Area of Panel} \qquad (9.5)$$

9.2.2 Design of a Grid-Tied PV System

In a grid-connected system the solar panels are connected to the local electricity grid which feeds energy back to the utility grid. Depending on the sunlight and the electrical demand, electricity flows back and forth from the grid. A grid tied system mainly consists of two components: Inverters and Power Meter [10]. A grid-tied inverter converts DC into sinusoidal AC of standard voltage and frequency. Solar modules usually generate excess power than what is actually required, this excess power is evacuated to the grid with net metering [11]. Usually in this system, bidirectional meters are utilized to measure the energy consumed and to measure the solar-powered electrical energy evacuated to the grid. The grid tied PV system is more efficient and economical without the usage of batteries, since maintaining batteries is an arduous task. It is also a simpler method of PV set-up available and is hence, used frequently. As per recent regulations of Indian Power Sector, installations of batteries in grid-tied PV systems are prohibited. Figure 9.2 depicts a grid-tied PV system.

For a grid tied system the user has an option to specify either the area available for PV panel installation or the power rating (kW_{peak}) of the PV panel which can be installed. When either of them is specified, the other components are designed. Since a non-storage grid tied system is considered battery is not required. The average daily units generated are the same

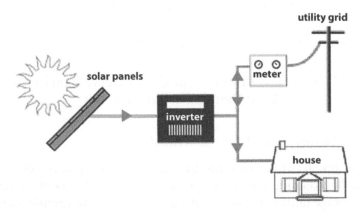

Figure 9.2 Schematic diagram of a grid-tied PV system.

as in a stand-alone system and is given by equation (9.5). The standard relationship between kW_{peak} rating and Area required by the PV panels is listed in Table 9.2.

9.2.3   Design of a Large Scale Power Plant

A large-scale PV system mainly consists of solar module arrays, grid tied inverters which can be either centralized or string type, transformers and utility or a grid system consisting of various loads. The power plants can have a single centralized inverter or multiple strings with each string having an inverter [11]. The latter ensures reliability as, if one of the many string inverters breakdown the complete power is not lost. This also has an economic advantage on the power plant in case of inverter failures. The loads can be of any type varying from an infinite bus to loads for various households in a particular area. One of the main challenges while designing a large-scale PV system is optimizing balance between performance and cost. Similar to a grid-tied network, this system is used for higher generational capacity and requires high capital investment. Figure 9.3 depicts a block diagram of a large solar power plant.

In case of large power plants, the design constraints are majorly the area available for the plant or the total cost that a producer can invest on the plant. By market survey, it is found that there are various designs for power plants which are mainly dictated by the investment cost. With greater investment the plant can accommodate a greater number of inverters and hence, is more reliable. Table 9.3 summarizes the various inverter configurations of large power plants. With increasing levels of configurations, the cost of the plant increases relatively but not linearly. These incremental percentage costs are inculcated in the gross economic evaluations performed in the GUI.

Table 9.3 Module cost estimate.

Type of Solar cell	Module cost per watt (in INR)
Monocrystalline	30
Polycrystalline	25
Thin Film	20

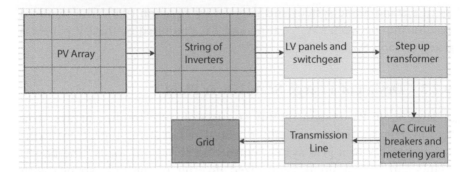

Figure 9.3 Block diagram of a large PV system.

9.3   Economic Considerations

Economic consideration for a system is done with the aid of market surveys of various companies concerning installations across India. The data gathered from these market surveys are shown in Table 9.1 which gives the total cost breakdown of installing a solar PV system. The main challenge while designing a large-scale PV system is optimizing balance between performance and cost. Module cost constitutes about 40% of the total cost breakdown. The module cost based on the type of solar cells is given in Table 9.3. The module cost is common for all the three systems.

The survey also gives an overview of the data of existing panels, which is given by Table 9.4. The market survey data are collected as of February 2019.

9.4   PV System Standards

The installations for all the three applications are done in norm with the standards provided in Table 9.4. Various IEEE and IEC standards are followed for items like Solar PV modules, Grid-tied inverters, cables, earthing, junction boxes, switches and circuit breakers [12–14]. A description for each of these items and the standards to be followed are also mentioned.

9.5   Design of GUI

To cater to those who opt installation of solar modules, a user-friendly open-source Graphical User Interface (GUI) using MATLAB has been

Table 9.4 Standards for PV installations.

Item	Standard description	Standard number
Solar PV modules	a) Crystalline Silicon Terrestrial PV modules.	IEC 61215 / IS 14286
	Thin film terrestrial PV modules.	IEC 61646
	b) Solar PV module safety qualification requirements	IEC 61730 (P1-P2)
	c) PV modules to be used in a highly corrosive atmosphere (Coastal area etc.,) must qualify salt mist corrosion testing.	IEC 61701 / IS 61701
Grid Tied Inverters	a) Environmental Testing	IEC 60068-2 (1,2,14,30) or Equivalent BIS Standard
	b) Efficiency Measurements	IEC 61683
	c) Product Safety standard	IEC 62109 -1 (2010) / IEC 62109-2 (2011)
	d) Grid Connectivity utility interface	IEC 61727: 2004 (as per IEEE 519 Specifications)
	e) Test procedure for islanding prevention measures for utility/ interconnected PV inverters	IEC 62116 or IEEE 1547 and IEEE 1547.1
	f) Electromagnetic compatibility & Electromagnetic Interference	IEC 61000-6-1:2007 IEC 61000-6-3:2007 IEC 61000-3-2:2006 IEC 61000-3-3:2006
	g) Ingress Protection	IP 54 (for outdoor) / IP 21 (for indoor)as per IEC 529

(Continued)

Table 9.4 Standards for PV installations. (*Continued*)

Item	Standard description	Standard number
Cables	General Test and Measuring Method PVC insulated cables for working voltage and UV resistant for outdoor installation for AC cables.	IEC 60227 / IS 694 / IEC 60502 / IS 1554 (Part I & II)
Earthing	Grounding	IS 3043: 1986
Switches/Circuit Breakers/ Connectors	General Requirements connectors safety A.C./D.C.	IEC 60947 part I,II,III / IS 60947 part I,II,III / EN 50521
Junction Boxes/ Enclosures for charge controllers/ Luminaries	General Requirements	IP 65 (for outdoor) IP 21 (for indoor) As per IEC 529

developed. This GUI gives the user an assessment of the gross economic evaluation with total investment cost, annual maintenance charges, loss of load, battery sizing and inverter specifications for various applications like stand alone, grid-tie and large power plants, considering different panel specifications. This section describes the complete design of the Graphical User interface. The Graphical User Interface (GUI) using MATLAB has been designed for three applications namely stand alone, grid-tie and large solar power plants. The GUI accepts user inputs like connected load, load usage pattern, area available for roof-top installations or the kW_{peak} rating of the solar system required by the user. The three options available in the GUI for the choice of panel along with their efficiencies are tabulated in Table 9.5.

The GUI provides economic evaluations and the generation related information to the user. To keep the economic estimates realistic, a detailed study of Bill of Materials (BoM) has been done by collecting data from market surveys of companies concerning PV installations across India. From the above study, the detailed breakdown was condensed to five main categories as shown in Table 9.1. Figure 9.4 depicts a flowchart for the GUI design.

Table 9.5 Panel efficiencies.

Type of solar cell	Efficiency
Monocrystalline	18%
Polycrystalline	14%
Thin Film	10%

9.6   Results

9.6.1   Design of a Stand-Alone System Using GUI

The GUI was used to design a stand-alone system by considering the sample load data of a household consumer. The data of load consumption is tabulated in Table 9.6.

Table 9.7 contains the data of lumped loads. Here Fans, and Lights are considered as one type of load. Refrigerator, Air Conditioners, and Heaters are considered as one load type. The average hours of usage per day is tabulated.

The load consumption pattern for the household for a stand-alone system is given in Table 9.8.

Figure 9.5 depicts a GUI for a stand-alone system considering the lumped load data and the load consumption pattern mentioned above.

The data is of a standard household and contains different appliances, their average hours of usage and their average watt rating. Using this data, we can categorize the loads into main categories by lumping the loads. By studying the usage pattern, we can develop the consumption pattern. The consumption pattern is a very important input for optimizing the energy storage capacity of the standalone system.

The GUI in Figure 9.5 depicts the design results and economic evaluations of a Stand Alone PV system for the sample load database input. For the given load database and 3 days of autonomy of battery, a 3.2 kW$_{peak}$ PV rating, 58.94 Ah Battery with a Voltage of 48V is given as the design output. Additionally, required rooftop area of around 19.5 sq. meters and total investment of INR 3,93,141.5 is also displayed to the user. The cost-breakdown is clearly displayed along with the available PV generation and Load Demand plots. The GUI also displays the Loss of Load for the given demand, type of PV panel and the location of installation. Thus, the design tool gives comprehensive and integrated design information to the user.

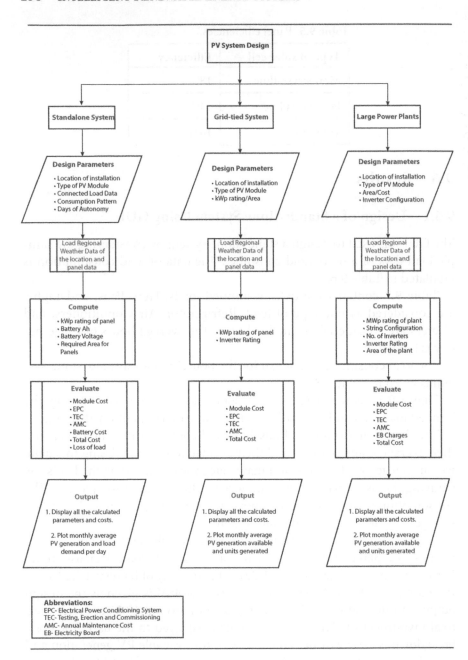

Figure 9.4 Flowchart for GUI design.

Table 9.6 Load description of a household consumer.

Category	Appliances	Average hours of usage per day	Average power rating (in watts)
General	Lighting	12	38
Entertainment	Radio	6	195
	CD Player		
	TV		
	DVD/VCR		
	Computer		
White Appliances	Washing Machine	1	2150
	Refrigerator	24	80
	Electric Oven	0.25	1248
	Toaster	0.1	1246
Heating/ Cooling	Water Heater	2	3000
	Fans	12	37
	Air Conditioners	2	1817

9.6.2 GUI for a Grid-Tied System

The GUI for a grid-tied system was used to design considering a sample load data. For instance, with the utility sanctioned load of 5kW and an area of 60m^2 the GUI is designed as shown in Figure 9.6.

Table 9.7 Lumped load data for a household.

Watt rating of lumped load	Hours of usage
75	12
195	6
5150	1
80	24

Table 9.8 Load consumption pattern.

Hours in a day	Average connected load in watts
00:00 – 03:59	155
04:00 – 07:59	842.5
08:00 – 11:59	80
12:00 – 15:59	177.5
16:00 – 19:59	875
20:00 – 23:59	155

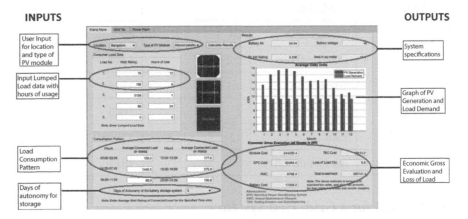

Figure 9.5 GUI front end for the design of a standalone PV system using sample household load database.

The GUI is Figure 9.6 gives the design of a Grid-Tied PV system for a building located at Bangalore with Monocrystalline PV panels. The tool takes into account the Utility Sanctioned load of the building to give the Inverter Specifications for tying the PV system to grid. The design output is for an available rooftop area of 8 sq. meters and a 5kW sanctioned load building. For the given input, a Single Phase 50 Hz, 230 V inverter is displayed as the Inverter specification. A kWp rating of 7.5kW along with a total investment of INR 8,66,250 and their breakdown costs are displayed. The GUI also gives the plots of available solar energy in every month (average) and the number of units that the rooftop PV system will generate in

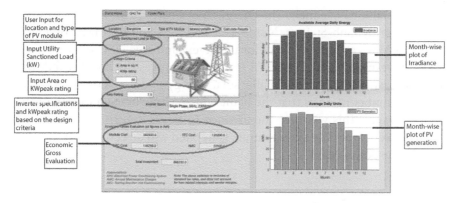

Figure 9.6 GUI front end for design of a grid-tied PV system for a rooftop area of 8m².

each month of the year (average) at the location of installation. This will help the customer to assess the revenue from the Grid-Tied system.

9.6.3   GUI for a Large PV Plant

The GUI for a large power plant was used to design considering a sample data with a large area and a choice for the inverter configuration. For instance, the area considered here is 5000m², and a Level 2 String inverter system. The GUI is as shown in Figure 9.7.

The GUI in Figure 9.7 gives the design of a Large PV Power Plant. The design tool is tested for an available land area of 8000 sq. meters. The design is for a Centralised Inverter configuration system at Bangalore with

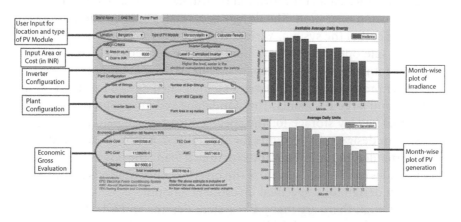

Figure 9.7 GUI front end for design of a PV power plant for an available land area of 8000m².

Monocrystalline PV panels. The Design Tool clearly gives the Plant configuration: String, Sub-Strings, Number of Inverters and Ratings along with
the Plant MW capacity of 1MW for the given land area. The tool also gives
a total investment of INR 5,00,78,160 and also gives the cost breakdown.
The tool gives the plots of available solar energy in every month (average)
and the number of units that the plant will generate in each month of the
year (average). This will help the investor to assess Return on Investment
in the power plant. The average units generated will directly affect the revenue of the power plant.

9.7   Discussions

The results obtained above were verified with leading Solar PV installation
companies and service providers in Karnataka State, India. All the figures
in costs and economic evaluation fields of the design tool are obtained
from market survey as of February 2019. The costs and design formulae
can be modified at the back end of the GUI as per user requirements. As
of February 2019, the design tool gives nearly accurate Electric System
Design Parameters and Economic Evaluations in agreement with Market
Standards.

9.8   Conclusion and Future Scope

The design of PV systems involves estimation of: PV capacity, battery
capacity, weather data at the location of installation, and cost estimates for
installation and operation. The design necessitates optimization to reduce
the overall cost of the system. Various design constraints like inverter specifications, safe operating current limits, power converter efficiencies, and
panel operating factor, play a major role in arriving at an optimal design.
This paper proposes a GUI that gives an integrated design for stand-alone,
grid-tied and large PV plants. The standalone system design encompasses
an optimal battery storage for the specified load usage pattern. The grid-
tied system design tool accounts for the utility sanctioned load and gives
the inverter design for the specific sanctioned load. The power plant design
tool provides options to customize the inverter configurations and gives an
exhaustive design for a specified investment amount.

Even though there are many PV system designs and GUIs available in
the market, the proposed GUI in this paper has some unique features,
which set in apart from typical GUIs. Most of the GUI tools available in

the market for PV system design are designed to be used by architects, engineers, and researchers. They are commercial in nature and are not very consumer friendly. The GUI proposed in this paper addresses both technical and financial aspects of PV system installations. It gives all possible PV system configurations from a simple rooftop to a large power plant along with economic aspects. It considers consumer inputs such as available rooftop/land area, type of panel, and the amount of money which a consumer is willing to invest in a power plant. This makes this tool unique and novel.

The future scope of this design tool would be to integrate Global Weather Data at specified latitudes/longitudes for designing the PV system at any user-defined location. Furthermore, the power plant design tool can incorporate financial aspects related to investments and returns. A Build-Operate-Maintain-Transfer (BOMT) model design, which gives detailed financial evaluations for investors of large-scale PV plants, can be incorporated.

9.9   Acknowledgement

We thank GTSS Infrastructure Private Limited (formerly GT Solar Solutions) and Spectrum Consultants for their valuable inputs on commercial scale Stand-alone PV System and Power Plant design, installation and economic evaluations. All the economic gross evaluations in the design tool are obtained from Government Sanctioned Bill of Materials and Quotations.

References

1. "Physical Progress (Achievements)", *Ministry of New & Renewable Energy*, Retrieved July 18, 2018.
2. "Government looking at 100,000 MW Solar Power by 2022", *IANS Business Standard*, New Delhi, November 17, 2014.
3. Can Wan, Jian Zhao, Yonghua Song, Zhao Xu, Jin Lin and Zechun Hu, "Photovoltaic and Solar Power Forecasting for Smart Grid Energy Management," CSEE Journal of Power and Energy Systems, 1, no. 4(2015): 38-46. https://doi.org/10.17775/CSEEJPES.2015.00046.
4. A. Rivai and N. A. Rahim, "GUI for Photovoltaic (PV) Array Monitoring System," *3rd IET International Conference on Clean Energy and Technology (CEAT) 2014*, Kuching, (2014): 1-5, doi: 10.1049/cp.2014.1484.

5. A. S. Ramya, N. Periyasamy, A. Vidhya, S. Sundrapandian and P. Raja, "Design and development of a GUI for an optimal hybrid energy system," *2014 Eighteenth National Power Systems Conference (NPSC)*, Guwahati, (2014): 1-6, doi: 10.1109/NPSC.2014.7103836.

6. Report IEA-PVPS T3-09: 2002, "Use of appliances in Stand Alone PV supply systems: Problems and Solutions".

7. M. Jariso, B. Khan, D. Tesfaye and J. Singh, "Modeling and Designing of Stand-alone Photovoltaic System: CaseStudy: Addis Boder Health Center South West Ethiopia," *2017 International conference of Electronics, Communication and Aerospace Technology (ICECA)*, Coimbatore, (2017): 168-173, doi: 10.1109/ICECA.2017.8203665.

8. Pal, Abhik Milan, Subhra Das, and N.B. Raju, "Designing of a Standalone Photovoltaic System for a Residential Building in Gurgaon, India, *Sustainable Energy* 3, no. 1 (2015): 14-24.

9. Chetan Singh Solanki, *Solar Photovoltaics Fundamentals, Technologies and Applications*, New Delhi, India: PHI Learning Private Limited, 2011.

10. M. H. Abbasi, A. Al-Ohaly, Y. Khan and H. M. Hasainen, "Design Phases for Grid Connected PV System," *2014 International Conference on Renewable Energy Research and Application (ICRERA)*, Milwaukee, WI, (2014): 684-688, doi: 10.1109/ICRERA.2014.7016473.

11. K. Dubey and M. T. Shah, "Design and Simulation of Solar PV System," *2016 International Conference on Automatic Control and Dynamic Optimization Techniques (ICACDOT)*, Pune, (2016): 568-573, doi: 10.1109/ICACDOT.2016.7877649.

12. Priyadarshi.; N;, Padmanaban, S.; Maroti, P.K.; Sharma. A.; An Extensive Practical Investigation of FPSO-Based MPPT for Grid Integrated PV System Under Variable Operating Conditions With Anti-Islanding Protection. IEEE System Journal, 2018, 13:1861-1871.

13. Priyadarshi, N.; Padmanaban, S.; Bhaskar, M.S.; Blaabjerg, F.; Sharma, A.; A Fuzzy SVPWM Based Inverter Control Realization of Grid Integrated PV-Wind System with FPSO MPPT Algorithm for a Grid-Connected PV/Wind Power Generation System: Hardware Implementation. IET Electric Power Appl., 2018, 12:962-971.

14. Priyadarshi, N.; Kumar, V.; Yadav, K.; Vardia, M.; An Experimental Study on Zeta buck-boost converter for Application in PV system. Handbook of distributed generation, Springer, DOI 10.1007/978-3-319-51343-0_13

15. Priyadarshi N.; Sharma A.K.; Priyam S.; An Experimental Realization of Grid-Connected PV System with MPPT Using dSPACE DS 1104 Control Board. Advances in Smart Grid and Renewable Energy. Lecture Notes in Electrical Engineering, Springer, Singapore 2018, 435.

16. Priyadarshi N.; Sharma A.K.; Priyam S.; Practical Realization of an Improved Photovoltaic Grid Integration with MPPT. International Journal of Renewable Energy Research 2017, 7:1180-1891.

17. Priyadarshi N.; Sharma A.K.; Azam F.; A Hybrid Firefly-Asymmetrical Fuzzy Logic Controller based MPPT for PV-Wind-Fuel Grid Integration. International Journal of Renewable Energy Research 2017, 7: 1546-1560.

18. Priyadarshi, N.; Anand, A.; Sharma, A.K.; Azam, F.; Singh, V.K.; Sinha, R. K.; An Experimental Implementation and Testing of GA based Maximum Power Point Tracking for PV System under Varying Ambient Conditions Using dSPACE DS 1104 Controller. International Journal of Renewable Energy Research, 2017, 7:255-265.

19. Priyadarshi, N.; Padmanaban S.; Mihet-Popa L.; Blaabjerg, F.; Azam F.; Maximum Power Point Tracking for Brushless DC Motor-Driven Photovoltaic Pumping Systems Using a Hybrid ANFIS-FLOWER Pollination Optimization Algorithm. MDPI Energies 2018, 11:1-16.

20. Priyadarshi, N.; Azam, F.; Bhoi, A.K.; Alam, S.; An Artificial Fuzzy Logic Intelligent Controller Based MPPT for PV Grid Utility. Lecture Notes in Networks and Systems 46, https://doi.org/10.1007/978-981-13-1217-5_88.

21. Padmanaban, S.; Priyadarshi, N.; Holm-Nielsen, J. B.; Bhaskar, M. S.; Azam, F.; Sharma, A.K.; A Novel Modified Sine-Cosine Optimized MPPT Algorithm for Grid Integrated PV System under Real Operating Conditions. IEEE Access, 2019, 7:10467-10477.

22. Padmanaban, S.; Priyadarshi, N.; Holm-Nielsen, J. B.; Bhaskar, M. S.; Hossain, E.; Azam, F.; A Hybrid Photovoltaic-Fuel Cell for Grid Integration With Jaya-Based Maximum Power Point Tracking: Experimental Performance Evaluation. IEEE Access, 2019, 7:82978-82990.

23. Priyadarshi, N.; Padmanaban, N.; Holm-Nielsen, J. B.; Blaabjerg, F.; Bhaskar, M.S.; An Experimental Estimation of Hybrid ANFIS–PSO-Based MPPT for PV Grid Integration Under Fluctuating Sun Irradiance. in IEEE Systems Journal. 2020, 14:1218-1229.

24. Priyadarshi, N.; Padmanaban, N.; Bhaskar, M. S.; Blaabjerg, F.; Holm-Nielsen, J. B.; Azam, F.; Sharma, A.K.; A Hybrid Photovoltaic-Fuel Cell-Based Single-Stage Grid Integration With Lyapunov Control Scheme. IEEE Systems Journal, 2020, 14: 3334-3342.

25. Priyadarshi, N.; Bhaskar, M. S.; Padmanaban, N.; Blaabjerg, F.; Azam, F.; New CUK–SEPIC converter based photovoltaic power system with hybrid GSA–PSO algorithm employing MPPT for water pumping applications. IET Power Electronics. 2020, 13:2824 – 2830.

26. Priyadarshi, N.; Padmanaban, N.; Holm-Nielsen, J. B.; Bhaskar, M.S.; Azam, F.; Internet of things augmented a novel PSO-employed modified zeta converter-based photovoltaic maximum power tracking system: hardware realisation. IET Power Electronics. 2020, 13:2775 – 2781.

27. Kamalapathi, K., Priyadarshi, N., Padmanaban, S., Holm-Nielsen, J.B., Azam, F., Umayal, C., Ramachandaramurthy, V.K. A Hybrid Moth-Flame Fuzzy Logic Controller Based Integrated Cuk Converter Fed Brushless DC Motor for Power Factor Correction. MDPI Electronics, 2018, 7: 288.

28. Priyadarshi, N., Padmanaban, S., Lonel, D., Mihet-Popa, L., Azam, F. Hybrid PV-Wind, Micro-Grid Development Using Quasi-Z-Source Inverter Modeling and Control—Experimental Investigation. MDPI Energies, 2018, 11:2277.

29. Priyadarshi, N.; Ramachandaramurthy, V, K.; Padmanaban, S.; Azam, A.; An Ant Colony Optimized MPPT for Standalone Hybrid PV-Wind Power System with Single Cuk Converter. MDPI Energies, 2019, 12: 167.

30. Azam, F.; Yadav, S.K.; Priyadarshi, N.; Padmanaban, S.; and Bansal, R.C.; A Comprehensive Review of Authentication Schemes in Vehicular Ad-Hoc Network, IEEE Access, 2021, 9:31309-31321, 2021, doi: 10.1109/ACCESS.2021.3060046.

31. Priyadarshi, N.; Sharma, A.K.; Bhoi, A. K.; Ahmad, S. N.; Azam, F.; Priyam, S.; A Practical performance verification of AFLC based MPPT for standalone PV power system under varying weather condition, International Journal of Engineering & Technology, 2018, 7:338-343.

32. Azam F.; Priyadarshi N.; Nagar H.; Kumar S.; Bhoi A.K.; An Overview of Solar-Powered Electric Vehicle Charging in Vehicular Adhoc Network. in: Electric Vehicles. Green Energy and Technology. Springer, Singapore. https://doi.org/10.1007/978-981-15-9251-5_5.

33. Azam, F.; Kumar, S.; Yadav, K.P.; Priyadarshi N.; Padmanaban, S.; An Outline of the Security Challenges in VANET, in Proc. of IEEE UPCON 2020, Nov, 2020.

34. Priyadarshi, N.; Azam, F.; Bhoi, A.K.; Sharma, A.K.; A Multilevel Inverter-Controlled Photovoltaic Generation. in Advances in Greener Energy Technologies. Springer, Singapore. 2020 https://doi.org/10.1007/978-981-15-4246-6_8.

35. Priyadarshi, N.; Azam, F.; Bhoi, A.K.; Sharma, A.K.; Dynamic Operation of Grid-Connected Photovoltaic Power System. in Advances in Greener Energy Technologies. Springer, Singapore. 2020 https://doi.org/10.1007/978-981-15-4246-6_13.

36. Priyadarshi, N.; Azam, F.; Bhoi, A.K.; Sharma, A.K.; A Proton Exchange Membrane-Based Fuel Cell Integrated Power System. in Advances in Greener Energy Technologies. Springer, Singapore. 2020 https://doi.org/10.1007/978-981-15-4246-6_18.

37. Priyadarshi, N.; Azam, F.; Bhoi, A.K.; Sharma, A.K.; A Closed-Loop Control of Fixed Pattern Rectifier for Renewable Energy Applications. in Advances in Greener Energy Technologies. Springer, Singapore. 2020 https://doi.org/10.1007/978-981-15-4246-6_25.

38. Priyadarshi, N.; Azam, F.; Bhoi, A.K.; Sharma, A.K.; A Four-Switch-Type Converter Fed Improved Photovoltaic Power System. in Advances in Greener Energy Technologies. Springer, Singapore. 2020 https://doi.org/10.1007/978-981-15-4246-6_29.

39. Vardia, M.; Priyadarshi, N.; Ali, I.; Azam, F.; Bhoi, A.K.; Maximum Power Point Tracking for Wind Energy Conversion System. in Advances in Greener

Energy Technologies. Springer, Singapore. 2020 https://doi.org/10.1007/978-981-15-4246-6_36.

40. Vardia, M.; Priyadarshi, N.; Ali, I.; Azam, F.; Bhoi, A.K.; Design of Wind Energy Conversion System Under Different Fault Conditions. in Advances in Greener Energy Technologies. Springer, Singapore. 2020 https://doi.org/10.1007/978-981-15-4246-6_41.

41. Choudhary, T.; Priyadarshi, N.; Kuma,r P.; Azam, F.; Bhoi A.K. (2020) A Fuzzy Logic Control Based Vibration Control System for Renewable Application. in Advances in Greener Energy Technologies. Springer, Singapore. 2020 https://doi.org/10.1007/978-981-15-4246-6_38.

42. Priyadarshi, N.; Azam F.; Solanki, S. S.; Sharma, A.K.; Bhoi, A.K.; Almakhles, D.; A Bio-Inspired Chicken Swarm Optimization-Based Fuel Cell System for Electric Vehicle Applications. in Bio-inspired Neurocomputing. Studies in Computational Intelligence, vol 903. Springer, Singapore. 2021 https://doi.org/10.1007/978-981-15-5495-7_1.

43. John H. Wohlgemuth, "Standards for PV Modules and Components – Recent Developments and Challenges,"*Proceedings of 27ᵗʰ European Photovoltaic Solar Energy Conference*, Frankfurt, Germany, (2012): 2976-2980, https://www.osti.gov/servlets/purl/1063692.

44. "Solar America Board for codes and Standards", 2011 - 2015 University of Central Florida.

45. "PV Codes and Standards Gap Issues", Prepared by Sherwood Associates, Inc., Solar ABCs, January 23, 2015.

10

Situational Awareness of Micro-Grid Using Micro-PMU and Learning Vector Quantization Algorithm

Kunjabihari Swain and Murthy Cherukuri*

Dept. of Electrical and Electronics Engineering, National Institute of Science and Technology, Berhampur, India

Abstract

The integration of distributed energy sources (DES) into the distribution grid of today's power system improves the generation capacity of the existing system to fulfill modern application requirements. The renewable energy sources are the main components of distribution grid. These renewable sources enable the system to operate parallelly along with the main grid or in an islanding mode in case of a grid faults. The penetration of DES raises the power and voltage level to fulfill the peak demand of the distribution grid and improves the voltage profile of the grid. However, DES penetration causes the steady-state voltage and current disturbances and power quality problems because of the harmonic disturbances induced by the DES to the grid, which necessitates the situational awareness (SA) of distribution grid and small energy generating micro-grids for timely decision making and protection, by the power system engineers. Real-time monitoring is required for adequate situational awareness of micro-grid. Phasor measurement units (PMUs) are instrumental in tracking the real-time behavior of the transmission line. Many researchers were focused on wide-area monitoring, control and protection of transmission lines for improving situational awareness of the transmission system. However, the micro-grid is still lacking in that respect. Due to its diverse environment and different level of measurement, distribution grid or micro-grid needs more precise and accurate measurement than that of the transmission line. It needs higher reporting, negligible instrumental error and reduced effect of white noise. Hence the special type of PMU called micro PMU can provide real-time monitoring in a micro-grid for efficient

Corresponding author: chmurthy2007@gmail.com

Neeraj Priyadarshi, Akash Kumar Bhoi, Sanjeevikumar Padmanaban, S. Balamurugan and Jens Bo Holm-Nielsen (eds.) Intelligent Renewable Energy Systems, (267–286) © 2022 Scrivener Publishing LLC

situational awareness. Situational awareness in a micro-grid is achieved by gathering the information, analyzing it to facilitate efficient and effective decision making in the critical emergency situation. It is mainly categorized into three parts.

This chapter presents a micro-grid situational awareness using the real-time measurements of a micro-grid using a National Instrument based micro-PMU interfaced with virtual instrumentation tool. The perception of fault is achieved by recognizing the deviations in voltage and frequency obtained from micro-PMU and thereby detect if any fault occurs in the micro-grid. The comprehension of the fault is accomplished by using the learning vector quantization (LVQ) algorithm for analyzing the information and understanding the type of fault. Based on the comprehension of the fault, the decision made to project the protective action need to be taken by sending the triggering signal to circuit breaker.

Keywords: Situational awareness, micro-grid, phasor measurement unit, learning vector quantization algorithm, micro-PMU, fast Fourier transform

10.1   Introduction

The integration of distributed energy sources (DES) into the distribution grid of today's power system improves the generation capacity of the existing system to fulfill modern application requirements [1–17]. The renewable energy sources are the main components of distribution grid. These renewable sources enable the system to operate parallelly along with the main grid or in an islanding mode in case of a grid faults [18–32]. The penetration of DES raises the power and voltage level to fulfill the peak demand of the distribution grid and improves the voltage profile of the grid. However, DES penetration causes the steady-state voltage and current disturbances and power quality problems because of the harmonic disturbances induced by the DES to the grid, which necessitates the situational awareness (SA) of distribution grid and small energy generating micro-grids for timely decision making and protection, by the power system engineers. Real-time monitoring is required for adequate situational awareness of micro-grid [33–50]. Phasor measurement units (PMUs) are instrumental in tracking the real-time behavior of the transmission line. Many researchers were focused on wide-area monitoring, control and protection of transmission lines for improving situational awareness of the transmission system. However, the micro-grid is still lacking in that respect. Due to its diverse environment and different level of measurement, distribution grid or micro-grid needs more precise and accurate measurement than that of the transmission line. It needs higher reporting, negligible instrumental error and reduced effect of white noise. Hence the special type of PMU called microPMU can provide real-time monitoring in a micro-grid for efficient situational awareness [2]. Situational awareness in a micro-grid is achieved by gathering the information, analyzing it to facilitate efficient and effective decision making in the critical emergency situation.

The proposed chapter presents a micro-grid situational awareness using the real-time measurements of a micro-grid using a National Instrument based micro-PMU interfaced with virtual instrumentation tool. The perception of fault is achieved by recognizing the deviations in voltage and frequency obtained from micro-PMU. The comprehension of the fault is accomplished by using the learning vector quantization (LVQ) algorithm. Based on the comprehension of the fault, the decision made to project the protective action need to be taken by sending the triggering signal to circuit breaker.

10.2   Micro Grid

The use of renewable energy technologies in the energy market has gained substantial attention due to environmental effects and volatility in the price of fossil fuels [51–60]. As a result, renewable energy options have become significant sources of power generation at the commercial scale due to their various advantages, as well as government subsidies and public support. The energy sources of micro grid are the photovoltaic system, wind turbine generator, combined heat power generator, hydro energy, tidal energy, geothermal energy, biomass energy etc. [3, 4]. It is a local electricity grid with a control capability, which ensures that it can work independently or along with the conventional grid. Typically, it works when attached to the grid, but most notably, in times of disaster such as floods or power outages, or for other reasons, it can split down and work on its own using local electricity generation. A micro grid not only delivers grid backup in the event of an emergency, it could also be used to reduce costs or to connect to a neighborhood network that is too limited or inefficient for conventional grid usage. This relies on the economic and financial limitations associated with it. It could be used to increase the reliability of the power grid with minimal operational expenses. Micro grids help cities to be more power-independent and, in certain cases, promote naturally sustainability. It is situated close to end users, which ensures that the costs associated with the transmission and distribution lines are minimized. Microgrids also contain technologies such as solar PV (with output signals as DC power) or micro turbines (higher frequencies AC power) required control electronic interfaces such as DC/AC or DC/AC/DC converters to communicate with the electrical grid. Inverters can perform a vital role in the regulation of voltage and frequency in island microgrids. The main grid interface with the micro grid can be a synchronous AC interface or an asynchronous interface using

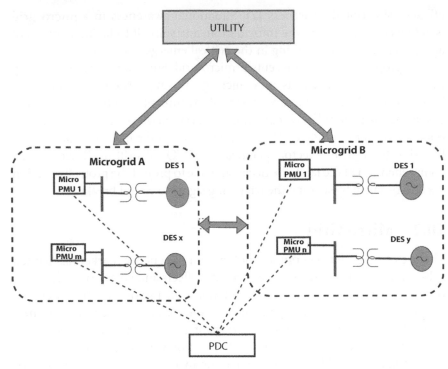

Figure 10.1 Micro-grid with micro-PMU.

a coupled direct current converter of electrical power. Some of the renewable resources involves fuel cells, solar energy PV and batteries, which provide or accept DC current to the loads like power electronics components, lights and variable speed drives, room heater, air conditioning systems, which may use direct current within. All DC microgrids have been required to reduce conversion losses power between DC and AC (and sometimes DC to AC and AC to DC). Microgrids have special control parameters and techniques conduct local balance to optimize their economic gains.

Figure 10.1 shows the block diagram of a microgrid. Microgrid A contains x number of micro-PMUs and microgrid B comprises of y number of micro-PMUs. All the micro-PMUs are connected to PDC for further processing to discover the situational awareness of the complete system.

10.3   Phasor Measurement Unit and Micro PMU

Phasor measurement unit/s (PMU) is fundamental instrument used in the wide area measuring system to sense the voltage and current phasor along with the frequency and the rate of change of frequency of the transmission systems [5]. PMU technology provides a highly automated measurement system that accurately monitor the state of the system and takes corrective measures [6]. It plays a major role in estimation of the state of power system, intelligent load shedding, temperature and sag estimation, analysis the power failure, detection and classifying the different types of fault occurred in the transmission line and the protection from different types of fault [7–9]. With the implementation of PMUs, it is easy to visualize the rapid transit through the representation of the dynamic behavior of the power system event with its higher sampling rate and time-stamped measurements of the transmission system [10]. The distribution grid and the micro grid however uses the voltage level different than that of the transmission line [11]. In the microgrids, the synchro phasor measurement needs a high-precision and more accurate measurement. The voltage angle variations between the two sites of the microgrid system can be up to two orders of magnitude less than that of the transmission network. When the percentage of error is small, the instrumental errors and white noise influence the microgrid measurement to a greater degree than that of transmission system. The cost of PMU that the transmission system uses are high. Therefore, there is a need of specialized PMU called as micro PMU, which can address all the factors to make it suitable to use in the micro grid with economic advantages. Micro PMU comprises all the basic blocks that of PMUs with the signal levels lower than that of the PMUs. The precision and the accuracy in the micro PMU is more compared PMU makes it efficiently monitor and analyze the micro grid events. With the higher sampling frequency, the micro PMU provides more phasor frames/ per second [12, 13]. Figure 10.2 shows the block diagram of the micro PMU. The microgrid voltage and currents are acquired by potential transformer (PT) and the current transformer (CT) respectively. Then the analogue voltage and currents are sent to low pass anti-aliasing filter for removing the high-frequency noise and keep the signal to fulfill Nyquist criterion. After filtering, analog to digital conversion is performed by ADC. The clock pulse is required for sampling in ADC and it is provided by GPS through phase-locked loop. The phase-locked loop receives 1 pulse per second (PPS) from the GPS receiver. The analog to digital converter does two things. It samples the data then it transforms the collected analogue data to the desired digital output. PPS signal is used for synchronization of the measurement. GPS receiver also receives the referenced time (universal coordinated time or UTC) and the geographical location (latitude and longitude) of the measurement site from the GPS satellite. The central processing unit (CPU) is an effectively a microprocessor or a DSP processor, capable of performing discrete Fourier Transform (DFT) or fast Fourier transformation (FFT) calculations to compute the phasor. After processing, the time-synchronized data along with the location will be sent to the phasor data concentrator (PDC) through a communication modem and the communication channel.

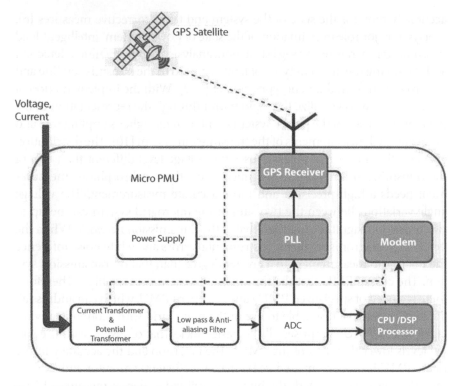

Figure 10.2 Micro PMU block diagram.

10.4 Situational Awareness: Perception, Comprehension and Prediction

Situational awareness is a crucial factor in micro-grid monitoring and protection [14]. It enables the effective and timely decision-making and operator response for the micro-grid event restoration. Inadequate situational awareness culminates in delayed, incorrect or deficient response, endangering micro-grid stability. It is mainly categorized into three parts.

1. Perception: Gathering valuable information such as current, voltage, frequency and thereby detect if any fault occurs in the micro-grid.
2. Comprehension: Analyzing the information and understand the type of fault from the three-phase voltage using the data computation algorithm, i.e., LVQ algorithm.
3. Projection: Anticipate what could happen and make the decision based on the comprehension and protect the micro-grid

by isolating the faulty line by sending the trip signal to the respective circuit breaker.

10.4.1   Perception

The perception of the microgrid is obtained by the acquiring the analog voltage phasor, current phasor and the frequency using micro PMU. There are several techniques used in the transmission line fault analysis. Fourier transformation, S-transformation, and Wavelet transformations are the mathematical tools used in analyzing the discrete signals to extract the features of the voltage and current signals to perceive the fault in the transmission line [15]. Fourier transform analyze the discrete signal in the frequency domain at DC, fundamental frequency, second harmonic, third harmonic, fourth and higher harmonic frequencies. The fault perception is accomplished by detecting the variation of these harmonics beyond certain threshold values. Wavelet transformation analyze the discrete signal in both time and frequency domain [16]. The fault perception accomplished using the variation of the detailed and approximation coefficients [10]. Alienation coefficient and Wigner distribution function based technique can perceive the transmission line fault over a period of quarter cycle [17]. All the mentioned techniques can also be applied in the microgrid fault perception. In this chapter, FFT based technique is proposed for the fault perception. In addition to FFT, the rate of change of the frequency also used in order to avoid false tripping. The voltage and current values are acquired using the National Instrument based micro PMU. It consists of a NI FPGA processor (cRIO-9066) [18], a PT (using c-series module NI-9242) for acquiring voltage at faster rate [19], a CT (using c-series module NI-9246) for high speed current acquisition [20], a NI-9467 c-series GPS receiver [21] and a NI-9401 [22], 8-channel digital I/O driver to operate the circuit breaker to isolate the faulty line to protect the healthy line. The micro PMU acquire the signals sent it to the personal computer (PC) having the RIO device driver and the LabVIEW software to analyze the signal captured by the micro PMU. Figure 10.3 shows the interfacing connections of micro grid with the micro PMU and PC. Figure 10.4 shows the connection diagram of micro-PMU. The three phase voltage and currents are acquired from the micro-grid using micro PMU and sent to PC through the gigabyte Ethernet cable. The voltage and current signal are performed the FFT transform to convert the time domain signal to frequency domain. The variation of the FFT coefficients at DC, fundamental frequency, second harmonic are monitored and the difference between consecutive coefficients beyond the threshold level indicates the perception of microgrid fault. Equation (10.1) shows the FFT transformation.

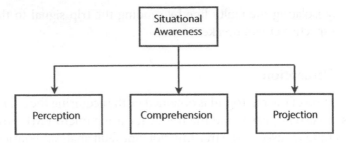

Figure 10.3 Situational awareness.

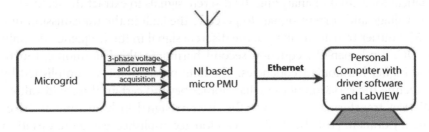

Figure 10.4 Connection diagram of micro-PMU.

$$\hat{\Omega}(z) = \frac{\sqrt{2}}{N} \sum_{m=0}^{N-1} x(m).\cos\left(\frac{2\pi mz}{N}\right) - j\frac{\sqrt{2}}{N} \sum_{m=0}^{N-1} x(m).\sin\left(\frac{2\pi mz}{N}\right) \quad (10.1)$$

Where $x(m)$ is the input AC signal; m is the mth sample; N is the total number of samples in a full cycle AC input signal. z=0,1,2,3……(N-1), are at DC, fundamental, second harmonic and higher harmonics respectively. In order avoid the false tripping, ROCOF $\left(\frac{df}{dt}\right)$ has also been used along with the FFT coefficient for perception [23].

10.4.2 Comprehension

There are several researches reported for the fault comprehension in the transmission line fault [24, 25]. Some of the methods used logical comparison for the fault comprehension, statistical methodology for fault comprehension in transmission line fault analysis [10]. Some of the researchers used artificial neural network (ANN) technique for fault comprehension [23, 26]. Probabilistic neural network is another powerful computation technique used for the fault comprehension [27]. Some of researchers preferred using support vector machine for fault comprehension in transmission line fault [28]. Fuzzy inference systems (FISs) has also been used in fault com-prehension [15]. All the mentioned techniques can also be applied for fault comprehension in micro-grid. K-nearest neighbors (K-NN) is the simplest algorithm. K-NN technique does not use any model other than storing the data. Therefore, there is no learning required. It can implement efficiently even complex data structure by matching during the classification. It classifies the data directly taking the training data set. K-NN uses the distance between the data points for classification [29, 30]. However, for fault comprehension in K-NN needs to hang on the entire training dataset. The algorithm for Learning Vector Quantization (LVQ) is an artificial neural network algorithm that enables one to choose how much training instances to hold on to and learn exactly what those instances should look like [29]. LVQ is a collection of codebook vectors. The model representation, learned from the training data, is a fixed pool of codebook vectors. The training data set are similar to new test data based on the Euclidian distance. For real valued data, the most used technique is Euclidean distance as shown in equation (10.2).

$$D = (\Omega_{new}(z), \Omega_{old}(z)) = \sqrt{\sum_{i=1}^{k} (\Omega_{new,i}(z), \Omega_{old,i}(z))^2} \qquad (10.2)$$

Where, $\Omega_{new}(z)$ is test data and $\Omega_{old}(z)$ is a data from the training data set; z=0, 1,2 presents the DC, fundamental and the second harmonic of FFT of the input signal; i is the serial number of the data set. The LVQ learns the code book vector from the training data set and the learning weight updates using equation (10.3) and (10.4).

$$w_{i+1} = w_i \pm \alpha \times (t - w_i) \qquad (10.3)$$

Where, w_{i+1} is the updated weight w_i is the weight in previous iteration, α is learning rate, and t is the new test data, whose fault comprehension has to determine. The sign '+/-' 'is decided during the training of each data set. If the predicted class is same as actual class(the codebook vector is moved closer to the training instance) of the training data set then it is '+'. If it does not match, it is moved further away and the sign is '-'.

Figure 10.5 shows the flow chart of the application of LVQ training and testing stage respectively. The prediction of the new test data is done using the updated weight after the training and the minimum Euclidian distance using the best matching unit (BMU) as depicted in the Figure 10.1.

Table 10.1 presents the fault class corresponding to the respective fault type. Table 10.2 presents the training data set consists of FFT at DC, fundamental and the second harmonics as in equation (10.4).

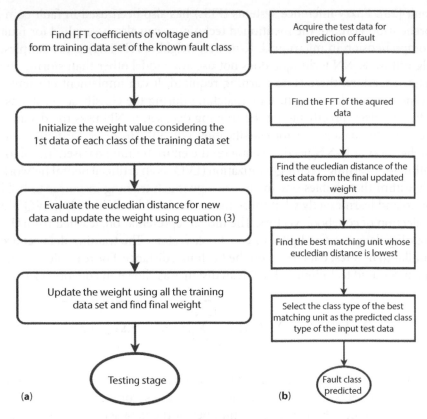

Figure 10.5 Flow chart of (a) comprehension algorithm (b) LVQ algorithm.

Table 10.1 Fault class corresponding to fault type.

Fault class	Type of fault
1	Normal operation
2	Line to ground fault
3	Line- Line Fault
4	Line-Line-Ground Fault
5	Line-Line-Line Fault

$$\Omega(0) = \left(\frac{1}{N}\right) \sum_{n=0}^{N-1} x(n) \qquad (10.4a)$$

Table 10.2 Training data set with known fault class.

FFT coefficients			Fault class
$\psi(0)$	$\psi(1)$	$\psi(2)$	
0.022964	0.003748	0.001928	1
0.02251	0.003674	0.00189	1
0.022355	0.003648	0.001877	1
0.022213	0.003625	0.001865	1
0.02129	0.003474	0.001788	1
0.582174	0.09501	0.048882	2
0.464819	0.075858	0.039029	2
0.466043	0.076058	0.039131	2
0.460156	0.075097	0.038637	2
0.581089	0.094833	0.048791	2
0.865728	0.141286	0.072691	3
0.584204	0.095342	0.049053	3
0.87362	0.142574	0.073354	3
0.587216	0.095833	0.049306	3
0.644604	0.105199	0.054124	3
0.939028	0.153248	0.078846	4
0.940435	0.153478	0.078964	4
1.131119	0.184597	0.094975	4
1.140445	0.186119	0.095758	4
0.947265	0.154593	0.079537	4
0.037882	0.006182	0.003181	5
0.000306	0.00005	0.000026	5
1.151669	0.187951	0.0967	5
0.004134	0.000675	0.000347	5
0.005576	0.00091	0.000468	5

$$\Omega(1) = \left(\frac{1}{N}\right) \sum_{n=0}^{N-1} x(n).e^{-\left(\frac{2\pi n}{N}\right)} \quad\quad (10.4b)$$

$$\Omega(2) = \left(\frac{1}{N}\right) \sum_{n=0}^{N-1} x(n).e^{-\left(\frac{4\pi n}{N}\right)} \qu\quad (10.4c)$$

Table 10.3 Initial weight vector.

Initial weight vector	Input			Target
$W_{(1,1)}$	0.022964	0.003748	0.001928	1
$W_{(1,2)}$	0.582174	0.09501	0.048882	2
$W_{(1,3)}$	0.865728	0.141286	0.072691	3
$W_{(1,4)}$	0.939028	0.153248	0.078846	4
$W_{(1,5)}$	0.037882	0.006182	0.003181	5

Table 10.4 Updated weight vector after training.

Updated weight vector	Input			Target
$W_{(n,1)}$	0.0290932	0.00474812	0.00244269	1
$W_{(n,2)}$	0.632633	0.103245	0.0531185	2
$W_{(n,3)}$	0.864939	0.141157	0.0726247	3
$W_{(n,4)}$	0.866713	0.141446	0.0727743	4
$W_{(n,5)}$	0.037882	0.006182	0.003181	5

Table 10.5 Euclidean distance test data.

Euclidean distance	BMU
0.713039	-
0.0994185	Yes
0.136768	-
0.138571	-
0.704103	-

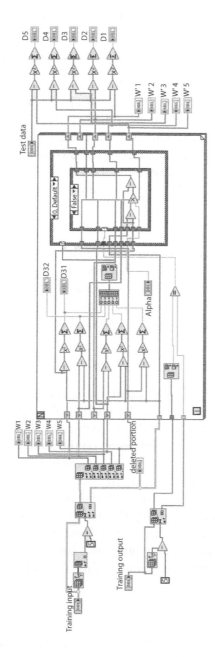

Figure 10.6 LVQ algorithm LabVIEW program.

Here $\Omega(0)$, $\Omega(1)$, and $\Omega(2)$ are the FFT at DC, fundamental and second harmonic.

The initial weight considered as presented in Table 10.3 below, via taking one element from each class.

The updated weight vector using the equation (10.3) considering the learning rate (α) = 0.1 after the training is as presented in Table 10.4.

A test data point is considered for comprehension, whose DC, fundamental and second harmonic are 0.730418, 0.119204, and 0.06133 respectively. The fault class can be found using Table 10.5.

Hence the fault class of the new test data set is second class i.e., LG fault. The test data verified using the SEL-311C transmission line protection relay. The simulation is carried out using the LabVIEW virtual instrumentation platform. The LabVIEW program is shown in the Figure 10.6.

10.4.3   Projection

Once the fault is perceived and comprehended in the micro-grid, the faulty part of the micro-grid need to be isolated from the healthy part. The circuit breaker is connected, which in turn operated by sending the trip signal from the NI 9401 digital I/O relay driver. Once the fault is comprehended, the line involved with fault is isolated without disturbing the healthy lines.

10.5   Conclusion

This chapter addresses micro-grid situational awareness using micro PMU. The perception of the fault is achieved using the voltage phasor deviation at different harmonics and the ROCOF. The comprehension is achieved using the algorithm learning vector quantization on the three-phase voltage only based on its frequency components at DC, fundamental and second harmonic to make the process immune to the fault resistance and fault inception angle. Additionally, a protection scheme is presented to isolate only the faulty phases, without disturbing the healthy phases. The future scope of the proposed work is that with the help of micro PMUs, the micro-grids can share the information of their situational information and the power flow amongst them keeping the function of micro-grid in a stable state.

References

1. Alsaidan, I.; Alanazi, A.; Gao, W.; Wu, H.; Khodaei A.; State-of-the-Art in micro-grid-integrated distributed energy storage sizing. Energies. 2017, doi:10.3390/en10091421.

2. Elbana, M. S.; Abbasy, N.; Meghed, A.; Shaker N.; "µPMU-based smart adaptive protection scheme for microgrids", Journal of Modern Power Systems and Clean Energy, 2019, 7, 887–898.

3. Ji, P.; Zhou, X. X.; Wu, S. Y.; "Review on sustainable development of island micro-grid". International Conference on advanced power system automation and protection. 2011, 3, 1806-1813. 4. Zhou, X.; Guo, T.; Ma, Y.; "An overview on microgrid technology". IEEE International Conference on Mechatronics Automation. 2015, 76–81, doi:10.1109/ICMA. 2015.7237460.

4. Phadke, A. G.; Thorp, J. S.; "Synchronized Phasor Measurements and Their Applications". Springer, 2008, doi:10.1007/978-0-387-76537-2.

5. Gopakumar, P.; Reddy, M. J. B.; Mohanta, D. K.; "Adaptive fault identification and classification methodology for smart power grids using synchronous phasor angle measurements". 2015, IET Generation Transmission and Distribution. 9, 133–145.

6. Rajaraman, P., N.A, S.; Mallikarjuna, B.; Reddy, M. J. B.; Mohanta, D. K.; "Robust fault analysis in transmission lines using Synchrophasor measurements". Protection and Control Modern Power System. 2018, 3.https://doi. org/10.1186/s41601-018-0082-4

7. Samantaray, S. R.; Kamwa, I.; Joos, G.; "Phasor measurement unit based wide-area monitoring and information sharing between micro-grids". IET Generation Transmission and Distribution, 2017, 11(5), 1293–1302. doi: 10.1049/iet-gtd.2016.1419.

8. Oleinikova, I.; Mutule, A.; Putnins, M.; "PMU measurements application for transmission line temperature and sag estimation algorithm development". 55th International Scientific Conference on Power and Electrical Engineering of Riga Technical University, 2014, 181–185. doi:10.1109/ RTUCON.2014.6998196.

9. Sundaravaradan, N. A.; Rajaraman, P.; Meyur, R.; Mallikarjuna, B.; Reddy, M. J. B.; Mohanta, D. K.; "Real-time fault analysis of transmission lines using wavelet multi resolution analysis based frequency domain approach". IET Science Measurement and Technology. 2016, 10(7), 693-703.

10. Jamei, M. et al. "Anomaly Detection Using Optimally-Placed µ PMU Sensors in Distribution Grids". IEEE Transactions on Power Systems. 2017, 33(4), 3611-3623.

11. https://www.PowerSensorsLtd.com MicroPMU Data Sheet Revision 1.2.

12. Das, H. P.; Micro-Phasor Measurement Unit (µPMU) Development and its Applications., 2016. doi:10.13140/RG.2.2.23606.96329.

13. Skok, S.; Ivankovic, I.; Microgrid monitoring protection and control based on synchronized measurements, CIGRE SC D2 Colloquium, 2017.

14. Chen, K.; Huang, C.; He, J.; "Fault detection, classification and location for transmission lines and distribution systems: a review on the methods." High voltage, 2016, 1(1), 25-33.

15. Silva, K. M.; Souza, B. A.; Brito, N. S. D.; Fault detection and classification in transmission lines based on wavelet transform and ANN. IEEE Transactions on Power Delivery, 2006. 21, 2058–2063.

16. Mahela, P.; Wigner distribution function and alienation coefficient-based transmission line protection scheme. IET Generation Transmission and Distribution, 2020, 14(10). doi:10.1049/iet-gtd.2019.1414.

17. NI cRIO-9066. http://www.ni.com/pdf/manuals/376341b.pdf.

18. NI 9242 Datasheet. 1–14 http://www.ni.com/pdf/manuals/376130b_02.pdf.

19. NI 9246 Datasheet. http://www.ni.com/pdf/manuals/376372a.pdf.

20. NI 9467 Datasheet. http://www.ni.com/pdf/manuals/373230c.pdf.

21. NI 9401 Datasheet. https://www.ni.com/pdf/manuals/374068a_02.pdf.

22. Picard, S. D.; Adamiak, M. G.; Madani, V.; Fault location using PMU measurements and wide-area infrastructure. 68thAnnual Conferencefor Protective Relay Engineers, 2015. doi:10.1109/CPRE.2015.7102170.

23. Hooshyar, A.; El-saadany, E. F.; Member, S.; Sanaye-pasand, M. & Member, S.; Fault type classification in Micro-grids including photovoltaic DGs, IEEE Transactions on Smart Grid,2016,7(5),2218-2229.

24. Dutta, S.; Sadhu, P. K.; Reddy, M. J. B.; Mohanta, D. K.; Smart inadvertent islanding detection employing P-Type micro-PMU for an active distribution network.IET Generation Transmission & Distribution, 2018, 12, 4615–4625.

25. Heo, S.; Lee, J. H.; Fault detection and classification using artificial neural networks. IFAC-Papers On Line, 2018, 51, 470–475.doi:10.1016/J.IFACOL.2018.09.380

26. Kinsner, W.; Probabilistic neural networksfor power line fault classification. IEEE Canadian Conference on Electrical and Computer Engineering, 1998, 585–588.

27. Gopakumar, P.; Mallikajuna, B.; Reddy, M. J. B.; Mohanta, D. K.; Remote monitoring system for real time detection and classification of transmission line faults in a power grid using PMU measurements. Protection and Control of Modern Power Systems, 2018, 3 (1),16.doi: 10.1186/s41601-018-0089-x

28. Brownlee, J.; Master Machine Learning Algorithms, 2019.

29. Asadi M. A.; Samet, H.; Ghanbari, T.; K-NN based fault detection and classification methods for power transmission systems. Protection and Control of Modern Power Systems,2017, 2. doi: 10.1186/s41601-017-0063-z.

30. Priyadarshi.; N;, Padmanaban, S.; Maroti, P.K.; Sharma. A.; An Extensive Practical Investigation of FPSO-Based MPPT for Grid Integrated PV System Under Variable Operating Conditions With Anti-Islanding Protection. IEEE System Journal, 2018, 13:1861 - 1871.

31. Priyadarshi, N.; Padmanaban, S.; Bhaskar, M.S.; Blaabjerg, F.; Sharma, A.; A Fuzzy SVPWM Based Inverter Control Realization of Grid Integrated PV-Wind System with FPSO MPPT Algorithm for a Grid-Connected PV/Wind Power Generation System: Hardware Implementation. IET Electric Power Appl., 2018, 12:962-971.

32. Priyadarshi, N.; Kumar, V.; Yadav, K.; Vardia, M.; An Experimental Study on Zeta buck-boost converter for Application in PV system. Handbook of distributed generation, Springer, DOI 10.1007/978-3-319-51343-0_13

33. Priyadarshi N.; Sharma A.K.; Priyam S.; An Experimental Realization of Grid-Connected PV System with MPPT Using dSPACE DS 1104 Control Board. Advances in Smart Grid and Renewable Energy. Lecture Notes in Electrical Engineering, Springer, Singapore 2018, 435.

34. Priyadarshi N.; Sharma A.K.; Priyam S.; Practical Realization of an Improved Photovoltaic Grid Integration with MPPT. International Journal of Renewable Energy Research 2017, 7:1180-1891.

35. Priyadarshi N.; Sharma A.K.; Azam F.; A Hybrid Firefly-Asymmetrical Fuzzy Logic Controller based MPPT for PV-Wind-Fuel Grid Integration. International Journal of Renewable Energy Research 2017, 7: 1546-1560

36. Priyadarshi, N.; Anand, A.; Sharma, A.K.; Azam, F.; Singh, V.K.; Sinha, R. K.; An Experimental Implementation and Testing of GA based Maximum Power Point Tracking for PV System under Varying Ambient Conditions Using dSPACE DS 1104 Controller. International Journal of Renewable Energy Research, 2017, 7:255-265

37. Priyadarshi, N.; Padmanaban S.; Mihet-Popa L.; Blaabjerg, F.; Azam F.; Maximum Power Point Tracking for Brushless DC Motor-Driven Photovoltaic Pumping Systems Using a Hybrid ANFIS-FLOWER Pollination Optimization Algorithm. MDPI Energies 2018, 11:1-16

38. Priyadarshi, N.; Azam, F.; Bhoi, A.K.; Alam, S.; An Artificial Fuzzy Logic Intelligent Controller Based MPPT for PV Grid Utility. Lecture Notes in Networks and Systems 46, https://doi.org/10.1007/978-981-13-1217-5_88.

39. Padmanaban, S.; Priyadarshi, N.; Holm-Nielsen, J. B.; Bhaskar, M. S.; Azam, F.; Sharma, A.K.; A Novel Modified Sine-Cosine Optimized MPPT Algorithm for Grid Integrated PV System under Real Operating Conditions. IEEE Access, 2019, 7:10467-10477.

40. Padmanaban, S.; Priyadarshi, N.; Holm-Nielsen, J. B.; Bhaskar, M. S.; Hossain, E.; Azam, F.; A Hybrid Photovoltaic-Fuel Cell for Grid Integration With Jaya-Based Maximum Power Point Tracking: Experimental Performance Evaluation. IEEE Access, 2019, 7:82978-82990.

41. Priyadarshi, N.; Padmanaban, N.; Holm-Nielsen, J. B.; Blaabjerg, F.; Bhaskar, M.S.; An Experimental Estimation of Hybrid ANFIS–PSO-Based MPPT for PV Grid Integration Under Fluctuating Sun Irradiance. in IEEE Systems Journal. 2020, 14:1218-1229

42. Priyadarshi, N.; Padmanaban, N.; Bhaskar, M. S.; Blaabjerg, F.; Holm-Nielsen, J. B.; Azam, F.; Sharma, A.K.; A Hybrid Photovoltaic-Fuel Cell-Based Single-Stage Grid Integration With Lyapunov Control Scheme. IEEE Systems Journal, 2020, 14: 3334 - 3342

43. Priyadarshi, N.; Bhaskar, M. S.; Padmanaban, N.; Blaabjerg, F.; Azam, F.; New CUK–SEPIC converter based photovoltaic power system with hybrid

GSA–PSO algorithm employing MPPT for water pumping applications. IET Power Electronics. **2020**, 13:2824 – 2830

44. Priyadarshi, N.; Padmanaban, N.; Holm-Nielsen, J. B.; Bhaskar, M.S.; Azam, F.; Internet of things augmented a novel PSO-employed modified zeta converter-based photovoltaic maximum power tracking system: hardware realisation. IET Power Electronics. **2020**, 13:2775 – 2781

45. Kamalapathi, K., Priyadarshi, N., Padmanaban, S., Holm-Nielsen, J.B., Azam, F., Umayal, C., Ramachandaramurthy, V.K. A Hybrid Moth-Flame Fuzzy Logic Controller Based Integrated Cuk Converter Fed Brushless DC Motor for Power Factor Correction. MDPI Electronics, **2018**, 7: 288.

46. Priyadarshi, N., Padmanaban, S., Lonel, D., Mihet-Popa, L., Azam, F. Hybrid PV-Wind, Micro-Grid Development Using Quasi-Z-Source Inverter Modeling and Control—Experimental Investigation. MDPI Energies, **2018**, 11:2277

47. Priyadarshi, N.; Ramachandaramurthy, V, K.; Padmanaban, S.; Azam, A.; An Ant Colony Optimized MPPT for Standalone Hybrid PV-Wind Power System with Single Cuk Converter. MDPI Energies, **2019**, 12: 167

48. Azam, F.; Yadav, S.K.; Priyadarshi, N.; Padmanaban, S.; and Bansal, R.C.; A Comprehensive Review of Authentication Schemes in Vehicular Ad-Hoc Network, IEEE Access, **2021,** 9:31309-31321, 2021, doi: 10.1109/ACCESS.2021.3060046.

49. Priyadarshi, N.; Sharma, A.K.; Bhoi, A. K.; Ahmad, S. N.; Azam, F.; Priyam, S.; A Practical performance verification of AFLC based MPPT for standalone PV power system under varying weather condition, International Journal of Engineering & Technology, **2018**, 7:338-343

50. Azam F.; Priyadarshi N.; Nagar H.; Kumar S.; Bhoi A.K.; An Overview of Solar-Powered Electric Vehicle Charging in Vehicular Adhoc Network. in: Electric Vehicles. Green Energy and Technology. Springer, Singapore. https://doi.org/10.1007/978-981-15-9251-5_5

51. Azam, F.; Kumar, S.; Yadav, K.P.; Priyadarshi N.; Padmanaban, S.; An Outline of the Security Challenges in VANET, in Proc. of IEEE UPCON 2020, Nov, 2020.

52. Priyadarshi, N.; Azam, F.; Bhoi, A.K.; Sharma, A.K.; A Multilevel Inverter-Controlled Photovoltaic Generation. in Advances in Greener Energy Technologies. Springer, Singapore. **2020** https://doi.org/10.1007/978-981-15-4246-6_8

53. Priyadarshi, N.; Azam, F.; Bhoi, A.K.; Sharma, A.K.; Dynamic Operation of Grid-Connected Photovoltaic Power System. in Advances in Greener Energy Technologies. Springer, Singapore. **2020** https://doi.org/10.1007/978-981-15-4246-6_13

54. Priyadarshi, N.; Azam, F.; Bhoi, A.K.; Sharma, A.K.; A Proton Exchange Membrane-Based Fuel Cell Integrated Power System. in Advances in Greener Energy Technologies. Springer, Singapore. **2020** https://doi.org/10.1007/978-981-15-4246-6_18

55. Priyadarshi, N.; Azam, F.; Bhoi, A.K.; Sharma, A.K.; A Closed-Loop Control of Fixed Pattern Rectifier for Renewable Energy Applications. in Advances in Greener Energy Technologies. Springer, Singapore. **2020** https://doi.org/10.1007/978-981-15-4246-6_25

56. Priyadarshi, N.; Azam, F.; Bhoi, A.K.; Sharma, A.K.; A Four-Switch-Type Converter Fed Improved Photovoltaic Power System. in Advances in Greener Energy Technologies. Springer, Singapore. **2020** https://doi.org/10.1007/978-981-15-4246-6_29

57. Vardia, M.; Priyadarshi, N.; Ali, I.; Azam, F.; Bhoi, A.K.; Maximum Power Point Tracking for Wind Energy Conversion System. in Advances in Greener Energy Technologies. Springer, Singapore. **2020** https://doi.org/10.1007/978-981-15-4246-6_36

58. Vardia, M.; Priyadarshi, N.; Ali, I.; Azam, F.; Bhoi, A.K.; Design of Wind Energy Conversion System Under Different Fault Conditions. in Advances in Greener Energy Technologies. Springer, Singapore. **2020** https://doi.org/10.1007/978-981-15-4246-6_41

59. Choudhary, T.; Priyadarshi, N.; Kuma,r P.; Azam, F.; Bhoi A.K. (2020) A Fuzzy Logic Control Based Vibration Control System for Renewable Application. in Advances in Greener Energy Technologies. Springer, Singapore. **2020** https://doi.org/10.1007/978-981-15-4246-6_38

60. Priyadarshi, N.; Azam F.; Solanki, S. S.; Sharma, A.K.; Bhoi, A.K.; Almakhles, D.; A Bio-Inspired Chicken Swarm Optimization-Based Fuel Cell System for Electric Vehicle Applications. in Bio-inspired Neurocomputing. Studies in Computational Intelligence, vol 903. Springer, Singapore. **2021** https://doi.org/10.1007/978-981-15-5495-7_1

11

AI and ML for the Smart Grid

Dr. M. K. Khedkar and B. Ramesh*

Electrical Engg. Deptt., Visvesvaraya National Institute of Technology, Nagpur, India

Abstract

Artificial Intelligence (AI) techniques such as Expert Systems (ES), Artificial Neural Networks (ANN), Fuzzy Logic (FL) and Genetic Algorithm (GA) have brought much advancement in modern day power systems. These techniques provide powerful tools to effectively deal with the ever increasing complexity of power system design, operation, control, estimation and fault diagnostics. Smart Grid is tomorrow's intelligent power grid that improves system reliability and security, achieves optimal distribution of energy to customers by integrating Distributed Energy Resources (DER) through state-of-art power electronics, communication systems, computers and machine intelligence. Machine Learning (ML) is a major application of AI which enables system's capability to learn automatically and improve through experience without being programmed exclusively. AI and ML can make smart grid capable of making intelligent decisions, ability to respond to intermittent nature of RES, sudden changes in energy demands of customers & power outages. Supervised Learning helps in forecasting future energy demand of customers through their energy consumption patterns obtained from smart meter data. Reinforcement Learning helps in making optimal decisions in energy markets so that the microgrid can maximize its cumulative reward. The use of wireless communication technologies in smart grid is prone to cyber-attacks. By employing ML, it is possible to detect & prevent cyber-attacks as well as pernicious activities. In this chapter role of AI & ML in smart grid entities such as Home Energy Management System (HEMS), Energy Trading, Adaptive Protection, Load Forecasting, and Smart Energy Meter are presented.

Corresponding author: ramesh.237@gmail.com

Neeraj Priyadarshi, Akash Kumar Bhoi, Sanjeevikumar Padmanaban, S. Balamurugan and Jens Bo Holm-Nielsen (eds.) Intelligent Renewable Energy Systems, (287–306) © 2022 Scrivener Publishing LLC

Keywords: Adaptive protection, artificial intelligence, energy trading, genetic algorithm, home energy management system, machine learning, smart energy meter, smart grid

Abbreviations

ANN	Artificial Neural Network
ANFIS	Adaptive Neuro Fuzzy Inference System
BPA	Back Propagation Algorithm
DER	Distributed Energy Resources
DL	Deep Learning
ES	Expert System
FL	Fuzzy Logic
GA	Genetic Algorithm
HEMS	Home Energy Management System
IED	Intelligent Electronic Device
LET	Local Energy Trading
ML	Machine Learning
RES	Renewable Energy Sources
RL	Reinforcement Learning
SEM	Smart Energy Meter
SVM	Support Vector Machine
STLF	Short Term Load Forecasting

11.1   Introduction

As the population is increasing worldwide, it has become difficult to meet the increasing energy demand [1–15]. Moreover fossil fuel based power generation is the major contributor to CO_2 emissions in the atmosphere [16–33]. To reduce global warming due to CO_2 emissions, governments of all countries are encouraging renewable based power generation. Conventional power grid becomes more complex with the integration of renewable based of DERs. The only solution to handle the complexity of power system is to make power grid intelligent by integrating advanced communication infrastructure and IEDs, widely referred as Smart Grid (SG) [1]. According to US DoE, "A Smart Grid uses digital technology to improve security, efficiency and reliability (both economic and energy) of electric system from large generation, through the delivery systems to electricity consumers and a growing number of distributed generation and storage resources". Table 11.1 shows the comparison between conventional grid and smart grid.

Table 11.1 Conventional grid versus smart grid.

Conventional grid	Smart grid
Electromechanical equipment	Digital equipment
Centralized Power Generation	Centralized and Distributed Power generation
One way communication	Two way communication
Manual restoration	Mostly automatic restoration as the grid is self-healing and resilient
Real time monitoring is not possible due to few sensors installed at desired locations	Real time monitoring of the power system is possible with WAMS (Wide area monitoring system) technology.
Heavy CO_2 emission which increases environmental pollution	Less pollution due to renewable based power generation
Limited customer choice	Customers have many choices

The following are the main features of Smart Grid:

- Ability to detect abnormal operating conditions before it actually happens
- Self-healing capability
- Integration of RES
- Advanced communication system which enables man to device communication and device to device communication which refers to communication between smart appliances and Smart Energy Meter (SEM)
- Ability to integrate communication infrastructure with power and control equipment

SG enables small scale utilities to generate and distribute power in a small distribution system. Such a small scale power system is termed as Microgrid. A microgrid can be operated independently or it can be integrated to main grid [1]. In Conventional power system, a consumer has to buy power from single utility only. In SG environment, a consumer is named as customer who has the choice of trading required energy in the market and purchase power from any utility. Wide Area Monitoring

System (WAMS) technology enables real time monitoring and control of the power system which uses time synchronized PMU data. With the development of DC microgrids and charging stations, all conventional vehicles can be replaced by Electric Vehicles (EV). EVs reduce pollution and can be integrated to grid to meet peak energy demand. The following are the benefits of smart grid:

- Reduced AT&C losses which in turn reduces price (Rs/kWh)
- Enhanced Grid stability
- Increased power system reliability and security with adaptive protection schemes
- Bidirectional communication facilitates more customer choices
- Reduced burden on conventional power plants and long distance transmission lines
- Increased utilization of resources
- ToU tariff decreases overall demand during peak load periods which facilitates effective peak demand management
- Chances of blackouts will be reduced
- Increased revenue
- Optimal scheduling of smart appliances is possible with smart energy meter
- Effective energy market framework
- Outage reduction
- Improved energy efficiency
- Renewable energy integration
- Real time monitoring of the power system through WAMS technology
- Effective use of Electric Vehicles

Major challenge in SG technology is to develop ultra-fast communication infrastructure, highly accurate measuring system and operating all communication, power and control equipment in synchronism. Another challenge is to bring awareness among people about Distributed Energy Resources (DER) and Energy Trading.

Artificial Intelligence (AI) techniques and Machine Learning (ML) algorithms are powerful tools to get best solution for most of the SG challenges [34–53]. AI is the ability of machines to think, understand and behave like humans and solve problems much faster and accurate than humans. AI is the process of making a machine intelligent.

11.2   AI Techniques

11.2.1   Expert Systems (ES)

ES is an intelligent computer program developed to solve highly complex problems in a specific domain at the level of remarkable human expertise and intelligence [2]. Basic structure of ES is shown in Figure 11.1. The basic capabilities of ES are instructing and assisting humans in decision making process, predicting result and suggesting alternative options to a problem.

Knowledge Base contains domain specific knowledge required to exhibit intelligence. Inference Engine (IE) is the major component of ES, contains all the rules required to solve a particular problem. User interacts with IE through the User Interface (UI). User's query is taken by UI in a readable format and communicates it to the IE.

11.2.2   Artificial Neural Networks (ANN)

The term ANN derives its origin from human brain. ANN imitates the behaviour of human brain to solve complex problems. Artificial Neural Networks (ANN) functions when some data input is fed to them. The interconnection among artificial neurons constitutes an ANN, which is able to solve many scientific and engineering problems [3].

These are usually classified in to recurrent and feed forward architectures depending upon the signal flow directions. The architecture of Back Propagation Algorithm (BPA) which is mostly used in feed forward network [2] is shown in Figure 11.2.

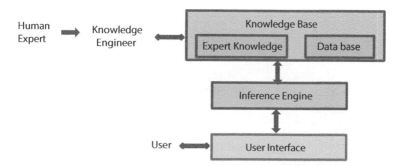

Figure 11.1 Basic structure of ES.

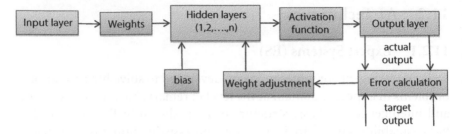

Figure 11.2 ANN architecture of BPA.

11.2.3   Fuzzy Logic (FL)

FL is based on the concept of relative graded membership as inspired by the process of human perception and cognition. FL deals with uncertainties due to inexact, approximate and vague data [4]. New methods based on FL may be used to develop intelligent systems.

A hybrid system is an intelligent system obtained by combining two or more intelligent technologies. ANFIS is the combination of Artificial Neural Networks (ANN) and Fuzzy Inference System (FIS) which integrates the benefits of both ANN and FL principles in a single framework [5]. It is a universal estimator. The functional block diagram of Fuzzy Inference System [5] is shown in Figure 11.3.

11.2.4   Genetic Algorithm (GA)

GA is a heuristic search and optimization algorithm that imitates the process of natural evolution [6]. It is a subset of evolutionary computation. In GA, initial population of possible optimal solution vector is considered. For each solution vector fitness value is calculated. Initial population

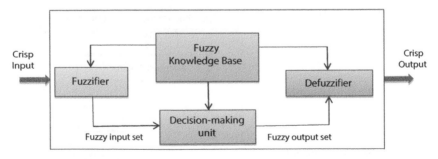

Figure 11.3 Functional block diagram of Fuzzy Inference System.

undergoes crossovers and mutations to produce new children. Fitness of new children is calculated and compared with the fitness values of initial population. Most fit solution vectors are treated as new population in the next generation. Least fit solution vectors are discarded. This procedure is repeated till optimal solution vector is obtained. High initial population with less number of iterations is better than low initial population with more number of iterations.

11.3 Machine Learning (ML)

Machine Learning (ML) is the field of study which enables computers the potential to learn on their own and improve their performance from experience without being programmed explicitly [7]. ML is a subset of Artificial Intelligenct (AI). It is the science of making machines to act by feeding them data and allowing them to learn so that it can interpret data, understand and analyse useful information to identify key features for solving complex problems. ML is classified in to Supervised Learning (SL), Unsupervised Learning (USL) and Reinforcement Learning (RL).

In SL, the machine needs to be supervised by feeding input and output data. First the machine needs to be trained with historical data. During training the machine maps the input and output data. After training the machine should be tested with some input data. If the output produced by machine exactly matches with the output data, the machine is eligible to be used in real time problems. SL is used to solve regression and classification problems. Linear regression, Logistic regression, Support Vector Machine (SVM) and K-Nearest neighbour are the most popular SL algorithms. SL can be implemented in Load Forecasting, Power System State Estimation etc. USL doesn't require any supervision. It is used to classify data/persons in to different groups called clusters based on similarities. USL can be used to categorize consumers based on their similarities like type of load; smart appliances based on their capacity, rated voltage, rated current and power factor; form all power system events in to clusters which may be useful in many power system studies.

Reinforced Learning (RL) is the most typical part of ML. The basic structure of RL consists of an agent put in an unknown stochastic environment. The agent interacts with and adapts to the environment. The agent transits from one state to another by choosing one of the available actions. Depending upon the action chosen, the agent receives a reward or punishment [8]. The main aim of the RL agent is to try all possible actions by trial and error approach to maximize its reward. Q-learning is the most popular

RL algorithm. It is very much useful in decision making process. Energy Trading among Multi Microgrids is the best Smart Grid entity in which multi agent RL can be implemented. Recently Deep Learning is gaining popularity which is a combination of ANN and ML.

The role of AI techniques and ML algorithms for the SG are explained in the following topics.

11.4 Home Energy Management System (HEMS)

Home Energy Management System (HEMS) is the process of managing energy consumption of household appliances in a most optimal way so as to reduce the energy bill, peak demand and to utilise Time of Use (ToU) tariff effectively. It is gaining popularity due to issues like energy deficit and atmospheric pollution. Use of conventional energy resources like coal, diesel increases carbon foot print. Moreover with ever increasing electricity demand, national power grid is being loaded heavily during the peak load period. In order to meet the increased load demand, distributed generation has become the only alternative. So, HEMS plays a crucial role in managing the energy efficiently in a smart distribution network [9]. It provides proper schedule for switching ON and OFF the home appliances in the order of their priority. The idea of HEMS was first implemented with a microprocessor based device and its performance was improved with the development of personal computers. Optimization algorithms were also developed to manage the peak demand and reduce the energy cost. Greatest improvement in HEMS took place in 2012 with the development of Demand Response (DR) based intelligent HEMS for reduction in electricity cost and energy consumption. In this work, few home appliances are considered with different priorities and comfort levels. The basic communication architecture of HEMS is shown in Figure 11.4.

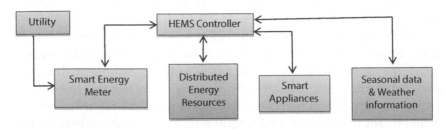

Figure 11.4 Communication architecture of HEMS.

Controllers based on AI techniques for scheduling home appliances in smart homes have been implemented. ANN, FL control and ANFIS are used to design schedule controllers. AI controllers consist of software programming which imitates human thinking. ANN which deals with non-linear systems has been used to develop intelligent controller for scheduling of home appliances [10]. Combination of ANN & GA has been used for weekly scheduling of appliances to achieve optimal energy consumption so that peak energy demand is reduced and usage of RES is maximized.

FL control can also be used to design and implement schedule controller for home appliances by reducing energy consumption and price. Air Conditioning units have been scheduled day ahead using FL based controller to obtain optimal temperatures in relation to weather forecast and energy prices [11]. Design and implementation of FL based controller is easy when compared to controllers based on other AI techniques. ANFIS based controller determines optimal scheduling of energy with respect to dynamic price without reducing energy consumption.

11.5   Load Forecasting (LF) in Smart Grid

Load Forecasting is the technique of estimating future load demand in the power system considering the duration of the day, seasonality factor and historical data of load curves, consumption patterns. It plays a crucial role in the future planning and reliable operation of power system and also in the effective development of smart grid technologies. It also helps to decide the energy price in certain duration of the day. In energy markets, highly accurate load forecasting provides reliable information to the market operator which helps in effective management of peak energy demand.

ANN is one of the most efficient methods to be implemented in load forecasting. The input data required for training the neural network includes weather information, list of working days and holidays, location information such as residential area, industrial area and so on [12]. Target outputs are the real time variations of load. All input data and target output data are normalised by dividing with absolute maximum value so that the normalised data lies between +1 and -1. Tanh function is used as activation function for the first layer and activation function for the output layer is chosen to be linear function. Network initialization has to be done which influences speed and probability of convergence. Network should be trained with suitable training algorithm. After training is completed another set of input and target output vectors are required for testing the network. If testing is completed successfully, network can be used for real time load forecasting.

STLF is implemented in [13] using ANN based on BPA. In this STLF, algorithm RL based identical day classification procedure is used. Measured data already available from previous load measurements is used to train identical day classification model. After training, the model is tested with other available load measurements. Output of the model consisting of identical days is used as one of the inputs to train BPNN based STLF model. By taking already available load measurements as another input, STLF model is trained. Once the model is trained, it is tested with another set of data and then used for real time STLF. The overall procedure of STLF based on RL and BPNN is shown in Figure 11.5, slightly modified as that of [13].

A standard ANN consists of one input layer, one output layer and one hidden layer. ML algorithms and standard ANN are not capable enough to deal with large data sets with more dimensions. To deal with such challenges, a new class of AI techniques has evolved called Deep Learning (DL). Architecture of DL is more complex when compared to other ANN models because of more layers and computations [14]. It is the most suitable technique for LF in SG.

1 – Historical Measurement data for training.
2 – Data for testing the trained model.
3 – Model obtained after training.

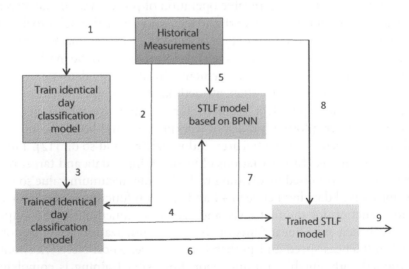

Figure 11.5 Overall STLF procedure based on RL and BPNN.

4 – Training data consisting of identical days.
5 – Historical measurement data for training STLF model.
6 – Testing data consisting of identical days.
7 – Model obtained after training.
8 – Testing data.
9 – Output (Forecasted load).

11.6   Adaptive Protection (AP)

With the massive penetration of Distributed Energy Resources (DERs) into the power grid, protection has become highly challenging in the SG environment. Many of the tasks performed by transmission system are now shifted to distribution system due to the development of microgrid technology [15]. When a DER is integrated to the main grid protection system is affected. In grid connected mode, if a fault occurs, fault will be fed by short circuit current from main grid as well as all microgrids. This increases the severity of the fault [16]. Hence upgradation of protection system has become inevitable for the reliable operation of modern day power system. Dynamics in fault current magnitude, Bi-directional flow of fault current and False tripping are the major issues of protection in smart grid.

Few factors like stochastic behaviour of RES which feeds variable current into the grid and variable short circuit level depending upon mode of operation of microgrid led to the development of AP schemes. AP refers to automatic adjustment of relays' settings and its operating characteristics in response to change in power system topology and mode of operation. WAMS technology is very much useful for AP. Highly accurate time synchronized phasor measurements obtained from PMU are useful to update the relay settings.

A rule based AP scheme based on ML is presented in [17]. This protection scheme requires database which is obtained by performing simulations on a smart distribution system consisting of DERs under different operating conditions. When computer in the control centre receives tripping signal, it gathers required measurements automatically and sends them to ANN model which estimates the actual occurrence of fault and faulted line. In the model presence of fault, identifying faulted line and location of the fault is estimated using SVM. For redundancy, output obtained from ANN-SVM model is compared with output of real time Least Square Estimation. Depending upon the requirement, on field actuators are used to reconfigure the network. If the ANN model doesn't confirm the presence of fault, the system is considered to be operating under normal state.

The status of DER interconnection is retrieved and protective settings are altered as per requirement. The detailed flowchart of rule based adaptive protection scheme is presented in [17].

11.7   Energy Trading in Smart Grid

With the development of DERs, it has become difficult to match generation and load because of dynamic behaviour of RES. So, it is necessary to have generation forecast from RES to plan the power to be generated from conventional sources [18]. Power system operators depend on LF and generation forecast to manage generation load balance and to avoid over loading of power grid. Smart grid facilitates supply demand balance irrespective of operating mode of power grid even though predicting energy usage patterns is difficult because of dynamic tariff and various demand side management techniques [19]. Energy Storage Systems play a significant role in meeting the peak demands. A battery can store energy during off peak periods or whenever there is excess generation and discharge during peak load periods or wherever there is energy deficit. A customer can sell energy from battery when the tariff is high and draw power from grid to charge battery when the tariff is low. In the present day power market scenario, customers have limited choice of buying energy from a particular utility as per their convenience. With the development of distributed generation small scale power generation utilities are evolved which enables customers the choice of buying required energy from any producer at the price acceptable to them by participating in the market. The structure of Centralized generation system and distributed generation system are shown in Figures 11.6 and 11.7 respectively.

Energy trading is the process of buying electrical energy from producers and selling it to customers at optimal price subjected to market rules. Energy trading among microgrids without the involvement of main grid is called Local Energy Trading (LET), operated under distribution level.

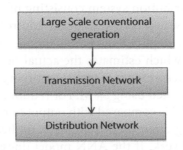

Figure 11.6 Centralized generation system.

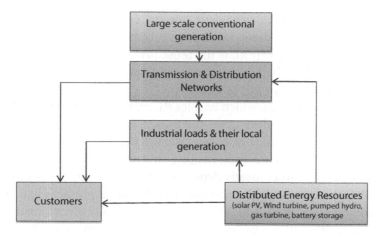

Figure 11.7 Structure of distributed generation system.

The structure of LET is shown in Figure 11.8. It facilitates all producers and customers to participate directly in the market. In LET model, market operator collects the data regarding excess energy available with producer microgrids and energy required by the customer microgrids. The data is shared among all the market players and energy allocation to customer microgrids is done by using any one of the market clearing mechanisms. Game Theory, Multi Objective Optimization, Auction methods are few conventional market clearing methods. Recently ML algorithms have been implemented in energy markets.

1 – Energy required by buyer microgrids.
2 – Energy supplied by seller microgrids.
3 – Energy allocated to buyer microgrids depending upon available surplus.
4, 5 – Money flow.

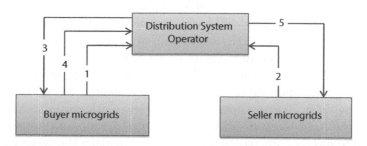

Figure 11.8 Structure of LET.

In [20] the prosumers' behaviour towards energy trading in the local market is modelled and decision making procedure is built as Markov decision process (MDP). Deep RL is the most advanced technique which has been proved to show better performance in several decision making circumstances. It is used to solve decision making procedure based on experience replay mechanism, which enables RL agents to memorize and reuse past experiences depending upon the present situation. Deep RL shares so many common features of conventional RL and is placed on the top of MDP model. As the decision making strategy of prosumers and their behaviour in the market mostly depend on different continuous variables. Deep RL is the most suitable technique to solve MDP problem like LET. It is the combination of RL and ANN. An MDP basically gives a mathematical representation of situations in which a system is mostly stochastic and slightly under the dominance of decision making. Dynamic programming can also solve this type of LET problem but it is very difficult to estimate transition probabilities under many circumstances.

11.8 AI Based Smart Energy Meter (AI-SEM)

Smart Energy Meter (SEM) is the advanced meter which not only records consumption of energy but also measures instantaneous active power, reactive power, power factor, THD, voltage, current and maximum demand as required by customers and utilities [21]. It facilitates the communication between utility and customer. It can maintain communication with household smart appliances; monitor, control and schedule them optimally to reduce total energy bill. It helps in effective implementation of ToU tariff structure which is highly beneficial to the utilities in managing peak demand. With the help of SEM data, customers can analyse their consumption patterns which helps them in bidding optimal values in the energy market.

Integrating AI technology in SEM improves its performance to large extent. In future, AI based SEM will become the first choice because it manages customers' energy consumption and provides improved quality of power under the supervision of AI based power quality diagnosis system [22]. The location of all appliances is recognised by AI-SEM based on smart multi power tap (SMPT) technology. SMPT can detect power flow from all active power socket outlets. Each power socket outlet uses Home Area Network (HAN)to share its location and identity with AI-SEM to monitor and record data. AI-SEM calculates the average energy consumption of each appliance for each day of the week and month and distinguishes between weekend and week days. It classifies all appliances into three groups, low capacity loads, medium capacity loads and high capacity loads, depending upon power rating and frequency of usage. The operation of AI-SEM is shown in flow chart in Figure 11.9.

Artificial Intelligence and Machine Learning are proven to be most promising technological developments without which smart grid can't be realised in practice. In this chapter, brief description of smart grid, AI techniques such as ES, FL, ANN, GA and ML types such as SL, USL & RL are presented. Role of AI techniques and ML algorithms in smart grid entities like HEMS, load forecasting, adaptive protection, energy trading and smart energy meter are explained.

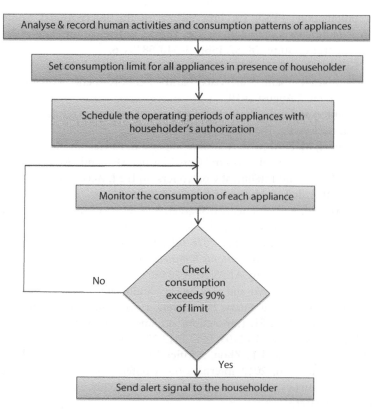

Figure 11.9 Operation of AI-SEM.

References

1. Ali, S.S.; Choi, B.J. State-of-the-Art Artificial Intelligence Techniques for Distributed Smart Grids: A Review. *Electronics* 2020, *9*, 1030.
2. B. K. Bose, Artificial intelligence techniques in smart grid and renewable energy systems in Proc. Keynote Present. Qatar Workshop Smart Grid Renew. Energy (SGRE), Doha, Qatar, Mar. 2015.
3. L. H. Tsoukalas and R. E. Uhrig, Fuzzy and Neural Approaches in Engineering. Hoboken, NJ, USA: Wiley, 1997.
4. Harpreet Singh, Madan M. Gupta, Thomas Meitzler, Zeng-GuangHou, KumKum Garg, Ashu M. G. Solo, Lotfi A. Zadeh, Real-Life Applications of Fuzzy Logic, Advances in Fuzzy Systems, vol. 2013, Article ID 581879, 3 pages, 2013. https://doi.org/10.1155/2013/581879.
5. J. R. Jang, ANFIS: adaptive-network-based fuzzy inference system, in *IEEE Transactions on Systems, Man, and Cybernetics*, vol. 23, no. 3, pp. 665-685, May-June 1993, doi: 10.1109/21.256541.
6. A. E. Eiben, P. E. Raue, Zs. Ruttkay, Genetic algorithms with multi-parent recombination". PPSN III: Proceedings of the International Conference on Evolutionary Computation. The Third Conference on Parallel Problem Solving from Nature: 78–87. ISBN 3-540-58484-6.
7. I. Salian, SuperVize Me: What's the Difference between Supervised, Unsupervised, Semi-Supervised and Reinforcement Learning, 2018. Accessed on: 5 August 2019.
8. R. S. Sutton and A. G. Barto, Reinforcement Learning: An Introduction, 2nd ed. Massachusetts: The MIT Press.
9. H. Shareef, M. S. Ahmed, A. Mohamed and E. Al Hassan, Review on Home Energy Management System Considering Demand Responses, Smart Technologies, and Intelligent Controllers, in IEEE Access, vol. 6, pp. 24498-24509, 2018, doi: 10.1109/ACCESS.2018.2831917.
10. M. S. Ahmed, A. Mohamed, H. Shareef, R. Z. Homod and J. A. Ali, Artificial neural network based controller for home energy management considering demand response events, *2016 International Conference on Advances in Electrical, Electronic and Systems Engineering (ICAEES)*, Putrajaya, 2016, pp. 506-509, doi: 10.1109/ICAEES.2016.7888097.
11. Y. Hong, J. Lin, C. Wu and C. Chuang, Multi-Objective Air-Conditioning Control Considering Fuzzy Parameters Using Immune Clonal Selection Programming, in IEEE Transactions on Smart Grid, vol. 3, no. 4, pp. 1603-1610, Dec. 2012, doi: 10.1109/TSG.2012.2210059.
12. H. Zhang, F. Xu and L. Zhou, Artificial neural network for load forecasting in smart grid, 2010 International Conference on Machine Learning and Cybernetics, Qingdao, 2010, pp. 3200-3205, doi: 10.1109/ICML C.2010.5580713.

13. Park, R.-J.; Song, K.-B.; Kwon, B.-S. Short-Term Load Forecasting Algorithm Using a Similar Day Selection Method Based on Reinforcement Learning. *Energies* 2020, *13*, 2640.
14. A. Almalaq and G. Edwards, A Review of Deep Learning Methods Applied on Load Forecasting, 2017 16th IEEE International Conference on Machine Learning and Applications (ICMLA), Cancun, 2017, pp. 511-516, doi: 10.1109/ICMLA.2017.0-110.
15. H. Lin, K. Sun, Z. Tan, C. Liu, J. M. Guerrero and J. C. Vasquez, Adaptive protection combined with machine learning for microgrids, in IET Generation, Transmission & Distribution, vol. 13, no. 6, pp. 770-779, 26 3 2019, doi: 10.1049/iet-gtd.2018.6230.
16. Chaitanya, B. K. , Soni, A. K. , Yadav, A., Communication assisted fuzzy based adaptive protective relaying scheme for microgrid Journal of Power of Technologies, 2018 | Vol. 98, nr 1 | 57-69.
17. Hengwei Lin, J. M. Guerrero, ChenxiJia, Zheng-hua Tan, J. C. Vasquez and Chengxi Liu, Adaptive overcurrent protection for microgrids in extensive distribution systems, IECON 2016 - 42nd Annual Conference of the IEEE Industrial Electronics Society, Florence, 2016, pp. 4042-4047, doi: 10.1109/IECON.2016.7793091.
18. S. Azad, F. Sabrina and S. Wasimi, Transformation of Smart Grid using Machine Learning, 2019 29th Australasian Universities Power Engineering Conference (AUPEC), Nadi, Fiji, 2019, pp. 1-6, doi: 10.1109/AUPEC48547.2019.211809.
19. M. Khorasany, Y. Mishra and G. Ledwich, Market framework for local energy trading: a review of potential designs and market clearing approaches, in IET Generation, Transmission & Distribution, vol. 12, no. 22, pp. 5899-5908, 11 12 2018, doi: 10.1049/iet-gtd.2018.5309.
20. T. Chen and W. Su, Local Energy Trading Behavior Modeling With Deep Reinforcement Learning, in IEEE Access, vol. 6, pp. 62806-62814, 2018, doi: 10.1109/ACCESS.2018.2876652.
21. Sivaneasan B, So PL, Gunawan E. Modeling and performance analysis of automatic meter reading systems using power line communications,presented at the 11th IEEE Singapore international conference on communication systems, 2008, ICCS 2008, Guangzhou; 2008.
22. A.F.A. Aziz, S.N. Khalid, M.W. Mustafa, H. Shareef, G. Aliyu,Artificial Intelligent Meter development based on Advanced Metering Infrastructure technology,Renewable and Sustainable Energy Reviews, Volume 27, 2013, Pages 191-197, ISSN 1364-0321, https://doi.org/10.1016/j.rser.2013.06.051
23. Priyadarshi.; N;, Padmanaban, S.; Maroti, P.K.; Sharma. A.; An Extensive Practical Investigation of FPSO-Based MPPT for Grid Integrated PV System Under Variable Operating Conditions With Anti-Islanding Protection. IEEE System Journal, **2018**, 13:1861-1871.

24. Priyadarshi, N.; Padmanaban, S.; Bhaskar, M.S.; Blaabjerg, F.; Sharma, A.; A Fuzzy SVPWM Based Inverter Control Realization of Grid Integrated PV-Wind System with FPSO MPPT Algorithm for a Grid-Connected PV/Wind Power Generation System: Hardware Implementation. IET Electric Power Appl., **2018**, 12:962-971.

25. Priyadarshi, N.; Kumar, V.; Yadav, K.; Vardia, M.; An Experimental Study on Zeta buck-boost converter for Application in PV system. Handbook of distributed generation, Springer, DOI 10.1007/978-3-319-51343-0_13

26. Priyadarshi N.; Sharma A.K.; Priyam S.; An Experimental Realization of Grid-Connected PV System with MPPT Using dSPACE DS 1104 Control Board. Advances in Smart Grid and Renewable Energy. Lecture Notes in Electrical Engineering, Springer, Singapore **2018**, 435.

27. Priyadarshi N.; Sharma A.K.; Priyam S.; Practical Realization of an Improved Photovoltaic Grid Integration with MPPT. International Journal of Renewable Energy Research **2017**, 7:1180-1891.

28. Priyadarshi N.; Sharma A.K.; Azam F.; A Hybrid Firefly-Asymmetrical Fuzzy Logic Controller based MPPT for PV-Wind-Fuel Grid Integration. International Journal of Renewable Energy Research **2017**, 7: 1546-1560

29. Priyadarshi, N.; Anand, A.; Sharma, A.K.; Azam, F.; Singh, V.K.; Sinha, R. K.; An Experimental Implementation and Testing of GA based Maximum Power Point Tracking for PV System under Varying Ambient Conditions Using dSPACE DS 1104 Controller. International Journal of Renewable Energy Research, **2017**, 7:255-265.

30. Priyadarshi, N.; Padmanaban S.; Mihet-Popa L.; Blaabjerg, F.; Azam F.; Maximum Power Point Tracking for Brushless DC Motor-Driven Photovoltaic Pumping Systems Using a Hybrid ANFIS-FLOWER Pollination Optimization Algorithm. MDPI Energies **2018**, 11:1-16.

31. Priyadarshi, N.; Azam, F.; Bhoi, A.K.; Alam, S.; An Artificial Fuzzy Logic Intelligent Controller Based MPPT for PV Grid Utility. Lecture Notes in Networks and Systems 46, https://doi.org/10.1007/978-981-13-1217-5_88.

32. Padmanaban, S.; Priyadarshi, N.; Holm-Nielsen, J. B.; Bhaskar, M. S.; Azam, F.; Sharma, A.K.; A Novel Modified Sine-Cosine Optimized MPPT Algorithm for Grid Integrated PV System under Real Operating Conditions. IEEE Access, **2019**, 7:10467-10477.

33. Padmanaban, S.; Priyadarshi, N.; Holm-Nielsen, J. B.; Bhaskar, M. S.; Hossain, E.; Azam, F.; A Hybrid Photovoltaic-Fuel Cell for Grid Integration With Jaya-Based Maximum Power Point Tracking: Experimental Performance Evaluation. IEEE Access, **2019**, 7:82978-82990.

34. Priyadarshi, N.; Padmanaban, N.; Holm-Nielsen, J. B.; Blaabjerg, F.; Bhaskar, M.S.; An Experimental Estimation of Hybrid ANFIS–PSO-Based MPPT for PV Grid Integration Under Fluctuating Sun Irradiance. in IEEE Systems Journal. **2020**, 14:1218-1229.

35. Priyadarshi, N.; Padmanaban, N.; Bhaskar, M. S.; Blaabjerg, F.; Holm-Nielsen, J. B.; Azam, F.; Sharma, A.K.; A Hybrid Photovoltaic-Fuel Cell-Based

Single-Stage Grid Integration With Lyapunov Control Scheme. IEEE Systems Journal, **2020**, 14: 3334-3342.

36. Priyadarshi, N.; Bhaskar, M. S.; Padmanaban, N.; Blaabjerg, F.; Azam, F.; New CUK–SEPIC converter based photovoltaic power system with hybrid GSA–PSO algorithm employing MPPT for water pumping applications. IET Power Electronics. **2020**, 13:2824-2830.

37. Priyadarshi, N.; Padmanaban, N.; Holm-Nielsen, J. B.; Bhaskar, M.S.; Azam, F.; Internet of things augmented a novel PSO-employed modified zeta converter-based photovoltaic maximum power tracking system: hardware realisation. IET Power Electronics. **2020**, 13:2775-2781.

38. Kamalapathi, K., Priyadarshi, N., Padmanaban, S., Holm-Nielsen, J.B., Azam, F., Umayal, C., Ramachandaramurthy, V.K. A Hybrid Moth-Flame Fuzzy Logic Controller Based Integrated Cuk Converter Fed Brushless DC Motor for Power Factor Correction. MDPI Electronics, **2018**, 7: 288.

39. Priyadarshi, N., Padmanaban, S., Lonel, D., Mihet-Popa, L., Azam, F. Hybrid PV-Wind, Micro-Grid Development Using Quasi-Z-Source Inverter Modeling and Control—Experimental Investigation. MDPI Energies, **2018**, 11:2277

40. Priyadarshi, N.; Ramachandaramurthy, V, K.; Padmanaban, S.; Azam, A.; An Ant Colony Optimized MPPT for Standalone Hybrid PV-Wind Power System with Single Cuk Converter. MDPI Energies, **2019**, 12: 167

41. Azam, F.; Yadav, S.K.; Priyadarshi, N.; Padmanaban, S.; and Bansal, R.C.; A Comprehensive Review of Authentication Schemes in Vehicular Ad-Hoc Network, IEEE Access, **2021,** 9:31309-31321, 2021, doi: 10.1109/ACCESS.2021.3060046.

42. Priyadarshi, N.; Sharma, A.K.; Bhoi, A. K.; Ahmad, S. N.; Azam, F.; Priyam, S.; A Practical performance verification of AFLC based MPPT for standalone PV power system under varying weather condition, International Journal of Engineering & Technology, **2018**, 7:338-343.

43. Azam F.; Priyadarshi N.; Nagar H.; Kumar S.; Bhoi A.K.; An Overview of Solar-Powered Electric Vehicle Charging in Vehicular Adhoc Network. in: Electric Vehicles. Green Energy and Technology. Springer, Singapore. https://doi.org/10.1007/978-981-15-9251-5_5

44. Azam, F.; Kumar, S.; Yadav, K.P.; Priyadarshi N.; Padmanaban, S.; An Outline of the Security Challenges in VANET, in Proc. of IEEE UPCON 2020, Nov, 2020.

45. Priyadarshi, N.; Azam, F.; Bhoi, A.K.; Sharma, A.K.; A Multilevel Inverter-Controlled Photovoltaic Generation. in Advances in Greener Energy Technologies. Springer, Singapore. **2020** https://doi.org/10.1007/978-981-15-4246-6_8

46. Priyadarshi, N.; Azam, F.; Bhoi, A.K.; Sharma, A.K.; Dynamic Operation of Grid-Connected Photovoltaic Power System. in Advances in Greener Energy Technologies. Springer, Singapore. **2020** https://doi.org/10.1007/978-981-15-4246-6_13

47. Priyadarshi, N.; Azam, F.; Bhoi, A.K.; Sharma, A.K.; A Proton Exchange Membrane-Based Fuel Cell Integrated Power System. in Advances in Greener Energy Technologies. Springer, Singapore. **2020** https://doi.org/10.1007/978-981-15-4246-6_18

48. Priyadarshi, N.; Azam, F.; Bhoi, A.K.; Sharma, A.K.; A Closed-Loop Control of Fixed Pattern Rectifier for Renewable Energy Applications. in Advances in Greener Energy Technologies. Springer, Singapore. **2020** https://doi.org/10.1007/978-981-15-4246-6_25

49. Priyadarshi, N.; Azam, F.; Bhoi, A.K.; Sharma, A.K.; A Four-Switch-Type Converter Fed Improved Photovoltaic Power System. in Advances in Greener Energy Technologies. Springer, Singapore. **2020** https://doi.org/10.1007/978-981-15-4246-6_29

50. Vardia, M.; Priyadarshi, N.; Ali, I.; Azam, F.; Bhoi, A.K.; Maximum Power Point Tracking for Wind Energy Conversion System. in Advances in Greener Energy Technologies. Springer, Singapore. **2020** https://doi.org/10.1007/978-981-15-4246-6_36

51. Vardia, M.; Priyadarshi, N.; Ali, I.; Azam, F.; Bhoi, A.K.; Design of Wind Energy Conversion System Under Different Fault Conditions. in Advances in Greener Energy Technologies. Springer, Singapore. **2020** https://doi.org/10.1007/978-981-15-4246-6_41

52. Choudhary, T.; Priyadarshi, N.; Kuma,r P.; Azam, F.; Bhoi A.K. (2020) A Fuzzy Logic Control Based Vibration Control System for Renewable Application. in Advances in Greener Energy Technologies. Springer, Singapore. **2020** https://doi.org/10.1007/978-981-15-4246-6_38

53. Priyadarshi, N.; Azam F.; Solanki, S. S.; Sharma, A.K.; Bhoi, A.K.; Almakhles, D.; A Bio-Inspired Chicken Swarm Optimization-Based Fuel Cell System for Electric Vehicle Applications. in Bio-inspired Neurocomputing. Studies in Computational Intelligence, vol. 903. Springer, Singapore. **2021** https://doi.org/10.1007/978-981-15-5495-7_1

12

Energy Loss Allocation in Distribution Systems with Distributed Generations

Dr. Kushal Manohar Jagtap

Electrical Engineering Department, National Institute of Technology Srinagar, Hazratbal, J & K, India

Abstract

In the deregulated power systems, setting the adequate price of electricity has emerged as a key issue. Likewise, other cost of distribution activities, energy losses are one of the costs to be allocated. Therefore, a meaningful loss allocation technique is required to reduce additional economic penalties or rewards for network participants. This paper presents a new method for energy loss allocation in the radial distribution network (RDN) with distributed generation in the context of the deregulated power system. The proposed method is dedicated to distribution networks and therefore a branch-oriented approach is employed to draw a solution. Based on the power summation algorithm, it decomposes the branch power flow into the injection/consumption of power by network participants. Therefore, allocated losses by the proposed method are based on the actual contribution of each participant into the network losses. To avoid reconciliation in the allocation procedure, it adopts a backward sweep network reduction technique. In order to test the proposed method, it has been applied to a 33-node test system. The effectiveness of the proposed method has been analyzed considering different static load models. The results obtained by the proposed method have been compared with those by existing methods in the literature.

Keywords: Distributed generation, radial distribution network, power flow, energy loss allocation

Email: jagtapkushal@nitsri.ac.in

Neeraj Priyadarshi, Akash Kumar Bhoi, Sanjeevikumar Padmanaban, S. Balamurugan and Jens Bo Holm-Nielsen (eds.) Intelligent Renewable Energy Systems, (307–344) © 2022 Scrivener Publishing LLC

12.1   Introduction

Under deregulated environment, the traditional horizontal structure of power systems is changing to the vertical structure of power systems. This change leads to unbundling of electrical power networks in a generation, transmission, and distribution entities [1]. Under such an environment, generation companies would be in competition with each other to serve more than one distribution utility. Generations are assigned by auction or trade contracts instead of economic dispatching orders. Unlike the generation, transmission, and distribution segments, however, are immune to competition and are generally considered to have a natural monopoly [1, 2]. Like a transmission network, a distribution network is also a service provider and charges the consumers for its services without any suitable technical and economic logic. The charges paid by consumers are affected by the network operating cost, and a large share of network operating cost is occupied due to the power losses. Therefore, equitable allocation of losses is very important for the efficient operation of the network.

Earlier, the problem of loss allocation was concerned with transmission networks only. After deregulation and introduction of distributed generations (DGs), problems of loss allocation in radial distribution networks (RDNs) have been given equal importance as in case of transmission networks. Since DG alters the power flows in the radial network from unidirectional to bidirectional, and thus affects the network losses [3, 4].

Practically, loss allocation is a complex issue because losses in the branches of a network are quadratic functions of power of generators and loads [1, 3]. Further, there is a strong interdependence among all the generators and consumers, expressed by the presence of cross-terms [5]. It is still under discussion to identify the exact contribution of generators and consumers into total network losses. Therefore, a loss allocation methodology must attain some essential attributes, as it should be simple, easy to understand/implement; utilize only on-site practical value of the network data; be accurate and consistent with equitable allocation of losses; consider both active and reactive power flow of the network; reflect the relative location of each generator and consumer; and send adequate economic signals to generator and consumer [6, 7].

Different methods have been reported in the literature for the allocation of losses and can be classified into five major categories as: 1) pro-rata (PR) method, 2) marginal loss coefficient (MLC) method, 3) proportional sharing method, 4) circuit based method, and 5) branch-oriented based method.

Pro-Rata method [6] is a simple, easy to implement, it is classical and widely used method for loss allocation. In this method, total network losses are assigned to network participants proportionally according to their apparent power ratings irrespective of their location within the network. While allocating the losses, Pro-Rata (PR) method does not consider network power flow. MLC method [8] is also known as incremental transmission loss (ITL) coefficient method, and it is a well-known method for loss allocation in transmission network. It allocates the losses to generators and loads through the ITL coefficients. In this method, different selection of slack/root node gives different value of ITL coefficients which further affect the allocated losses among generators and loads. Also, the method results in over-recovery of losses and therefore an additional step of reconciliation is needed [6, 8]. In proportional sharing method [6, 9], losses are allocated to generators and loads by using the results of a converged power flow along with a linear proportional sharing principle. Due to linear proportional sharing principle, 50% of the total network losses are first assigned to generators and remaining 50% of losses are assigned to loads. However, a 50-50% scheme of loss allocation is not suitable for RDN because power generated by DGs meets small percentage of total load of the network as compare to that of root node. Conejo *et al.* [10] proposed a Z-bus method which is a circuit-based procedure for allocating distribution losses to generators and loads. By using this method, negative losses are also assigned to those generators and loads which assist to reduce network losses by placing them well position in the network strategically. These negative losses can be interpreted as cross-subsidies. This method is having its own limitations when applied to RDNs due to the fact that building of Z-bus is difficult with negligible shunt elements as in most of the distribution networks. Conejo *et al.* [6] presented a comparison of different practical algorithms available for loss allocation in transmission networks.

In a deregulated environment, Mishra *et al.* [11] presented a branch-oriented approach to allocate losses to loads in RDN using exact method of loss allocation. Savier and Das [12] presented an energy loss allocation at various load levels, and also explained the proportional and quadratic methods to allocate and compare energy loss allocation. Carpaneto *et al.* [13] presented a branch current decomposition method for loss allocation in the RDN with DGs. This method allocates the losses based on a relation between branch current and load current at a node. Carpaneto *et al.* [17] presented a detailed characterization of different loss allocation techniques for RDNs with DG.

In order to solve the mutual relation (cross-terms) among network participants, authors in [5] proposed several techniques for careful allocation of the cross-terms. But while allocating the losses, method in [5] considers only active power flow and neglects reactive power flow of network participants.

Pankaj Kumar *et al.* [3] presented loss allocation methods by exact decomposing of cross-term of network participants by considering their active and reactive power flow. Cross-terms of each participants are handled individually and contributions of DGs in network losses are calculated based on the principle of superposition theorem. Atanasovski and Taleski [7] proposed a power summation method which allocates the network losses by using quadratic scheme of allocation. Atanasovski and Taleski [14] presented a branch-oriented approach for allocation of energy losses. It is a statistical based approach which utilizes daily load and daily generation curves.

Jahromi *et al.* [15] presented a loss allocation method for RDNs with DG in which the loss is allocated in three steps: in first step, loss is allocated to consumer node where load is more than generation; in second step, loss is allocated to generator node where generation is more than load, and in last step, the remaining portion of losses is allocated by the proportionality principle based on the voltage variation. During the loss allocation, this method avoids losses in the downstream branches fed by an upstream branch and therefore this method performs a step of normalization to recover the avoided losses. Kushal Manohar Jagtap and Dheeraj Kumar Khatod [16] proposed a method which allocates the network losses among participants by improving their cross subsidies and to do this, they have developed a relation between two different power flow condition of the network i.e., network with DGs and network without DGs. Hortensia Amaris *et al.* [17] solved problem of loss allocation by combining the principle of electric circuits and Aumann-Shaply as game theory. To calculate coefficients of participants, current demand/injection of participants and the network topology are employed.

The proposed methodology is suitable for energy loss allocation in RDN with and without integration of DG in the network. The contributions of the paper can be summarized as:

1. Proposed method overcomes the drawback of the PR method [6] by employing the power flow solutions for allocation of the energy losses in the network.
2. To avoid the unfairness in the results, it assigns network losses to both DG and load simultaneously, and avoid 50-50% scheme of loss allocation [6, 8].
3. It considers not only active/real power but also reactive power flows for allocation of active energy loss in the network [5].
4. It does not make any assumption or approximation, and therefore it is exempted from additional steps of reconciliation [7, 8, 15].

In this paper, a new method is proposed for allocation of energy losses in RDN with DG. The proposed method considers branch power flow and allocates energy losses based on power injection and consumption of generators and consumers, respectively, at specified period of time. It allocates the energy losses based on decomposition of the energy flow at the receiving end of a branch. The proposed method is simple, efficient and easy to implement. It is circuit-based branch-oriented approach. It allocates energy losses to each generator and consumer of various load models by finding their actual contribution in the power losses, without making any approximation regarding the sharing of energy losses. In order to allocate the energy losses, it requires the network data and the power flow solution only. Further, to avoid approximation and the additional step of reconciliation, proposed method employs backward sweep network reduction technique. This technique starts from terminal branch and moves towards root node after allocating the energy losses of a branch to all participants supplied by it, and treating the branch under consideration lossless.

The rest of the paper is organized in five sections. Section 12.2, is about the theoretical and mathematical explanation of various load models. Section 12.3, presents the mathematical model of the proposed method. Section 12.4, shows flowchart of the proposed algorithm. Section 12.5, discusses and compares the results obtained by proposed method with PR method, power summation method of loss allocation (PSMLA), and branch current decomposition of loss allocation (BCDLA) method; and finally, Section 12.6, draws the conclusion of the work.

12.2 Load Modelling

While allocating the network losses, most of the loads on the network are considered as constant sink of active and reactive power and such type of load model is known as constant power (CP) load model. In this model, loads are independent on the magnitude of voltages. But in practical power system operation, network comprises industrial, commercial, residential load *etc.* Active and reactive power of such loads are dependent on the magnitude of voltage and system frequency [18].

Allocated losses of network participants have been significantly affected by the load characteristic. Unlike CP load model, load can be modeled as constant current (CC) and constant impedance (CI) load models. In RDN, most of the static loads are mainly affected by the voltage variation rather than frequency variation [18, 19], and therefore in this study, load can be considered only effect of magnitude of voltage and neglected the frequency deviation. Common static load models for active and reactive power can be expressed in an exponential form without considering the effect of frequency deviation as:

$$p(i,l) = P(i,l)\left[\frac{v(i)}{V(i)}\right]^{\tau} \tag{12.1}$$

$$q(i,l) = Q(i,l)\left[\frac{v(i)}{V(i)}\right]^{\psi} \tag{12.2}$$

where $p(i, l)$ and $q(i, l)$ are active and reactive, respectively, power of load l at i^{th} node;
$P(i, l)$ and $Q(i, l)$ are nominal value of active and reactive, respectively, power of load l at i^{th} node;
$v(i)$ is magnitude of voltage at i^{th} node;
$V(i)$ is magnitude of nominal value of voltage at i^{th} node; and
τ and ψ are load exponents.

When values of τ and ψ become same and equal to the 0, 1, and 2 then load can be represented as CP, CC, and CI load models, respectively [18, 19].

12.3   Mathematical Model

In order to formulate the proposed algorithm in a simple manner, let us consider the RDN which has a branch connected between substation to root node (marked as branch '0') is assumed to be lossless as shown in Figure 12.1. Also, root node acts as reference node and therefore it is marked as 1 and assigns unique integer numbers on different nodes sequentially. After this, a branch is assigned a number equal to one less than the number assigned to its receiving end node as shown in Figure 12.1. Apart from this, RDN is comprised with various consumers and DG which are modelled as positive load and negative load, respectively. Further, it is assumed that the effect of shunt conductance and susceptance has been neglected.

In the proposed energy loss allocation method, first study period is divided into a number of intervals, and power losses are allocated to DGs and loads for each intervals. Finally, considering the allocated losses to network participants during individual interval, energy losses are assigned to them.

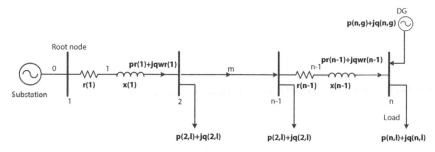

Figure 12.1 Single line diagram of n-node RDN.

From Figure 12.1, power loss in the ith branch during a tth time interval can be expressed in terms of power injection/consumption by DG/load and power at the receiving end of branch connected beyond it as follows:

$$ps(t,i) = pr(t,i) - \sum_{k=1}^{\alpha_i} \big(p(t,k,l) - p(t,k,g) \big) \qquad (12.3\text{a})$$

$$qs(t,i) = qr(t,i) - \sum_{k=1}^{\alpha_i} \big(q(t,k,l) - q(t,k,g) \big) \qquad (12.3\text{b})$$

where, $ps(t, i)$ and $qs(t, i)$ are active and reactive, respectively, power loss in i^{th} branch at t^{th} time interval;

$pr(t, i)$ and $qr(t, i)$ are active and reactive, respectively, power at the receiving end of ith branch at t^{th} time interval.

$p(t, k, l)$ and $q(t, k, l)$ are active and reactive, respectively, power of load l at k^{th} node at t^{th} time interval.

$p(t, k, g)$ and $q(t, k, g)$ are active and reactive, respectively, power of DG g at k^{th} node at t^{th} time interval.

α_i is the number of nodes at downstream of ith branch.

Active and reactive power losses in the ith branch are calculated using the following expression:

$$ps(i,t) + jqs(i,t) = \left(\frac{r(i) + jx(i)}{v(t,i)} \right) \big\{ \big(pr(t,i) \times pr(t,i) \big) + \big(qr(t,i) \times qr(t,i) \big) \big\}$$

$$(12.4\text{a})$$

$$= \left(\frac{r(i)+jx(i)}{v(t,i)} pr(t,i) \right) pr(t,i) + \left(\frac{r(i)+jx(i)}{v(t,i)} qr(t,i) \right) qr(t,i) \qquad (12.4b)$$

$$= (PR(t,i) + jPX(t,i))pr(t,i) + (QR(t,i) + jQX(t,i))qr(t,i) \qquad (12.4c)$$

where $\dfrac{r(i)}{v(t,i)} pr(t,i) = PR(t,i);\ \dfrac{x(i)}{v(t,i)} pr(t,i) = PX(t,i);\ \dfrac{r(i)}{v(t,i)} qr(t,i) = QR(t,i);$

$\dfrac{x(i)}{v(t,i)} qr(t,i) = QX(t,i)r(i)$ and $x(i)$ are resistance and reactance, respectively, of ith branch;

$v(t, i)$ is the voltage at the receiving end of ith branch at t^{th} time interval.

Modify and substitute Eqs. (12.3a) and (12.3b) in Eq. (12.4c), the active and reactive power loss in the ith branch can be expressed as:

$$ps(t,i)\left[PR(t,i) \left\{ \sum_{k=1}^{\alpha_i} (p(t,k,l) - p(t,k,g)) + \sum_{k=1}^{\beta_i} ps(t,k) \right\} \right] +$$

$$\left[QR(t,i) \left\{ \sum_{k=1}^{\alpha_i} (q(t,k,l) - p(t,k,g)) + \sum_{k=1}^{\beta_i} qs(t,k) \right\} \right] \qquad (12.5a)$$

$$qs(t,i)\left[PX(t,i) \left\{ \sum_{k=1}^{\alpha_i} (p(t,k,l) - p(t,k,g)) + \sum_{k=1}^{\beta_i} ps(t,k) \right\} \right] +$$

$$\left[QX(t,i) \left\{ \sum_{k=1}^{\alpha_i} (q(t,k,l) - q(t,k,g)) + \sum_{k=1}^{\beta_i} qs(t,k) \right\} \right] \qquad (12.5b)$$

where β_i is the total number of branches at downstream of ith branch.

It can easily be observed from above equations that power losses in the ith branch have two components – first due to loads/DGs at various nodes ahead of it and second due to power losses in various branches fed by it. The first component is easy to identify, while the second component is difficult to trace. To simplify the formulation, some authors have neglected the second components while allocating the network losses [15]. This leads to unfair distribution of losses among network participants. The proposed method does not make such approximation and hence uses backward sweep network reduction technique for allocation of losses.

The proposed method starts the allocation of losses with terminal branch as this branch has no further branch to supply. Using Eq. (12.5a), the power losses in the terminal branch n-1 can be expressed as:

$$ps(t, n\text{-}1) = \{PR(t, n\text{-}1)(p(t, n, l) - p(t, n, g))\} + \{QR(t, n\text{-}1)(q(t, n, l) - q(t, n, g))\}$$
$$(12.6)$$

Now, power loss in the $n\text{-}1^{th}$ branch is allocated to load and DG connected at n^{th} node, as:

For load: $\nabla ps(t, n, l, n - 1) = PR(t, n\text{-}1)p(t, n, l) + QR(t, n\text{-}1)q(t, n, l)$ (12.7)

For DG: $\nabla ps(t, n, g, n - 1) = -PR(t, n\text{-}1)p(t, n, g) - QR(t, n\text{-}1)q(t, n, g)$ (12.8)

where $\nabla ps(t, n, l, n - 1)$ and $\nabla ps(t, n, g, n - 1)$ are allocated active power loss of $n\text{-}1^{th}$ branch to load l and DG g, respectively, at n^{th} node at t^{th} time interval.

Reactive power loss allocation to load and DG at n^{th} node is also calculated in a similar way as active power loss allocation.

After allocating the losses of terminal branch $n\text{-}1$ to end node n, the DG/load connected at node n is removed and connected to node $n\text{-}1$ after adding their allocated losses to their corresponding ratings. The updated ratings of load and DG, initially connected at node n, at node $n\text{-}1$ is computed by the following expressions:

$$\text{For load: } up(t, n - 1, l_n) = p(t, n, l) + \nabla ps(t, n, l, n - 1) \quad (12.9)$$

$$uq(t, n - 1, l_n) = q(t, n, l) + \nabla qs(t, n, l, n - 1) \quad (12.10)$$

$$\text{For DG: } up(t, n - 1, g_n) = p(t, n, g) + \nabla ps(t, n, g, n - 1) \quad (12.11)$$

$$uq(t, n - 1, g_n) = q(t, n, g) + \nabla qs(t, n, g, n - 1) \quad (12.12)$$

where $up(t, n - 1, l_n)$ and $uq(t, n - 1, l_n)$ are updated active and reactive, respectively, power of load l (initially connected at n^{th} node) connected at $n\text{-}1^{th}$ node at t^{th} time interval.

$up(t, n - 1, g_n)$ and $uq(t, n - 1, g_n)$ are updated active and reactive, respectively, power of DG g (initially connected at n^{th} node) connected at $n\text{-}1^{th}$ node at t^{th} time interval.

Since the losses of terminal branch $n\text{-}1$ has been allocated to end nodes and DG/load at end node has been removed, the terminal branch $n\text{-}1$ is also eliminated. These results from the network reduction from n node to $n\text{-}1$ node with branch $n\text{-}2$ as terminal branch.

Next, power loss in the branch $n\text{-}2$ is allocated to its original load, and updated rating of DG and load, which were removed from node n and connected to node $n\text{-}1$. After this, a similar procedure is adopted as described earlier for branch $n\text{-}1$ till all lossy branches of network are eliminated and all updated loads and DGs are connected at root node. At this point, power injected at root node becomes equal to the updated power of all loads and DGs connected at it as:

$$p(t,0) + jq(t,0) = \sum_{k=1}^{\alpha_0} \{up(t,1,l_k) + up(t,1,g_k)\} + j \sum_{k=1}^{\alpha_0} \{uq(t,1,l_k) + juq(t,1,g_k)\}$$

$$(12.13)$$

Now, total active and reactive power loss allocated to load/DG at any node m can be calculated by subtracting the actual power rating from their corresponding updated power of load/DG connected at root node as:

For load: $\Delta ps(t, m, l) = up(t, 1, l_m) - p(t, m, l)$; and
$\Delta qs(t, m, l) = uq(t, 1, l_m) - q(t, m, l)$ (12.14)

For DG: $\Delta ps(t, m, g) = up(t, 1, g_m) - p(t, m, g)$; and
$\Delta qs(t, m, g) = uq(t, 1, g_m) - q(t, m, g)$ (12.15)

where $\Delta ps(t, m, l)$ and $\Delta qs(t, m, l)$ are total allocated active and reactive, respectively, power loss of load l connected at m^{th} node at t^{th} time interval.

$\Delta ps(t, m, g)$ and $\Delta qs(t, m, g)$ are total allocated active and reactive, respectively, power loss of DG g connected at m^{th} node at t^{th} time interval.

Finally, for entire calculation period of time, total active and reactive energy losses allocated to load and DG are expressed as:

For load: $\Delta pes(m,l) = \Delta T \sum_{k=1}^{nt} \{up(1,m,l_k) - p(m,k,l)\}$; and $(12.16a)$

$$\Delta qes(m,l) = \Delta T \sum_{k=1}^{nt} \{uq(1,m,l_k) - q(m,k,l)\} \qquad (12.16b)$$

$$\text{For DG: } \Delta pes(m,g) = \Delta T \sum_{k=1}^{nt} \{up(1,m,g_k) - p(m,k,g)\}; \text{and} \quad (12.17a)$$

$$\Delta qes(m,g) = \Delta T \sum_{k=1}^{nt} \{uq(1,m,g_k) - q(m,k,g)\} \qquad (12.17b)$$

where $\Delta pes(m, l)$ and $\Delta qes(m, l)$ are allocated active and reactive, respectively, energy loss to load l at m^{th} node; nt is total number of time period; ΔT is interval of the time period;
$\Delta pes(m, g)$ and $\Delta qes(m, g)$ are allocated active and reactive, respectively, energy loss to DG g at m^{th} node.

The sum of allocated energy losses of load and DG at every node in the network gives the total energy losses in the network as:

$$pes + jqes = \sum_{k=1}^{\alpha_0} \{\Delta pes(k,l) + \Delta pes(k,g)\} + j \sum_{k=1}^{\alpha_0} \{\Delta qes(k,l) + \Delta qes(k,g)\}$$

$$(12.18)$$

where pes and qes are active and reactive, respectively, energy loss of the network.

12.4   Solution Algorithm

A flow chart indicating different steps involved in the proposed method for energy loss allocation to DGs and loads in RDN is shown in Figure 12.2.

12.5   Results and Discussion

The proposed method has been applied to 33-node RDN, and line data as well as peak active and reactive power at different nodes of this test system

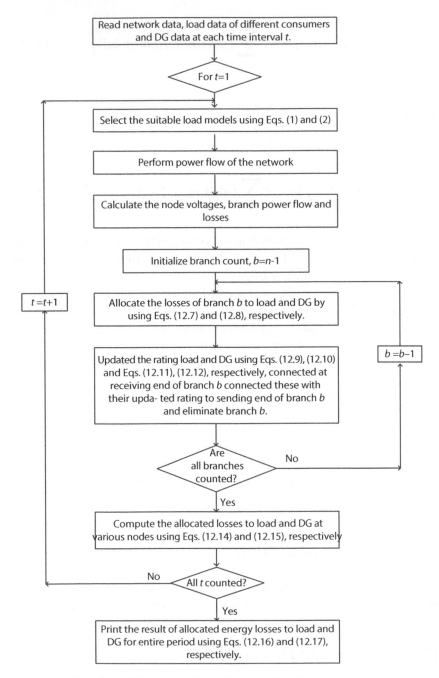

Figure 12.2 Flowchart of the proposed loss allocation algorithm.

have been taken from [20]. Consumers connected in the test network have different characteristics, and therefore their load profile is also different. However, the test network has been modified by connecting different consumers in a particular sequence as shown in Table 12.1. The daily load profile of individual consumers is obtained from [21].

In addition to this, various load models such as CP, CC and CI load models, are also considered, and their impact is analyzed on the loss allocation. The test network has further been modified by connecting three DGs at node 8, node 18 and node 33. Details of DG connection, its power injection corresponding to time and its types are mentioned in Table 12.2.

For each hour (h) of a day under consideration, power flow solution has been obtained using the method as described in [22] taking CP, CC and CI load models under two scenarios: 1) without DG integration, and 2) with DG integration. After performing power flow, the energy losses at both the scenarios have been computed for each hour and it is shown in Figure 12.3.

After calculating the network losses for each hour, from Figure 12.3, it is observed that network has attained minimum losses at 4 AM considered as off-peak hour while network has attained maximum losses at 11 AM considered as peak hour. Network losses without DG at 4 AM are 19.768 kW,

Table 12.1 Consumers type and their connected nodes.

Consumer types	Connected at nodes
Household	2, 7, 12, 17, 22, 27, 32
Commercial	3, 8, 13, 18, 23, 28, 33
Light industries	4, 9, 14, 19, 24, 29
Rural	5, 10, 15, 20, 25, 30
Heavy industries	6, 11, 16, 21, 26, 31

Table 12.2 DG data at different nodes.

DG nodes	Period	Power (kVA)	Type
DG at node 8	For 24-h period	240.00 + j96.00	PQ
DG at node 18	From 8 AM to 6 PM	400.00 + j160.00	PQ
DG at node 18	From 6 PM to 8 AM	240.00 + j96.00	PQ
DG at node 33	For 24-h period	400.00 + j85.00	PQ

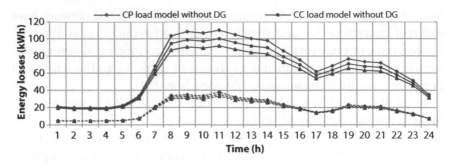

Figure 12.3 Total energy losses in the network at 1-h interval for scenario without and with DG.

19.023 kW and 18.330 kW on CP, CC and CI load models, respectively; while network losses without DG at 11 AM are 110.349 kW, 100.451 kW and 91.951 kW on CP, CC and CI load models, respectively. Similarly, network losses with DG at 4 AM are 4.637 kW, 4.603 kW and 4.569 kW on CP, CC and CI load models, respectively; while network losses with DG at 11 AM are 34.848 kW, 32.828 kW and 30.959 kW on CP, CC and CI load models, respectively.

Now the proposed method has been applied to the test network under consideration and results obtained have been compared with those computed by other methods, namely, PR method, PSMLA and BCDLA method for the sake of comparison. Tables 12.3 and 12.4 show the node-wise allocated losses at 4 AM and 11 AM, respectively, of a network without DG on various load models. From those tables it indicates that positive allocated losses are represented as penalty for increasing the network losses whereas negative allocated losses are represented as reward for reducing the network losses. From Table 12.3 it is seen that all the methods assign positive losses to consumers connected in the network except by BCDLA method. It assigns negative losses to consumer at node 19 and node 21, which is unacceptable by the electricity market, because consumers consumed power from only one source i.e., root node and hence they must be penalized for increasing network losses.

It is fact that a consumer close to root node has get more economical benefits than a consumer far away from root node, and therefore from the Tables 12.3 and 12.4 it is seen that consumer at node 2 gets less penalty as compared to that of consumer at node 33. At 4 AM network without DG, it is observed from Table 12.3 that proposed method provides less penalty to consumers at node 2 and more penalty to consumer at node 33 as compared to other methods. Also, same observation is also made for consumer at node 2 and node 33 at 11 AM network without DG as shown in Table 12.4.

Table 12.3 Allocated losses (kW) at 4 AM with different load models in scenario without DG.

Node no.	CP load model				CC load model				CI load model			
	PR method	PSMLA	BCDLA method	Proposed method	PR method	PSMLA	BCDLA method	Proposed method	PR method	PSMLA	BCDLA method	Proposed method
1	0.000	0.000	0.000	0.000	0.000	0.000	0.000	0.000	0.000	0.000	0.000	0.000
2	0.529	0.048	0.071	0.041	0.509	0.045	0.072	0.040	0.491	0.043	0.074	0.039
3	0.269	0.070	0.046	0.139	0.259	0.069	0.043	0.135	0.249	0.069	0.039	0.133
4	0.512	0.174	0.184	0.254	0.493	0.171	0.178	0.248	0.475	0.168	0.172	0.242
5	0.516	0.216	0.248	0.308	0.497	0.211	0.24	0.299	0.479	0.207	0.232	0.291
6	0.269	0.086	0.163	0.237	0.258	0.084	0.155	0.229	0.249	0.081	0.147	0.221
7	1.095	1.704	1.408	1.280	1.054	1.645	1.365	1.235	1.016	1.589	1.323	1.192
8	0.571	1.165	1.072	0.998	0.550	1.122	1.035	0.961	0.530	1.082	1.001	0.926
9	0.264	0.124	0.242	0.303	0.254	0.119	0.230	0.291	0.245	0.115	0.218	0.280
10	0.519	0.545	0.636	0.633	0.499	0.522	0.609	0.606	0.481	0.500	0.584	0.582
11	0.198	0.075	0.187	0.257	0.19	0.072	0.175	0.246	0.183	0.069	0.165	0.236

(Continued)

Table 12.3 Allocated losses (kW) at 4 AM with different load models in scenario without DG. (*Continued*)

Node no.	CP load model				CC load model				CI load model			
	PR method	PSMLA	BCDLA method	Proposed method	PR method	PSMLA	BCDLA method	Proposed method	PR method	PSMLA	BCDLA method	Proposed method
12	0.319	0.369	0.536	0.549	0.307	0.352	0.512	0.526	0.296	0.337	0.490	0.504
13	0.159	0.215	0.386	0.423	0.154	0.205	0.366	0.404	0.148	0.196	0.347	0.387
14	0.512	0.717	0.816	0.784	0.493	0.682	0.779	0.748	0.475	0.650	0.745	0.715
15	0.522	0.680	0.763	0.74	0.502	0.647	0.728	0.706	0.484	0.616	0.696	0.674
16	0.269	0.186	0.354	0.397	0.258	0.177	0.334	0.378	0.249	0.168	0.316	0.361
17	0.347	0.419	0.606	0.608	0.334	0.397	0.576	0.579	0.322	0.377	0.548	0.553
18	0.269	0.482	0.662	0.655	0.259	0.457	0.630	0.624	0.249	0.434	0.600	0.595
19	0.392	0.014	-0.087	0.027	0.377	0.014	-0.088	0.027	0.363	0.014	-0.089	0.027
20	0.776	0.121	0.013	0.111	0.747	0.120	0.011	0.109	0.719	0.119	0.010	0.108
21	0.400	0.038	-0.045	0.063	0.385	0.038	-0.046	0.062	0.371	0.037	-0.047	0.061
22	0.502	0.09	0.001	0.101	0.483	0.089	0.000	0.100	0.466	0.089	-0.001	0.099

(*Continued*)

Table 12.3 Allocated losses (kW) at 4 AM with different load models in scenario without DG. (*Continued*)

Node no.	CP load model				CC load model				CI load model			
	PR method	PSMLA	BCDLA method	Proposed method	PR method	PSMLA	BCDLA method	Proposed method	PR method	PSMLA	BCDLA method	Proposed method
23	0.245	0.087	0.089	0.175	0.236	0.085	0.085	0.171	0.227	0.084	0.081	0.167
24	1.823	1.106	1.117	1.036	1.755	1.082	1.097	1.013	1.691	1.059	1.079	0.991
25	3.616	3.286	2.647	2.318	3.481	3.207	2.602	2.264	3.353	3.131	2.559	2.212
26	0.267	0.089	0.175	0.247	0.257	0.086	0.166	0.238	0.248	0.084	0.158	0.230
27	0.338	0.209	0.352	0.395	0.325	0.203	0.338	0.381	0.313	0.196	0.324	0.367
28	0.195	0.096	0.245	0.306	0.188	0.092	0.233	0.294	0.181	0.089	0.221	0.283
29	0.516	0.454	0.680	0.670	0.497	0.435	0.652	0.643	0.479	0.418	0.626	0.617
30	1.584	3.398	2.693	2.357	1.525	3.252	2.594	2.257	1.469	3.115	2.501	2.165
31	0.666	0.742	0.973	0.916	0.641	0.708	0.933	0.876	0.618	0.677	0.895	0.839
32	1.159	2.595	2.273	2.005	1.116	2.477	2.184	1.917	1.075	2.366	2.102	1.835
33	0.148	0.178	0.400	0.435	0.142	0.170	0.380	0.416	0.137	0.162	0.351	0.398

Table 12.4 Allocated losses (kW) at 11 AM with different load models in scenario without DG.

Node no.	CP load model				CC load model				CI load model			
	PR method	PSMLA	BCDLA method	Proposed method	PR method	PSMLA	BCDLA method	Proposed method	PR method	PSMLA	BCDLA method	Proposed method
1	0.000	0.000	0.000	0.000	0.000	0.000	0.000	0.000	0.000	0.000	0.000	0.000
2	1.792	0.154	0.184	0.121	1.631	0.154	0.136	0.116	1.494	0.154	0.140	0.112
3	2.893	0.743	0.528	1.098	2.633	0.721	0.936	1.041	2.41	0.698	0.886	0.990
4	3.917	2.180	2.150	2.225	3.566	2.081	2.039	2.091	3.265	1.986	1.923	1.973
5	1.961	0.542	1.029	1.169	1.785	0.518	0.989	1.091	1.634	0.496	0.920	1.022
6	2.112	1.078	1.885	1.976	1.922	1.003	1.749	1.816	1.759	0.936	1.610	1.676
7	3.665	3.875	3.950	3.921	3.336	3.570	3.616	3.593	3.054	3.301	3.333	3.309
8	6.336	11.348	8.196	7.920	5.768	10.341	7.425	7.22	5.280	9.471	6.821	6.615
9	2.099	1.590	2.570	2.621	1.910	1.443	2.335	2.374	1.748	1.316	2.122	2.162
10	1.983	1.425	2.432	2.491	1.805	1.280	2.198	2.243	1.652	1.158	1.985	2.032
11	1.488	1.104	2.260	2.329	1.355	0.990	2.043	2.095	1.240	0.894	1.842	1.896

(Continued)

Table 12.4 Allocated losses (kW) at 11 AM with different load models in scenario without DG. (Continued)

Node no.	CP load model				CC load model				CI load model			
	PR method	PSMLA	BCDLA method	Proposed method	PR method	PSMLA	BCDLA method	Proposed method	PR method	PSMLA	BCDLA method	Proposed method
12	1.079	0.543	1.637	1.742	0.983	0.486	1.485	1.564	0.900	0.438	1.333	1.413
13	1.859	2.289	3.433	3.434	1.693	2.025	3.060	3.064	1.550	1.807	2.745	2.751
14	3.917	8.964	7.515	7.279	3.566	7.911	6.648	6.481	3.265	7.044	5.970	5.808
15	2.004	1.788	2.924	2.955	1.824	1.572	2.601	2.627	1.669	1.394	2.323	2.351
16	2.112	2.347	3.512	3.508	1.922	2.058	3.113	3.115	1.759	1.822	2.780	2.785
17	1.14	0.612	1.883	1.974	1.037	0.534	1.679	1.749	0.949	0.47	1.488	1.561
18	2.893	5.344	5.599	5.474	2.633	4.674	4.933	4.848	2.410	4.128	4.403	4.323
19	3.078	0.174	0.024	0.223	2.801	0.173	0.068	0.215	2.564	0.171	0.061	0.208
20	2.953	0.318	0.175	0.365	2.687	0.314	0.216	0.356	2.46	0.309	0.209	0.348
21	3.104	0.447	0.272	0.456	2.825	0.441	0.31	0.445	2.586	0.434	0.301	0.435
22	1.669	0.143	0.067	0.263	1.519	0.141	0.112	0.257	1.391	0.139	0.107	0.251

(Continued)

Table 12.4 Allocated losses (kW) at 11 AM with different load models in scenario without DG. (Continued)

Node no.	CP load model				CC load model				CI load model			
	PR method	PSMLA	BCDLA method	Proposed method	PR method	PSMLA	BCDLA method	Proposed method	PR method	PSMLA	BCDLA method	Proposed method
23	2.810	0.837	1.254	1.381	2.558	0.808	1.218	1.31	2.342	0.778	1.156	1.245
24	14.269	12.271	8.911	8.595	12.989	11.61	8.385	8.135	11.89	10.99	7.986	7.719
25	13.751	10.672	8.506	8.213	12.515	10.071	7.996	7.764	11.454	9.509	7.604	7.357
26	2.080	1.137	1.999	2.083	1.893	1.056	1.850	1.912	1.733	0.982	1.701	1.762
27	1.120	0.293	1.066	1.204	1.019	0.272	1.000	1.103	0.933	0.253	0.912	1.014
28	1.984	1.221	2.382	2.444	1.805	1.114	2.175	2.221	1.653	1.021	1.982	2.029
29	3.987	5.992	5.956	5.810	3.629	5.405	5.357	5.251	3.323	4.904	4.877	4.772
30	5.461	14.224	10.465	10.058	4.973	12.777	9.365	9.067	4.554	11.55	8.514	8.220
31	5.152	9.148	7.971	7.708	4.689	8.178	7.117	6.927	4.292	7.361	6.448	6.261
32	3.868	5.921	6.199	6.139	3.521	5.286	5.438	5.432	3.223	4.753	5.011	4.900
33	1.818	1.726	3.259	3.270	1.655	1.539	2.925	2.936	1.516	1.382	2.639	2.651

Further at 4 AM, all the methods assign positive losses to all the consumers, however BCDLA method assigns reward to some of the consumers.

Table 12.5 shows the node-wise allocated energy loss without DGs for 24-h on various load models. From Table 12.5 it is seen that proposed-0method assigns less positive energy loss to consumer at node 2 and assigns more positive energy loss to consumer at node 33 as compared to other methods. Also at some pair of nodes, such as node 7 and node 8; node 12 and node 13; node 16 and node 17; node 18 and node 19; node 26 and node 27, have small difference in the consumed power. Energy losses assigned by the PR method to nodes in each pair are nearly closed to each other while they are entirely different from each other by proposed method, PSMLA and BCDLA method. However, difference obtained by the proposed method is better than those by PR method, PSMLA and BCDLA method.

Tables 12.6 and 12.7 show the node-wise allocated losses at 4 AM and 11 AM, respectively, of a network with DG on various load models. Due to integration DG along with root node, DG feeds power to meet consumer demand. Therefore, negative loss allocation may occur in scenario with DGs. Negative loss is represented as reward for reducing the network losses. But reward and penalty are depending on the participants location and corresponding contribution in the improvement of system performances.

At 4 AM on CP, CC and CI load models, PR method and PSMLA allocate positive losses to consumers due to consumption of power and negative losses to generators due to injection of power into the network. But, proposed method and BCDLA method allocates either positive or negative losses to consumers and generators according to their location and corresponding to their power injection/consumption at specific time period.

At 11 AM, all the methods allocate positive losses to consumers and-0negative losses to generators. At node 18, node 19, node 20 and node 21 consumers consumed entirely different power from each other; however, PR method assigns nearly same losses to all consumers while on the other hand proposed method, PSMLA and BCDLA method can easily differentiate their power consumption and contribution into the network losses and therefore their allocated losses by proposed method, PSMLA and BCDLA method are different from each other.

From both the tables it is further observed that as compared to other methods, proposed method provides less penalty to consumers at node 2 and more penalty to consumer at node 33 in scenario with DG. It shows that proposed method consistently provides fair loss allocation to consumers which are close and far away from root node in both scenarios of the network.

Table 12.8 shows the total allocated energy loss (kWh) for 24-h on various load models and network with DGs. From Table 12.8 it is seen

Table 12.5 Node-wise allocated energy losses (kWh) without DGs for entire day on different load models.

Node no.	CP load model				CC load model				CI load model			
	PR method	PSMLA	BCDLA method	Proposed method	PR method	PSMLA	BCDLA method	Proposed method	PR method	PSMLA	BCDLA method	Proposed method
1	0.000	0.000	0.000	0.000	0.000	0.000	0.000	0.000	0.000	0.000	0.000	0.000
2	38.592	1.835	2.867	2.595	35.777	1.820	2.824	2.515	33.302	1.802	2.768	2.441
3	36.429	9.128	9.239	14.361	33.584	8.896	8.669	13.719	31.101	8.657	8.090	13.135
4	46.235	21.793	21.762	25.694	42.654	20.951	20.614	24.355	39.529	20.136	19.443	23.149
5	33.085	11.148	15.319	19.863	30.642	10.739	14.346	18.774	28.499	10.344	13.368	17.791
6	24.681	10.312	19.013	23.206	22.763	9.685	17.492	21.576	21.089	9.114	16.025	20.134
7	78.931	105.79	86.765	84.520	73.173	98.995	81.762	78.804	68.112	92.882	76.788	73.727
8	79.461	140.70	108.20	103.92	73.250	129.88	101.10	96.029	67.833	120.37	94.213	89.095
9	24.671	15.439	27.059	30.488	22.754	14.174	24.709	28.001	21.081	13.071	22.487	25.833
10	33.397	28.876	39.602	41.839	30.929	26.544	36.420	38.430	28.764	24.511	33.397	35.456
11	17.422	10.244	22.939	26.760	16.073	9.307	20.698	24.431	14.895	8.504	18.609	22.413

(Continued)

Table 12.5 Node-wise allocated energy losses (kWh) without DGs for entire day on different load models. (*Continued*)

Node no.	CP load model				CC load model				CI load model			
	PR method	PSMLA	BCDLA method	Proposed method	PR method	PSMLA	BCDLA method	Proposed method	PR method	PSMLA	BCDLA method	Proposed method
12	23.243	21.050	33.925	36.701	21.547	19.346	31.098	33.691	20.057	17.86	28.418	31.064
13	23.166	27.896	42.499	44.461	21.354	25.103	38.592	40.364	19.773	22.743	34.962	36.836
14	46.235	90.463	84.975	82.901	42.654	81.102	77.536	75.041	39.529	73.236	70.634	68.298
15	33.708	36.273	47.857	49.309	31.216	32.829	43.630	44.850	29.03	29.902	39.691	41.007
16	24.681	22.560	38.038	40.423	22.763	20.105	34.267	36.512	21.089	18.058	30.803	33.168
17	24.552	24.783	39.501	41.748	22.761	22.401	35.863	37.934	21.187	20.376	32.479	34.647
18	36.429	65.439	71.646	70.838	33.584	58.305	65.021	63.897	31.101	52.362	58.919	57.966
19	36.230	1.738	2.893	2.618	33.417	1.727	2.853	2.540	30.963	1.711	2.799	2.469
20	49.783	6.360	2.840	6.570	46.107	6.295	7.235	6.442	42.881	6.216	7.169	6.323
21	36.296	4.452	1.725	5.561	33.478	4.405	6.119	5.448	31.019	4.345	6.058	5.343
22	35.955	5.186	2.451	6.218	33.333	5.130	6.853	6.102	31.027	5.065	6.795	5.993

(*Continued*)

Table 12.5 Node-wise allocated energy losses (kWh) without DGs for entire day on different load models. (*Continued*)

Node no.	CP load model				CC load model				CI load model			
	PR method	PSMLA	BCDLA method	Proposed method	PR method	PSMLA	BCDLA method	Proposed method	PR method	PSMLA	BCDLA method	Proposed method
23	35.086	10.356	15.410	17.946	32.342	10.044	12.519	17.147	29.948	9.730	11.814	16.420
24	168.03	128.89	105.29	99.288	154.99	122.88	99.613	94.699	143.61	117.19	95.814	90.507
25	231.906	193.459	151.10	140.74	214.78	184.68	144.26	134.45	199.75	176.38	139.09	128.67
26	24.318	10.850	22.556	24.413	22.43	10.165	18.718	22.667	20.782	9.544	17.148	21.124
27	24.116	12.026	24.449	26.126	22.357	11.325	20.598	24.341	20.81	10.687	18.998	22.756
28	25.182	14.638	31.329	32.352	23.217	13.504	26.731	29.803	21.503	12.505	24.454	27.568
29	47.012	59.065	70.442	67.748	43.367	53.907	62.968	62.069	40.187	49.443	57.962	57.122
30	94.700	233.153	176.678	163.88	87.795	213.406	162.183	150.414	81.73	196.297	150.392	138.645
31	60.251	91.309	95.913	90.799	55.574	82.662	86.213	82.768	51.493	75.271	79.149	75.809
32	83.314	163.34	141.625	132.16	77.236	149.302	129.315	121.147	71.894	137.155	119.646	111.527
33	22.495	21.025	43.677	43.527	20.733	19.014	37.818	39.674	19.197	17.296	34.393	36.334

Table 12.6 Allocated losses (kW) at 4 AM with different load models in scenario with DG.

Node no.	CP load model				CC load model				CI load model			
	PR method	PSMLA	BCDLA method	Proposed method	PR method	PSMLA	BCDLA method	Proposed method	PR method	PSMLA	BCDLA method	Proposed method
1	0.000	0.000	0.000	0.000	0.000	0.000	0.000	0.000	0.000	0.000	0.000	0.000
2	0.275	0.031	0.066	0.015	0.273	0.031	0.065	0.015	0.270	0.031	0.065	0.015
3	0.123	0.067	0.08	0.04	0.122	0.067	0.080	0.04	0.121	0.067	0.079	0.04
4	0.300	0.165	0.086	0.052	0.298	0.165	0.086	0.051	0.296	0.165	0.086	0.051
5	0.313	0.205	0.081	0.042	0.310	0.205	0.081	0.042	0.308	0.205	0.081	0.042
6	0.162	0.083	0.064	0.012	0.161	0.082	0.064	0.012	0.160	0.082	0.063	0.012
7	0.589	1.45	0.084	0.047	0.584	1.451	0.084	0.048	0.580	1.452	0.084	0.049
8	0.246	0.992	0.041	-0.028	0.244	0.994	0.042	-0.027	0.242	0.996	0.042	-0.026
9	0.158	0.118	0.054	-0.005	0.157	0.118	0.054	-0.004	0.156	0.118	0.054	-0.004
10	0.315	0.508	0.051	-0.011	0.313	0.509	0.051	-0.01	0.311	0.51	0.051	-0.009
11	0.118	0.072	0.054	-0.006	0.117	0.072	0.054	-0.005	0.116	0.072	0.054	-0.005

(Continued)

Table 12.6 Allocated losses (kW) at 4 AM with different load models in scenario with DG. (Continued)

Node no.	CP load model				CC load model				CI load model			
	PR method	PSMLA	BCDLA method	Proposed method	PR method	PSMLA	BCDLA method	Proposed method	PR method	PSMLA	BCDLA method	Proposed method
12	0.167	0.345	0.044	-0.022	0.166	0.346	0.044	-0.022	0.164	0.347	0.045	-0.021
13	0.061	0.199	0.034	-0.040	0.061	0.200	0.035	-0.039	0.060	0.201	0.035	-0.039
14	0.300	0.662	0.020	-0.066	0.298	0.666	0.020	-0.065	0.296	0.670	0.021	-0.064
15	0.318	0.628	0.015	-0.074	0.316	0.633	0.016	-0.073	0.313	0.637	0.016	-0.072
16	0.162	0.175	0.026	-0.054	0.161	0.177	0.026	-0.054	0.160	0.179	0.026	-0.053
17	0.196	0.390	-0.017	-0.13	0.195	0.395	-0.017	-0.13	0.193	0.400	-0.017	-0.130
18	0.123	0.440	-0.047	-0.182	0.122	0.447	-0.046	-0.182	0.121	0.454	-0.046	-0.182
19	0.233	0.014	0.064	0.013	0.232	0.014	0.064	0.013	0.230	0.014	0.064	0.013
20	0.470	0.119	0.104	0.083	0.467	0.118	0.104	0.083	0.463	0.118	0.103	0.083
21	0.241	0.037	0.085	0.048	0.239	0.037	0.084	0.048	0.237	0.037	0.084	0.048
22	0.275	0.089	0.102	0.079	0.273	0.088	0.101	0.078	0.270	0.088	0.101	0.078
23	0.098	0.082	0.098	0.071	0.097	0.081	0.097	0.071	0.097	0.081	0.097	0.071

(Continued)

Table 12.6 Allocated losses (kW) at 4 AM with different load models in scenario with DG. (*Continued*)

Node no.	CP load model				CC load model				CI load model			
	PR method	PSMLA	BCDLA method	Proposed method	PR method	PSMLA	BCDLA method	Proposed method	PR method	PSMLA	BCDLA method	Proposed method
24	1.083	0.963	0.400	0.601	1.075	0.957	0.395	0.595	1.067	0.951	0.390	0.589
25	2.191	2.613	0.907	1.492	2.174	2.591	0.894	1.474	2.158	2.569	0.832	1.457
26	0.161	0.085	0.063	0.011	0.160	0.085	0.063	0.011	0.159	0.085	0.053	0.011
27	0.186	0.199	0.065	0.014	0.185	0.199	0.065	0.015	0.184	0.199	0.055	0.015
28	0.099	0.091	0.058	0.002	0.098	0.091	0.058	0.003	0.097	0.091	0.058	0.003
29	0.304	0.426	0.047	-0.017	0.302	0.426	0.048	-0.016	0.300	0.426	0.048	-0.016
30	0.898	2.733	0.002	-0.097	0.891	2.739	0.003	-0.097	0.884	2.744	0.004	-0.093
31	0.401	0.683	-0.006	-0.110	0.397	0.686	-0.005	-0.110	0.395	0.689	-0.005	-0.109
32	0.628	2.171	-0.093	-0.263	0.623	2.182	-0.092	-0.261	0.618	2.193	-0.091	-0.260
33	0.049	0.163	0.022	-0.061	0.049	0.164	0.022	-0.061	0.048	0.165	0.022	-0.060
DG at 8	-1.689	-3.671	0.110	0.093	-1.676	-3.680	0.108	0.089	-1.663	-3.689	0.105	0.086
DG at 18	-1.689	-3.960	0.948	1.563	-1.676	-3.985	0.939	1.552	-1.663	-4.010	0.929	1.541
DG at 33	-3.226	-4.728	0.927	1.525	-3.201	-4.747	0.919	1.517	-3.177	-4.767	0.911	1.508

Table 12.7 Allocated losses (kW) at 11 AM with different load models in scenario with DG.

Node no.	CP load model				CC load model				CI load model			
	PR method	PSMLA	BCDLA method	Proposed method	PR method	PSMLA	BCDLA method	Proposed method	PR method	PSMLA	BCDLA method	Proposed method
1	0.000	0.000	0.000	0.000	0.000	0.000	0.000	0.000	0.000	0.000	0.000	0.000
2	0.832	0.150	0.233	0.080	0.783	0.150	0.229	0.078	0.738	0.150	0.225	0.076
3	1.342	0.668	0.743	0.692	1.264	0.658	0.714	0.666	1.192	0.647	0.687	0.642
4	1.817	1.880	1.232	1.28	1.712	1.839	1.175	1.225	1.614	1.798	1.120	1.173
5	0.911	0.494	0.688	0.627	0.858	0.483	0.657	0.597	0.810	0.472	0.627	0.569
6	0.98	0.969	0.967	0.961	0.924	0.936	0.912	0.907	0.871	0.906	0.861	0.855
7	1.701	3.303	1.730	1.877	1.602	3.189	1.623	1.769	1.511	3.084	1.523	1.668
8	2.94	8.599	3.096	3.518	2.769	8.290	2.888	3.304	2.611	8.008	2.696	3.106
9	0.974	1.414	1.100	1.120	0.918	1.359	1.030	1.049	0.866	1.308	0.964	0.982
10	0.921	1.270	1.017	1.021	0.868	1.217	0.951	0.954	0.819	1.170	0.889	0.891
11	0.691	0.988	0.951	0.942	0.650	0.946	0.889	0.879	0.613	0.909	0.832	0.820
12	0.501	0.490	0.740	0.689	0.472	0.469	0.694	0.642	0.445	0.450	0.651	0.599

(Continued)

Table 12.7 Allocated losses (kW) at 11 AM with different load models in scenario with DG. (Continued)

Node no.	CP load model				CC load model				CI load model			
	PR method	PSMLA	BCDIA method	Proposed method	PR method	PSMLA	BCDIA method	Proposed method	PR method	PSMLA	BCDIA method	Proposed method
13	0.863	2.009	1.198	1.239	0.812	1.925	1.113	1.150	0.766	1.851	1.033	1.067
14	1.817	7.306	2.271	2.527	1.712	7.021	2.096	2.343	1.614	6.766	1.933	2.171
15	0.931	1.577	0.984	0.982	0.877	1.516	0.914	0.909	0.828	1.462	0.849	0.841
16	0.98	2.055	1.053	1.065	0.924	1.981	0.975	0.983	0.871	1.916	0.902	0.906
17	0.529	0.545	0.582	0.499	0.498	0.531	0.542	0.457	0.470	0.518	0.504	0.417
18	1.342	4.489	1.177	1.213	1.264	4.370	1.072	1.101	1.192	4.268	0.976	0.997
19	1.428	0.161	0.299	0.159	1.346	0.161	0.293	0.155	1.269	0.160	0.287	0.151
20	1.371	0.302	0.425	0.310	1.292	0.300	0.416	0.305	1.219	0.297	0.408	0.300
21	1.441	0.426	0.493	0.392	1.357	0.422	0.483	0.386	1.280	0.417	0.473	0.379
22	0.775	0.137	0.356	0.228	0.730	0.136	0.35	0.224	0.688	0.134	0.343	0.221
23	1.304	0.753	0.966	0.960	1.228	0.737	0.927	0.925	1.158	0.721	0.890	0.891
24	6.622	9.748	5.663	6.601	6.239	9.413	5.391	6.340	5.884	9.096	5.134	6.094

(Continued)

Table 12.7 Allocated losses (kW) at 11 AM with different load models in scenario with DG. (Continued)

Node no.	CP load model				CC load model				CI load model			
	PR method	PSMLA	BCDLA method	Proposed method	PR method	PSMLA	BCDLA method	Proposed method	PR method	PSMLA	BCDLA method	Proposed method
25	6.384	8.692	5.590	6.513	6.016	8.369	5.312	6.245	5.676	8.065	5.05	5.992
26	0.965	1.021	1.010	1.013	0.909	0.986	0.952	0.955	0.858	0.953	0.898	0.900
27	0.520	0.268	0.653	0.584	0.489	0.258	0.618	0.550	0.462	0.249	0.585	0.517
28	0.921	1.093	1.133	1.161	0.867	1.047	1.061	1.087	0.818	1.004	0.994	1.019
29	1.850	5.002	2.437	2.726	1.743	4.781	2.263	2.545	1.643	4.581	2.102	2.377
30	2.533	10.711	4.097	4.720	2.384	10.230	3.794	4.403	2.247	9.797	3.513	4.108
31	2.391	7.337	2.889	3.270	2.253	7.014	2.668	3.037	2.125	6.725	2.463	2.820
32	1.795	4.922	2.247	2.498	1.691	4.706	2.076	2.318	1.595	4.512	1.917	2.151
33	0.843	1.501	1.273	1.328	0.794	1.435	1.181	1.232	0.749	1.377	1.097	1.145
DG at 8	-3.693	-10.846	-3.478	-4.377	-3.478	-10.668	-3.287	-4.188	-3.28	-10.507	-3.109	-4.012
DG at 18	-6.155	-23.498	-4.542	-5.654	-5.797	-22.826	-4.121	-5.200	-5.466	-22.234	-3.721	-4.762
DG at 33	-6.518	-20.986	-6.425	-7.916	-6.142	-20.452	-6.02	-7.504	-5.793	-19.973	-5.637	-7.112

Table 12.8 Node-wise allocated energy losses (kWh) with DGs for entire day on different load models.

Node no.	CP load model				CC load model				CI load model			
	PR method	PSMLA	BCDLA method	Proposed method	PR method	PSMLA	BCDLA method	Proposed method	PR method	PSMLA	BCDLA method	Proposed method
1	0.000	0.000	0.000	0.000	0.000	0.000	0.000	0.000	0.000	0.000	C.000	0.000
2	16.867	1.693	1.684	1.591	16.131	1.689	1.690	1.558	15.441	1.683	1.695	1.526
3	16.131	8.318	6.777	8.404	15.348	8.209	6.519	8.140	14.618	8.099	6.271	7.887
4	20.865	19.277	12.28	13.603	19.882	18.929	11.78	13.10	18.965	18.589	11.314	12.621
5	14.987	10.252	7.816	9.385	14.339	10.079	7.452	9.019	13.734	9.911	7.103	8.668
6	11.185	9.406	8.604	10.130	10.662	9.145	8.101	9.630	10.174	8.899	7.623	9.156
7	34.676	84.920	34.252	34.364	33.172	82.911	32.64	32.75	31.762	81.033	31.124	31.218
8	35.061	109.557	40.530	40.295	33.349	106.489	38.35	38.12	31.752	103.661	36.334	36.109
9	11.193	13.932	10.197	11.635	10.668	13.483	9.537	10.98	10.179	13.07	8.914	10.368
10	15.143	25.941	13.618	14.867	14.489	25.209	12.78	14.04	13.878	24.537	12.006	13.271
11	7.859	9.287	8.133	9.684	7.490	8.964	7.552	9.113	7.145	8.669	7.005	8.576
12	10.167	18.982	10.930	12.328	9.724	18.464	10.23	11.63	9.308	17.986	9.572	10.985

(Continued)

Table 12.8 Node-wise allocated energy losses (kWh) with DGs for entire day on different load models. (Continued)

Node no.	CP load model				CC load model				CI load model			
	PR method	PSMLA	BCDLA method	Proposed method	PR method	PSMLA	BCDLA method	Proposed method	PR method	PSMLA	BCDLA method	Proposed method
13	10.164	24.791	12.726	14.024	9.664	23.973	11.81	13.12	9.197	23.235	10.952	12.281
14	20.865	76.185	25.013	25.634	19.882	73.777	23.31	23.95	18.965	71.611	21.711	22.382
15	15.300	32.249	12.818	14.111	14.639	31.410	11.91	13.21	14.022	30.656	11.054	12.377
16	11.185	20.086	9.320	10.807	10.662	19.512	8.545	10.04	10.174	19.003	7.812	9.334
17	10.874	22.023	6.988	8.603	10.407	21.644	6.319	7.952	9.969	21.312	5.680	7.332
18	16.131	55.940	11.530	12.895	15.348	54.832	10.32	11.72	14.618	53.877	9.192	10.629
19	16.409	1.628	1.891	1.787	15.639	1.623	1.897	1.753	14.920	1.617	1.904	1.719
20	22.558	6.099	3.707	5.503	21.584	6.056	3.645	5.433	20.672	6.009	3.585	5.365
21	16.425	4.273	2.890	4.731	15.655	4.238	2.832	4.667	14.937	4.199	2.775	4.605
22	15.839	5.001	3.528	5.333	15.155	4.960	3.468	5.266	14.513	4.916	3.410	5.201
23	15.424	9.434	10.332	11.762	14.666	9.268	9.977	11.39	13.959	9.103	9.637	11.047
24	76.068	104.513	75.877	73.694	72.497	101.59	73.50	71.23	69.164	98.806	71.26	68.896

(Continued)

Table 12.8 Node-wise allocated energy losses (kWh) with DGs for entire day on different load models. (Continued)

Node no.	CP load model				CC load model				CI load model			
	PR method	PSMLA	BCDLA method	Proposed method	PR method	PSMLA	BCDLA method	Proposed method	PR method	PSMLA	BCDLA method	Proposed method
25	105.07	156.039	112.19	108.009	100.525	151.587	108.8	104.4	96.28	147.352	105.59	101.12
26	11.009	9.890	9.135	10.631	10.493	9.605	8.598	10.09	10.012	9.338	8.088	9.593
27	10.638	11.000	9.210	10.703	10.179	10.735	8.696	10.19	9.749	10.485	8.207	9.704
28	11.226	13.275	12.146	13.476	10.687	12.814	11.39	12.73	10.184	12.390	10.681	12.027
29	21.245	50.781	27.165	27.667	20.246	48.932	25.51	26.03	19.313	47.244	23.97	24.502
30	42.137	175.197	64.364	62.816	40.298	169.592	60.68	59.15	38.575	164.486	57.215	55.711
31	27.257	76.15	32.267	32.488	25.979	73.460	30.13	30.38	24.787	71.024	28.134	28.411
32	36.645	127.275	41.966	41.653	35.058	123.711	39.31	39.02	33.570	120.467	35.801	36.547
33	9.811	18.554	13.121	14.398	9.323	17.934	12.15	13.44	8.867	17.375	11.253	12.563
DG at 8	-61.347	-187.26	-53.41	-61.407	-58.753	-184.97	-51.1	-59.1	-56.323	-182.89	-48.960	-56.96
DG at 18	-82.284	-317.10	-45.64	-53.641	-78.655	-310.67	-41.1	-49.1	-75.261	-304.93	-36.740	-44.740
DG at 33	-110.997	-345.815	-92.187	-100.187	-106.382	-339.138	-87.14	-95.14	-102.062	-333.069	-82.284	-90.284

that proposed method assigns less losses to consumer at node 2, however PSMLA assigns more losses to consumer at node 33 as compared to other method. Further, proposed method assigns appropriate reward to DGs according to their contribution in the reduction of network losses whereas PSMLA method provides excess reward to DGs which successively increases the penalty of consumers.

Table 12.9 shows the summary of total allocated energy losses for ahead of a day. By all the methods, total allocated energy losses to consumers is positive and total allocated energy losses to generators is negative. From above discussion it is concluded that proposed method has capability to send correct signal of active and reactive power injection/consumption of participants to allocate fair energy losses among them.

Table 12.9 Summary of total allocated energy losses (kWh) ahead of a day.

Load model	Methods	Without DG	With DG		
			Load	DG	Total
CP	PR method	1599.592	716.408	-254.628	461.78
	PSMLA	1599.592	1311.948	-850.171	
	BCDLA method	1599.592	653.009	-191.235	
	Proposed method	1599.592	677.011	-215.235	
CC	PR method	1478.632	683.84	-243.79	440.05
	PSMLA	1478.632	1274.824	-834.773	
	BCDLA method	1478.632	619.503	-179.382	
	Proposed method	1478.632	643.433	-203.382	
CI	PR method	1372.765	653.403	-233.646	419.35
	PSMLA	1372.765	1240.642	-820.886	
	BCDLA method	1372.765	587.872	-167.982	
	Proposed method	1372.765	611.735	-191.982	

12.6   Conclusion

In this paper, a new method for the allocation of energy losses in RDN with DGs has been proposed. The proposed method is a circuit-based branch-oriented approach and is derived from the power summation algorithm. It establishes a direct relation between branch losses and complex power at the receiving end of the branch. Proposed method is simple, efficient, and easy to implement. It has decomposed power flow naturally and proceed for achieving objectives. Advantage of the proposed method is that it allocates the energy losses without any assumptions and approximations. Further, it does not require any additional step of reconciliation. In addition to this, proposed method requires only network data and the power flow solution for allocation of energy losses.

Results of the proposed method have been compared with a classical technique named as PR method, PSMLA, and BCDLA method and all the methods are tested on a 33-node RDN with CP, CC, and CI load models. From the obtained results, few features of the proposed method have been observed. Proposed method is based on decomposition of power flow considering power absorption/injection locations of participants while PR method is based on the proportionality principle and does not consider the geographical location of participants. Allocating the active energy loss, proposed method considers not only active power but also reactive power flow of network participants. The performance of proposed method is comparatively better for CP, CC, and CI load models as far as economic benefit of a node is concerned. Further, the proposed method assigns not only positive losses but also negative losses to participants based on their power consumption/injection and corresponding to their location at a given period of time. These features make the proposed method more applicable and justified for the fair allocation of losses.

References

1. Dibya Bharti, Mala De, "A new graph theory based loss allocation framework for bilateral power market using diakoptics". *Elect. Power and Energy Syst.* 77, 395-403 (2016).
2. Nalin B. Dev Choudhury, Mala De, Swapna K. Goswami, "Transmission loss allocation in a power market using artificial neural network". *Electr. Eng.* 95, 87-98 (2013).

3. Pankaj Kumar, Nikhil Gupta, K.R. Niazi, Anil Swarnkar, "Exact cross-term decomposition method for loss allocation in contemporary distribution systems". *Arabian Journal for Science and Engineering.* 44, 1977-1988 (2019).

4. Shashank Shekhar Kashyap, Mala De, "Loss allocation and loss minimization for radial distribution system including DGs". *IET Renewable Power Gener.* 11(6), 806-818 (2017).

5. Antonio Gomez Exposito, Jesus Manuel Riquelme Santos, Tomas Gonzalez Garcia, Enrique A. Ruiz velasco, Fair allocation of transmission power losses. IEEE Trans. Power Syst. 15(1), 184-188 (2000).

6. A.J. Conejo, J.M. Arroyo, N. Alguacil, A.L. Guijarro, Transmission loss allocation: "A comparison of different practical algorithms". *IEEE Trans. Power Syst.* 17(3), 571-575 (2002).

7. M. Atanasovski, R. Taleski. "Power summation method for loss allocation in radial distribution networks with DG". *IEEE Trans. Power Syst.* 26(4), 2491-2498 (2011).

8. J. Mutale, G. Strbac, S. Curcic, N. Jenkins. "Allocation of losses in distribution systems with embedded generation". *Proc. Inst. Elect. Eng., Gener. Transm. Distrib.* 147(1), 7-13 (2000).

9. J.W. Bialek, P.A. Kattuman, "Proportional sharing assumption in tracing methodology". *IEE Proc. Gener. Transm. Distrib.* 151(4), 526-532 (2004).

10. A.J. Conejo, F.D. Galiana, I. "Kockar, Z-bus loss allocation". *IEEE Trans. Power Syst.* 16(1), 105-110 (2001).

11. S. Mishra, D. Das, S. Paul, A simple algorithm to implement active power loss allocation schemes in radial distribution systems, Journal of The Institute of Engineering (India): Series B, 93(3), 123-132 (2012).

12. J.S. Savier, D. Das, Energy loss allocation in radial distribution systems: A comparison of practical algorithms. IEEE Trans. power del. 24(1), 260-266 (2004).

13. E. Carpaneto, G. Chicco, J.S. Akilimali, Branch current decomposition method for loss allocation in radial distribution systems with distributed generation. IEEE Trans. Power Syst. 21(3), 1170-1178 (2006).

14. M. Atanasovski, R. Taleski, Energy summation method for loss allocation in radial distribution networks with DG. IEEE Trans. Power Syst. 27(3) 1433-1439 (2012).

15. Z.G. Jahromi, Z Mahmoodzadeh, M. Ehsan. Distribution loss allocation for radial systems including DGs. IEEE Trans. Power Del. 2(1), 72-80 (2014).

16. Kushal Manohar Jagtap, Dheeraj Kumar Khatod, Novel approach for loss allocation of distribution network with DGs, Elect. Power Syst. Research. 143, 303-311 (2017).

17. Hortensia Amaris, Yuri P. Molina, Monica Alonso, Jaime E. Luyo, Loss allocation in distribution networks based on Aumann-Shapley, IEEE Trans. Power Syst. 33(6) 6655-6667 (2018).

18. M.E. EI-Hawary, L.G. Dias, Incorporation of load models in load-flow studies: Form of model effects. IEE Proc. C, 134, 27-30 (1987).

19. IEEE task force on load representation for dynamic performance. Load representation for dynamic performance analysis. IEEE Trans. Power Syst. 8, 472-482 (1993).
20. M. Baran, F.F. Wu, Network reconfiguration in distribution systems for loss reduction and load balancing. IEEE Trans. Power Del. 4, 1401-1707 (1989).
21. A.L. Shenkman, Energy loss computation by using statistical techniques, IEEE Trans. Power Del. 5, 254-258 (1990).
22. Ghosh S, Das D. Method for load-flow solution of radial distribution networks. Proc. Inst. Elect. Eng. Gen. Transm. Distrib. 146, 641-648 (1999).

13

Enhancement of Transient Response of Statcom and VSC Based HVDC with GA and PSO Based Controllers

Nagesh Prabhu[1]*, R. Thirumalaivasan[2] and M.Janaki[3]

[1]NMAM Institute of Technology, Nitte, Karnataka, India
[2]Vellore Institute of Technology, Vellore, Tamil Nadu, India

Abstract

Power flow in parallel AC networks is determined according to the impedance of individual lines and cannot be restricted to desired transmission corridors as it is governed by Kirchhoff's laws. Power flow is also limited due to stability considerations. As a consequence, some of the lines are overloaded while the others left with large margins. The problem of under-utilization of AC transmission network and increasing the transmission loadings close to their thermal limits can be alleviated by the use of FACTS controllers. The deregulation or restructuring in electric utilities pose challenges in secure system operation which can be met by the introduction of FACTS controllers in appropriate locations to control power flow in the network while maintaining stability.

FACTS controllers based on Voltage Source Converter (VSC) are emerging controllers that have several advantages over the conventional ones using thyristors. VSC HVDC power transmission enables simultaneous and independent control of active and reactive power at a converter without any problems of commutation failure.

However, the transient performance of the power converter depends primarily on the parameters of controllers. A systematic method is essential to choose the controller parameters in order to get the satisfactory response and desired output. Also, the transient performance of the power converter devices with designed controller is to be satisfactory at various operating conditions. The optimization methods are effective in guaranteeing global or near global optimum of the problem and are applied to get the suitable parameters of controller with desired

*Corresponding author: prabhunagesh@nitte.edu.in

Neeraj Priyadarshi, Akash Kumar Bhoi, Sanjeevikumar Padmanaban, S. Balamurugan and Jens Bo Holm-Nielsen (eds.) Intelligent Renewable Energy Systems, (345–390) © 2022 Scrivener Publishing LLC

performance. This chapter presents GA and PSO based optimization of controller parameters of STATCOM and VSC based HVDC keeping in view of improvement of stability and transient response.

Keywords: VSC, FACTS controllers, HVDC, GA, PSO

13.1 Introduction

There are many techniques to find the global minimum of a nonlinear optimization problem [1–25]. These techniques employ an element of randomness in the iterations which helps to escape local minimum. Genetic Algorithm is a nature-inspired approach, derivative free, more effective random exploration technique in searching and guaranteeing global or near global optimum of the problem. GA is efficient in searching global minimum, fast convergence, less computational time, and guarantees global or near global minimum with less number of function evaluations. Another nature-based class of global optimization problems is Particle Swarm Optimization. This approach utilizes the concepts borrowed from the field of social psychology. Particle Swarm Optimization (PSO) is an iteration based optimization tool, and the particle does not only have ability to search global minimum, but also has memory, and it can be convergent directionally.

Genetic Algorithm (GA) has been used as optimizing the parameters of control system that are complex and difficult to solve by conventional optimization methods [5]. It maintains a set of candidate solutions called population and repeatedly modifies them. Each member of the population is evaluated using a fitness function. The population undergoes reproduction in a number of iterations. One or more parents are chosen stochastically, but strings with higher fitness values have higher probability of contributing the offspring Genetic operators, such as crossover and mutation are applied to parents to produce offspring. The offspring are inserted into the population and the process is repeated. The (meta)heuristic algorithms are used to optimize the solution in power systems for load flow, optimal power flow (OPF), expansion planning, transmission cost allocation etc. [6–10]. In ac transmission system, the Flexible AC Transmission System (FACTS) controllers are used for fast control of reactive power so as to regulate the voltage, increase transmission line loading close to their thermal limits and improve system damping [11, 12]. However, the response or performance of the FACTS devices depends primarily on the parameters of controller. This chapter presents GA and PSO based optimization of controller parameters of STATCOM and VSC based HVDC [26–59].

The optimization is based on GA and PSO keeping in view of improvement of stability and transient response.

13.2   Design of Genetic Algorithm Based Controller for STATCOM

The STATic synchronous COMpensator (STATCOM) is a voltage source converter (VSC) based FACTS controller. It is a shunt connected reactive power controller and most suitable in long transmission line for regulating voltage, improving stability and enhancing power transfer capability. STATCOM consists of a voltage source converter which is connected to the high voltage transmission line through a step up transformer as shown in Figure 13.1.

The principle of operation is similar to that of a synchronous condenser. The VSC is connected to the system through a small reactance which is the leakage reactance of the coupling transformer. The VSC produces a set of three phase voltages which are in phase with the corresponding bus voltages. A small phase difference exists in steady state (depending on reactive power output) for compensating the losses in VSC. In steady state, no real power is drawn by VSC (except for losses), and the DC voltage can be maintained by a capacitor. The provision of an energy source at the DC terminals enables the STATCOM to exchange real power with the AC system by controlling the phase of the inverter output voltages with respect to corresponding bus voltages.

The major advantages of the STATCOM over SVC are [14]:

1. The STATCOM can supply required reactive current even at low bus voltage, whereas the reactive current capability

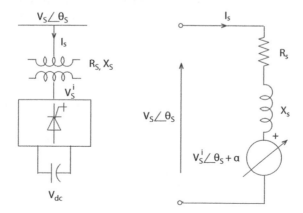

Figure 13.1 Schematic and equivalent circuit of STATCOM.

of SVC at its capacitive susceptance limit decreases linearly with decrease in the bus voltage.

2. With proper choice of device rating and thermal design, STATCOM can have a short time overload capacity. This is not possible with SVC as it has inherent susceptance limit.
3. Significant size reduction can be achieved as reduced number of passive components with smaller size are involved.
4. STATCOM can allow real power modulation with energy source at its DC terminals.

In Figure 13.1, the STATCOM is connected to the bus (voltage V_s) through a coupling transformer with resistance and reactance of Rs and X_s respectively. In the power circuit of a STATCOM, the converter has either a multi-pulse and/or a multilevel configuration. In the power circuit of a STATCOM, the converter has either a multi-pulse and/or a multilevel configuration.

13.2.1   Two Level STACOM with Type-2 Controller

With a 2-level VSC, the reactive current control can be achieved by varying α alone as shown in Figure 13.2. When STATCOM regulates the bus voltage, the reactive current reference i_{Ref} in Figure 13.2 is obtained as the output of the bus voltage controller.

In this controller, the modulation index is constant. The capacitor voltage is not regulated but depends upon the phase difference between the converter output voltage and the bus voltage. The reactive current control is effected by converter output voltage magnitude (which is a function of dc voltage) and achieved by phase angle control [11, 13]. This causes the variation of capacitor voltage over a small range with change in operating point.

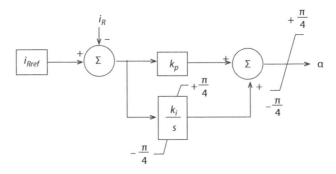

Figure 13.2 Type-2 controller for 2-level VSC based STATCOM.

From control view point, it is convenient to define active (i_p) and reactive (i_R) currents drawn from the STATCOM as

$$i_P = \frac{V_{sD}i_{sD} + V_{sQ}i_{sQ}}{V_s} = i_{sD}sin\theta_s + i_{sQ}cos\theta_s.$$ (13.1)

$$i_R = \frac{V_{sD}i_{sQ} + V_{sQ}i_{sD}}{V_s} = -i_{sD}cos\theta_s + i_{sQ}sin\theta_s.$$ (13.2)

The reactive current (i_R) is positive when STATCOM is operating in the inductive region and negative when STATCOM is operating in the capacitive region. The active current (i_p) is positive when STATCOM draws active power from the system. To simplify the design procedure we design the reactive controller assuming the voltage at STATCOM bus is constant (neglecting the dynamics in the transmission network). Hence, the reactive current reference i_{Rref} is kept constant.

STATCOM with PI controller based reactive current control experiences oscillatory instability in inductive mode. The incorporation of nonlinear state variable feedback with PI controller can overcome the oscillatory instability predicted in the inductive operation mode of STATCOM.

13.2.1.1   Simulation Results with Suboptimal Controller Parameters

The eigenvalue analysis and transient simulation are carried in MATLAB-SIMULINK. The results are given without and with nonlinear feedback.

13.2.1.2   PI Controller Without Nonlinear State Variable Feedback

The Eigenvalue analysis is performed by linearizing the system equations (of Figure 13.1) for capacitive and inductive mode of operation of 12-pulse 2-Level STATCOM and are given in Table 13.1. It is to be noted that the system is unstable in the inductive mode of operation of STATCOM.

The movement of the critical eigenvalues for operating points in the inductive region and capacitive region with PI controller (refer Figure 13.1.) is shown in Figure 13.3. Referring to Figure 13.3 it is observed that, in the inductive region the poles move towards the imaginary axis resulting in oscillatory instability. The instability in the inductive mode of operation of a STATCOM is also reported in literature [11, 13].

As detailed in [14], the condition for stability can be expressed as

$$i_R < \frac{\omega C}{k}V_{dc}.$$ (13.3)

Table 13.1 Eigenvalues of 2-level STATCOM with PI controller.

Capacitive region $i_R = -1$	Inductive region $i_R = 1$
-834.58	-775.36
$-81.819 \pm j1429.8$	$12.969 \pm j\,485.8$
-10	-10
-9.9137	-9.9137

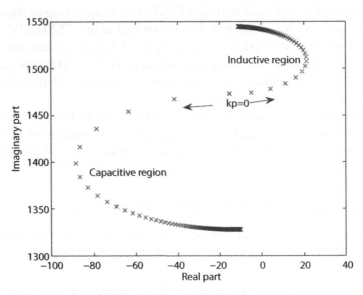

Figure 13.3 Movement of the critical eigenvalues with PI controller for $k_p = 0$ *to* 10 and $k_i/k_p = 10$.

The above condition is always satisfied when $i_R < 0$ (when the converter is operating in the capacitive mode). Thus, the problem of instability can arise only while operating in the inductive mode and is also verified in the present study. The important point is that, the variation of locations of zeros with the operating point, the angle of departure for this complex mode varies from 0 to -180° as the operating point is changed [14]. Thus design of a compensator in cascade with the PI controller which is suitable for all operating points is also difficult.

It is to be noted that the system is unstable in the inductive mode of operation. To validate the linearized analysis (which neglects harmonics in the switching functions) and to check the performance for large deviations from an operating point, the transient simulation of a 12-pulse 3 phase STATCOM is carried out using MATLABSIMULINK [15]. The action of the converter is modeled using the switching functions. (Switching instants are obtained from θ_s and the controller output α) [13], [14], and [16]. The instability predicted by linearized analysis in the inductive region (when a PI controller is used) is also brought out by simulation as shown in Figure 13.4.

13.2.1.3   PI Controller with Nonlinear State Variable Feedback

Schauder and Mehta [13] proposed a nonlinear feedback controller to overcome the problem of instability in the inductive mode of operation of STATCOM. The block diagram of the controller is shown in Figure 13.5.

The root locus of the critical eigenvalues with nonlinear feedback controller for inductive and capacitive mode of operation is shown in Figure 13.6. It is observed from the root locus plot that, the critical modes are stable.

The eigenvalues of the system with nonlinear feedback and suboptimal controller parameters [11] are given in Table 13.2. It is to be noted that, the eigenvalues are stable with good stability margin for both inductive and capacitive mode of operation of STATCOM.

The transient simulation of the 3 phase model of the STATCOM for step change in the reactive current is shown in Figure 13.7 and Figure 13.8.

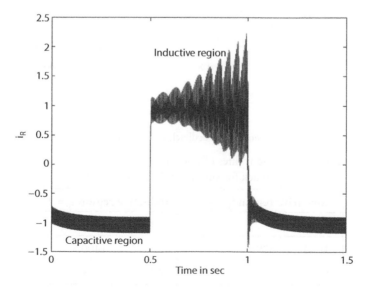

Figure 13.4 Step response of STATCOM with PI controller.

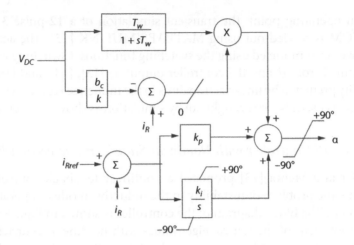

Figure 13.5 PI controller with nonlinear feedback controller.

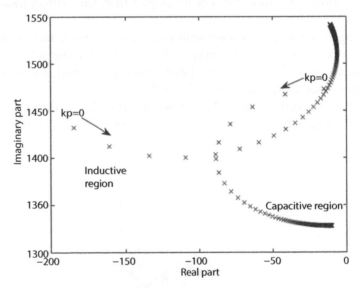

Figure 13.6 Root locus with nonlinear feedback for $k_p = 0$ *to* 10 and $k_i/k_p = 10$.

Table 13.2 Eigenvalues of 2-level STATCOM with nonlinear feedback for suboptimal controller parameters.

Capacitive region $i_R = -1$	Inductive region $i_R = 1$
-834.58	-1173.2
$-81.819 \pm j\,429.8$	$-102.73 \pm j\,1400.7$
-10	$-7.3766 \pm j\,4.3491$
-9.9137	

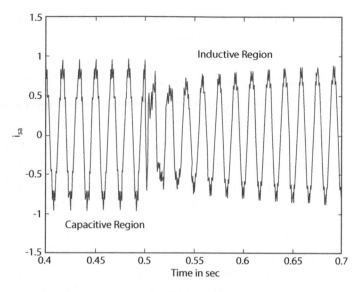

Figure 13.7 Phase 'a' current of STATCOM with nonlinear feedback controller.

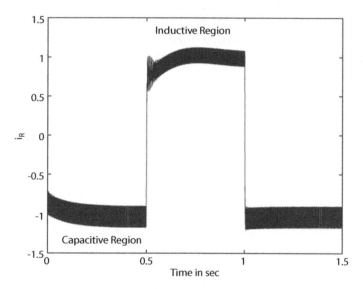

Figure 13.8 Response of STATCOM with nonlinear feedback controller.

It can be seen that, transition from capacitive to inductive mode of operation of STATCOM is slow and steady state is reached after 0.2 sec following the step change in reactive current. It is to be noted that, although the system is stable during inductive operation, the transient response of the

STATCOM is slow. Hence there is a need to optimize the controller parameters to improve the transient response of the STATCOM.

13.2.2   Structure of Type-1 Controller for 3-Level STACOM

With three-level converter topology the magnitude of ac output voltage of the converter can be changed by varying dead angle β with fundamental switching frequency [16, 17]. The time period in a cycle during which the converter pole voltage is zero is $\dfrac{4\beta}{\omega}$. The three-level converter topology greatly reduces the harmonic distortion on the ac side [14, 16, 18]. Here the STATCOM is realized by a combination 24-pulse three level configuration.

The real current drawn by the VSC is controlled by phase angle and reactive current by modulating the converter output voltage magnitude as a function of β. Figure 13.9 shows the schematic representation of Type-1 controller for three level STATCOM current control. The reactive current reference of STATCOM can be kept constant or regulated to maintain bus voltage magnitude at the specified value.

For control of shunt current, we proceed in a way similar to the one outlined in references [13] as described below.

The derivative of i_R can be expressed as

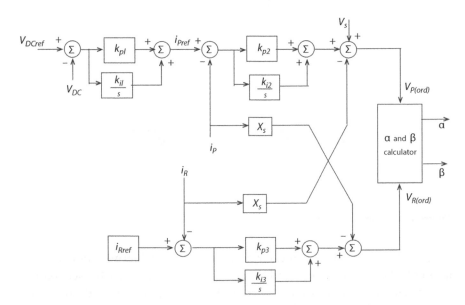

Figure 13.9 Schematic of type1controller for STATCOM.

$$\frac{di_R}{dt} = i_{sQ}\cos\theta_s \frac{d\theta_s}{dt} + \frac{di_{sQ}}{dt}\sin\theta_s + i_{sD}\sin\theta_s \frac{d\theta_s}{dt} - \frac{di_{sD}}{dt}\cos\theta_s$$

$$= i_P \frac{d\theta_s}{dt} + \sin\theta_s\left[-\frac{R_s\omega_B}{X_s}i_{sQ} + \omega_o i_{sD} + \frac{\omega_B}{X_s}\left(V_{sQ} - V_{sQ}^i\right)\right]$$

$$-\cos\theta_s\left[-\frac{R_s\omega_B}{X_s}i_{sD} - \omega_o i_{sQ} + \frac{\omega_B}{X_s}\left(V_{sD} - V_{sQ}^i\right)\right]$$

$$= -\frac{R_s\omega_B}{X_s}i_R + \omega' i_P + \frac{\omega_B}{X_s}\left[-V_{sQ}^i\sin\theta_s + V_{sD}^i\cos\theta_s\right]$$

$$= -\frac{R_s\omega_B}{X_s}i_R + \omega' i_P + \frac{\omega_B}{X_s}V_R$$

(13.4)

The derivative of i_p can be expressed as

$$\frac{di_P}{dt} = i_{sD}\cos\theta_s \frac{d\theta_s}{dt} + \frac{di_{sD}}{dt}\sin\theta_s + i_{sQ}\sin\theta_s \frac{d\theta_s}{dt} + \frac{di_{sQ}}{dt}\cos\theta_s$$

$$= i_R \frac{d\theta_s}{dt} + \sin\theta_s\left[-\frac{R_s\omega_B}{X_s}i_{sD} - \omega_o i_{sQ} + \frac{\omega_B}{X_s}\left(V_{sD} - V_{sD}^i\right)\right]$$

$$+\cos\theta_s\left[-\frac{R_s\omega_B}{X_s}i_{sQ} - \omega_o i_{sD} + \frac{\omega_B}{X_s}\left(V_{sQ} - V_{sQ}^i\right)\right]$$

$$= -\frac{R_s\omega_B}{X_s}i_P - \omega' i_R + \frac{\omega_B}{X_s}\left[V_{sD}\sin\theta_s + V_{sQ}\cos\theta_s - V_{sD}^i\sin\theta_s - V_{sQ}^i\cos\theta_s\right]$$

$$= -\frac{R_s\omega_B}{X_s}i_P - \omega' i_R + \frac{\omega_B}{X_s}(V_s - V_P)$$

(13.5)

where $\omega' = \omega_o + \dfrac{d\theta_s}{dt}$, $V_s = \sqrt{V_{sQ}^2 + V_{sD}^2}$ and V_P and V_R are the in-phase and quadrature components of converter output voltage V_s^i with respect to STATCOM bus voltage which are defined as

$$V_P = V_{sD}^i\sin\theta_s + V_{sQ}^i\cos\theta_s$$

(13.6)

$$V_R = V_{sD}^i \cos\theta_s - V_{sQ}^i \sin\theta_s \tag{13.7}$$

If we control the converter output voltages as,

$$V_R = V_{R(ord)} = -\frac{\omega'}{\omega_B} X_s i_P + \frac{X_s}{\omega_B} u_R \tag{13.8}$$

$$V_P = V_{P(ord)} = -\frac{\omega'}{\omega_B} X_s i_R + V_s + \frac{X_s}{\omega_B} u_P \tag{13.9}$$

Substituting these in equations (13.4) and (13.5), the differential equations governing i_R and i_P are decoupled as follows.

$$\frac{di_R}{dt} = -\frac{R_s \omega_B}{X_s} i_R + u_R \tag{13.10}$$

$$\frac{di_P}{dt} = -\frac{R_s \omega_B}{X_s} i_P - u_P \tag{13.11}$$

u_R and u_P are chosen as follows.

$$u_R(s) = G_{s1}(s)\left[i_{Rref}(s) - i_R(s)\right] \tag{13.12}$$

$$u_P(s) = G_{s2}(s)\left[i_{Pref}(s) - i_P(s)\right] \tag{13.13}$$

Where

$$G_{s1}(s) = K_{p3}' + \frac{K_{i3}'}{s} \tag{13.14}$$

$$G_{s2}(s) = K_{p2}' + \frac{K_{i2}'}{s} \tag{13.15}$$

Type-1 controller is shown in Figure 13.9, where $K_{p2} = \dfrac{X_s}{\omega_B}K'_{p2}$, $K_{i2} = \dfrac{X_s}{\omega_B}K'_{i2}$, $K_{p3} = \dfrac{X_s}{\omega_B}K'_{p3}$ and $K_{i3} = \dfrac{X_s}{\omega_B}K'_{i3}$.

In Figure 13.9, α and β are calculated as:

$$\alpha = tan^{-1}\left[\frac{V_{R(ord)}}{V_{P(ord)}}\right] \tag{13.16}$$

$$\beta = cos^{-1}\left[\frac{\sqrt{V_{P(ord)}^2 + V_{R(ord)}^2}}{kV_{dc}}\right] \tag{13.17}$$

To simplify the design procedure we design the controller assuming the voltage at STATCOM bus to be a constant (neglecting the dynamics in the transmission network).

13.2.2.1 Transient Simulation with Suboptimal Controller Parameters

The transient simulation of STATCOM is carried out using both D-Q and 3-phase model using MATLAB-SIMULINK [15]. The step response with 3-phase model of three-level STATCOM with non-optimized controller parameters is shown in Figure 13.10. It is to be noted that the step response of STATCOM reactive current with non-optimized controller parameters has overshoot during the transition from capacitive to inductive mode of operation of STATCOM and reaches steady state after 0.04 sec.

Hence there is a requirement to optimize the controller parameters to improve the transient response of the STATCOM. The optimization of reactive current controller parameters based on GA to improve the transient response will be discussed in the section to follow.

13.2.3 Application of Genetic Algorithm for Optimization of Controller Parameters

For damping oscillations, the damping factor of around 10% to 20% is considered to be adequate. A damping factor of 10% would be acceptable to most utilities and can be adopted as the minimum requirement. Further, having the real part of eigenvalue restricted to be less than a value, say α, guarantees a minimum decay rate α. A value $\alpha = -0.5$ is to be considered adequate for an acceptable settling time. The closed loop mode location

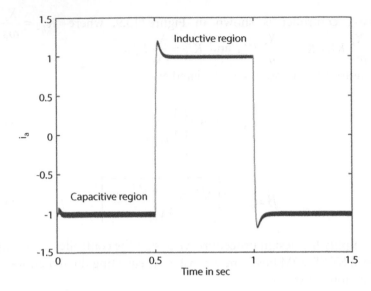

Figure 13.10 Step response with 3phase model of STATCOM with non-optimized controller parameters.

should simultaneously satisfy these two constraints for an acceptable small disturbance response of the controlled system.

If all the closed loop poles are located to the left of the contour shown in Figure 13.11, then the constraints on the damping factor and the real part of eigenvalues are satisfied and a well damped small disturbance response is guaranteed. This contour is referred as the D-contour [14]. The system is said to be D-stable if it is stable with respect to this D-contour, i.e. all its pole lie on the left of this contour. This property is referred to as generalized stability in control literature. This generates a neat specification- the closed loop system should be robustly D-stable i.e. D-stable for the entire range of operating and system conditions. Hence a system is said to be 'robust', if, in spite of changes in system and operating conditions, the closed loop poles remain on the left of the D-contour for the specified range of system and operating conditions.

The D-contour in Figure 13.11 can be mathematically described as,

$$f(Z) = Real(Z) - min[-imag(Z), \alpha] = 0 \qquad (13.18)$$

where, is a point on D-contour, C represents the complex plane.

Defining J

$$J = \max_i \left[Real(\lambda_i) - min[-\varsigma|imag(Z)|, \alpha] \right] \qquad (13.19)$$

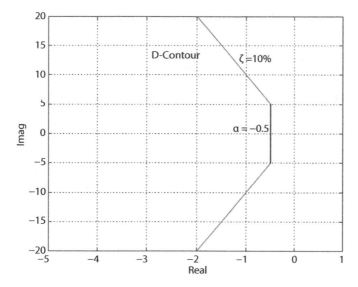

Figure 13.11 D-contour with $\alpha = -0.5$ and $\zeta = 10\%$.

where $i = 1, 2, 3 \ldots n$. n is the number of eigenvalues. λ_i is the ith eigenvalue of the system at an operating point. A negative value of J implies that all the eigenvalues lie on the left of the D-contour. Similarly some or all eigenvalues lie on the right of the D-contour if J is positive. On the basis of these facts, objective function E is defined as:

$$\text{Sum Squared Error} = \Sigma e^2 \tag{13.20}$$

Where $e = i_{Rref} - i_R$

Where i_{Rref} and i_R are the reactive current reference input and reactive current output of the STATCOM respectively.

Hence the optimization problem can be stated as:

$$\text{Minimize } E$$

$$\text{Subjected } J \le 0$$

The parameters used with GA are given in Table 13.3.

13.2.3.1 Boundaries of Type-2 Controller Parameters in GA Optimization

The boundaries of optimal parameters of type-2 controller are

$$g_{min} \le g \le g_{max}$$

Table 13.3 Parameters used for optimization with genetic algorithm.

Parameter	Value/type
Maximum Generations	100
Population Size	200
Type of Selection	Normal Geometric [0 0.08]
Type of Crossover	Arithmetic [4]
Type of mutation	Non uniform [4 20 3]
Termination method	Maximum Generation

$$T_{wmin} \leq T_w \leq T_{wmax}$$

$$k_{pmin} \leq k_p \leq k_{pmax}$$

$$k_{imin} \leq k_i \leq k_{imax}$$

13.2.3.2 Boundaries of Type-1 Controller Parameters in GA Optimization

The boundaries of optimal parameters of type-1 controller are

$$k_{p1min} \leq k_{p1} \leq k_{p1max}$$

$$k_{i1min} \leq k_{i1} \leq k_{i1max}$$

$$k_{p2min} \leq k_{p2} \leq k_{p2max}$$

$$k_{i2min} \leq k_{i2} \leq k_{i2max}$$

$$k_{p3min} \leq k_{p3} \leq k_{p3max}$$

$$k_{i3min} \leq k_{i3} \leq k_{i3max}$$

13.2.4 Optimization Results of Two Level STATCOM with GA Optimized Controller Parameters

The eigenvalues of the system with nonlinear feedback and optimized controller parameters are given in Table 13.4. Comparing with the eiganvalue

Table 13.4 Eigenvalues of 2-level STATCOM with non-linear feedback for suboptimal controller parameters.

Capacitive region $i_R = -1$	Inductive region $i_R = 1$
-1856.7	-2194.6
$-83.949 \pm j1373.6$	$-58.401 \pm j1398.3$
-55.556	$-32.538 \pm j4.9879$
-23.842	

results given in Table 13.2, it is to be noted that, although the damping of critical mode is decreased (in inductive region), the damping of other modes is increased. The GA based optimization ensures that, the system is robustly D-stable for various operating points under consideration.

13.2.4.1 Transient Simulation with GA Optimized Controller Parameters

The transient simulation of the 3 phase model of the STATCOM for step change in the reactive current is shown in Figure 13.12 and Figure 13.13. It can be seen from that the transition from capacitive to inductive mode of operation of STATCOM is very fast and takes less time about 0.04 sec to reach steady state. It is to be noted that, the transient response of the

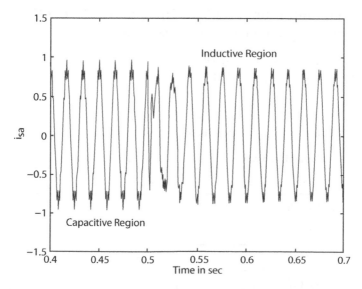

Figure 13.12 Phase 'a' current of STATCOM with optimal controller parameters.

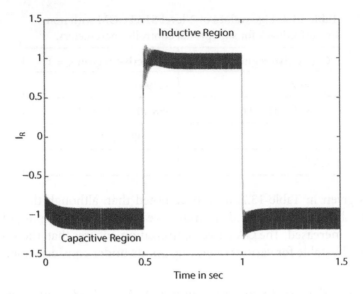

Figure 13.13 Step response with 3-phase model of STATCOM and optimal controller parameters.

STATCOM is significantly improved. The steady state oscillations in the reactive current of Figure 13.13 are due to harmonics in the converter output voltage. Thus with optimal controller parameters the transient response of the STATCOM is improved.

13.2.5 Optimization Results of Three Level STATCOM with Optimal Controller Parameters

Eigenvalues of the system with Type-1 controller and optimized controller parameters are shown in Table 13.5.

Table 13.5 Eigenvalues of 3-level STATCOM with optimal controller parameters based on GA.

Capacitive region $i_R = -1$	Inductive region $i_R = 1$
-733.87 ± j 1297.9	-733.37 ± j 1570.6
-649.88	-649.88
-25.134	-25.134
-1.4425	-1.4442
-11.137	-11.137

Figure 13.14 shows location of eigenvalues of the STATCOM in the complex plane for the entire inductive and capacitive range of operation. The eigenvalues are lying on left half of the D-contour with optimal controller parameters. Thus the GA based optimization ensures that, the system is robustly D-stable for various operating points under consideration.

13.2.5.1   Transient Simulation with GA Optimized Controller Parameters

The transient simulation of STATCOM is carried out using both D-Q and 3-phase model using MATLAB-SIMULINK. The step response with 3-phase model of three-level STATCOM with optimal controller parameters is shown Figure 13.15.

It can be seen from Figure 13.15 and Figure 13.16 that the transition from capacitive to inductive mode of operation of STATCOM is very fast and takes less time about 0.005 sec to reach steady state. It is to be noted that, the transient response of the STATCOM is significantly improved. The steady state oscillations in the reactive current of Figure 13.15 are due to harmonics in the converter output voltage. Thus with optimal controller parameters the speed of response of the STATCOM is increased and hence the transient response.

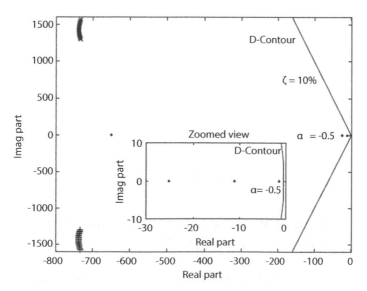

Figure 13.14 Location of eigenvalues of STATCOM with optimal controller parameters.

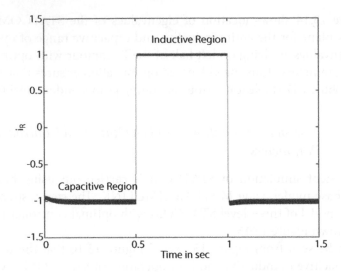

Figure 13.15 Step response with 3-phase model of STATCOM with optimal controller parameters.

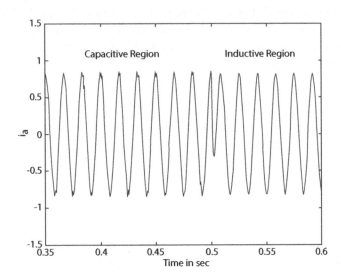

Figure 13.16 Phase 'a' current of STATCOM with optimal controller parameters.

13.3   Design of Particle Swarm Optimization Based Controller for STATCOM

Another nature-based class of global optimization problems is PSO [1–4], [19]. This approach utilizes the concepts borrowed from the field of social psychology. The basic idea behind the Particle Swarm Optimization (PSO) technique is to imagine a swarm of particles (points) travelling together in the parameter space. Initially a swarm of particles or start population is formed in a random way. PSO does not employ mutation and crossover as GA tool. Instead, the particles move through a predetermined search space, and in each iteration move near to the optimal value. At every iteration, every particle moves in a certain way in search of better local minima. Each individual particle remembers the position in the parameter space where this particle achieved the best value of the objective function. This is called the individual best position. In addition, the whole swarm keeps track of the position where the best value of the whole swarm was achieved. The memory capability of PSO makes all the particles to remember its local best position as well as global best position of the group. Each member of the swarm moves according to a relationship that is influenced by its individual best value and the swarm best value. This approach integrates the collective cognitive experience of the swarm into the optimization process. The process is repeated until either maximum generations or convergence criterion is met.

The parameters used with PSO are given in Table 13.6.

13.3.1   Optimization Results of Two Level STATCOM with GA and PSO Optimized Parameters

The optimization of controller parameters is performed with maximum iteration of 100 in both GA and PSO. Figure 13.17 and Figure 13.18 show the value of objective function (OFV) at every function evaluation (for two ranges of y-axis) and iteration with GA and PSO respectively. It is observed

Table 13.6 Parameters used for optimization with PSO.

Parameter	Value/type
Maximum Generations	100
Population Size	200
Cognitive Acceleration	1
Social Acceleration	0.5
Constriction factor	0.2
Termination method	Maximum Generation

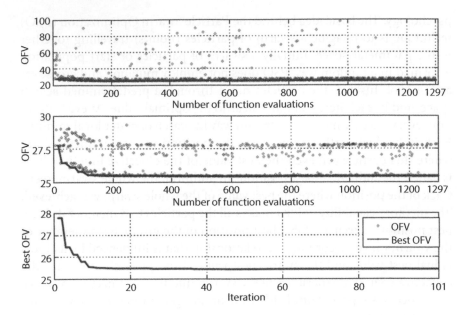

Figure 13.17 Value of objective function at every function evaluation and iteration with GA.

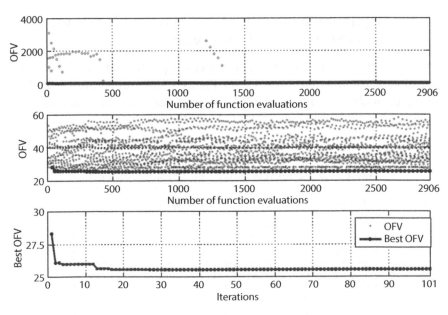

Figure 13.18 Value of objective function at every function evaluation and iteration with PSO.

that, for the same population size, boundary conditions and iterations, PSO performs more function evaluations than GA, however in both methods the best objective function value reduces in successive iterations and reaches a final value. In Figure 13.19, it is to be noted that the final value of best objective function is less in GA than PSO and indicating the ability of GA in searching global optimum than PSO.

The performance of optimization technique is as well determined by the computational time for optimization. Figure 13.20 shows time for every iteration up to 50 iterations where it is indicated by asterisks. It is seen that GA takes minimum of 1.5 sec and maximum of 3.2 sec for an iteration whereas PSO takes minimum of 18.5 sec and maximum of 20 sec for an iteration due to more number of function evaluations. It demonstrates GA takes less computational time than PSO for optimization.

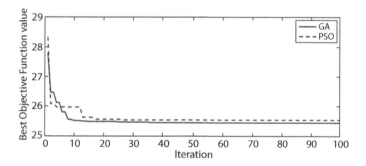

Figure 13.19 Best value of objective function at every iteration with GA and PSO.

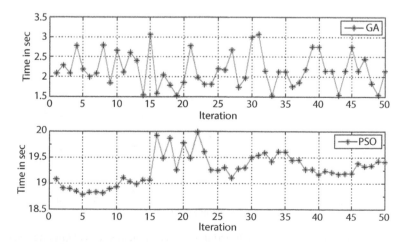

Figure 13.20 Time for iteration with GA and PSO.

However GA and PSO are stochastic techniques and employ an element of randomness in the iterations which helps to escape local minima. Hence these techniques may convergence to local minimum in few runs. The best value of objective function is calculated in multiple runs with GA and PSO for the same settings of maximum generation and population size (for PSO Table 13.6). Figure 13.21 shows best value of objective function (indicated by dots) for ten continuous runs of optimization program. It is observed that GA gives global minimum or near global minimum in most number of the runs than PSO, and shows the efficiency of GA in searching and guaranteeing global minimum or near global minimum. Though PSO performs more function evaluations, in most of the runs it results in local minimum. However, comparing with GA, deviations in best objective value is less in PSO and guarantees near global minimum in many runs.

From the results it is observed that GA is efficient in searching global minimum or near global minimum, fast convergence and comparatively less computational time with less number of function evaluations. GA guarantees global minimum or near global minimum and outperforms PSO significantly.

The eigenvalues of the system with non-linear feedback and optimized controller parameters are given in Table 13.7. Comparing with the eiganvalue results given in Table 13.1, it is to be noted that, though the damping of critical mode is decreased in inductive region, the damping of other modes is

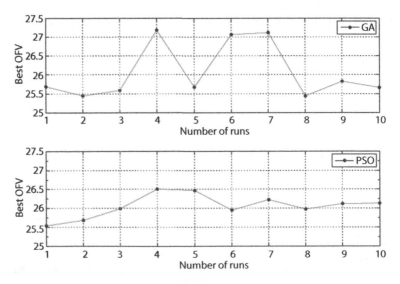

Figure 13.21 Best value of objective function for ten continuous runs of GA and PSO optimization.

Table 13.7 Eigenvalues of 2-level STATCOM with nonlinear feedback for optimal controller parameters.
a) Eigenvalues with GA optimized controller parameters

Capacitive region $i_R = -1$	Inductive region $i_R = 1$
-978.48	1045.7
-88.3 ± j1417.4	-58.819 ± j 8.9574
-85.324	-27.905 ± j 1458.3
-46.762	

b) Eigenvalues with PSO optimized controller parameters

Capacitive region $i_R = -1$	Inductive region $i_R = 1$
-978.06	-1058.2
-89.334	-65.864
-87.963 ± j 1417.7	-50.173
-42.044	-31.108 ± j 1455.6

increased significantly. Figure 13.22 shows the location of eigenvalues from maximum capacitive to inductive operation of STATCOM with GA and PSO optimized controller parameters. It is observed that, with optimized controller parameters the real part of all eigenvalues lie in L.H.S of s-plane, indicating that STATCOM is stable for various operating points.

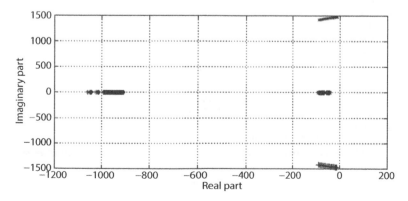

Figure 13.22 Plot of eigenvalues from maximum capacitive to inductive operation of STATCOM with optimized controller parameters.

The transient simulation of three-phase model of the STATCOM (with GA and PSO optimized controller parameters) for step change in the reactive current is carried out. Figure 13.23 and Figure 13.24 show phase 'a' current and reactive current of STATCOM respectively.

In Figure 13.23 it can be seen from that, for large deviation (step change) in reactive current reference, the transition in STATCOM reactive current from capacitive to inductive mode is very fast and reaches steady state in

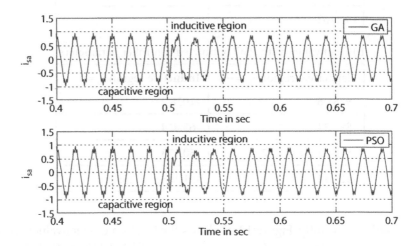

Figure 13.23 Phase 'a' current of STATCOM with optimal controller parameters.

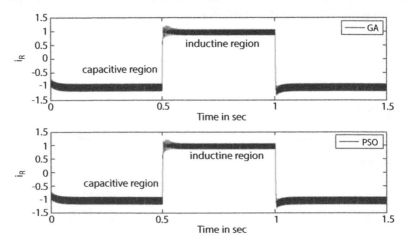

Figure 13.24 Step response with three phase model of STATCOM and optimal controller parameters.

less time about 0.025 sec. In Figure 13.24 is to be observed that, the transient response of the STATCOM with optimized controller parameters is fast and significantly improved. In reactive current response shown in Figure 13.24, the steady state oscillations indicate the presence of harmonics in the converter output voltage.

STATCOM with optimized controller parameters exhibits excellent transient response for large deviation in the reactive current reference. The GA and PSO based optimization methods ensure that, the system is robustly stable for various operating points under consideration. Further, the transient performance with GA and PSO optimized parameters is closely matching. The difference in computational effort between GA and PSO is problem dependent. Comparing to PSO, GA is efficient in searching global minimum or near global minimum, fast convergence and comparatively takes less computational time with less number of function evaluations. The results demonstrate that GA outperforms PSO significantly and efficient when applied to constrained nonlinear problem optimization.

13.4 Design of Genetic Algorithm Based Type-1 Controller for VSCHVDC

The VSC based HVDC is based on turn-off devices which has several advantages over conventional HVDC based on thyrister [20, 21]. The point to point VSC based HVDC transmission system consists of two converter stations connected by a dc cable. The active and reactive power can be controlled independently in all four quadrants by controlling the magnitude and phase angle of the converter output voltage. When one converter operates on dc voltage control, the other converter operates on active power control for balanced active power flow [22]. When power flow is zero in dc line, the two converters operate as independent STATCOMs.

This section presents GA based design of controller for VSC based HVDC. The VSC is realized with twenty four pulse three level converter, and Type-I controller [23, 24] is used for controlling both the magnitude and phase angle of converter output voltage. A systematic approach is used for selecting the controller parameters and Genetic Algorithm (GA) is used for tuning the controller parameters.

13.4.1 Modeling of VSC HVDC

The system diagram of HVDC transmission system with two VSCs is shown in Figure 13.25. The electromechanical system consists of generator

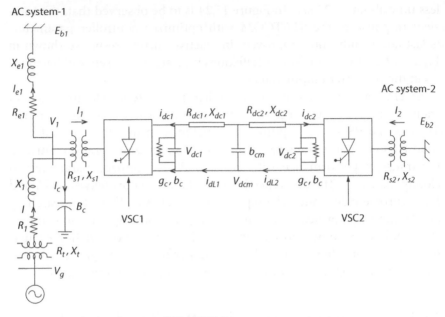

Figure 13.25 System diagram of VSC HVDC.

2.2 model, six mass mechanical system, Power System Stabilizer (PSS) and the transmission line. The VSC HVDC and long transmission ac line are originated from a substation which receives power from the turbine-generator whose data is adapted from IEEE First Benchmark model [7, 25, 26]. VSC HVDC provides asynchronous link between AC system-1 and AC system-2. The details of the study system are depicted in Figure 13.25.

Neglecting the harmonics and approximating the switching functions by their fundamental components, VSC based HVDC is modelled by transforming the 3-phase voltages and currents to D-Q using Kron's transformation [26, 27].

The two converters are of three level twenty four pulse configuration. The magnitude and phase angle of converter output voltage can be controlled simultaneously for controlling active and reactive power flows respectively.

The VSC equivalent circuit viewed from ac bus is shown in Figure 13.26. In Figure 13.26, R_{sj} and X_{sj} are the resistance and reactance of the interfacing transformer of VSC_j.

The converter output voltage in D-Q frame is given by

$$V_j^i = \sqrt{V_{jD}^{i\,2} + V_{jQ}^{i\,2}} \tag{13.21}$$

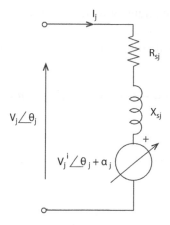

Figure 13.26 Equivalent circuit of VSC viewed from ac bus.

where V_{jD}^i and V_{jQ}^i are the D and Q components of VSC output voltage. The jth converter current in D-Q is given by the following equations as

$$\frac{dI_{jD}}{dt} = -\frac{R_{sj}\omega_B}{X_{sj}}I_{jD} - \omega_o I_{jQ} + \frac{\omega_B}{X_{sj}}\left[V_{jD} - V_{jD}^i\right] \qquad (13.22)$$

$$\frac{dI_{jQ}}{dt} = -\frac{R_{sj}\omega_B}{X_{sj}}I_{jQ} + \omega_o I_{jD} + \frac{\omega_B}{X_{sj}}\left[V_{jQ} - V_{jQ}^i\right] \qquad (13.23)$$

In this system $j = 1, 2$. The dc-side capacitors of the VSCs are described by the dynamical equations as,

$$\frac{dV_{dc1}}{dt} = -\frac{\omega_B}{b_c R_p}V_{dc1} - \frac{\omega_B}{b_c}I_{dc1} + \frac{\omega_B}{b_c}I_{dL1} \qquad (13.24)$$

$$\frac{dV_{dc2}}{dt} = -\frac{\omega_B}{b_c R_p}V_{dc2} - \frac{\omega_B}{b_c}I_{dc2} + \frac{\omega_B}{b_c}I_{dL2} \qquad (13.25)$$

Where

$$I_{dcj} = -[k_{mj}\sin(\theta_s + \alpha_j)I_{jD} + k_{mj}\cos(\theta_s + \alpha_j)I_{jQ}]$$

Where α_j is the phase angle by which the fundamental component of jth converter output voltage leads the jth ac bus voltage V_j. I_{dL1} and I_{dL2} are the dc link currents in the left and right hand side sections and are described as

$$\frac{dI_{dL1}}{dt} = -\frac{\omega_B}{X_{dc1}}[V_{dc1} - V_{dcm} - R_{dc1}I_{dL1}] \qquad (13.26)$$

$$\frac{dI_{dL2}}{dt} = -\frac{\omega_B}{X_{dc2}}[V_{dcm} - V_{dc2} - R_{dc2}I_{dL2}] \qquad (13.27)$$

$$\frac{dV_{dcm}}{dt} = -\frac{\omega_B}{b_{cm}}I_{dL1} - \frac{\omega_B}{b_{cm}}I_{dL2} \qquad (13.28)$$

Where $k_{mj} = k'cos\beta_j$ is the modulation index. $k' = k\rho_j \frac{V_{dcb}}{V_{acb}}$. For a 24-pulse converter $k = \frac{4\sqrt{6}}{\pi}$. ρ_j is the transformation ratio of the interfacing transformer for j^{th} converter. V_{dcb} and V_{acb} are the base voltages of the dc and ac side respectively.

13.4.1.1   Converter Controller

In a VSC HVDC system, one converter has to control the DC voltage and other converter can operate on constant DC power control. Accordingly, in a VSC HVDC terminal the various modes of control, like DC link voltage(V_{dcj})/power(P_j) and constant ac bus voltage(V_j)/reactive current(I_{Rj}) are considered. The DC voltage/power controller sets the reference value for real current(I_{Pjref}) and the reference value of reactive current (I_{Rjref}) of VSCs is set by ac bus voltage controller, or it can be a constant. These two controllers form the outer loop. The real and reactive current controllers form the inner loop. Hence for each converter there are four controllers as shown in Figure 13.27.

The magnitude control of the jth converter output voltage V_j^i is achieved by modulating the conduction period affected by the dead angle β_j of the individual converters. α_j and β_j are calculated as,

$$\alpha_j = tan^{-1}\left[\frac{V_{Rj(ord)}}{V_{Pj(ord)}}\right] \qquad (13.29)$$

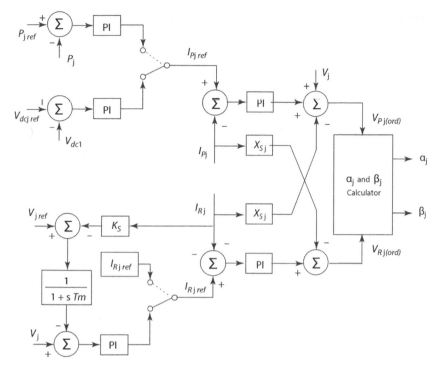

Figure 13.27 Controller for one of the VSCs of HVDC.

$$\beta_j = cos^{-1}\left[\frac{\sqrt{V_{Pj(ord)}^2 + V_{Rj(ord)}^2}}{k'V_{dcj}}\right] \quad (13.30)$$

The various operating combinations of the VSC HVDC are given in Table 13.8. The reference value of reactive current (IRjref) of VSCs is set by ac bus voltage controller, or it can be a constant. Since converter-2 is connected to infinite bus, the reactive current reference is kept constant.

In each case there are several controllers gains to be selected for HVDC link. The selection of controller parameters is based on a systematic approach using Genetic Algorithm. The parameter optimization based on GA [28] considers the various operating cases of VSC HVDC as given in Table 13.8.

13.4.2   A Case Study

The system diagram of HVDC transmission system with two VSCs is shown in Figure 13.25. The controller design and analysis is performed with the following assumptions and initial operating conditions.

Table 13.8 Operating combinations of VSC HVDC controllers.

Case	VSC1(Rectifier)		VSC2(Inverter)	
	Controller-1	Controller-2	Controller-1	Controller-2
1	Power	Reactive Current	DC Voltage	Reactive Current
2	Power	AC Voltage	DC Voltage	Reactive Current
3	DC Voltage	Reactive Current	Power	Reactive Current
4	DC Voltage	AC Voltage	Power	Reactive Current
	VSC1(Inverter)		VSC2(Rectifier)	
5	Power	Reactive Current	DC Voltage	Reactive Current
6	Power	AC Voltage	DC Voltage	Reactive Current
7	DC Voltage	Reactive Current	Power	Reactive Current
8	DC Voltage	AC Voltage	Power	Reactive Current

1. The generator supplies 0.125 p.u power to transmission system.
2. The generator terminal voltage is 1.0 p.u.
3. The converter bus voltage magnitudes are set at 1.0 p.u.
4. In rectifier operation, HVDC cable power P1 is set at 0.9 p.u. The reactive powers drawn by the two converters are set to zero $Q_1 = Q_2 = 0$. The base values of ac system are 300 MVA, 500 kV and the dc voltage base is 300 kV.
5. The ESCR of the system at bus1 is 3.5.
6. In all the transient simulation a step change of 10% decrease in reference value is applied at 1 sec and removed at 3 sec.

13.4.2.1 Transient Simulation with Suboptimal Controller Parameters

The transient simulation of VSC HVDC is carried out using D-Q model in MATLAB-SIMULINK [15]. The step responses with D-Q of three-level VSC HVDC with non-optimized controller parameters are shown in Figure 13.28 and Figure 13.29. It is to be noted that the step response of VSC HVDC with non-optimized controller parameters is slow and having overshoot.

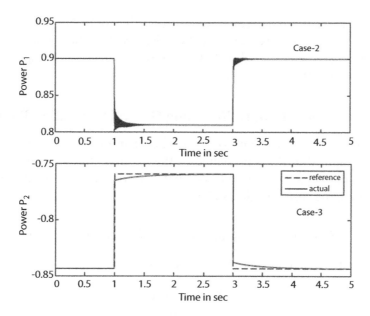

Figure 13.28 Step response 3-level VSC HVDC with non-optimized controller parameters in case-2 and case-3.

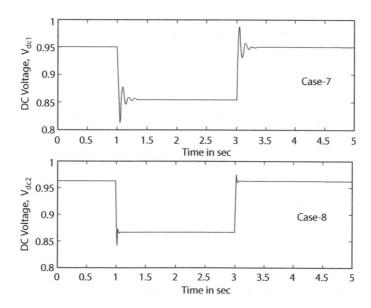

Figure 13.29 Step response 3-level VSC HVDC with non-optimized controller parameters in case-7 and case-8.

Hence there is a requirement to optimize the controller parameters to improve the transient response of the VSC HVDC. The optimization of controller parameters based on GA to improve the transient response will be discussed in the section to follow.

13.4.3   Design of Controller Using GA and Simulation Results

The optimization problem for controller parameters selection using Genetic Algorithm [5] is presented in this section. The selection of controller parameters is based on a systematic approach [24] considering the eight operating cases of VSC HVDC.

13.4.3.1   Description of Optimization Problem and Application of GA

Consider a system described by the equation

$$\dot{X} = [A(r)]X \qquad (13.31)$$
$$Y = [C]X$$

In Equation 13.31, matrix $[A(r)]$ contains one or more adjustable parameters. $[r]$ is the set of controller gains need be optimized. The optimization of controller parameters is based on minimizing the standard infinite time quadratic performance index and can be stated as,

$$J = \int_t^\infty Y^t Y \, dt \qquad (1.32)$$

Considering the system is stable, J can be expressed as

$$J = X^T P X \qquad (13.33)$$

Where P is a positive definite matrix and solved from the following liapunov equation

$$PA + A^T P = -Q \qquad (13.34)$$

Where $Q = C^T C$.
From this the objective function is obtained as

$$\hat{J} = \sum_i tr[P_i] \qquad (13.35)$$

which is to be minimized. where 'i' is 1 to 8 cases of VSC HVDC. Genetic Algorithm is used for tuning the controller parameters based on the objective function defined in Equation 13.35. The parameter optimization based on GA considers the various operating cases of VSC HVDC as given in Table 13.8. The GA enables the usage of the same controller gains for all operating cases while maintaining the system stability.

13.4.3.2   Transient Simulation

The transient simulation of the combined system with optimal controller parameters obtained using GA is carried out in MATLABSIMULINK [15]. The results for step change in reactive current, power and DC voltage references in case-1 to case-8 are shown in Figure 13.30 to Figure 13.37; it is clear that, the transient responses are good with optimal controller parameters.

13.4.3.3   Eigenvalue Analysis

The eigenvalues of the combined system linearized at an operating point are computed from system matrix and are given in Table 13.9 and Table 13.10 for eight operating cases. It is to be noted from Table 13.9 and Table 13.10 that, all the eigenvalues have negative real part in case-1 to case-8. Hence, it is evident that the system is stable in all eight operating cases with optimal controller parameters. The Genetic Algorithm enables the usage of the same controller gains for all operating cases while maintaining the system stability.

13.5   Conclusion

This chapter presents the optimization of controller parameters for FACTS and VSC based HVDC. The controller parameters are selected based on a systematic approach using GA and PSO. The GA and PSO enable the usage of the same controller gains for all operating cases while maintaining the system stability. The analysis is based on eigenvalue and transient simulation is carried out to validate the performance of the system with same controller parameters in various operating cases. The transient response is excellent in all the operating cases with optimal controller parameters. The results show the robustness and suitability of designed controller for various operating cases.

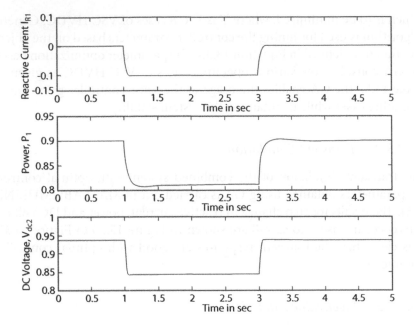

Figure 13.30 Step response of reactive current, power and DC voltage for case-1 with optimal controller parameters.

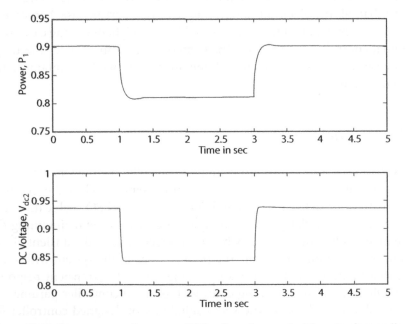

Figure 13.31 Step response of power and DC voltage for case-2 with optimal controller parameters.

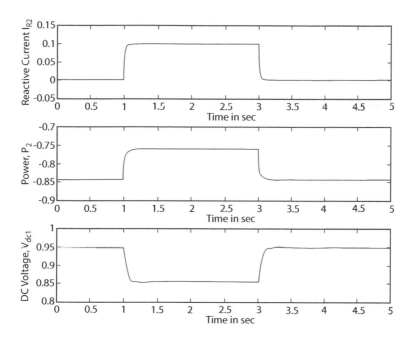

Figure 13.32 Step response of reactive current, power and DC voltage for case-3 with optimal controller parameters.

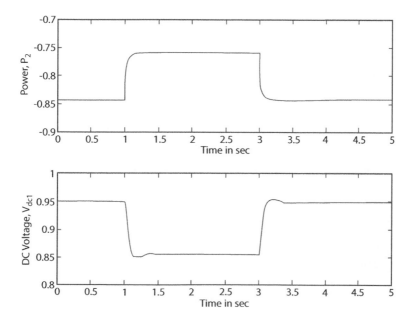

Figure 13.33 Step response of power and DC voltage for case-4 with optimal controller parameters.

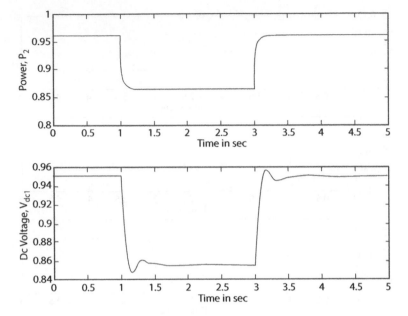

Figure 13.36 Step response of power and DC voltage for case-7 with optimal controller parameters.

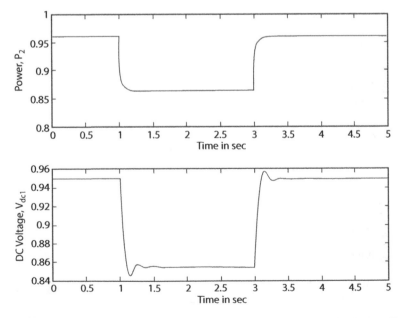

Figure 13.37 Step response of power and DC voltage for case-8 with optimal controller parameters.

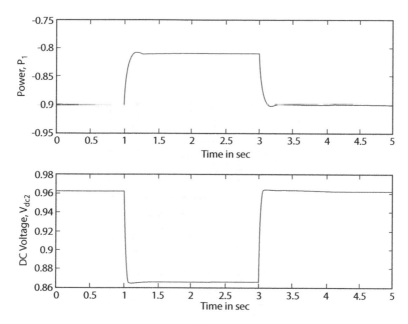

Figure 13.34 Step response of reactive current, power and DC voltage for case-5 with optimal controller parameters.

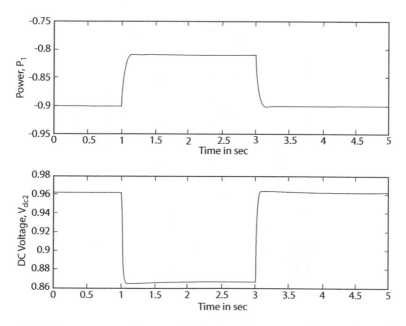

Figure 13.35 Step response of power and DC voltage for case-6 with optimal controller parameters.

Table 13.9 Eigenvalues of the combined system in case-1 to case-4.

Torsional mode	Eigenvalue			
	Case-1	Case-2	Case-3	Case-4
0	-1.0033 ± j 6.8833	-1.2937 ± j 6.9322	-0.9897 ± j 6.8563	-1.2862 ± j 6.9333
1	-0.2167 ± j 98.928	-0.2146 ± j 98.927	-0.2328 ± j 98.921	-0.2323 ± j 98.918
2	-0.0738 ± j 127.01	-0.0737 ± j 127.01	-0.0745 ± j 127.01	-0.0745 ± j 127.01
3	-0.6449 ± j 160.58	-0.6449 ± j 160.58	-0.6464 ± j 160.58	-0.6465 ± j 160.58
4	-0.3607 ± j 202.94	-0.3607 ± j 202.94	-0.3620 ± j 202.95	-0.3622 ± j 202.95
5	-1.8504 ± j 298.17	-1.8504 ± j 298.17	-1.8504 ± j 298.17	-1.8504 ± j 298.17

Table 13.10 Eigenvalues of the combined system in case-5 to case-8.

Torsional mode	Eigenvalue			
	Case-5	Case-6	Case-7	Case-8
0	-1.3567 ± j 6.2744	-1.1941 ± j 6.7270	-1.3861 ± j 6.2864	-1.2013 ± j 6.7227
1	-0.2579 ± j 98.918	-0.2604 ± j 98.915	-0.2364 ± j 98.925	-0.2365 ± j 98.923
2	-0.0755 ± j 127.01	-0.0756 ± j 127.01	-0.0745 ± j 127.01	-0.0745 ± j 127.01
3	-0.6484 ± j 160.58	-0.6485 ± j 160.58	-0.6464 ± j 160.58	-0.6465 ± j 160.58
4	-0.3638 ± j 202.95	-0.3640 ± j 202.95	-0.3621 ± j 202.94	-0.3622 ± j 202.94
5	-1.8504 ± j 298.17	-1.8504 ± j 298.17	-1.8504 ± j 298.17	-1.8504 ± j 298.17

References

1. Rega Rajendra, Dilip K. Pratihar, "Particle Swarm Optimization Algorithm vs Genetic Algorithm to Develop Integrated Scheme for Obtaining Optimal Mechanical Structure and Adaptive Controller of a Robot", *Intelligent Control and Automation*, vol.56, No.2, pp. 1348-1354, 2011.
2. Sidhartha Panda, Narayana Prasad Padhy, "Comparison of particle swarm optimization and genetic algorithm for FACTS-based controller design", *Applied Soft Computing*, vol.8, No.4, pp. 1418-1427, Sep 2008.
3. M. Peyvandi M. Zafarani, E Nasr, "Comparison of Particle Swarm Optimization and Genetic Algorithm in the Improvement of Power System Stability by an SSSC-based Controller", *Journal of Electrical Engineering and Technology*, vol.6, No.2, pp. 182-191, 2011.
4. Rania Hassan Babak Cohanim, Olivier de Weck and Venter, Gerhard, "A comparison of Particle Swarm Optimization and Genetic Algorithm", *American Institute of Aeronautics and Astronautics*, 2004.
5. Goldberg, *Genetic Algorithm In search, Optimization and Machine Learning*, Addison Wesley Reading, 1989.
6. R. Thirumalaivasan, M. Janaki and Nagesh Prabhu, "Damping of SSR Using Subsynchronous Current Suppressor With SSSC", *IEEE Trans. on Power Syts*, vol.28, No.1, pp. 64-74, Feb 2013.
7. M. Janaki, Nagesh Prabhu, R Thirumalaivasan and Kothari, D P, "Mitigation of SSR by Subsynchronous Current Injection with VSC HVDC ", *Electrical Power and Energy Systems*, vol.57, pp. 287-297, 2014.
8. R. Thirumalaivasan, M. Janaki and Yunjian Xu, "Kalman Filter Based Detection and Mitigation of Subsynchronous Resonance with SSSC ", *IEEE Trans. on Power Syts*, vol.32, No.2, pp. 1400-1409, Mar 2017.
9. Yanhui Xi, Xin Tang, Zewen Li, Yonglin Cui, Ting Zhao, Xiangjun Zeng, Jun Guo and Wei Duan, "Harmonic estimation in power systems using an optimised adaptive Kalman filter based on PSO-GA", *IET Gen. Trans and Distribution*, vol.13, No.17, pp. 3968-3979, Sep 2019.
10. Penghan Li, Jie Wang, Linyun Xiong, Meiling Ma, Ziqiang Wang and Sunhua Huang, "Robust sub-synchronous damping controller to mitigate SSCI in series-compensated DFIG-based wind park", *IET Gen. Trans and Distribution*, vol. 14, no. 9, pp. 1762-1769, May 2020.
11. Padiyar. K. R and Kulkarni. A. M, "Design of Reactive Current and Voltage Controller of Static Condenser", *International Journal of Electrical Power and Energy Systems*, vol. 19, no. 6, pp. 397-410, 1997.
12. M. Janaki, R. Thirumalaivasan and Nagesh Prabhu, "Design of Robust Current Controller for Two-Level 12-Pulse VSC-based STATCOM", *Advances in Power Electronics*, article ID 912749, 2011.
13. C. Schauder and H. Mehta, "Vector Analysis and Control of Advanced Static Var Compensator", *IEE Proceedings-C*, vol. 140, no. 4, pp. 299-306, July 1993.

14. Padiyar. K. R, *FACTS controllers in Power Transmission and Distribution*, New Delhi, India. New age International (P) Ltd, 2007.

15. Natick. M. A, *Using MATLAB-SIMULINK*, The MathWorks, Inc., 1999.

16. Padiyar. K. R and Nagesh Prabhu, "Analysis of sub synchronous resonance with three level twelve-pulse VSC based SSSC", *in Proc.IEEE TENCON-2003*, Bangalore, India, 2003.

17. K.R.Padiyar and V. Swayam Prakash, "Tuning and performance evaluation of damping controller for a STATCOM", Int. J. Electr. Power and Energy Syst., vol. 25, pp. 155-166, 2003.

18. Padiyar. K. R and Nagesh Prabhu, "Design and Performance Evalution of Subsynchronous Damping Controller with STATCOM", *IEEE Transactions on Power Delivery*, vol. 21, no. 3, pp. 1398-1405, 2006.

19. Kennedy, J and Eberhart, R, "Particle Swarm Optimization, *in proceedings of IEEE International Conference on Neural Networks*, 1995.

20. G. Asplund K. Eriksson and Stevenson, K, "DC transmission based on voltage source converters", *in Proc. CIGRE SC14 Colloq.*, South Africa, 1997.

21. Ooi. B. T and Wang. X, "Voltage angle lock loop control of the boost type PWM Converter for HVDC application", *IEEE Trans. Power Electron.*, vol. 5, no. 2, pp. 229-235, Apr 1990.

22. Nagesh Prabhu and Padiyar. K. R, "Investigation of Subsynchronous Resonance with VSC based HVDC Transmission Systems", *IEEE Trans. on Power Delivery*, vol. 24, no. 1, pp. 433-440, Jan 2009.

23. Padiyar. K. R and Kulkarni. A. M, "Control design and simulation of unified power flow controller", *IEEE Trans. on Power Del.*, vol. 13, no. 4, pp. 1348-1354, Oct 1998.

24. Padiyar. K. R and Nagesh Prabhu, "Modelling, control design and analysis of VSC based HVDC transmission systems", *POWERCON*, Singapore, 2004.

25. Working group, IEEE, "First bench mark model for computer simulation of Subsynchronous resonance", *IEEE Transactions on PAS*, vol. 96, no. 5, pp. 1565-1572, Sept 1977.

26. K.R.Padiyar, Analysis of Subsynchronous Resonance in power systems, Boston: Kluwer Academic Publishers, 1999.

27. K.R.Padiyar, Power System Dynamics - Stability and Control- Second edition, Hyderabad: B.S.Publications, 1999.

28. Janaki. M, Thirumalaivasan. R and Nagesh Prabhu, "Design of Robust Current Controller Using GA for Three Level 24-Pulse VSC Based STATCOM", Journal of Power Electronics, vol. 11, no. 3, pp. 375-380, May 2011.

29. Priyadarshi.; N;, Padmanaban, S.; Maroti, P.K.; Sharma. A.; An Extensive Practical Investigation of FPSO-Based MPPT for Grid Integrated PV System Under Variable Operating Conditions With Anti-Islanding Protection. IEEE System Journal, 2018, 13:1861 - 1871.

30. Priyadarshi, N.; Padmanaban, S.; Bhaskar, M.S.; Blaabjerg, F.; Sharma, A.; A Fuzzy SVPWM Based Inverter Control Realization of Grid Integrated PV-Wind System with FPSO MPPT Algorithm for a Grid-Connected PV/

Wind Power Generation System: Hardware Implementation. IET Electric Power Appl., 2018, 12:962-971.

31. Priyadarshi, N.; Kumar, V.; Yadav, K.; Vardia, M.; An Experimental Study on Zeta buck-boost converter for Application in PV system. Handbook of distributed generation, Springer, DOI 10.1007/978-3-319-51343-0_13

32. Priyadarshi N.; Sharma A.K.; Priyam S.; An Experimental Realization of Grid-Connected PV System with MPPT Using dSPACE DS 1104 Control Board. Advances in Smart Grid and Renewable Energy. Lecture Notes in Electrical Engineering, Springer, Singapore 2018, 435.

33. Priyadarshi N.; Sharma A.K.; Priyam S.; Practical Realization of an Improved Photovoltaic Grid Integration with MPPT. International Journal of Renewable Energy Research 2017, 7:1180-1891.

34. Priyadarshi N.; Sharma A.K.; Azam F.; A Hybrid Firefly-Asymmetrical Fuzzy Logic Controller based MPPT for PV-Wind-Fuel Grid Integration. International Journal of Renewable Energy Research 2017, 7: 1546-1560.

35. Priyadarshi, N.; Anand, A.; Sharma, A.K.; Azam, F.; Singh, V.K.; Sinha, R. K.; An Experimental Implementation and Testing of GA based Maximum Power Point Tracking for PV System under Varying Ambient Conditions Using dSPACE DS 1104 Controller. International Journal of Renewable Energy Research, 2017, 7:255-265.

36. Priyadarshi, N.; Padmanaban S.; Mihet-Popa L.; Blaabjerg, F.; Azam F.; Maximum Power Point Tracking for Brushless DC Motor-Driven Photovoltaic Pumping Systems Using a Hybrid ANFIS-FLOWER Pollination Optimization Algorithm. MDPI Energies 2018, 11:1-16.

37. Priyadarshi, N.; Azam, F.; Bhoi, A.K.; Alam, S.; An Artificial Fuzzy Logic Intelligent Controller Based MPPT for PV Grid Utility. Lecture Notes in Networks and Systems 46, https://doi.org/10.1007/978-981-13-1217-5_88.

38. Padmanaban, S.; Priyadarshi, N.; Holm-Nielsen, J. B.; Bhaskar, M. S.; Azam, F.; Sharma, A.K.; A Novel Modified Sine-Cosine Optimized MPPT Algorithm for Grid Integrated PV System under Real Operating Conditions. IEEE Access, 2019, 7:10467-10477.

39. Padmanaban, S.; Priyadarshi, N.; Holm-Nielsen, J. B.; Bhaskar, M. S.; Hossain, E.; Azam, F.; A Hybrid Photovoltaic-Fuel Cell for Grid Integration With Jaya-Based Maximum Power Point Tracking: Experimental Performance Evaluation. IEEE Access, 2019, 7:82978-82990.

40. Priyadarshi, N.; Padmanaban, N.; Holm-Nielsen, J. B.; Blaabjerg, F.; Bhaskar, M.S.; An Experimental Estimation of Hybrid ANFIS–PSO-Based MPPT for PV Grid Integration Under Fluctuating Sun Irradiance. in IEEE Systems Journal. 2020, 14:1218-1229.

41. Priyadarshi, N.; Padmanaban, N.; Bhaskar, M. S.; Blaabjerg, F.; Holm-Nielsen, J. B.; Azam, F.; Sharma, A.K.; A Hybrid Photovoltaic-Fuel Cell-Based Single-Stage Grid Integration With Lyapunov Control Scheme. IEEE Systems Journal, 2020, 14: 3334 - 3342.

42. Priyadarshi, N.; Bhaskar, M. S.; Padmanaban, N.; Blaabjerg, F.; Azam, F.; New CUK–SEPIC converter based photovoltaic power system with hybrid GSA–PSO algorithm employing MPPT for water pumping applications. IET Power Electronics. 2020, 13:2824 – 2830.

43. Priyadarshi, N.; Padmanaban, N.; Holm-Nielsen, J. B.; Bhaskar, M.S.; Azam, F.; Internet of things augmented a novel PSO-employed modified zeta converter-based photovoltaic maximum power tracking system: hardware realisation. IET Power Electronics. 2020, 13:2775 – 2781.

44. Kamalapathi, K., Priyadarshi, N., Padmanaban, S., Holm-Nielsen, J.B., Azam, F., Umayal, C., Ramachandaramurthy, V.K. A Hybrid Moth-Flame Fuzzy Logic Controller Based Integrated Cuk Converter Fed Brushless DC Motor for Power Factor Correction. MDPI Electronics, 2018, 7: 288.

45. Priyadarshi, N., Padmanaban, S., Lonel, D., Mihet-Popa, L., Azam, F. Hybrid PV-Wind, Micro-Grid Development Using Quasi-Z-Source Inverter Modeling and Control—Experimental Investigation. MDPI Energies, 2018, 11:2277.

46. Priyadarshi, N.; Ramachandaramurthy, V, K.; Padmanaban, S.; Azam, A.; An Ant Colony Optimized MPPT for Standalone Hybrid PV-Wind Power System with Single Cuk Converter. MDPI Energies, 2019, 12: 167.

47. Azam, F.; Yadav, S.K.; Priyadarshi, N.; Padmanaban, S.; and Bansal, R.C.; A Comprehensive Review of Authentication Schemes in Vehicular Ad-Hoc Network, IEEE Access, 2021, 9:31309-31321, 2021, doi: 10.1109/ACCESS.2021.3060046.

48. Priyadarshi, N.; Sharma, A.K.; Bhoi, A. K.; Ahmad, S. N.; Azam, F.; Priyam, S.; A Practical performance verification of AFLC based MPPT for standalone PV power system under varying weather condition, International Journal of Engineering & Technology, 2018, 7:338-343.

49. Azam F.; Priyadarshi N.; Nagar H.; Kumar S.; Bhoi A.K.; An Overview of Solar-Powered Electric Vehicle Charging in Vehicular Adhoc Network. in: Electric Vehicles. Green Energy and Technology. Springer, Singapore. https://doi.org/10.1007/978-981-15-9251-5_5

50. Azam, F.; Kumar, S.; Yadav, K.P.; Priyadarshi N.; Padmanaban, S.; An Outline of the Security Challenges in VANET, in Proc. of IEEE UPCON 2020, Nov, 2020.

51. Priyadarshi, N.; Azam, F.; Bhoi, A.K.; Sharma, A.K.; A Multilevel Inverter-Controlled Photovoltaic Generation. in Advances in Greener Energy Technologies. Springer, Singapore. 2020 https://doi.org/10.1007/978-981-15-4246-6_8

52. Priyadarshi, N.; Azam, F.; Bhoi, A.K.; Sharma, A.K.; Dynamic Operation of Grid-Connected Photovoltaic Power System. in Advances in Greener Energy Technologies. Springer, Singapore. 2020 https://doi.org/10.1007/978-981-15-4246-6_13

53. Priyadarshi, N.; Azam, F.; Bhoi, A.K.; Sharma, A.K.; A Proton Exchange Membrane-Based Fuel Cell Integrated Power System. in Advances in

Greener Energy Technologies. Springer, Singapore. 2020 https://doi.org/10.1007/978-981-15-4246-6_18

54. Priyadarshi, N.; Azam, F.; Bhoi, A.K.; Sharma, A.K.; A Closed-Loop Control of Fixed Pattern Rectifier for Renewable Energy Applications. in Advances in Greener Energy Technologies. Springer, Singapore. 2020 https://doi.org/10.1007/978-981-15-4246-6_25

55. Priyadarshi, N.; Azam, F.; Bhoi, A.K.; Sharma, A.K.; A Four-Switch-Type Converter Fed Improved Photovoltaic Power System. in Advances in Greener Energy Technologies. Springer, Singapore. 2020 https://doi.org/10.1007/978-981-15-4246-6_29

56. Vardia, M.; Priyadarshi, N.; Ali, I.; Azam, F.; Bhoi, A.K.; Maximum Power Point Tracking for Wind Energy Conversion System. in Advances in Greener Energy Technologies. Springer, Singapore. 2020 https://doi.org/10.1007/978-981-15-4246-6_36

57. Vardia, M.; Priyadarshi, N.; Ali, I.; Azam, F.; Bhoi, A.K.; Design of Wind Energy Conversion System Under Different Fault Conditions. in Advances in Greener Energy Technologies. Springer, Singapore. 2020 https://doi.org/10.1007/978-981-15-4246-6_41

58. Choudhary, T.; Priyadarshi, N.; Kuma,r P.; Azam, F.; Bhoi A.K. (2020) A Fuzzy Logic Control Based Vibration Control System for Renewable Application. in Advances in Greener Energy Technologies. Springer, Singapore. 2020 https://doi.org/10.1007/978-981-15-4246-6_38

59. Priyadarshi, N.; Azam F.; Solanki, S. S.; Sharma, A.K.; Bhoi, A.K.; Almakhles, D.; A Bio-Inspired Chicken Swarm Optimization-Based Fuel Cell System for Electric Vehicle Applications. in Bio-inspired Neurocomputing. Studies in Computational Intelligence, vol 903. Springer, Singapore. 2021 https://doi.org/10.1007/978-981-15-5495-7_1

14

Short Term Load Forecasting for CPP Using ANN

Kirti Pal* and Vidhi Tiwari

*Department of Electrical Engineering, Gautam Buddha University,
Greater Noida, India*

Abstract

The irregularity of Indian grid system increases, with increase in the power demand. The quality of power supplied by the power grid is also poor due to continuous variation in frequency and voltage. For any industry, an electric power grid is required as an input. To overcome this problem of power deficit and quality faced by all industries, *captive power plants* (CPP) installed capacity has grown at a faster rate as compared to the utilities. Power intensive industries such as fertilizers, textiles and cement have started setting their own captive power plants to protect themselves from an unreliable grid power supply.

Here short term load forecasting of Yara Fertilizers India Private limited installed at Babrala, Uttar Pradesh is performed using multi-layer feed-forward Neural network in MATLAB. The algorithm used is a Levenberg Marquardt algorithm. Yara fertilizers India Private limited is mainly a combined cycle power plant (CCPP) which mainly consists of both gas turbine and steam turbine in order to produce electricity. For accurate generation, CCPP is used by Yara Fertilizers which is the main concern by the operators. However, the training and results from ANN are very fast and accurate; it may be used for on-line load prediction for CPP. For load prediction of CPP Neural Network toolbox of MATLAB is used and the output from the Neural Network is then compared with the actual data which is taken from Yara Fertilizer India Private Limited. Inputs given to the Neural Network are time, ambient air temperature from the compressor, cool air temperature at the compressor and IGV opening. The need, benefits and growth of CPP in India and use of ANN for short term load forecasting of CPP has been explained in detail in the paper.

**Corresponding author*: kirti.pal@gbu.ac.in

Neeraj Priyadarshi, Akash Kumar Bhoi, Sanjeevikumar Padmanaban, S. Balamurugan and Jens Bo Holm-Nielsen (eds.) Intelligent Renewable Energy Systems, (391–408) © 2022 Scrivener Publishing LLC

Keywords: Artificial intelligence, artificial neural network, captive power plant, Levenberg–Marquardt Back-propagation, short-term load forecasting

14.1 Introduction

Electricity has now become a part of everyone's life. In India, demand is increasing day by day and also facing problems such as power quality issue, lack of latest technology, losses etc. Stress on existing energy resources has also increased drastically due to increase in electricity demand and thus, leads to shortage of power.

Electrical load forecasting is a process which helps in planning and expansion of the electrical system which helps in increasing the reliability of the system reduces the cost of maintenance and operation and helps in future development of the electricity sector. Electrical load forecasting can be done on hourly, daily, weekly, monthly, and yearly basis [1–25]. It is classified as short term load forecasting, which is done for hourly or weekly basis. Secondly, medium term load forecasting which is done for 1 week to 1 year and lastly, the long term load forecasting which is done for more than 1 year.

Now-a-days demand of CPP is increasing day by day due to its various advantages such as high efficiency, low environmental impact, low investment cost, simple operation and many more. The load demand prediction and generation of CPP must be accurate. Electrical load Prediction is the process of future load prediction in the blocks of hours, days, weeks, months or for a year. It is mainly done in order to prognosticate the power consumption of electrical utilities and help them to plan their future decisions related to generation, transmission and distribution system. Electrical load prediction also helps in managing demand and supply of electricity at every moment which is managed by utilities. Load forecasting is used for power supply planning, transmission & distribution planning, demand side management, maintenance and financial planning. So accurate load prediction is very essential for the effective working of the power system otherwise it may leads to the equipment's failure and supply loss [26–60].

An author [2, 3] presented case study of the captive power plant in Maharashtra and Bangladesh respectively. A study by [4] has shown that the scenario of captive power plants in India can be broadly assigned to (a) manage the backup power system, (b) checks the quality of the supply, (c) ensures the benefits of co-generation process of industries, and (d) also generate electricity at lower costs than the high industrial tariffs. In view of designing the Captive power generation from coolant jet author [5] suggested some guidelines for executing the captive hydro power plant at low head of coolant jet for developers.

There are various factors which affect load forecasting such as weather variables (temperature, rain, wind and humidity), holidays, festivals, economic growth and new load demand [6]. The two main classification of load forecasting techniques are parametric and non-parametric. Examples of parametric technique are auto regressive moving average (ARMA), linear regression, general exponential technique and stochastic time series techniques. These techniques are also known as statistical or traditional techniques. The main limitations of traditional methods are its capability to cover up the changes due to environment.

However, this can be resolved by using non-parametric techniques. This method is also known as modern techniques as it uses artificial intelligence. Modern techniques include Neuro-Fuzzy Method, Artificial Neural Network (ANN) method, Genetic Algorithm (GA), Fuzzy Logic Method, and Particle Swamp Optimization (PSO). Among these methods of artificial intelligence based technique called artificial neural network is appeared to be most appropriate and has received attention of many researchers [7–10]. ANN has the capacity to make decisions for uncertain environment, tosolve complex problems, image recognition, and prediction capability. Thus ANN has emerged as a useful techniques as compared to the other traditional techniques [11, 12].

In hybrid networks, stochastic learning techniques like genetic algorithm (GA), particle swarm optimization (PSO) are applied in combination with the artificial neural network for short term load forecasting. An author [13] has discussed about the various applications of several stochastic learning techniques with the artificial neural network for short term load forecasting.

In the paper [14] author proposes an architecture of deep neural network for load forecasting of an hourly load of North China city. Deep neural network architecture is also used by other various authors for load forecasting [15–17].

In the present work ANN is used for short term load prediction of Captive Power Plant, Yara Fertilizers India Private limited installed at Babrala, Uttar Pradesh, India. The MATLAB tool box is used to train and predict the load using ANN. Basic overview of captive power plant, Gas Turbine with introduction is discussed in section 14.1. The section 14.2 describes about the working of combined cycle power plant in section 14.3 ANN is implemented for CPP. Training and testing results are discussed in section 14.4. Conclusion of proposed methodology is illustrated in section 14.5.

14.1.1 Captive Power Plant

Captive Power Plants are mainly constructed within a locality or campus because of its advantages such as it's quite cheaper, less distribution and transmission losses, no power cuts, no problem electric theft etc. Captive power plants are kind of distributed generation where electricity is generated very close to the load. Captive power plants can be connected to the grid or can operate in off-grid mode.

There are two types of power generation entities in India such as Generation Non-Utilities or Captive Power Plants (CPPs) and Generation Utilities. Captive Power Plant (CPP) is a power plant which is set up by any person in order to generate electricity for his own use. It is set up by any association of persons or co-operative society for their own consumption of electricity (Electricity Act, 2003) [18]. After the introduction of the Electricity Act 2003, surplus power from captive plants, after meeting self-requirements, could be sold to third parties [19].

Yara fertilizerIndia Private limited, Babrala (captive Power plant) consist of two gas turbines units, two waste heat recovery boilers, steam and turbo pump, auxiliary electrical and mechanical equipment's. The main plant block consists of two modules, each of 1 GTGs (Gas Turbine Generator) placed on each side and 1 HRSG (Heat Recovery Steam Generator).

14.1.2 Gas Turbine

A rotating device in which the action of a fluid is used to produce work is called a Turbine. These fluids may be: helium, steam, air, wind, water and gas etc. Major components of gas turbine are air intake filter with evaporative cooler, the shaft driven compressor and the combustion chamber. A gas turbine mainly consist of a compressor which is used to extract air from the environment. In compressor air got compressed and then passes to the combustor. In combustor, fuel is added to the compressed air in order to increase its temperature. That hot air is then given to the turbine to extract power from the flow to hot air and get expanded. These Gas turbines are capable of attaining full load within 10 to 15 minutes. The operating speed of gas turbine is 5178 rpm and other specifications are mentioned in Table 14.1.

Table 14.1 Gas turbine specifications.

1.	Type	Impulse turbine
2.	Speed	5178 rpm
3.	Air inlet temperature	45 degree Celsius
4.	Exhaust temperature of flue gases	516 degree Celsius
5.	Exhaust pressure of flue gases	756 mm Hg

14.2 Working of Combined Cycle Power Plant

Here, CPP is a combined cycle power plant which mainly consists of both the gas turbine and steam turbine to produce electricity. Atmospheric air is taken as the input for the compressor where air is compressed and then the air moves to the combustion chambers where it is ignited and that high temperature air moves to the gas turbine which drives a generator and hence electricity is produced.

Heat recovery steam generator (HRSG) captures the exhaust from the gas turbine which is further used to produce steam and that steam is used to drive the steam turbine in order to produce further additional electricity. This whole system increases the overall efficiency. So, from Figure 14.1, cool air temperature to the compressor is the air going into the compressor

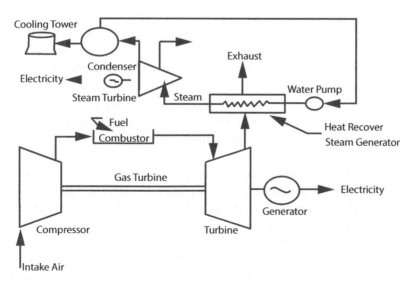

Figure 14.1 Combined cycle power plant.

and ambient air temperature from the compressor is air coming out of the compressor and IGV is *inlet guide vane* controls the air flow to the compressor, in which air is allowed to flow at the proper angle.

14.3   Implementation of ANN for Captive Power Plant

ANN is mainly composed of highly connected structure in order to process the information. Multi-layer feed forward neural network is used for load forecasting as it can approximate nonlinear function with high accuracy. Selection of input and output data is very important for prediction [20]. Input is given to the input layer, which is then given to the hidden layer where the information is processed and output from the hidden layer is finally given to the final layer which is called output layer.

The ANN is a huge parallel implementation whose processing speed is very high and due which ANN has a great potential in the field of research [21]. Now-a-days ANNs is used for various applications such as natural language processing, image recognition, and many more. An ANN model made use of the Levenberg-Marquadt Back-Propagation, two-layer feed forward ANN model with the help of MALTAB which showed a high degree of accuracy in future load forecasting [22].

The most common algorithm is back propagation algorithm as it is fast, simple and easy to program. Back propagation algorithm is very flexible as well. AI can be extensively applied to in petroleum exploration and industrial production [23] and business [24] setting for optimization. Since ANN model resembles to the functioning of human brain due to which its applications are increasing globally [25].

Figure 14.2 shows the block diagram of the overall model of feed-forward neural network which is trained by Levenberg-Marquardt Back Propagation algorithm. Data which is taken from Yara Fertilizers is of six months and that data are used for training, validation and testing. For training 70% data is used, 15% for validation and 15% for testing.

For prediction, data is imported into Neural Network Toolbox of the MATLAB and prediction procedure is carried out to predict the load for the month of March 2020 and the network is trained with the past six month's data. From the, Figure 14.2 inputs given to the model are time, ambient air temperature from the compressor, cool air temperature at the compressor, and the IGV opening from which the forecasted load is obtained.

Two variables X and Y are created in the workspace of the MATLAB which are input and target data respectively. Both input and Target data is imported in the neural network toolbox. The feed-forward network

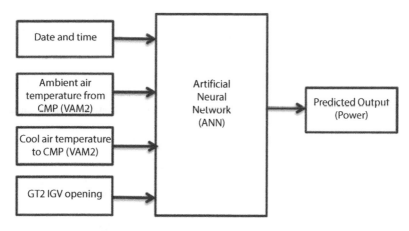

Figure 14.2 Block diagram of ANN structure.

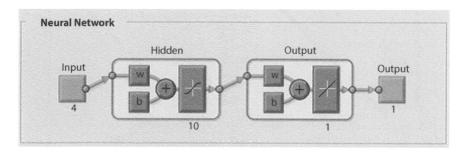

Figure 14.3 Neural network model.

as shown in Figure 14.3 with two layer structure in which sigmoid activation function is used in hidden layer and linear activation function in output layers. This network is trained with a Levenberg-Marquardt backpropagation algorithm. There is no specific approach to calculate the number of hidden layer nodes and the numbers of neurons are taken as 10.

14.4 Training and Testing Results

After training the network the following results are obtained.

14.4.1 Regression Plot

Figure 14.4 shows the plot of regression, which mainly comprises of four plots as shown below. The regression plot is mainly the plot between set

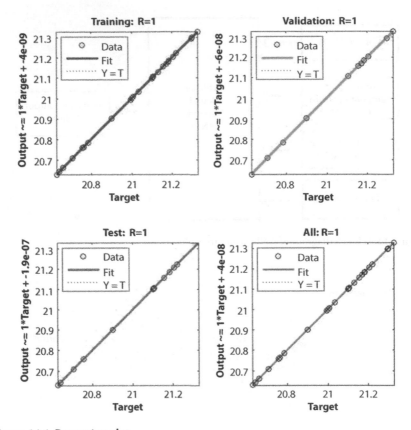

Figure 14.4 Regression plot.

target and the output obtained from the network. In Figure 14.4, the first plot is the plot of the data which was set for training; the second plot is the plot of data which was set for Validation; the third plot is the plot of the data which was set for testing, and the forth plot is the overall plot of the network.

From the plots it can be observe that the value of R is coming as 1, which shows the accurate and reasonable good fit of data. Therefore, the relationship between output obtained after training the network and the target is linear and accurate.

14.4.2 The Performance Plot

Performance plot is the plot between the number of epochs and Mean Squared Error (MSE). It mainly shows the performance of the network by

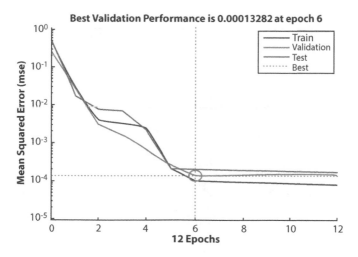

Figure 14.5 Performance plot.

showing Validation error, Train error, and Test error. Validation error in the performance plot is shown by green line, train error is shown by blue line and test error is shown by red line. From the given plot, we can see that the result is reasonable as the final mean square error is extremely small. From the Figure 14.5, at 6th iteration the best validation performance of 0.00013282 is achieved.

14.4.3   Error Histogram

In Error Histogram, errors are plotted against the instances and error is given by target subtracting the output. The Figure 14.6 shows the plot of the error histogram in which the *blue* bar, *green* bar, and *red* bar represents: Training data, Validation data, and Testing data respectively. The *orange* line shows the zero error and the error is concentrated towards the zero line. From the Figure 14.6, it can be seen that most of the error fall between − 0.02179 and 0.01845.

14.4.4   Training State Plot

The Figure 14.7 shows the training state plot which mainly consists of three plots. The first plot is a plot between gradient and number of Epochs. The value of a gradient is obtained as 0.00062898 at 11 epochs. The second plot of Figure 14.7 is the plot between learning rate (mu) and the number of epochs and it can also be seen that with the increase in epochs mu

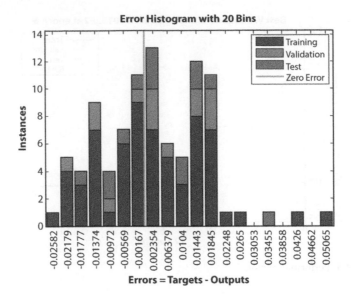

Figure 14.6 Error Histogram.

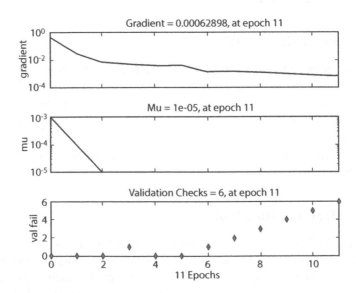

Figure 14.7 Training state plot.

decreases and becomes constant. It shows that with the increase in training process error of the network reduces. The value of mu is coming as 1e-05 at 11 epochs. The third plot of Figure 14.7 performs a validation check which is coming as 6 at 11 epochs.

14.4.5   Comparison between the Predicted Load and Actual Load

The Figure 14.8 shows the plot between Predicted Load in Megawatt (Output) after the training of the network and the actual load for the month of March 2020. The graph mainly consist of the two plots. The *red* line plot shows the predicted load and the blue line plot shows the *actual* load (Target) in which is given for training as a target to the neural network.

From the Figure 14.8, it can be seen that both plots of the actual load and predicted load are almost overlapping which shows that there is very less deviation between the predicted load and the actual load. Thus, an output after training is accurate. Table 14.2 shows the comparison between the Absolute percentage error of the actual load and the predicted load.

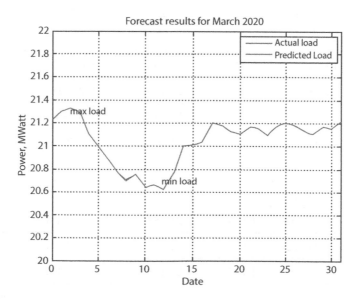

Figure 14.8 Forecast results for the month of March.

Table 14.2 Comparison between the actual load and predicted load.

S no.	Date	Load in megawatts		Absolute percentage error (%)
		Actual load	**Predicted load**	
1.	01-03-2020	21.221	20.906	1.484%
2.	02-03-2020	21.299	20.785	2.413%
3.	03-03-2020	21.328	20.710	2.897%
4.	04-03-2020	21.295	20.761	2.507%
5.	05-03-2020	21.104	20.655	2.127%
6.	06-03-2020	20.992	20.661	1.576%
7.	07-03-2020	20.900	20.629	1.29%
8.	08-03-2020	20.785	20.763	0.105%
9.	09-03-2020	20.708	21.001	1.414%
10.	10-03-2020	20.757	21.004	1.189%
11.	11-03-2020	20.643	21.031	1.879%
12.	12-03-2020	20.661	21.205	2.632%
13.	13-03-2020	20.628	21.185	2.700%
14.	14-03-2020	20.763	21.125	1.743%
15.	15-03-2020	21.000	21.106	0.505%
16.	16-03-2020	21.007	21.169	0.771%
17.	17-03-2020	21.032	21.155	0.58%
18.	18-03-2020	21.204	21.097	0.504%
19.	19-03-2020	21.184	21.179	0.024%
20.	20-03-2020	21.130	21.204	0.350%
21.	21-03-2020	21.106	21.182	0.374%
22.	22-03-2020	21.170	21.130	0.188%
23.	23-03-2020	21.157	21.108	0.231%

(*Continued*)

Table 14.2 Comparison between the actual load and predicted load. (*Continued*)

S no.	Date	Load in megawatts		Absolute percentage error (%)
		Actual load	**Predicted load**	
24.	24-03-2020	21.098	21.170	0.341%
25.	25-03-2020	21.179	21.112	0.316%
26.	26-03-2020	21.204	21.105	0.466%
27.	27-03-2020	21.184	20.906	1.312%
28.	28-03-2020	21.130	20.785	1.632%
29	29-03-2020	21.106	20.701	1.918%
30.	30-03-2020	21.175	20.761	1.955%
31.	31-03-2020	21.106	21.122	0.075%

14.5   Conclusion

The load forecasting by ANN is suitable because of its various advantages. Moreover, the ANN is used for load forecasting because utilization of power output of CPP is fixed. The data was collected for all the 24 hours. The patterns include the features like load (MW), date, time, ambient air temperature from the compressor, cool air temperature at the compressor and IGV opening. The designed network is trained with supervised algorithm (Back propagation algorithm). Implementation of this network is showing reasonably good results with the Mean absolute Percentage Error (MAPE) of 1.210% which is very less. The error will be less by the use of large data set with very less variation. The result from the ANN model reflects good prediction performance with a least error. Thus, short term load forecasting using ANN is an effective method for load forecasting.

14.6   Acknowlegdement

The sincere gratitude goes to Yara Fertilizers, India Private Limited for providing required data and their contributions are sincerely appreciated and gratefully acknowledged.

References

1. Jaswal, R.; Naveen; "Short Term Electric Load Prediction Using Artificial Neural Network", Kurukshetra University, ISSN: 2278-0181, Vol. 2 Issue 7, 2013.
2. Oak, R. A.; Patil, D. B.; "Captive power plant- A case study of CEPT Ichalkaranji, Maharashtra (Volume 1, Issue 3)", *International Research Journal of Engineering and Technology*, 2016.
3. Alam, M. S.; Islam, K. K.; "Halim Z.E.; Study on Gas Based Captive Power Generation in Bangladesh", *Proceedings of 2013 2nd International Conference on Advances in Electrical Engineering* 19-21, Dhaka, Bangladesh, 2013.
4. David G.V.; Debashish B.; Shukla, P.R.; Tirthankar N.; Thomas H.; Yajnik, A.; "Captive Power Plants: Case Study of Gujarat", India, *Programme on Energy and Sustainable Development Working Paper 22*, Stanford University, 2004.
5. Pooja P. K.; Rohit C.C.; Tushar B. R.; Tejaswini V. K.; "Design, Manufacturing & Testing of Captive Power Plant Using Liquid Coolant Jet" (Vol. 6, Issue 5, 34-39) "International Journal of Innovative Research in Electrical, Electronics", *Instrumentation and Control Engineering* ,2018.
6. Gupta, P.; Mangalvedhekar,H.A.; Mantri,R.; "Weather sensitive short term load forecasting using fully connected feed forward neural network," Vol. 2 Issue 9, *International Journal of Engineering Research and Technology* , ISSN-2278-0181, 2013.
7. Bello, Ishaku.;Harrison, I.; "Short Term Load Forecasting OF 132/33Kv Maiduguri Transmission Substation Using Artificial Neural Network University of Maiduguri Computer Engineering Department", (Vol 4, Issue 5), 2015.
8. Hippert, H.S.; Pedreira, C.E.; Souza, R.C.; "Neural networks for short-term load forecasting: A review and evaluation", *Institute of Electrical and Electronics Engineers, Trans.Power System* vol. 16, no. 1, pp. 44–55, 2001.
9. Atlas, L. E.; Damborg. M. J.; El-Sharkawi, M. A.; Park, D. C.; Marks II, R. J.; "Electric load forecasting using an artificial neural network", (Vol. 6, no. 2, pp. 442-449) *Institute of Electrical and Electronics Engineers, Transactions on Power Systems*, 1991.
10. Karthikeyan, V.; Reddy C.; Sujatha, B., Veerendra K.K.; "Power Load Forecasting using Back Propagation Algorithm", (Volume-8 Issue-10), *International Journal of Innovative Technology and Exploring Engineering* ISSN: 2278-3075, 2019.
11. Abiodun, O.I.; Arshad, H.; Dada K.V.; Jantan, A.; Mohamed, N.A.E. & Omolara, A.E.State-of-the-art in artificial neural network Applications: A survey. Heliyon4 e00938, 2018.
12. Araque, O.; CorcueraPlatas, I.; Iglesias, C.A.; Sanchez, J.F.; Enhancing deep learning sentiment analysis with ensemble techniques in social application, Expert Syst. Appl. 77 236e246 , 2017.

13. Baliyan, A.; Kumar, G.; Mishra, S.K.; A Review of Short Term Load Forecasting using Artificial Neural Network Models(pp. 121 – 125) Elsevier Procedia Computer Science, **2015**.
14. He,Wan.; Load forecasting via Deep Neural Networks, Elsevier Procedia Computer Science 122 308–314, **2017**.
15. Graziani, S.; Xibilia, M.G.; Innovative Topologies and Algorithms for Neural Networks, MDPI,Future Internet, 12, 117, 1-4., **2020**.
16. Sun, H.; Xue, B.; Zhao, H.; Zhang, W.; Embedded deep learning for ship detection and recognition. Future Internet, 11, 53., **2019**.
17. Li, W.; Liu, P.; Liu, W.; Zhang, Q.; An improved approach for text sentiment classification based on a deep neural network via a sentiment attention mechanism. Future Internet, 11, 96, **2019**.
18. Ministry of Power. Discussion Paper on Rural Electrification Policies, Government of India, New Delhi, **2003**.
19. Tirthankar N.;Captive Generation in India-The Dilemma of DualismIndia (pp. 197-207) Infrastructure Report, **2010**.
20. Bello, I.; Dibal, P.; Harrison, I.; Short Term Load Forecasting of 132/33Kv Maiduguri Transmission Substation Using Artificial Neural Network (Vol 4, Issue 5) University of Maiduguri Computer Engineering Department, **2015**.
21. Pal K., Pandit M. and Srivastava L, Market Power Assessment Using Hybrid Fuzzy Neural Network, published in Springer book series, Innovations in Intelligent Machines-3, Contemporary Achievements in Intelligent Systems, chapter 2, pp. 15–35, 2012.
22. Agarwal A. and Pal K., Optimization of Unit Commitment Problem using Genetic Algorithm, International Journal of System Dynamics Applications (IJSDA), Volume 10, Issue 3, pp. 21–37, 2021.
23. Pal K., Pandit M. and Srivastava L, Levenberg-Marquardt Algorithm Based ANN for Nodal Price Prediction in Restructured Power System, Springer book series Energy Systems, Intelligent Solutions for Electricity Transmission and Distribution Networks, March 2016, pp. 297–318, Energy Systems ISBN 978-3-662-49432-5.
24. Jayasankar V. *et al.*: Estimation of voltage stability index for power system employing artificial neural network technique and TCSC placement. Neurocomputing, 73(16–18), 3005–3011 (2010).
25. Liu, D.; He, H.; Wang D.; Adaptive critic nonlinear robust control: a survey, Institute of Electrical and Electronics Engineers, Trans. Cybern. 47 (10) 3429e3451, **2017**.
26. Asbury, C. E.; Weather load model for electric demand and energy forecasting, *IEEE Trans. on Power Appr. And Sys.* Vol. PAS-94, pp. 1111-1116, **1975.**
27. Castrode L. N.; Von Zuben, F. J.; Learning and Optimisation Using the Clonal Selection Principle, *IEEE Trans. Evolutionary Computation*, vol. 6, pp. 239-251, June **2002**.

28. Al-Shakarchi, M.R.G.; Ghulaim, M.M.; Short-term load forecasting for bagh-dad electricity region, Electric Machines and Power Systems, 28 pp. 355-371, **2000.**

29. Hahn, H.; Meyer-Nieberg, S.; Pickl S.; Electric load forecasting methods: tools for decision making European Journal of Operational Research, 199 pp. 902-907, **2009.**

30. Priyadarshi.; N; Padmanaban, S.; Maroti, P.K.; Sharma. A.; An Extensive Practical Investigation of FPSO-Based MPPT for Grid Integrated PV System Under Variable Operating Conditions With Anti-Islanding Protection. IEEE System Journal, 2018, 13:1861 - 1871.

31. Priyadarshi, N.; Padmanaban, S.; Bhaskar, M.S.; Blaabjerg, F.; Sharma, A.; A Fuzzy SVPWM Based Inverter Control Realization of Grid Integrated PV-Wind System with FPSO MPPT Algorithm for a Grid-Connected PV/Wind Power Generation System: Hardware Implementation. IET Electric Power Appl., 2018, 12:962-971.

32. Priyadarshi, N.; Kumar, V.; Yadav, K.; Vardia, M.; An Experimental Study on Zeta buck-boost converter for Application in PV system. Handbook of distributed generation, Springer, DOI 10.1007/978-3-319-51343-0_13

33. Priyadarshi N.; Sharma A.K.; Priyam S.; An Experimental Realization of Grid-Connected PV System with MPPT Using dSPACE DS 1104 Control Board. Advances in Smart Grid and Renewable Energy. Lecture Notes in Electrical Engineering, Springer, Singapore 2018, 435.

34. Priyadarshi N.; Sharma A.K.; Priyam S.; Practical Realization of an Improved Photovoltaic Grid Integration with MPPT. International Journal of Renewable Energy Research 2017, 7:1180-1891.

35. Priyadarshi N.; Sharma A.K.; Azam F.; A Hybrid Firefly-Asymmetrical Fuzzy Logic Controller based MPPT for PV-Wind-Fuel Grid Integration. International Journal of Renewable Energy Research 2017, 7: 1546-1560.

36. Priyadarshi, N.; Anand, A.; Sharma, A.K.; Azam, F.; Singh, V.K.; Sinha, R. K.; An Experimental Implementation and Testing of GA based Maximum Power Point Tracking for PV System under Varying Ambient Conditions Using dSPACE DS 1104 Controller. International Journal of Renewable Energy Research, 2017, 7:255-265.

37. Priyadarshi, N.; Padmanaban S.; Mihet-Popa L.; Blaabjerg, F.; Azam F.; Maximum Power Point Tracking for Brushless DC Motor-Driven Photovoltaic Pumping Systems Using a Hybrid ANFIS-FLOWER Pollination Optimization Algorithm. MDPI Energies 2018, 11:1-16.

38. Priyadarshi, N.; Azam, F.; Bhoi, A.K.; Alam, S.; An Artificial Fuzzy Logic Intelligent Controller Based MPPT for PV Grid Utility. Lecture Notes in Networks and Systems 46, https://doi.org/10.1007/978-981-13-1217-5_88.

39. Padmanaban, S.; Priyadarshi, N.; Holm-Nielsen, J. B.; Bhaskar, M. S.; Azam, F.; Sharma, A.K.; A Novel Modified Sine-Cosine Optimized MPPT Algorithm for Grid Integrated PV System under Real Operating Conditions. IEEE Access, 2019, 7:10467-10477.

40. Padmanaban, S.; Priyadarshi, N.; Holm-Nielsen, J. B.; Bhaskar, M. S.; Hossain, E.; Azam, F.; A Hybrid Photovoltaic-Fuel Cell for Grid Integration With Jaya-Based Maximum Power Point Tracking: Experimental Performance Evaluation. IEEE Access, 2019, 7:82978-82990.

41. Priyadarshi, N.; Padmanaban, N.; Holm-Nielsen, J. B.; Blaabjerg, F.; Bhaskar, M.S.; An Experimental Estimation of Hybrid ANFIS–PSO-Based MPPT for PV Grid Integration Under Fluctuating Sun Irradiance. in IEEE Systems Journal. 2020, 14:1218-1229.

42. Priyadarshi, N.; Padmanaban, N.; Bhaskar, M. S.; Blaabjerg, F.; Holm-Nielsen, J. B.; Azam, F.; Sharma, A.K.; A Hybrid Photovoltaic-Fuel Cell-Based Single-Stage Grid Integration With Lyapunov Control Scheme. IEEE Systems Journal, 2020, 14: 3334 - 3342.

43. Priyadarshi, N.; Bhaskar, M. S.; Padmanaban, N.; Blaabjerg, F.; Azam, F.; New CUK–SEPIC converter based photovoltaic power system with hybrid GSA–PSO algorithm employing MPPT for water pumping applications. IET Power Electronics. 2020, 13:2824 – 2830.

44. Priyadarshi, N.; Padmanaban, N.; Holm-Nielsen, J. B.; Bhaskar, M.S.; Azam, F.; Internet of things augmented a novel PSO-employed modified zeta converter-based photovoltaic maximum power tracking system: hardware realisation. IET Power Electronics. 2020, 13:2775 – 2781.

45. Kamalapathi, K., Priyadarshi, N., Padmanaban, S., Holm-Nielsen, J.B., Azam, F., Umayal, C., Ramachandaramurthy, V.K. A Hybrid Moth-Flame Fuzzy Logic Controller Based Integrated Cuk Converter Fed Brushless DC Motor for Power Factor Correction. MDPI Electronics, 2018, 7: 288.

46. Priyadarshi, N., Padmanaban, S., Lonel, D., Mihet-Popa, L., Azam, F. Hybrid PV-Wind, Micro-Grid Development Using Quasi-Z-Source Inverter Modeling and Control—Experimental Investigation. MDPI Energies, 2018, 11:2277.

47. Priyadarshi, N.; Ramachandaramurthy, V, K.; Padmanaban, S.; Azam, A.; An Ant Colony Optimized MPPT for Standalone Hybrid PV-Wind Power System with Single Cuk Converter. MDPI Energies, 2019, 12: 167.

48. Azam, F.; Yadav, S.K.; Priyadarshi, N.; Padmanaban, S.; and Bansal, R.C.; A Comprehensive Review of Authentication Schemes in Vehicular Ad-Hoc Network, IEEE Access, 2021, 9:31309-31321, 2021, doi: 10.1109/ACCESS.2021.3060046.

49. Priyadarshi, N.; Sharma, A.K.; Bhoi, A. K.; Ahmad, S. N.; Azam, F.; Priyam, S.; A Practical performance verification of AFLC based MPPT for standalone PV power system under varying weather condition, International Journal of Engineering & Technology, 2018, 7:338-343.

50. Azam F.; Priyadarshi N.; Nagar H.; Kumar S.; Bhoi A.K.; An Overview of Solar-Powered Electric Vehicle Charging in Vehicular Adhoc Network. in: Electric Vehicles. Green Energy and Technology. Springer, Singapore. https://doi.org/10.1007/978-981-15-9251-5_5

51. Azam, F.; Kumar, S.; Yadav, K.P.; Priyadarshi N.; Padmanaban, S.; An Outline of the Security Challenges in VANET, in Proc. of IEEE UPCON 2020, Nov, 2020.

52. Priyadarshi, N.; Azam, F.; Bhoi, A.K.; Sharma, A.K.; A Multilevel Inverter-Controlled Photovoltaic Generation. in Advances in Greener Energy Technologies. Springer, Singapore, 2020. https://doi.org/10.1007/978-981-15-4246-6_8

53. Priyadarshi, N.; Azam, F.; Bhoi, A.K.; Sharma, A.K.; Dynamic Operation of Grid-Connected Photovoltaic Power System. in Advances in Greener Energy Technologies. Springer, Singapore, 2020. https://doi.org/10.1007/978-981-15-4246-6_13

54. Priyadarshi, N.; Azam, F.; Bhoi, A.K.; Sharma, A.K.; A Proton Exchange Membrane-Based Fuel Cell Integrated Power System. in Advances in Greener Energy Technologies. Springer, Singapore, 2020. https://doi.org/10.1007/978-981-15-4246-6_18

55. Priyadarshi, N.; Azam, F.; Bhoi, A.K.; Sharma, A.K.; A Closed-Loop Control of Fixed Pattern Rectifier for Renewable Energy Applications. in Advances in Greener Energy Technologies. Springer, Singapore, 2020. https://doi.org/10.1007/978-981-15-4246-6_25

56. Priyadarshi, N.; Azam, F.; Bhoi, A.K.; Sharma, A.K.; A Four-Switch-Type Converter Fed Improved Photovoltaic Power System. in Advances in Greener Energy Technologies. Springer, Singapore, 2020. https://doi.org/10.1007/978-981-15-4246-6_29

57. Vardia, M.; Priyadarshi, N.; Ali, I.; Azam, F.; Bhoi, A.K.; Maximum Power Point Tracking for Wind Energy Conversion System. in Advances in Greener Energy Technologies. Springer, Singapore, 2020. https://doi.org/10.1007/978-981-15-4246-6_36

58. Vardia, M.; Priyadarshi, N.; Ali, I.; Azam, F.; Bhoi, A.K.; Design of Wind Energy Conversion System Under Different Fault Conditions. in Advances in Greener Energy Technologies. Springer, Singapore, 2020. https://doi.org/10.1007/978-981-15-4246-6_41

59. Choudhary, T.; Priyadarshi, N.; Kuma,r P.; Azam, F.; Bhoi A.K. (2020) A Fuzzy Logic Control Based Vibration Control System for Renewable Application. in Advances in Greener Energy Technologies. Springer, Singapore, 2020. https://doi.org/10.1007/978-981-15-4246-6_38

60. Priyadarshi, N.; Azam F.; Solanki, S. S.; Sharma, A.K.; Bhoi, A.K.; Almakhles, D.; A Bio-Inspired Chicken Swarm Optimization-Based Fuel Cell System for Electric Vehicle Applications. in Bio-inspired Neurocomputing. Studies in Computational Intelligence, vol 903. Springer, Singapore, 2021. https://doi.org/10.1007/978-981-15-5495-7_1

15

Real-Time EVCS Scheduling Scheme by Using GA

Tripti Kunj* and Kirti Pal

Dept. of Electrical Engineering, School of Engineering, Gautam Buddha University, Greater Noida, India

Abstract

In order to support the implementation of EVs, it becomes important to look forward to designing an EV (Electric Vehicle) infrastructure that supports EV planning. Modeling of EVCS (Electric Vehicle Charging Station) with charging scheme cycle is explained by taking the example of two types of EVs Hatchback and SUV. To successfully instigate this study, two scenarios are incorporated under which EV charging takes place. Scenario 1 includes incoming of EV with anticipated EV charging upon receiving the response from GA, whereas Scenario 2 includes incoming of EV with a reserved time slot in response to charging request and as well as considering those consumers who couldn't reach on time at charging station for charging. For calculation of available time for charging, slot allocations and expected waiting time for both scenarios MATLAB environment is used. An office building is considered for evaluation of effectiveness and validity of the operation of both the scenarios with total number of 60 EVs, 30 EVs being each of SUV and Hatchback type for three different time slots.

Keywords: EV, EV charging station, EV planning, EVCS management scheme, global aggregator (GA)

Nomenclature

Ø	Number of charging slots
$Ø_d$	Charging slot allotted
nm	Name of the customer

---

*Corresponding author: triptikunj210509@gmail.com

Neeraj Priyadarshi, Akash Kumar Bhoi, Sanjeevikumar Padmanaban, S. Balamurugan and Jens Bo Holm-Nielsen (eds.) Intelligent Renewable Energy Systems, (409–434) © 2022 Scrivener Publishing LLC

Rg   Registration ID of customer
Ty   Type of vehicle
t_{pd} Discharged percentage of battery
σ_{char}^{SUV} Battery charging rate of SUV
$\sigma_{char}^{Hatchback}$ Battery charging rate of Hatchback
LIST   Output including available time per charging slot at CS
t_d Time taken by EV to fully charge
t_{dp}^{ev} Time taken by previous EV to fully charge
t_{curr} Current time of system
t_{av} Available time slot for charging
N_c Queue of EVs under charging
N_r Queue of EVs reserved for charging
t_g Buffer time gap between two arriving EVs
t_{arr}^{ev} Arrival time of EV
EVCS   Electric Vehicle Charging Station
EV   Electric Vehicle

15.1   Introduction

Increasing pollution across the globe has now started to take a toll on human existence. Accounting for millions of deaths, it has now become a matter of concern for the administration and governance of all countries [1–31]. Talking of air pollution itself, has taken over 4 million deaths of people below 60 years of age in 2012, says [32]. (WHO, 2017) says children are most vulnerable to this, summing of 1.7 million deaths and (CNBC September, 2019) accounts for over 18% premature births across globe. From (Wikipedia contributors, n. d.) it is known that India contributes 21 cities out of 30 having worst air pollution. 27% of out of which is contributed by only vehicular pollution. Hence, to address this problem *electric vehicles* (EVs) are starting to get a wide approval towards them. Due to the numerous benefits offered by EVs and governments continuous steps towards implementation of EV planning continuous efforts are being made to make EV planning successful. In order to convince the consumer to buy EV over other conventional petrol and diesel driven vehicle continuous research is carried out on both EV charging station and EV side.

Mukherjee & Gupta [33] present a charging case scenario for a parked EV in garage and reducing frequency instabilities, [34] elaborate a method for minimizing peak load and [35] to minimize cost functions. Cao *et al.*, [36] discusses a charging scheduling problem to promote the total utility for charging operator in order to maximize the profit of [37] both consumer and the charging station provider under a PV system. Kuran *et al.*, [38] elaborates a smart charging management system for a parking lot using a real-world parking pattern. A similar real time charging scheme by Yao *et al.*, [39] is presented to coordinate with E. A day time charging scenario by Zhang and Li [40] is devised for an EVCS near a commercial building. Whereas, Liu *et al.* [41] offer an optimal approach to determine location for an *electric vehicle charging station* EVCS using an adaptive particle swarm optimization (APSO) algorithm. Qin and Zhang [42] propose a charging management scheme to minimize the charging time for customers whereas a contrasting approach for EV charging is presented by Yang *et al.* [43] for a highway scenario where unlike the previous charging station are placed along a highway and it is assumed that EV passes through all CS.

A distributed communication infrastructure consisting of both wired and wireless is proposed by Gharbaoui *et al.*, [44] in order to minimize the communication network for EV installation. Hausler, Crisostomi, Schlote, Radusch, & Shorten, (2014, p. 899) [45] present a stochastic approach to model a CS charging behavior and observe the results of reducing the charging queue for four hours.

Sortomme [46], Fasugba and Krein [47] and Gallardo-Lozano *et al.* [48] especially in the transportation area, inquiries about on electric vehicles are effectively in progress as a push to decrease air toxins and EV's are accepted to turn into a significant means of transport by 2030. If EV supplant alive inner burning motors, substantially more power resolve be charge the EV, which will influence the Power System (PS). To manage this developing supply need, it's important to figure and dissect the charge example of electric vehicles (EV). Author utilizes Bayesian assumption strategies with complexity to estimate the 24-hour charging scheme & the outcome is compare with linear regression analysis (LRA).

Da-Han *et al.* [49] Here the author optimally assigning resource for public charging organisation. The provision model is expressed as a mathematical program with balancing constraints and resolved by active set algorithm. Gil-Aguirre *et al.* [50] Partial least squares (PLS) way model procedure is utilized for Technique to order preference by similarity to ideal solution (TOPSIS) model and bunch model, a far reaching city status appraisal of charging foundation is made dependent on the trial exploration of 25 exhibit urban communities in China. The outcomes show that, a few urban areas are deed better in the four zones of strategy backing and venture, charging station structure and arranging, activity extension and impact, activity administration and security. There are 6 pointers of the amount of charging heaps, amount of total charging times, vehicle types in administration, amount of combined charge for power, amount of preparing individuals and absolute venture that impact on city readiness.

According to Seddig, Jochem, and Fishtner, authors developed a static model of smart charging plug-in system of electric vehicle for public use, also reduce the price of electricity, destination and plug-in route choice of compact traffic area [51]. This allocation model solved through active-set algorithm. This model is based on the mathematical program in equilibrium state.

According to Rei, Soares, Almeida and Lopez in 2010 [52], here the authors talked about a model dependent on Trip Success Ratio (TSR) so as to improve CS comfort for PEV drivers. Assortment of custom and distinctive driving practices are thought of, just as differing trip types (In-city, Highway). The administration scope of charging stations has been evaluated utilizing TSR with consideration of the vulnerability of excursion separations and the vulnerability in the Remaining Electric Range (RER) of PEVs and CS distribution stage [52].

Due to the EV, development in the interest for power to charge these vehicles could present generous difficulties to the electrical grid as far as extra burden due to unmanaged charge strategies [53–54]. So as to facilitate these issues, the charging of the electrical vehicles must be adapted. The paper presents the improvement of a system intending to progressively control the charging of electric vehicles to keep the best possible activity of the nearby appropriation operation and decrease the ecological impact.

Researchers report an optimization model is discussed in order to maximize the profit for the grid operator [55]. A detailed risk analysis for grid operator study is given in [56, 57].

As per the literature review, any previous work have not discussed the arrival of delayed consumers who could not make it on time for the charging reservation. Our proposed work focuses on charging management scheme concerning delayed arrivals as well as on time arrival of EV drivers and propose an EV charging station (EVCS) management scheme which would help the EV consumers to schedule his charging reservation, scheme is designed such that it benefits both the consumer and the charging station owner. For this purpose concept of a global aggregator (GA) is proposed which acts as a communication medium between EV and EVCS in order to provide the EV driver with information regarding his charging reservation status. A well-executed charging infrastructure would certainly help to uplift the EV consumer's quality of experience and benefit the EVCS owner as well.

The paper is divided into five sections. Section 1 discusses the system model, followed by the proposed system design in section 2. Results are discussion in section 3 & 4. The paper is concluded in section 5.

15.2 EV Charging Station Modeling

15.2.1 Parts of the System

1. Electric Vehicle (EV): Each EV to be considered is assumed to have a particular state of charge (SOC) in the battery of EV. When the EV driver feels there is a need of charging then driver requests the charging station (CS) for a charging request via global aggregator (GA). For an effective study here two types of EV cars are considered namely Kia e-soul and MG ZS there specifications are given in Table 15.1.

2. Charging station (CS): It acts as a refill station for discharged EVs where multiple EVs can be charged in parallel. GA continuously monitors the condition of it. Charging station is assumed to be equipped with 250 kWh fast charger.

3. Global aggregator (GA): It schedules the reservation upon receiving the charging request from EVs. It acts as a middleman between EVs and CS for effective working of EV infrastructure. Figure 15.1 shows a basic work model of GA which is used to develop a charging station and management scheme.

Table 15.1 Car specification.

Specification of cars	EVs to be considered	
	Kia e-soul	MG EZs
Car type	Hatchback	SUV
Driving range	350-400 km	250-300 km
Battery capacity	64 kWh	44.5 kWh
Charging time (from 50kW fast charger)	0 to 80 % in 50 minutes	0 to 80% in 30 minutes

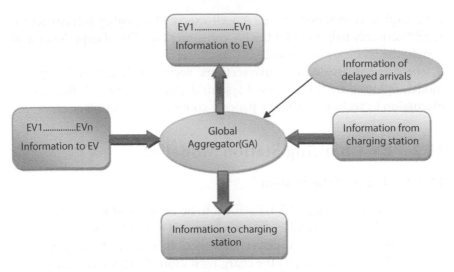

Figure 15.1 Basic work model of global aggregator (GA).

15.2.2   Proposed EV Charging Station

For analyzing the role of Global Aggregator between charging station (CS) and EV driver in the proposed model a charging station is deployed at an office building, as a large concentration of EVs could be seen around such places. EVs are equipped with wireless communication in order to communicate with *global aggregator* GA in order to book a reservation slot for charging of EVs.

Multiple chargings can take place at the CS as parallel charging ports are employed in order to serve more customers at a given instance of time.

Charging station are bound to serve the customers in a first come first serve (FCFS) order, that means no breaching in between the reservations is entertained. GA monitors the condition of CS and arranges the reservations accordingly.

15.2.3   Proposed Charging Scheme Cycle

The proposed charging scheme cycle consists of following parts as described in Figure 15.2

1. **Full charged battery:** EV battery is fully charged either from a CS or any home charging facility.
2. **Driving stage of EV:** Now the EV battery is fully charged it is ready to go to the desired destination. If the EV driver feels that there is a need of charging then he requests CS to make charging reservation via GA.

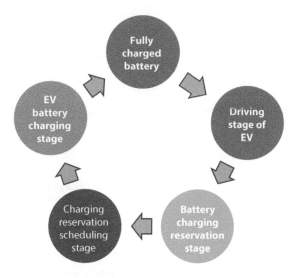

Figure 15.2 Proposed charging scheme cycle.

3. **Battery charging reservation stage:** Input from EV is taken via wireless communication device from GA.
4. **Charging reservation scheduling stage:** GA continuously monitors the condition of CS and as per receiving the charging request from EV it schedules a charging slot for it.
5. **EV battery charging stage:** Upon receiving the charging reservation slot in response to charging request EV travels towards CS and get its battery charged.

15.3   Real Time System Modeling for EVCS

To successfully instigate this study, two scenarios are incorporated under which EV charging takes place. Scenario 1 includes incoming of EV with anticipated EV charging upon receiving the response from *global aggregator* GA whereas Scenario 2 includes incoming of EV with a reserved time slot in response to charging request and as well as considering those consumers who couldn't reach on time at CS for charging. Below sections will discuss these scenarios in detail.

15.3.1   Scenario 1

As referred from Figure 15.3, this scenario progresses the charging management scheme in following chronological order. EV starts to travel with fully

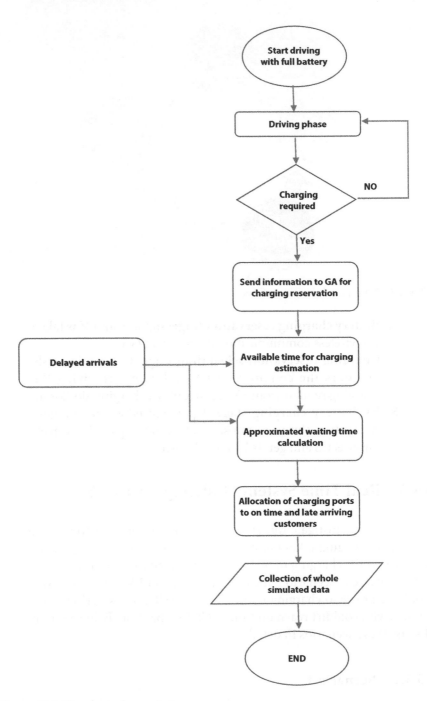

Figure 15.3 Flowchart of scenario 1.

charged battery with a full top up. As the EV driver feels that there is a need of charging, he requests a need for charging from CS. GA being the middleman communicates with EV to get the required input for scheduling it's charging reservation. GA now calculates the available time of charging and the expected waiting time for charging to start in the CS. This calculation is performed on the CS side and finally a charging port and a charging available time is allotted to the EV driver in response to the charging request. But some delayed arrivals who had initially requested for charging but didn't came on time may also interfere while other consumers charging request is being processed. So, a charging slot with an available time of charging is also allotted to them along with the consumers requesting for first time charging request (Table 15.2).

Table 15.2 Nomenclature table.

$\emptyset$	Number of charging slots
$\emptyset_d$	Charging slot allotted
nm	Name of the customer
Rg	Registration ID of customer
Ty	Type of vehicle
t_{pd}	Discharged percentage of battery
σ_{char}^{SUV}	Battery charging rate of SUV
$\sigma_{char}^{Hatchback}$	Battery charging rate of Hatchback
LIST	Output including available time per charging slot at CS
t_d	Time taken by EV to fully charge
t_{dp}^{ev}	Time taken by previous EV to fully charge
t_{curr}	Current time of system
t_{av}	Available time slot for charging
N_c	Queue of EVs under charging
N_r	Queue of EVs reserved for charging
t_g	Buffer time gap between two arriving EVs
t_{arr}^{EV}	Arrival time of EV

15.3.2   Design of Scenario 1

To assign EV customers with a charging slot GA needs to know some information for scheduling the reservation and as well as for ensuring no breaching of reservation queue is done as represented between lines 1 and 5.

Once the required information for making reservation is completed, between lines 6 and 10 the time taken to fully charge EV, whether it is a SUV or hatchback is calculated on the CS side by GA with a help of the discharge percentage of respective batteries and the rate of charging of battery. As soon as an EV makes a request for charging at CS it must be given a charging slot and an available time slot in which he can arrive at CS. Line 13 represents that t_{curr} is estimated only if there are no EVs currently at charging.

Algorithm 1: Calculation of available time for charging, slot allocation and expected waiting time for Scenario 1

---

1. Input
2. nm
3. rg
4. ty
5. t_{pd}
6. initialize $\emptyset_1$, LIST
7. if ty $==$ 'SUV' then
8. $t_d = \sigma_{char}^{SUV} \times t_{pd}$
9. else
10. $t_d = \sigma_{char}^{Hatchback} \times t_{pd}$
11. end if
12. if no EV is under charging then
13. add t_{curr} in LIST with $\emptyset_1$ times
14. return LIST
15. end if
16. if ($\emptyset_1 > N_c$) then
17. for (j=1 ; j $\leq$ ($\emptyset_1 - N_c$) ; j++) do
18. LIST.ADD (t_{curr})
19. end for
20. end if
21. if no EV is waiting for charging then
22. return LIST
23. else
24. sort N_r according to FCFS
25. sort the obtained LIST from above steps in ascending order
26. if ($t_{arr(i)}^{ev} < t_{arr(r)}^{ev}$) then

27. LIST.ADD ($t_{curr} + t_{wt}$)

28. ($t_{wt} = t_g + (n-1) \times t_{dp}^{ev}$)   % n= number of EV in N_c

29. return LIST

30. end if

31. end if

32. $\emptyset_{1d} = \emptyset_{1d} \cdot (\min(t_d^{SUV}))$

33. $\emptyset_{1d} = \emptyset_{1d} \cdot (\min(t_d^{Hatchback}))$

34. end

35. Algo. GET (all data)

36. end procedure

Now, when all the incoming EVs are provided with a charging slot and an available time for charging, to ensure that no slot is left unoccupied, t_{curr} is estimated as represented between lines 16 and 18. Now, GA receives a second row of charging requests which also must be fulfilled as well. Hence, GA monitors the present condition of charging slots and allot a charging port as shown in line 32 and 33. An available time slot for charging according to least time taken by an EV to fully charge before its departure is allotted in line 24 and 29. Hence, in this way all the incoming charging reservations are processed at the charging station.

But delayed arrivals due possible traffic jams cause some EVs to unable to come at CS at their allotted time and eventually interfere in between the reserved charging time and slots to which GA is completely unaware of. Hence, creating a discomfort and an increased waiting time for the consumers who had made their reservations earlier. Now, this condition causes a negative impact on the EV consumer and may cause a heavy loss for the charging station provider as well. EV driver may abstain from making reservations next time. In order to cope with this scenario 2 is devised and discussed in following section.

15.3.3   Scenario 2

From Scenario 1 it is understood that, implementation of this scenario can cause a potential hotspot at the CS. To avoid this condition, we have devised a second scenario under which the delayed arrivals are processed separately as referred in Figure 15.4. In the primary stage, reservation procedure is carried out as same as scenario 1. But the difference between scenario 1 and Scenario 2 lies in the processing of the delayed arrivals. Delayed arrivals in scenario 1 were incorporated with on time consumers whereas in scenario 2 delayed arrivals are arranged separately to ensure that on time arriving customers don't feel any kind of discomfort and increased

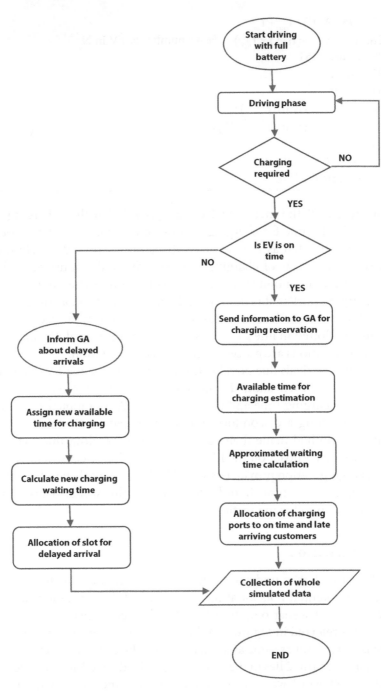

Figure 15.4 Flowchart of scenario 2.

charging waiting time for those who have reserved their charging earlier. This would be a win-win for both EV user and EV CS owner.

15.3.4   Design of Scenario 2

The advantage of this scenario is that it eliminates the problem of potential hotspot causing at the CS caused due to delay arrivals of EV. Delayed arrivals are caused due to possible traffic jams in city. The designing of Scenario 2 is essentially broken into two parts. First part of designing deals with allotment of charging port and available time for charging in response to charging request made at CS while the second part is allotment of charging port and available time for charging for the delayed arrivals. For the first part the user input is taken for reservation, and allotment is carried out just as same as algorithm 1 as shown between line 1 and 10.

Algorithm 2: Calculation of available time for charging, slot allocation and expected waiting time for Scenario 2

---

1. Input
2. nm
3. rg
4. ty
5. t_{pd}
6. initialize $\emptyset_1$, LIST
7. Algo. GET ($\emptyset_{1d}$) % from algorithm 1
8. Algo. GET (t_{wt})   % from algorithm 1
9. Algo. GET (t_{av})   % from algorithm 1
10. end
11. consumer arrives late at CS
12. take input data of steps 1 to 5
13. initialize $\emptyset_2$, LIST
14. if ty == 'SUV' then
15. $t_d = \sigma_{char}^{SUV} \times t_{pd}$
16. else
17. $t_d = \sigma_{char}^{Hatchback} \times t_{pd}$
18. end if
19. if no EV is under charging then
20. add t_{curr} in LIST with $\emptyset_2$ times
21. return LIST
22. end if
23. sort N_r according to FCFS

24. if ($t^{ev}_{arr(i)} < t^{ev}_{arr(r)}$) then
25.   LIST.ADD ($t_{curr} + t_{wt}$)
26.   ($t_{wt} = t_g + (n-1) \times t^{ev}_{dp}$)   % n= number of EV in N_c
27.   end if
28. $\emptyset = \emptyset_{2d}$
29.   end
30.   Algo. GET (all data)
31.   end procedure

Now, as per the second part of designing if consumer arrives late if no EV is under charging then slot is allotted to the arriving customer as per line 20. Now, if another customer arrives at CS late while one late arriving customer is already plugged to the port, his expected waiting time is shown between lines 23 and 2.

15.3.5   Simulation Settings

An office building is considered for evaluation of effectiveness and validity of the operation of both the scenarios. A number of 60 EVs to be served, 30 EVs being each of SUV and Hatchback type. Simulation is run for 9 hours of the day (5a.m. to 2 p.m.).

Based on the statistical data of EVs on time and late coming arrivals is fitted in a probability density function curve Figure 15.5 and Figure 15.6 described by as follows:

$$f(x) = \frac{1}{\sigma} \exp\left(-(1+kz)^{-\frac{1}{k}}\right)(1+kz)^{-1-1/k} \, k \neq 0$$

$$\frac{1}{\sigma} \exp(-z - \exp(-z)) \, k = 0$$

where, $k = 0.37$, $\sigma = 1.52$, $\mu = 8.23$, $z = (x-\mu)/\sigma$(for on time arrivals)

$k = 0.38$, $\sigma = 1.68$, $\mu = 9.36$, $z = (x-\mu)/\sigma$ (for late arrivals)

Also, in Figure 15.7 considering EVs to be used as a household car the daily driving distance is fitted in a probability distribution function described as:

$$f_D(x) = \frac{1}{x\sigma_D\sqrt{2\pi}} \exp\left[\frac{-(lnx - \mu)^2}{2\sigma_D^2}\right] \text{where } \mu = 3.20, \sigma_D = 0.88$$

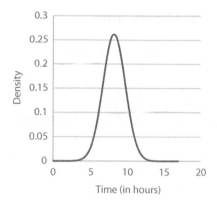

Figure 15.5 Fitting result of on time arrival.

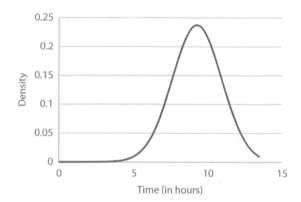

Figure 15.6 Fitting result of late arrivals.

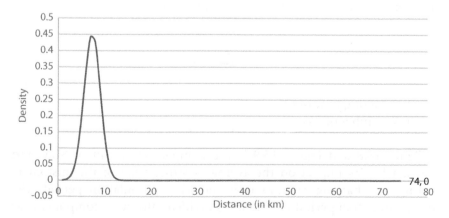

Figure 15.7 Fitting result of daily driving distance.

15.4   Results and Discussion

For effective realization of both scenarios total of five charging slots are considered in scenario 1 whereas in scenario 2 five charging slots are reserved for EV consumers reaching the CS on time and one charging slot for late arriving EV consumer. Arrival time of EVs were randomly generated, based on above section. Additionally, initial SOC is calculated on the basis of daily driving distance.

In order to effectively study the charging requests behavior of the incoming EV it becomes necessary that the simulation must be observed between different phases of the day. Hence, the simulation is carried out for 9 hours of day (simulation hours 1 is equal to 5 a.m. to 6 a.m. and hence increasing in that order) from early 5 a.m. to afternoon 2 p.m. The charging scheme is designed such that it benefits both the customer and EVCS owner so that EV planning could sustain and fulfill both the needs of customer and the provider, it becomes essential to realize the impact of the charging schemes on both ends.

In order to effectively analyze the results, the result section is broken down into two sections. First, being the influence of charging scheme on the average waiting time of customer waiting for processes his charging request and the second part of result, being the influence of charging schemes on total number of charged EVs in whole simulation period.

15.4.1   Influence on Average Waiting Time

To effectively illustrate the results on influence on average waiting time of the customer a comparative graph is shown in Figure 15.8 and Figure 15.9. The average time calculation is carried out as follows:

$$t_{av} = \sum_{i=0}^{n} \frac{fi}{n}$$

fi = waiting time of EV
n = number of EV

Figure 15.8 and Figure 15.9 is the comparative result of SUV and Hatchback EVs impact on the average waiting time of the customers waiting for charging requests over the whole simulation period. The whole simulation period of 9 hours is divided into three components as discussed below:

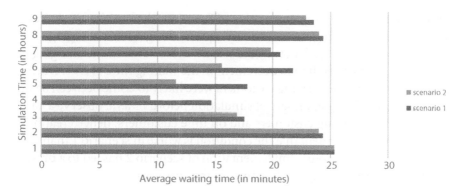

Figure 15.8 SUV's average waiting time in both scenarios.

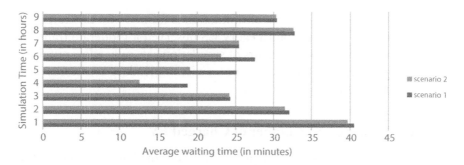

Figure 15.9 Hatchback's average waiting time in both scenarios.

15.4.1.1   Early Morning

The time between 5 a.m. to 8 a.m. is categorized into early morning arrivals. Since the number of charging requests to be processed are less hence, both the charging scenarios perform equally well. Between 5 a.m. to 6 a.m. a very few numbers of EVs come for charging and hence the average waiting time for EVs in both the scenarios is higher. As the number of EVs start to increase, by the time the average waiting time reduces between 6 a.m. to 7 a.m. Between 7 a.m. to 8 a.m. the average waiting time is drastically reduced in comparison to 1st hour of simulation because of office opening hours.

15.4.1.2   Forenoon

The simulation period between 9 a.m. to 11 a.m. is categorized into forenoon period. This is termed as "rush hours" as a large influx of EVs are observed in this. Between 8 a.m. to 9 a.m. it is clearly evident from the figure that impact of adding extra charging slots for sole purpose of serving late arriving customers or implementation of Scenario 2 has resulted in decreasing the average waiting time of the EV approaching CS for charging. This happened due to delayed arrivals did not interfere between the charging of on time consumers leading to decrement in the waiting time of EVs. During whole simulation late arriving customers were likely to come between 8a.m. to 9 a.m. The subsequent hours of simulation before 11 a.m. observe a large number of late coming customers and on time customers, hence creating a hotspot at CS. It is evident that the condition is worse in scenario 1 than scenario 2 during rush hours. Implementation of scenario 2 has led to a drastic decrement in the average waiting time of the customers.

15.4.1.3 Afternoon

Time between 11 a.m. to 2 p.m. of simulation is framed into this category. In the first hour of afternoon category CS observed a moderate traffic of EVs, whereas the subsequent hours of simulation saw only a few numbers of EVs approaching CS in the afternoon session, leading to increase the average waiting time for EVs again.

15.4.2 Influence on Number of Charged EV

Figure 15.10 and Figure 15.11 depict the number of charged EVs over the whole simulation period. Just like previous section of result, to study the impact on the average waiting time this section is also divided into three parts as below:

a. Early morning: Between 5 a.m. to 6 a.m. no significant difference is observed between two scenarios. Between 6 a.m. to 7 a.m. hatchback EVs did not see any significant increase in number of charged EVs but in case of SUVs the increment could be seen. Between 7 a.m. to 8 a.m. a larger number of EV charging request is processed in case of SUV and a very slight increment can be seen in case of hatchbacks. Almost zero number of extra hatchbacks were charged during early morning hours due to the fact that hatchbacks take a significantly larger time to charge than SUVs or the charging rate of SUV is larger in comparison to hatchback. As a result of which a lesser number of hatchbacks charging requests were fulfilled. Whereas due to lesser charging rate than hatchback more SUVs charging requests were processed and hence creating a difference in curve line in scenario 1 and scenario 2.

b. Forenoon: During the rush hours of the day, hatchback saw an increment in number of processed requests between 3rd and 4th hour of simulation and creating a slight difference between curve of scenario 1 and scenario 2, whereas a relatively larger difference in the number of processed charging requests could be seen in case of SUVs for same. Between 8a.m. to 9 a.m. both the EVs saw the maximum difference between the two scenario curves, both type of EVs and their respective scenarios have the maximum difference in this slot of time. The subsequent hours of simulation (between 9a.m to 11 a.m.) also have a significant difference between the two scenarios. Also, it is very evident that the number of SUV charged are more than hatchbacks.

c. Afternoon: In between 6th and 7th hour of simulation, declination in observed in the curve but still scenario 2 curve leads the scenario 1 by a slight difference due to a moderate influx of late arrival customers. Further declination in both the curves could be observed in both the curves because the influx of the vehicles reduces in the 8th to 9th hour of simulation.

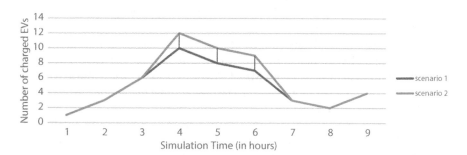

Figure 15.10 Total charged hatchback in both scenarios.

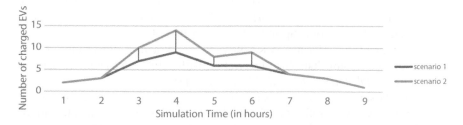

Figure 15.11 Total charged SUV in both scenarios.

15.5 Conclusion

In this paper an EV charging management scheme is presented and reviewed two different scenarios under which the EV charging takes place. For successful execution of both scenarios GA has employed which schedules the charging reservation. GA upon receiving the charging request from EV customer contacts CS and book a reservation slot for the consumer. Scenario 1 includes EV which came on time for charging whereas Scenario 2 includes EV on time and EV who got late. Simulation results showed the advantage of proposed algorithm in the two scenarios in terms of reducing the average waiting time and an increment in number of charged EVs. Decrement in the average waiting time of customers for processing of their charging reservations increases the quality of experience of EV customer and a larger number of charged EVs would benefit the EVCS (electrical vehicle charging station) owner as the owner could extract the maximum benefit out of his investment in installation of charging station.

References

1. Priyadarshi.; N;, Padmanaban, S.; Maroti, P.K.; Sharma. A.; "An Extensive Practical Investigation of FPSO-Based MPPT for Grid Integrated PV System Under Variable Operating Conditions With Anti-Islanding Protection". *IEEE System Journal*, 2018, 13:1861 - 1871.
2. Priyadarshi, N.; Padmanaban, S.; Bhaskar, M.S.; Blaabjerg, F.; "Sharma, A.; A Fuzzy SVPWM Based Inverter Control Realization of Grid Integrated PV-Wind System with FPSO MPPT Algorithm for a Grid-Connected PV/ Wind Power Generation System: Hardware Implementation". *IET Electric Power Appl.*, 2018, 12:962-971.
3. Priyadarshi, N.; Kumar, V.; Yadav, K.; Vardia, M.; "An Experimental Study on Zeta buck-boost converter for Application in PV system". *Handbook of Distributed Generation*, Springer, DOI 10.1007/978-3-319-51343-0_13
4. Priyadarshi N.; Sharma A.K.; Priyam S.; "An Experimental Realization of Grid-Connected PV System with MPPT Using dSPACE DS 1104 Control Board". *Advances in Smart Grid and Renewable Energy*. Lecture Notes in Electrical Engineering, Springer, Singapore 2018, 435.
5. Priyadarshi N.; Sharma A.K.; Priyam S.; "Practical Realization of an Improved Photovoltaic Grid Integration with MPPT". *International Journal of Renewable Energy Research 2017*, 7:1180-1891.
6. Priyadarshi N.; Sharma A.K.; Azam F.; "A Hybrid Firefly-Asymmetrical Fuzzy Logic Controller based MPPT for PV-Wind-Fuel Grid Integration". *International Journal of Renewable Energy Research 2017*, 7: 1546-1560

7. Priyadarshi, N.; Anand, A.; Sharma, A.K.; Azam, F.; Singh, V.K.; Sinha, R. K.; "An Experimental Implementation and Testing of GA based Maximum Power Point Tracking for PV System under Varying Ambient Conditions Using dSPACE DS 1104 Controller". *International Journal of Renewable Energy Research*, 2017, 7:255-265

8. Priyadarshi, N.; Padmanaban S.; Mihet-Popa L.; Blaabjerg, F.; Azam F.; "Maximum Power Point Tracking for Brushless DC Motor-Driven Photovoltaic Pumping Systems Using a Hybrid ANFIS-FLOWER Pollination Optimization Algorithm". *MDPI Energies 2018*, 11:1-16

9. Priyadarshi, N.; Azam, F.; Bhoi, A.K.; Alam, S.; "An Artificial Fuzzy Logic Intelligent Controller Based MPPT for PV Grid Utility". *Lecture Notes in Networks and Systems* 46, https://doi.org/10.1007/978-981-13-1217-5_88.

10. Padmanaban, S.; Priyadarshi, N.; Holm-Nielsen, J. B.; Bhaskar, M. S.; Azam, F.; Sharma, A.K.; A "Novel Modified Sine-Cosine Optimized MPPT Algorithm for Grid Integrated PV System under Real Operating Conditions". *IEEE Access*, 2019, 7:10467-10477.

11. Padmanaban, S.; Priyadarshi, N.; Holm-Nielsen, J. B.; Bhaskar, M. S.; Hossain, E.; Azam, F.; A Hybrid Photovoltaic-Fuel Cell for Grid Integration With Jaya-Based Maximum Power Point Tracking: Experimental Performance Evaluation. IEEE Access, 2019, 7:82978-82990.

12. Priyadarshi, N.; Padmanaban, N.; Holm-Nielsen, J. B.; Blaabjerg, F.; Bhaskar, M.S.; An Experimental Estimation of Hybrid ANFIS–PSO-Based MPPT for PV Grid Integration Under Fluctuating Sun Irradiance. in IEEE Systems Journal. 2020, 14:1218-1229

13. Priyadarshi, N.; Padmanaban, N.; Bhaskar, M. S.; Blaabjerg, F.; Holm-Nielsen, J. B.; Azam, F.; Sharma, A.K.; A Hybrid Photovoltaic-Fuel Cell-Based Single-Stage Grid Integration With Lyapunov Control Scheme. IEEE Systems Journal, 2020, 14: 3334 - 3342

14. Priyadarshi, N.; Bhaskar, M. S.; Padmanaban, N.; Blaabjerg, F.; Azam, F.; New CUK–SEPIC converter based photovoltaic power system with hybrid GSA–PSO algorithm employing MPPT for water pumping applications. IET Power Electronics. 2020, 13:2824 – 2830

15. Priyadarshi, N.; Padmanaban, N.; Holm-Nielsen, J. B.; Bhaskar, M.S.; Azam, F.; Internet of things augmented a novel PSO-employed modified zeta converter-based photovoltaic maximum power tracking system: hardware realisation. IET Power Electronics. 2020, 13:2775 – 2781

16. Kamalapathi, K., Priyadarshi, N., Padmanaban, S., Holm-Nielsen, J.B., Azam, F., Umayal, C., Ramachandaramurthy, V.K. A Hybrid Moth-Flame Fuzzy Logic Controller Based Integrated Cuk Converter Fed Brushless DC Motor for Power Factor Correction. MDPI Electronics, 2018, 7: 288.

17. Priyadarshi, N., Padmanaban, S., Lonel, D., Mihet-Popa, L., Azam, F. Hybrid PV-Wind, Micro-Grid Development Using Quasi-Z-Source Inverter Modeling and Control—Experimental Investigation. MDPI Energies, 2018, 11:2277

18. Priyadarshi, N.; Ramachandaramurthy, V, K.; Padmanaban, S.; Azam, A.; An Ant Colony Optimized MPPT for Standalone Hybrid PV-Wind Power System with Single Cuk Converter. MDPI Energies, 2019, 12: 167

19. Azam, F.; Yadav, S.K.; Priyadarshi, N.; Padmanaban, S.; and Bansal, R.C.; A Comprehensive Review of Authentication Schemes in Vehicular Ad-Hoc Network, IEEE Access, 2021, 9:31309-31321, 2021, doi: 10.1109/ACCESS.2021.3060046.

20. Priyadarshi, N.; Sharma, A.K.; Bhoi, A. K.; Ahmad, S. N.; Azam, F.; Priyam, S.; A Practical performance verification of AFLC based MPPT for standalone PV power system under varying weather condition, International Journal of Engineering & Technology, 2018, 7:338-343

21. Azam F.; Priyadarshi N.; Nagar H.; Kumar S.; Bhoi A.K.; An Overview of Solar-Powered Electric Vehicle Charging in Vehicular Adhoc Network. in: Electric Vehicles. Green Energy and Technology. Springer, Singapore. https://doi.org/10.1007/978-981-15-9251-5_5

22. Azam, F.; Kumar, S.; Yadav, K.P.; Priyadarshi N.; Padmanaban, S.; An Outline of the Security Challenges in VANET, in Proc. of IEEE UPCON 2020, Nov, 2020.

23. Priyadarshi, N.; Azam, F.; Bhoi, A.K.; Sharma, A.K.; A Multilevel Inverter-Controlled Photovoltaic Generation. in Advances in Greener Energy Technologies. Springer, Singapore. 2020 https://doi.org/10.1007/978-981-15-4246-6_8

24. Priyadarshi, N.; Azam, F.; Bhoi, A.K.; Sharma, A.K.; Dynamic Operation of Grid-Connected Photovoltaic Power System. in Advances in Greener Energy Technologies. Springer, Singapore. 2020 https://doi.org/10.1007/978-981-15-4246-6_13

25. Priyadarshi, N.; Azam, F.; Bhoi, A.K.; Sharma, A.K.; A Proton Exchange Membrane-Based Fuel Cell Integrated Power System. in Advances in Greener Energy Technologies. Springer, Singapore. 2020 https://doi.org/10.1007/978-981-15-4246-6_18

26. Priyadarshi, N.; Azam, F.; Bhoi, A.K.; Sharma, A.K.; A Closed-Loop Control of Fixed Pattern Rectifier for Renewable Energy Applications. in Advances in Greener Energy Technologies. Springer, Singapore. 2020 https://doi.org/10.1007/978-981-15-4246-6_25

27. Priyadarshi, N.; Azam, F.; Bhoi, A.K.; Sharma, A.K.; A Four-Switch-Type Converter Fed Improved Photovoltaic Power System. in Advances in Greener Energy Technologies. Springer, Singapore. 2020 https://doi.org/10.1007/978-981-15-4246-6_29

28. Vardia, M.; Priyadarshi, N.; Ali, I.; Azam, F.; Bhoi, A.K.; Maximum Power Point Tracking for Wind Energy Conversion System. in Advances in Greener Energy Technologies. Springer, Singapore. 2020 https://doi.org/10.1007/978-981-15-4246-6_36

29. Vardia, M.; Priyadarshi, N.; Ali, I.; Azam, F.; Bhoi, A.K.; Design of Wind Energy Conversion System Under Different Fault Conditions. in Advances

in Greener Energy Technologies. Springer, Singapore. 2020 https://doi.org/10.1007/978-981-15-4246-6_41

30. Choudhary, T.; Priyadarshi, N.; Kuma,r P.; Azam, F.; Bhoi A.K. (2020) A Fuzzy Logic Control Based Vibration Control System for Renewable Application. in Advances in Greener Energy Technologies. Springer, Singapore. 2020 https://doi.org/10.1007/978-981-15-4246-6_38

31. Priyadarshi, N.; Azam F.; Solanki, S. S.; Sharma, A.K.; Bhoi, A.K.; Almakhles, D.; A Bio-Inspired Chicken Swarm Optimization-Based Fuel Cell System for Electric Vehicle Applications. in Bio-inspired Neurocomputing. Studies in Computational Intelligence, vol 903. Springer, Singapore. 2021 https://doi.org/10.1007/978-981-15-5495-7_1

32. Carlsen, L., Bruggemann, R., & Kenessov, B. (2018). Use of partial order in environmental pollution studies demonstrated by urban BTEX air pollution in 20 major cities worldwide. *Science of The Total Environment, 610–611*, 234–243. https://doi.org/10.1016/j.scitotenv.2017.08.029

33. Mukherjee, J. C., & Gupta, A. (2015). A Review of Charge Scheduling of Electric Vehicles in Smart Grid. *IEEE Systems Journal, 9*(4), 1541–1553. https://doi.org/10.1109/jsyst.2014.2356559

34. Flath, C. M., Gottwalt, S., &Ilg, J. P. (2012). A Revenue Management Approach for Efficient Electric Vehicle Charging Coordination. *2012 45th Hawaii International Conference on System Sciences.* https://doi.org/10.1109/hicss.2012.79

35. Wei, Z., Li, Y., Zhang, Y., & Cai, L. (2018). Intelligent Parking Garage EV Charging Scheduling Considering Battery Charging Characteristic. *IEEE Transactions on Industrial Electronics, 65*(3), 2806–2816. https://doi.org/10.1109/tie.2017.2740834

36. Cao, Y., Wang, N., Kamel, G., & Kim, Y.-J. (2017). An Electric Vehicle Charging Management Scheme Based on Publish/Subscribe Communication Framework. *IEEE Systems Journal, 11*(3), 1822–1835. https://doi.org/10.1109/jsyst.2015.2449893

37. Jiang, W., & Zhen, Y. (2019). A Real-Time EV Charging Scheduling for Parking Lots With PV System and Energy Store System. *IEEE Access, 7*, 86184–86193. https://doi.org/10.1109/access.2019.2925559

38. Kuran, M. S., Carneiro Viana, A., Iannone, L., Kofman, D., Mermoud, G., &Vasseur, J. P. (2015). A Smart Parking Lot Management System for Scheduling the Recharging of Electric Vehicles. *IEEE Transactions on Smart Grid, 6*(6), 2942–2953. https://doi.org/10.1109/tsg.2015.2403287

39. Yao, L., Lim, W. H., & Tsai, T. S. (2017). A Real-Time Charging Scheme for Demand Response in Electric Vehicle Parking Station. *IEEE Transactions on Smart Grid, 8*(1), 52–62. https://doi.org/10.1109/tsg.2016.2582749

40. Zhang, L., & Li, Y. (2017). Optimal Management for Parking-Lot Electric Vehicle Charging by Two-Stage Approximate Dynamic Programming. *IEEE Transactions on Smart Grid, 8*(4), 1722–1730. https://doi.org/10.1109/tsg.2015.2505298

41. Liu, Z., Zhang, W., Ji, X., & Li, K. (2012). Optimal Planning of charging station for electric vehicle based on particle swarm optimization. *IEEE PES Innovative Smart Grid Technologies*. https://doi.org/10.1109/isgt-asia.2012.6303112

42. Qin, H., & Zhang, W. (2011). Charging scheduling with minimal waiting in a network of electric vehicles and charging stations. *Proceedings of the Eighth ACM International Workshop on Vehicular Inter-Networking - VANET '11*. https://doi.org/10.1145/2030698.2030706

43. Yang, S.-N., Cheng, W.-S., Hsu, Y.-C., Gan, C.-H., & Lin, Y.-B. (2013). Charge scheduling of electric vehicles in highways. *Mathematical and Computer Modelling, 57*(11–12), 2873–2882. https://doi.org/10.1016/j.mcm.2011.11.054

44. Gharbaoui, M., Valcarenghi, L., Brunoi, R., Martini, B., Conti, M., &Castoldi, P. (2012). An advanced smart management system for electric vehicle recharge. *2012 IEEE International Electric Vehicle Conference*. https://doi.org/10.1109/ievc.2012.6183171

45. Hausler, F., Crisostomi, E., Schlote, A., Radusch, I., & Shorten, R. (2014). Stochastic Park-and-Charge Balancing for Fully Electric and Plug-in Hybrid Vehicles. *IEEE Transactions on Intelligent Transportation Systems, 15*(2), 895–901. https://doi.org/10.1109/tits.2013.2286266

46. E. Sortomme, "Combined bidding of regulation and spinning reserves for unidirectional vehicle-to-grid," IEEE PES ISGT 2012, innovative smart grid technologies 2012, pp. 16–20.

47. M. A. Fasugba and P. T. Krein, "Cost benefits and vehicle-to-grid regulation services of unidirectional charging of electric vehicles," Proceedings of the IEEE ECCE 2011: energy conversion congress and exposition, pp. 827–34, Sep 17–22.

48. J. Gallardo - Lozano, M. I. Milanés-Montero, M. A. Guerrero-Martínez and E.R. Cadaval, "Electric vehicle battery charger for smart grids," Electr. Power Syst. Res 2012, Vol. 90, pp. 18–29.

49. L. Da-Han, M.S. Kim, J.H. Roh, J.P. Yang and J.B.Park, "Forecasting of Electric Vehicles Charging Pattern Using Bayesians method with the Convolustion," IFAC 2019, pp. 413–418.

50. J. Gil-Aguirre, S. Perez-Londono and J. Mora-Florez, "A measurement-based load modelling methodology for electric vehicle fast charging stations," Electric Power System Research 2019.

51. K. Seddig, P. Jochem and W. Fichtner, "Two-stage stochastic optimization for cost-minimal charging of electric vehicles at public charging stations with photovoltaics," Applied Energy 2019, vol.242, pp. 769–781.

52. R. J. Rei, F. J. Soares,P. M. R. Almeida and J. A. Peças Lopes, "Grid Interactive Charging Control for Plug-in Electric Vehicles," 13th International IEEE Annual Conference on Intelligent Transportation Systems Madeira Island 2010.

53. J. Jung, Y.J. Joseph, R. Jayakrishnan and J.Y.Park, "Stochastic dynamic itinerary interception refuelling location problem with queue delay for electric taxi charging stations, "Transportation Research 2014, vol. 40, pp. 123–142.
54. C. Lee and J.Han, "Benders-and-Price approach for electric vehicle charging station location problem under probabilistic travel range," Transportation Research 2017, pp. 1–23.
55. R.Faria, P. Moura, J. Delgado and A.T.D Almeida, "Managing the Charging of Electrical Vehicles: Impacts on the Electrical Grid and on the Environment, 2010.
56. E. S. Rigas,S. D. Ramchurn and N. Bassiliades, "Managing Electric Vehicles in the Smart Grid Using Artificial Intelligence: A Survey," IEEE Transactions On Intelligent Transportation Systems 2014.
57. A.M. Hariri, M.M. Hejazi, H.H. Dezaki, "Reliability optimization of smart grid based on optimal allocation of protective devices, distributed energy resources, and electric vehicle plug-in hybrid electric vehicle charging stations," Journal of Power Sources 2019, vol. 436.

About the Editors

Neeraj Priyadarshi, PhD, works in the Department of Energy Technology, Aalborg University, Denmark, from which he also received a post doctorate. He received his M. Tech. degree in power electronics and drives in 2010 from the Vellore Institute of Technology (VIT), Vellore, India, and his PhD from the Government College of Technology and Engineering, Udaipur, Rajasthan, India. He has published over 60 papers in scientific and technical journals and conferences and has organized several international workshops. He is a reviewer for a number of technical journals, and he is the lead editor for four edited books, including from Scrivener Publishing.

Akash Kumar Bhoi, PhD, is an assistant professor in the Department of Electrical and Electronics Engineering at Sikkim Manipal Institute of Technology (SMIT), India. He is also a research associate at Wireless Networks (WN) Research Laboratory, Institute of Information Science and Technologies, National Research Council (ISTI-CRN) Pisa, Italy. He is a member of several technical associations and is an editorial board member for a number of journals. He has published several papers in scientific journals and conferences and is currently working on several edited volumes for various publishers, including from Scrivener Publishing.

Sanjeevikumar Padmanaban, PhD, is a faculty member with the Department of Energy Technology, Aalborg University, Esbjerg, Denmark and works with CTIF Global Capsule (CGC), Department of Business Development and Technology, Aarhus University, Denmark. He received his PhD in electrical engineering from the University of Bologna, Italy. He has almost ten years of teaching, research and industrial experience and is an associate editor on a number of international scientific refereed journals. He has published more than 300 research papers and has won numerous awards for his research and teaching.

S. Balamurugan is the Head of Research and Development, QUANTS IS & Consultancy Services, India. He has authored or edited 40 books, more than 200 papers in scientific and technical journals and conferences and has 15 patents to his credit. He is either the editor-in-chief, associate editor, guest editor, or editor for many scientific and technical journals, from many well-respected publishers around the world. He has won numerous awards, and he is a member of several technical societies.

Jens Bo Holm-Nielsen currently works at the Department of Energy Technology, Aalborg University and is head of the Esbjerg Energy Section. He helped establish the Center for Bioenergy and Green Engineering in 2009 and served as the head of the research group. He has served as technical advisor for many companies in this industry, and he has executed many large-scale European Union and United Nation projects. He has authored more than 300 scientific papers and has participated in over 500 various international conferences.

Index

Also of Interest

Check out these published and forthcoming titles in the "Artificial Intelligence and Soft Computing for Industrial Transformation" series from Scrivener Publishing

The New Advanced Society
Artificial Intelligence and Industrial Internet of Things Paradigm
Edited by Sandeep Kumar Panda, Ramesh Kumar Mohapatra, Subhrakanta Panda and S. Balamurugan
Forthcoming 2022. ISBN 978-1-119-82447-3

Digitization of Healthcare Data using Blockchain
Edited by T. Poongodi, D. Sumathi, B. Balamurugan and K. S. Savita
Forthcoming 2022. ISBN 978-1-119-79185-0

Tele-Healthcare
Applications of Artificial Intelligence and Soft Computing Techniques
Edited by R. Nidhya, Manish Kumar and S. Balamurugan
Forthcoming 2020. ISBN 978-1-119-84176-0

Impact of Artificial Intelligence on Organizational Transformation
Edited by S. Balamurugan, Sonal Pathak, Anupriya Jain, Sachin Gupta, and Sachin Sharma and Sonia Duggal
Forthcoming 2022. ISBN 978-1-119-71017-2

Artificial Intelligence for Renewable Energy Systems
Edited by Ajay Kumar Vyas, S. Balamurugan, Kamal Kant Hiran Harsh S. Dhiman
Forthcoming 2022. ISBN 978-1-119-76169-3

Artificial Intelligence Techniques for Wireless Communication and Networking
Edited by Kanthavel R., K. Ananthajothi, S. Balamurugan and R. Karthik Ganesh
Forthcoming 2022. ISBN 978-1-119-82127 4

Advanced Healthcare Systems
Empowering Physicians with IoT-Enabled Technologies
Edited by Rohit Tanwar, S. Balamurugan, R. K. Saini, Vishal Bharti and Premkumar Chithaluru
Forthcoming 2022. ISBN 978-1-119-76886-9

Smart Systems for Industrial Applications
Edited by C. Venkatesh, N. Rengarajan, P. Ponmurugan and S. Balamurugan
Published 2022. ISBN 978-1-119-76200-3

Human Technology Communication
Internet of Robotic Things and Ubiquitous Computing
Edited by R. Anandan. G. Suseendran, S. Balamurugan, Ashish Mishra and D. Balaganesh
Published 2021. ISBN 978-1-119-75059-8

Nature-Inspired Algorithms Applications
Edited by S. Balamurugan, Anupriya Jain, Sachin Sharma, Dinesh Goyal, Sonia Duggal and Seema Sharma
Published 2021. ISBN 978-1-119-68174-8

Computation in Bioinformatics
Multidisciplinary Applications
Edited by S. Balamurugan, Anand Krishnan, Dinesh Goyal, Balakumar Chandrasekaran and Boomi Pandi
Published 2021. ISBN 978-1-119-65471-1

Fuzzy Intelligent Systems
Methodologies, Techniques, and Applications
Edited by E. Chandrasekaran, R. Anandan, G. Suseendran, S. Balamurugan and Hanaa Hachimi
Published 2021. ISBN 978-1-119-76045-0

Biomedical Data Mining for Information Retrieval
Methodologies, Techniques and Applications
Edited by Sujata Dash, Subhendu Kumar Pani, S. Balamurugan and Ajith Abraham
Published 2021. ISBN 978-1-119-71124-7

Design and Analysis of Security Protocols for Communication
Edited by Dinesh Goyal, S. Balamurugan, Sheng-Lung Peng and O.P. Verma
Published 2020. ISBN 978-1-119-55564-3

www.scrivenerpublishing.com

Printed and bound by CPI Group (UK) Ltd, Croydon, CR0 4YY

27/10/2024

14580131-0004